T0323678

Business Ethics for a Material World

Increasingly, conscientious consumers and green marketers are recognizing that material things, not firms, are the locus of social and ecological responsibility. Even so, many scholars in ethics, sustainability, and governance focus on people and organizations, ignoring the flows of things.

In this book, Ryan Burg argues that material things are fundamental features of moral life, serving as both valuable instruments and guides for responsibility. Unless care is taken for these nonliving entities, living things cannot be protected. Viewing the global economy as a network of material transfers, Burg argues that to facilitate object care, professionals must act as stewards. By tracing the origins and disposal of workplace objects through this material network, businesses and employees can discover the outcomes for which they are responsible, and managers can align ethics, sustainability, and governance with a truly global formulation of responsibility.

RYAN BURG is Visiting Assistant Professor in the College of Management at Bucknell University. He holds a joint PhD in Business Ethics and Sociology from the Wharton School of Business, University of Pennsylvania, and his dissertation was a finalist for the Social Issues in Management Dissertation award. Professor Burg is also a cofounder of the Responsible Endowments Coalition, a national organization that supports the student-led responsible investment movement on college and university campuses.

Business, Value Creation, and Society

SERIES EDITORS:

R. Edward Freeman, *University of Virginia*
Jeremy Moon, *Copenhagen Business School*
Mette Moring, *Copenhagen Business School*

The purpose of this innovative series is to examine, from an international standpoint, the interaction of business and capitalism with society. In the twenty-first century it is more important than ever that business and capitalism come to be seen as social institutions that have a great impact on the welfare of human society around the world. Issues such as globalization, environmentalism, information technology, the triumph of liberalism, corporate governance, and business ethics all have the potential to have major effects on our current models of the corporation and the methods by which value is created, distributed and sustained among all stakeholder—customers, suppliers, employees, communities, and financiers.

Business Ethics for a Material World

An Ecological Approach to Object Stewardship

RYAN BURG
Visiting Assistant Professor, Bucknell University

CAMBRIDGE
UNIVERSITY PRESS

CAMBRIDGE
UNIVERSITY PRESS

University Printing House, Cambridge CB2 8BS, United Kingdom

One Liberty Plaza, 20th Floor, New York, NY 10006, USA

477 Williamstown Road, Port Melbourne, VIC 3207, Australia

314–321, 3rd Floor, Plot 3, Splendor Forum, Jasola District Centre,
New Delhi – 110025, India

79 Anson Road, #06–04/06, Singapore 079906

Cambridge University Press is part of the University of Cambridge.

It furthers the University's mission by disseminating knowledge in the pursuit of
education, learning, and research at the highest international levels of excellence.

www.cambridge.org
Information on this title: www.cambridge.org/9781107183018
DOI: 10.1017/9781316869147

© Ryan Burg 2018

First published 2018

Printed in the United Kingdom by Clays, St Ives plc

A catalogue record for this publication is available from the British Library.

Library of Congress Cataloging-in-Publication Data
Names: Burg, Ryan, author.
Title: Building market ethics of material things : an ecological approach to object
stewardship / Ryan Burg, National Research University, Moscow.
Description: Cambridge, United Kingdom ; New York, NY : Cambridge University
Press, 2017.
Identifiers: LCCN 2017024709 | ISBN 9781107183018
Subjects: LCSH: Sustainable development – Moral and ethical aspects. | Business
ethics. | Material culture. | Materials.
Classification: LCC HD75.6 .B863 2017 | DDC 174/.4–dc23
LC record available at https://lccn.loc.gov/2017024709

ISBN 978-1-107-18301-8 Hardback

For Sherman and Marlo, collectors of stuff
and stewards of things

Contents

Figures and Tables

Foreword

Ryan Burg suggests that the normal way we think about business ethics is in need of a radical reorientation. He suggests that the sheer complexity of modern business requires new narratives and new ways of thinking. The complexity of business today obscures the important relationships between people and objects, and most of contemporary business ethics starts with people, and adds the context of business.

Burg's reorientation will seem quite strange to many. He suggests that we start with things and objects, rather than people. He says that we need to understand "the physical, tangible materials with which business deals." It is only by starting with things, and in particular the things that matter and affect the stakeholders of a business, that we can even begin to assign responsibility in a meaningful way.

It is easiest to see Burg's view if we look at the physical environment, but he goes far beyond sustainability in his analysis and prescriptions. If we are to address many of our societal issues, we must address the stewardship of objects, and that is impossible without understanding the objects themselves and the roles they play in human society.

Philosophically, Burg is a pragmatist. He is deeply rooted in practice and in the phenomena he writes about. Starting ethics with "things" engenders a raised eyebrow and a "why in the world would you do that" look. This is precisely the kind of new narrative that we need for the twenty-first century. And it is precisely that kind of book that this series on Business, Value Creation, and Society is proud to publish.

My hope is that this book will be one of many more to come that will help us develop a better business ethics, and continue to make business and capitalism a system of value creation and trade that is truly fit for human beings.

R. Edward Freeman
Series Co-Editor
January 2017

Acknowledgments

This book benefitted from a passel of supportive teachers, colleagues, and friends. Tom Donaldson and Diana Robertson read early drafts and provided helpful feedback. Bill Laufer gave invaluable advice on organizing the manuscript. Ruben Flores, Manuel Maroto, and Yuval Weber provided constructive scrutiny on a more mature (and much longer) draft. Ryan Fehr collaborated on a paper on the moralization of objects and challenged me to clarify several concepts in the process. Three anonymous reviewers contributed helpful suggestions.

The Higher School of Economics in Moscow provided the time and resources to write. At HSE, Nikolay Filinov, Veronika Kabalina, and Valentina Kuskova deserve special thanks for their collegiality and guidance. The Zicklin Center for Business Ethics Research at the Wharton School of Business provided the research assistantship of Emma James, who was endlessly helpful in gathering and organizing materials that were unavailable in Russia.

On the subject of Russia, I should not write a book about material things without acknowledging my own entanglements. My ecological imagination owes a special allegiance to South Dakota, my productivity to Moscow's weather, and my income to a petrostate-funded university. Make of these entanglements what you will; an ecological consciousness admits of many contradictions.

Writing is a solitary activity, but publishing is an act of engagement. This book is an invitation to anyone who is ready to make room for things in the crowded moral space of the modern firm. There is much to be done, and we will need to work together.

I have been fortunate to find a community of thoughtful and creative scholars who take ideas seriously. I will single out Robbin Derry, Eric Orts, Mollie Painter-Morland, Stephen Pavelin, Rob Phillips, Caddie Putnam Rankin, Noah Buckley, Lili Di Puppo, Benjamin Lind, David Szakonyi, and Valery Yakubovich among the many important interlocutors in my academic life. Ed Freeman deserves special mention. His scholarship and leadership in the field of business ethics made this project possible. I am grateful to these friends and mentors, and to numerous others who make the study of organizational ethics a joyful undertaking.

At Cambridge University Press, Valerie Appleby has been efficient and encouraging. Daniel Brown conscientiously guided this manuscript and its moving parts to completion. The text benefited from their professionalism. It was a special pleasure to work with Todd McLellan to develop the cover image. His worldmaking deserves special acknowledgement.

Some of my debts in writing this book can never be repaid, most notably my debt to Thomas Dunfee. Aspects of this book's thesis emerged a decade ago in a conversation with Tom, who has since passed away. We disagreed about whether business ethics scholars expect too little from corporations. I said that shareholder activists and conscientious consumers are right to set high expectations for firms. I defended the way that some consumers moralize objects and demand product stewardship across the length of a supply chain. In a sense, Tom agreed, but he stipulated that firms must also be free to define and pursue their interests. Law, he argued, creates boundaries around firms so that they can do so. I make a case that the responsibilities of object stewardship exceed the legal boundaries of the firm, but I have tried to keep Tom's insights in mind. His passing was a great loss for his family, friends, colleagues, and students. This book would likely be better if Tom Dunfee were here to read it.

Beyond professional tributes, I wish to thank my parents and sister for their continuous support. The newest member of our family, Stella, has played the least constructive role in this book's completion, but I could not be more delighted by the distractions she provides. Her mother is a different story. My deepest gratitude is to Imanni for making my life more livable and my writing more readable. Without her, I would be bearded and lost in the wilderness. Other textual cleanups are thanks to Dominic Fean, Seraphina Davey, Anna Gomberg, Andrew Matheny, and Laura Mills. All mistakes are my own.

Introduction

"Business is a human enterprise. To be good in business is to be a good human being."[1] These two sentences sum up the great majority of research and writing on business ethics. Ordinarily, business ethics is a humanistic undertaking. Its key proponents ask businesspeople to be as decent, honest, caring, cooperative, and respectful at work as they are in other contexts.

Robert Solomon wanted to change the narrative about business by writing about business as a humanistic enterprise. He believed that the theory of business ethics should derive from practice and from positive stories about how people become successful by behaving responsibly. Solomon was right that narratives have power in our imaginations and actions, and he may also have been right to describe a business humanism grounded in classical virtues. But classical virtues are not sufficient to traverse the convoluted expanse of modern business responsibility.

The business world is bewilderingly complex, and businesses are often structured in ways that multiply these complexities, intentionally obfuscating responsibility. We have long since departed from the realm of sensible responsibility where a professional can manage the consequences of her work by taking care of the people with whom she has contact. As long as we apply kin-based interpersonal responsibility to the modern workplace, business ethics will fail to account for the global scope of business impact. Such a morality, born in the nuclear family, becomes unreliable as complexity increases.

Traditional business ethics is arguably part of the problem. It may seem like progress to say that managers are responsible to employees for substantive provisions like a living wage and a safe workplace. It may seem like progress to place managers and employees in the same moral community and to acknowledge the obligations that follow from their interdependence. But if we allow organizational boundaries to define the scope of responsibility and managers to define the scope of organizational boundaries, then we empower managers to distance themselves from whomever they choose, even if their actions directly affect these parties. Since it is often costly to treat people responsibly, offloading these costs can improve (or seem to improve) business performance. Things take a perverse turn when managers are able to use the language of business responsibility as camouflage for a campaign to limit their real moral obligations.

The call to move business ethics beyond the narrow scope of in-group loyalty is not new; it has been a central theme in both critical management studies and supply chain ethics for more than a decade. But while the question is well established, my answer is not. I propose that we expand the circles of moral regard around businesses through a better understanding of the physical, tangible materials with which businesses deal. The human scope of a business entity's moral community is the conclusion in my analysis rather than the point of departure. Material stuff forms the reaching tendrils of our economy. As such, we will not start with people, but with the things that bring people together. By looking closely at these things and our relationships to them, we will find new ways of organizing our moral responsibilities and moral communities. The shift in focus allows us to transcend the firm and its boundaries, to know the moral scope of our work without reference to the distortions of managerial fiat.

Often, objects will lead us back to people and to the same forms of dignity with which we should treat everyone, but through objects we can assemble a moral system that is much more elaborate and comprehensive than we could ever develop without them. Thus, material things function as a sort of moral scaffolding that we will erect in order to build an ethical system. The scaffolding is not the substance of the ethic, and it can even be removed once construction is complete, but without moral scaffolding it is impossible to build a system of morality with the reach that the modern economy requires.

Starting with Objects

Every living thing is entangled in a complex web of material relationships. Humans are no exception. We rely upon physical, chemical, and biological processes, depending on things at every scale.

Many of our relationships with material things exist in a balance. The Earth's massive core draws us to the ground, and it is the combination of this gravitational force and the adequate thickness of the atmosphere pushing oxygen into our lungs that allows us to breathe. Our evolved fitness to a specific material environment is such that if the Earth were bigger or its atmosphere thinner, the structure of our lungs would cause us to be poisoned or to asphyxiate. The specific properties of these things, of the Earth's mass, the gases in the atmosphere, and the membranes in our lungs make our lives possible.

Yet traditional moral theories take little interest in material stuff. We are taught that ethics works from intentions and agency. Material things lack both. This book will complicate the simplified understanding of objects as inert, meaningless props in an anthropocentric morality. It will show that objects act, and that people can find a sense of responsibility in objects.

Both social science and humanistic writing have recently turned toward material things. The turn is partly caused by the proliferation of human-made things in the world and the rising significance of these objects for the way that we work, live, and communicate. But the more pressing global cause of the materialist turn is ecological. The relationship between people and material objects is of special interest now as we place unprecedented pressure on our biophysical environment. Our ancestors had no reason to think that the oxygen a fire consumed and the carbon dioxide it released would eventually change the weather. Until recently, that thought was unthinkable. But as our impact has increased, so has our scientific knowledge. Human conduct, having no precedent at the present scale, is a massive environmental experiment with only one trial and an uncertain result. As preliminary findings accumulate, we begin to realize that the relationships between things are much more complicated than we previously imagined. Today, the threat of global climate change forces us to confront species-level impact as a matter of public policy and private responsibility. To do so, we must think about things.

New Understanding, New Norms

This is a transformative moment, one where new norms are born and old conventions crushed. History may eventually look at our disregard for CO_2 emissions with as much disgust as we now feel when we imagine the sewage-filled streets of a medieval city. "How could they live that way?" our descendants may ask of us.

Relationships between people and things do change over time. The trouble with CO_2 emissions is that we cannot see them and we have to infer their consequences. But again, there is precedent. Our eyes also cannot see the germs that make us sick. Before germ theory, custom alone gave cause to wash hands. Doctors did not think twice about moving directly from autopsies to obstetrics. When Ignác Semmelweis observed high death rates among mothers whose babies were delivered by doctors and further observed that these doctors came directly from autopsies, he inferred the existence of germs and gave medical professionals a new reason to wash their hands.[2] Now, we look back on these practices and pass judgment. Everything seems wrong. It seems revolting that a doctor would not wash his hands before delivering a baby, but Semmelweis was widely disbelieved at the time. Then, as now, perceptions of things were ripe for change.

What will these changes be? What kinds of insights will guide them? Climate change interventions may begin with science, but the norms of environmentalism depend on a much wider application and a new public consciousness of the environmental consequences of material consumption. Nonhuman things give order to this new consciousness. New linkages are already being formed between the energy intensity of production and use, and the things that require this intensity. As Jane Bennett argues in her book, *Vibrant Matter*, "the image of dead or thoroughly instrumentalized matter feeds human hubris and our earth-destroying fantasies of conquest and consumption."[3]

In writing this book, I hope to improve the language and methods that business ethicists use to talk about responsibility. Looking at objects more closely can guide our moral ascriptions more efficiently to apply the right responsibilities to the right firms and employees. But blame is not my cause; responsible business practice is the primary objective. I wish to change the way that business is done, to starve rather than feed firms' "earth-destroying fantasies of conquest and consumption." It is not only business ethicists but also managers who must change the way that they see things. Chapters 1, 7, and 8 all speak directly to practical problems in the business application of object-based stewardship. In practice, we discover problems and try out solutions. And yet, fundamental problems do not get solved by practice alone; we need to use practice to hone our insights and to develop better theories for action. I explore objects and the problems that objects can solve as a theory for action that prescribes practical change. As Semmelweis showed, to learn to wash, first we must see that our hands are dirty.

Objects for Humans' Sake and Objects for Objects' Sake

Though the threat of an ecological crisis raises some of the most pressing calls to ascribe moral meaning to material objects, there are other forces in play. Many consumers, activists, and researchers are deeply concerned about the human costs of global production. Fair-trade labeling schemes provide moral cues to consumers, embedding moral meaning about human welfare into material products. Fair-trade labels remind purchasers that coffee is more than a flavor profile and stimulant, and that the beans they grind have a very different meaning to the people who grow them.

Coffee is an interesting character in the development of global capitalism. The proliferation of its cultivation across numerous small patches of mountainous soil began with the observation that coffee was expensive. Historically, the obscure mountain origins of the beans set the price, but as cultivation spread to new regions, supply increased more rapidly than demand and prices fell. Coffee roasters benefited most significantly from a rise in consumption and the decrease in input costs.

Fair-trade labeling schemes are designed to emphasize the human aspects of a supply chain. But coffee's tale is also one of soils, plants, and coffee cherries. It is the mountainous terrain where coffee grows and coffee cherries' tendency to ripen unevenly that gives manual labor an advantage relative to mechanized harvesters. The lives of the pickers who scour the hills are shaped as much by the attributes of the plants as they are by the structure of the market for coffee. The plants do not play an inert role: they act to shape human behavior. They become what Bruno Latour calls actants, which *"emerge in surprising fashion, lengthening the list of beings that must be taken into account."*[4]

Placing our species at the center of the system of meaning skews our perspective on material entanglements. While we play a special role insofar as we are the ones perceiving and evaluating, we must decide what else to make special and to endow with meaning. Doing so is

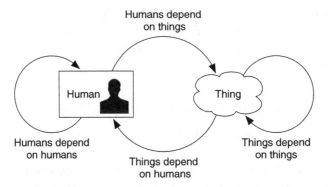

Figure 1.1 Dependences

initially an empirical matter. As Ian Hodder has argued, we depend upon things and things depend upon us, just as things depend upon other things.[5]

In the case of coffee, people depend upon plants and plants depend upon weather conditions. Increasingly, these climate conditions are believed to be precarious. A 2016 report on the future of coffee cultivation warned that as much as half of the land where coffee is currently being cultivated may not be suitable for coffee production by 2050.[6]

Climate change is one of many forces in play that is helping people to construct new meaning around objects, but material dependence is an important part of everyday life. Think of the things that you carry when you leave your house: a phone, some keys, and probably a wallet. Each thing serves as a gateway to a whole system of communication, resources, and exchange. We cover ourselves in things, ride around in things, fix things at work, and buy things for play. Our relationships with these things are not simple. Some of them afford us benefits that we desire; others make us dependent upon them in ways that are not desirable. Some things bring us together; other things, like flies and the SARS coronavirus, force us to create boundaries. Hodder distinguishes between dependence and dependency, reserving the latter term for the kinds of reliances that reduce options. Dependence is the more general category, which includes some historical relationships. For example, the development of telephones was unlikely to precede the discovery of the telegraph. The possibility of transmitting signals through wires needed to be discovered before that signal could be refined to transmit a complex sound. The relationship between the phone and the tele-graph is one of dependence, not dependency.

There are situations in which the historical origins of ideas and cultural artifacts warrant moral consideration, especially where these elements have special significance to an unacknowledged group or when someone unfairly profits from expropriation.[7] The commerciali-zation of culture raises a number of questions about indigenous rights and ownership,[8] and these are worthy of study. However, I will focus on the more general system of functional object dependence, where things need other things in an immediate sense rather than a historical or developmental sense. The extensive network of interdependence is important for understanding how systems work and how we take care of their elements. Though historical dependence is a part of this story, the fact that the Internet comes after modems which come after phone lines is less significant for our normative analysis than the fact that computers require energy, materials, and eventually disposal. In fact, as we will discuss later, computers are sometimes put forth as a characteristic example of dematerialized production (see Materiality for Business Ethics in Chapter 8).

Tracing these dependences acknowledges the social and physical complexity of entirely mundane tasks. Imagine that you need to make a shopping list to cook a simple dinner. Your task begins with the ingredients. If you're cooking at home, the list may be short, but if you're camping, it gets longer. Campers cannot rely upon the avail-ability of kitchen implements. They cannot get salt and pepper from the shelf. The list grows again if we account for the knowledge that makes a meal possible, knowledge of hygiene, flavor, cooking time, the operation of equipment, etc. Now suppose we add the resources that were necessary to create our ingredients. We use energy to prepare, package, and refrigerate ingredients. Adding these items to our list further expands the dependence we have on things. Cows eat grass and grain. One pound of beef also requires almost 7,000 liters of water.[9] These are secondary ingredients. Now imagine that we add the tertiary inputs. Tertiary ingredients include fertile soil, pesticides, roads, and additional water used to create secondary ingredients.

Many of the things in this web have dependences of their own. Things depend on people as well. Edible plants, for example, are ecologically precarious. The hybrids that are best for human consump-tion would not thrive on their own. With a few exceptions, such as mint, most plants that people eat are outcompeted by more vigorous plants that people do not like to eat. In service of the preferred plants, humans maintain a delicate ecological niche. Thus, even as people rely upon these plants for food, the plants also rely upon people for care and protection from competition. In the introduction to *Botany of Desire*, Michael Pollan compares a gardener to a bumblebee, and asks whether both the gardener and the bee are deceiving themselves to imagine that they are the ones choosing which plants and flowers to favor. Instead, "the flower has cleverly manipulated the bee into hauling its pollen from blossom to blossom."[10] Pollan's project is an imaginative one, a perspective-taking exercise that recognizes how plants rely on people for their ecological success in a coevolution that shapes both organisms.

These reliances go far beyond biological forms. Think of the aging infrastructure of a city. Water flows under streets and washes foundations away; it freezes and thaws, creating cracks and fissures. Walls lean and crumble; paint cracks. In time, glass pools downward and thins at the top. Everything degrades. Even things that seem relatively stable in a human lifespan require people to make them useful. A toll bridge is not especially ephemeral, but its economic and regulatory structure is only sustained through human labor.

In philosophy, the movement to reappraise the meaning of things began with Kant, who recognized that all things, whether people or objects, are mediated by mental representations in the way that we understand them. But where Kant wished to reify the distinction between morally free subjects who make choices and these mental representations, postmodernists have since sought to dismantle or complicate this distinction, leveling the playing field of subjects and objects.

This book is not necessarily a work of postmodernist philosophy. With the exception of a short discussion of Heidegger, it makes only episodic references to the literatures that inspire postmodern thinkers. Instead, it is grounded in a pragmatic reappraisal of things as key factors in the way that we decide to be responsible. Pragmatists deal with many of the same problems that concern postmodernists. However, postmodern philosophy is not as open to the uses of modern social systems and technology as pragmatism tends to be. As Ryder describes, postmodern philosophy "is guilty of an abuse of modernity in failing to recognize its contributions to intellectual development and in rejecting it more or less wholesale." In comparison, pragmatism provides "a positive alternative."[11] Rather than despair of the challenges that modernity presents, pragmatists augment critique with adaptation in an effort to realize better possibilities. Likewise, objects and their networks of dependence provide the substance for both critique and adaptation.

This text will highlight the chains of dependence in which people and things are entangled, demonstrating the relevance of these chains for business responsibility. It will show that objects have their own stories, and that telling these stories helps us to develop a more comprehensive account of social and environmental responsibility for businesses and businesspeople.

How to Think Things

In this text, I will argue that complex networks of things and people are morally relevant to us in ways that we often forget. I explore the stewardship of material objects as a way to address social and environmental issues within a complex global economy. To make this argument, we will have to think much more sensitively than we normally do about the histories and consequences of the things with which we are entangled.

Thoughts in this vein are increasingly fashionable. A lively conversation about things, materials, matter, and stuff has already caught on in anthropology, archaeology, sociology, and in interdisciplinary fields like science and technology studies. Though many scholars trace the material conversation through figures like Aristotle, Hegel, Marx, Heidegger, and Darwin, the proximate cause of our captivation with things is much closer to hand. In the uncertain ecological future of our planet and a materialistic economy, it is hard not to take notice of the ways that matter matters. Scholars are drawn into writing about things, not so much by the history of scholarship as by the present and future of our societies and cultures. Now, more than ever before, it is necessary that we confront the place of things in our social, political, and economic systems.

As fashionable as it may be, writing about things presents significant challenges. Things are everything. As we confront them, we face what Theodor Adorno calls the "preponderance of the object."[12] Faced with the plurality of things, it is impossible to categorize and control the whole range. Academic knowledge ordinarily develops by breaking the world into small pieces of expertise, but material things cannot always be structured and studied in this way.

Scholars often approach objects from the perspective of their academic disciplines. The boundaries of professionalized scholarship partition the intellectual encounter with things, separating the functions of objects within the psychology of identity, the communication of symbolic meaning,[13] the structure of interpersonal and intergroup power,[14] and the formation of political groups.[15] These specific roles each yield different examples, and objects become touchstones in the process. Thus, the pumps in laboratories become an object of inquiry into the relationships with things in science,[16] the transformation of uses and techniques of ceramics organizes a wide array of studies into ancient civilizations, and the treatment of the human body becomes a study of the extent and form of political domination.[17] While these things and their interactions operate in distinctive ways within a disciplinary dialogue, the objects themselves remain undisciplined. Vacuum pumps are not only a character in the discovery of Boyle's law, but also a character in factories that vacuum seal food and in the production of lightbulbs. Moreover, objects allow for multiple perspectives from different people and different objects: "[w]indow panes are designed to be looked through rather than to be looked at, unless one is a window cleaner."[18] In order to understand objects, we must also understand their relationships to each other and the distinctive perspectives that different people with different expertise bring to them.

Academic studies of material objects must also work through a fraught intellectual history. Marx's materialism juxtaposed the power of things with the power of ideas, claiming that historical materialism could help us to understand the false consciousness of ideas. As Shiping Tang explains, "epistemologically, materialism holds ... it is always better to explain social facts with material forces than with ideational forces."[19] Tang proposes that these ways of thinking can be complementary, that materialism can augment other ways of theorizing. To argue otherwise places the dogmatic Marxist in an illogical position, since historical materialism is itself an idea.

While I use materials as Marx did to develop ideas about social processes, the approach taken here gives objects much more room to be objects. As a result, materialism tells a story that goes far beyond class dynamics in social, political, and economic history. Objects differ across the universe of things, and these differences matter for the way that we understand them, use them, care for them, and care for the people to whom these objects connect.

The recent influence of Marx's materialism is arguably overwhelmed by work on science and technology that considers the active role that objects play in numerous contexts. Contrary to Marx, these actor-network theorists do not juxtapose things and ideas. Instead, they juxtapose an anthropocentric view of the world where objects are inert and inactive with a view that recognizes that the objects themselves play a key role in guiding behavior and ideas. The approach towards objects as actants prescribed by Latour allows ideas to matter, as long as they take their place within the structure of material relations that represents an actual and embodied reality.

As with Marx's materialism, most actor-network theorists use materials for a descriptive analysis. They do not seek to develop the moral position of objects. Like actor-network theorists, I seek to acknowledge that objects accomplish many things in society: bringing people together, shaping the way that they understand reality, satisfying their preferences, and constraining them in important ways. But I take an additional step to consider objects' moral position. This move suggests that we need to do more than describe the role that things play; we must choose what role they ought to play.

While social science may sometimes require a disinterested and non-judgmental perspective to credibly represent observations, this will not be our approach. In this book, the question is not if and how objects matter, but how objects ought to matter.

Answering this question is a thoroughly normative undertaking. Several social theorists have framed their inquiries in these terms. Bennett's work is fundamentally engaged with normative questions of publicness and participation as well as the distribution of harm to persons and objects that helps to explain the formation of a political community. Aihwa Ong and Stephen Collier suggest another avenue for using studies in object relationships to employ a complex and reflexive view of society, politics, and ethics.[20] Philosophical responses have struggled to account for the ethics of objects in complex ways. As Ian Bogost explains:

The ethics of the spark plug are no more clear to us than would be those of the vegan to the soybean plant, even as the former strips and devours the latter's salted, boiled babies in a tasty appetizer of edamame. Worse yet, there might be multiple, conflicting theories of soybean ethics.[21]

Bogost goes on to argue that ethics "is a self-centered practice," and that the useful applications of object-focused observations work as metaphor rather than as a real object ethic. Still, some scholars are working from the perspective that nonhuman objects can be fruitfully studied not only as objects of curiosity with their own distinctive world of connections, but as centers of moral worth that deserve our attention.

Beyond People

Because ethics is chiefly concerned with caring for people, the move towards object relevance is controversial. Developmentally and historically, ethics expands from egoism through kin-based loyalties to other configurations of moral sympathies. Philosophical ethics tends to privilege humans over other species and to ignore things that are not alive.

There are many reasons why ethicists prioritize people. People are capable of suffering and making promises, they have rights and preferences, and their actions are sometimes goal-directed and intentional. Any of these human qualities can be engaged in normative terms. By describing human rights, we advance a set of responsibilities to avoid infringing upon these rights. Taking preferences into account grants the importance of people's happiness. The capacity to aspire and plan and to choose between different kinds of goals is one of several excuses for privileging humans over other species.

Business ethics takes an additional interest in people because they have special relationships with firms. The people who are morally relevant to firms are known as stakeholders. Clarifying the responsibilities that firms and stakeholders have to each other allows us to make judgments about how organizations behave and it allows organizations to find better ways to be useful to people.[22] Unfortunately, this focus on people creates two basic biases. First, it relegates the interests of nonhuman organisms and living systems to a secondary status. If the natural environment is not a stakeholder, its value can only be appreciated insofar as it proves directly useful to a firm's human stakeholders.[23]

Second, thinking about people tends to place them into containers according to people's specific relationships to each other. It is easy enough to recognize a firm's stakeholder relationships to its own employees, shareholders, managers, customers, and suppliers. But what about the employees of a firm's suppliers or the employees of a firm's supplier's supplier? In a complex production network, these relationships seem very distant as a matter of ownership structure.[24] And yet, when we focus on a firm's products and equipment and the materials that constitute them, these people are inescapably drawn into the same productive scenario.

As soon as we shift our focus from people to products and other organizational objects, it is immediately apparent that business ethics is bursting with things. It is also clear that these objects are undertheorized. Almost every case we discuss in a business ethics class is organized around a product, facility, or material, yet we manage to say little about these elements. We talk about sweatshops without talking seriously about shoes and the manufacturing processes that create them, the glues that hold them together, and the stitching that requires the most labor. We talk about the Dalkon Shield as product liability and a legal quagmire of bankruptcy and risk-shifting without thinking about the intrauterine contraceptive device as a thing itself.[25] It should be obvious that the Dalkon Shield invites a qualitatively different kind of acrimony from injured customers because of its function as a thing, but these issues have not been developed in any coherent way. We talk about sustainably harvested lumber without thinking much about trees and forests. We talk about BP's Deepwater Horizon oil spill without feeling, touching, or smelling crude oil, or understanding the uncertainty of the environmental consequences of a deep-sea leak.

Several assumptions about objects make them seem uninteresting from the perspective of ethics. First, it is often assumed that objects are inert and incapable of action. Formal distinctions between subject and object, agent and patient, artisan and tool make material things seem like mere manifestations of human intentionality. Second, we assume that objects exist for humans to use. Ownership, anthropocentrism, and the everyday practice of material culture transforms objects into extensions of individuals and their identities without questioning what other role the things might play. Third, we assume that objects can be standardized as commodities. We do not need to talk about the specific history of a given shoe, and we should instead think about shoes on a massive scale, about the number of shoes being produced in China, and the specific firms producing them.

Meaningful Things

Recognizing the influence of things invites an inquiry into the ethics of material entanglement. It invites us to ask what things we ought to value and care for, and how we should make such a determination. Many societies invest a sense of meaning into material things. From icons to animism, there is much to rediscover in the moral relevance of objects. But it seems doubtful that we can undertake this journey by moving to an earlier historical period or by adopting another society's symbolism. How could we decide which norms to adopt and which to discard? Instead, we must move forward by developing new ways to inculcate a sense of responsibility for objects within an economy that encourages a critical inquiry about its things, their origins, their relationships, and their consequences.

Social theorists have long been interested in the economy of objects and in the value ascribed to them. For instance, in the mid-nineteenth century John Ruskin explored the production conditions that give rise to different forms of artistic expression. He argued that important aspects of human well-being and freedom follow directly from stylistic preferences; when we pay for things that are made to look a certain way, we also pay for the production conditions that produce them.[26] Accordingly, an object is as beautiful as the expressive conditions that produce it.

We have a vested interest in the material world. It nourishes our biological, cognitive, and emotional selves. Learning about objects brings us closer to our jobs, our communities, our habitats, and our planet. Learning about objects brings us closer to the things that we think are beautiful, and perhaps it may bring our sense of beauty closer to the way that our objects are made.

It follows that an object should be valuable when it has been created under responsible conditions, used responsibly and when it can be discarded without destructive results. Thinking of objects' value in these terms encourages people and economic entities to deal with a wider set of social and ecological outcomes than a direct focus on interpersonal responsibility.

Though I focus on legitimate businesses and industries, black market trade is a hotbed of object awareness. Sometimes, this awareness involves symbolic exercises that demonstrate the extent to which harm and hardship are invested in material things. For example, at the ceremonial destruction of a stockpile of ivory confiscated in Sri Lanka, a Buddhist priest apologized to the elephants. "Those elephants were victimized by the cruelty of certain people. But all of human society is responsible. We destroyed those innocent lives to take those tusks. We have to ask for pardon from them."[27] Morality is often invested in things; every society must decide how and when to invest moral meaning into material things.

This is the right time to think more carefully about the role that material objects play in ethics and especially in business ethics. Modern technologies present firms with multiple opportunities to account for the real impact of the specific resources that they make, sell, and consume. Production is more traceable and more specifiable than ever before. The same can be said for use and disposal. Even agricultural products can be tracked from field to fork. I will suggest that the market does not encourage us to appreciate the value of objects and the consequences of their use. However, as we look more closely at these material things and begin to value their unique histories, we will formulate an improved configuration of supply chain responsibility.

These are the subjects that I investigate in this book. It is worth noting a few of the many categories of objects that are not extensively developed. First, this is not a book about money. Money is arguably among the most interesting objects from a business ethics perspective, but it warrants so many considerations that are unique to its issuance and exchange that I make only passing reference to it. Second, for many anthropologists, objects have an important ritualistic and cultural meaning as gifts, centers of symbolic meaning, and systems of symbols. Like money, these systems of symbols and ritualism are important for thinking about business ethics, but they operate within cultural systems that are specific enough to require more focused study than this book can provide. Suffice it to say that anyone who wishes to do business in a certain culture must endeavor to understand the symbolic role that objects play within that culture or risk unintended consequences. The third limitation of this text is its treatment of virtual objects. From computer viruses to corporate surveillance, many important things have a digital nature for which the physical location may be its least significant attribute. Questions of moral obligations for such objects are beyond the scope of this text, but are deeply important for making sense of corporate responsibility in the information age.

A Plan

To follow the argument in this book, it helps to think like a pragmatist. Pragmatists develop principles by discovering practical problems and trying out solutions. For pragmatists, workability is a higher aim than rational consistency or conceptual clarity. Sometimes, practice reveals principles that can be defended on rational grounds, but the moral prioritization of objects is not such a case.

The best reason to care for things is that the human relationship with the natural environment will never be sustainable and the global commercial system will never be responsible unless we do so. The principle that people have a special moral priority is perfectly clear in conceptual terms, but absolutely toxic in practice.

I approach the argument by working from practice, to the problems of practice, to principles, and then back to practice. After this introduction, Chapter 1 begins with practice. It contrasts the treatment of objects as commodities and as singularities to show how trees, toys, and gold are sometimes granted unique, historical identities. Recognizing this uniqueness highlights the social and ecological impact of forestry, consumer products, and commerce. Forestry provides the key example with an extensive discussion of how foresters make sense of forest ecologies. The disagreement between ecological and commodity forestry shows how the ethics and politics of things are already guiding a key debate in an important industry. Moving to toys shifts the focus from cultivation to manufacturing, another part of the supply chain. In a product liability case, toys serve as key signifiers of managerial responsibility. Purchasers assume the suitability of toys for children's play, but when their assumptions prove ill-founded, they react vehemently. Later in this book, I will emphasize why the consumers are more justified than producers in claiming that they were ignorant of product inputs' content and suitability for use. The third and final discussion focuses on gold and exchange responsibility. As previously mentioned, money is one of the objects that this book does not purport to address. However, I briefly discuss responsible transactions and gold to characterize the network of responsibility linked together by transactional media.

Chapter 2 explores schema by which singularization manifests. Usefulness, sentimentality, personification, and stewardship are four mechanisms that emerge in cultural narratives across settings, reinforcing the unique meaning of specific things. The first and second chapters differ also in the substance of their explorations. Where Chapter 1 develops its examples in key industries and exemplary ethics issues, Chapter 2 focuses on cultural works, especially animated films. In so doing, I try to express an important element of singularization's breadth, to demonstrate that this cognitive framework, while still obscure to the field of business ethics, is demonstrably manifest in popular culture.

Up to this point, the story of singularization rests on its positive potential. However, Chapter 3 takes a darker turn to propose a negative justification for singularization. Some problems can only be resolved by stewarding objects. Movements for the singularization of things among "conscientious consumers," consumers who take responsibility for the things they buy, and within environmental labeling organizations are driven forward by the exhaustion of alternative approaches. Chapter 3 shows the limits of markets, states, and personal responsibility, and uses these limits to justify why creative moral actors are searching for alternatives.

Chapter 4 demonstrates the limited capabilities of market, state, and personal ethic by looking at three key social problems: inequality, climate change, and financial instability. These examples demonstrate the limits of responsibilities as allocated by states' laws, markets' incentives, and ethics' personal norms. I revisit these cases in Chapter 7 to show how object stewardship would address them.

Chapter 5 establishes a pluralistic theory of value as one collaborative solution to basic problems in business ethics. The chapter extends a humanistic moral theory by recognizing that the boundaries between people and things are never entirely clear. I show that material things are important because they connect with valuable persons and living things.[28]

Chapter 6 goes one step further to describe the complex system of contextual worth in which appreciating the value of any one element requires us to understand its entanglements. I show that, in both organic and inorganic systems, disregarding aggregate complexity and failing to appreciate the interconnectedness of valued entities makes us more likely to harm them. The chapter concludes by applying an ecological theory of value to inequality, climate change, and financial instability, the three failures of regulatory capitalism described in Chapter 4.

Chapter 7 and Chapter 8 demonstrate the role that objects could play in business ethics. In Chapter 7, I argue that business ethicists make a mistake when they equate businesses with the closed moral communities that are at the center of Aristotelian theories of virtue. Instead, I propose that objects be used as a locus of professional ethics.

Finally, Chapter 8 concludes by showing how material objects can be a platform for normative thinking about firms and the way that they are governed, regardless of how a firm's governance is first conceptualized. Applying this argument to the 2015 Volkswagen emissions scandal helps to demonstrate the kind of ethic that we can build by using objects as moral scaffolding. Because objects help us to build more elaborate moral structures, they help to hold together responsibilities that might otherwise be disconnected.

This is the task that I define for objects. I do not enlist them as a cause for being moral, but as a means by which morality is directed. If managers can learn to manage things responsibly, I suggest that they will learn to manage people more responsibly in the process.

1 | *The Singularization of Everything*

I began writing this book on an iPad.[1] The device arrived on my doorstep in a brown box just like millions of other iPads arrived on millions of other doorsteps. I have no relationship to any person who assembled, sold, or delivered it. I do not understand what makes it work, could not name its parts, and do not know their origins. I am a user in the most pejorative sense; I take without contributing.

Yet I call it mine. Why? What special claim do I have to this thing? Perhaps it is my feeling of dependence, the custom text burnt into its aluminum shell, the personal information it contains, or the potentially useful work that I do with it. Attachment, identification, privacy, and public utility are good reasons to allow someone to own a thing, but the only reason that matters to Apple Incorporated is that I paid for it.

This is global capitalism's prototypical arrangement. Consumers and producers are mediated by brands and currency. Knowing little about each other, we are chained together by complex products that no single person understands. In this global capitalism, we pay money for products without knowing the origins of either the money or the goods. We produce without knowing consumers and consume without knowing producers. When a television reporter interviewed a worker who cuts plastic burrs off iPads in a Foxconn factory, the worker had never seen or touched an assembled tablet.[2] Her perspective of the product was even more limited than mine, and she makes it.

The Richness of Things

Talking about ownership, commodities, and global capitalism limits the range of things that we imagine, and the range of relationships that people can have with these things. This is a necessary consequence of my effort, at least at this stage of the argument, to focus on tangible and relatable examples. However, different societies and different objects

19

within our societies are not all treated similarly. I am not, for example, speaking of the exchange of gifts to enhance one's prestige, such as those which are called Moka among the Highlands people of Papua New Guinea. The social regulatory features of such person-thing interactions bear little resemblance to commodities. From an anthropological perspective, these differences warrant recognition, particularly because observing the diversity helps remind us that the relationships between persons and things change with context, as Strathern has described in the context of the Highlands.[3] If I limited this text to contexts in which people already believe that "The thing itself possess a soul," as Maus described, the book would miss the opportunity to think critically about today's dominant modes of economic organization.[4]

Focusing on a finite and culturally circumscribed expression of what it means to have and own a thing highlights the increasing dominance of a particular form of exchange and its attendant problems. Status-gift cultures are not being promulgated as the cross-cultural standard for person-thing relations, but relations characterized by social distance between transacting parties and a broad disregard for the origins of things have diffused into a range of contexts and products. This propagation alone motivates research on how such interactions can be managed responsibly. Moreover, in contrast to localized transactional cultures, there is a special need to situate commodity exchange within a global production network and to map out the kinds of responsibilities that such relationships require.

Even while focusing on commodities, it is sometimes important to return to the diverse anthropological record of cultural differences in exchange. Business ethicists Donaldson and Dunfee have written most extensively on global businesses' obligations to respect local cultures. They contend that businesspeople must understand local cultures and values in order to behave responsibly within them. My approach will affiliate these values with the moral histories of objects. It will ask managers and employees to act as stewards of things, as evaluative actors who seek to understand the consequences of the way that they deal with things and to improve these consequences in ways that esteem the moral systems that they value. I make no attempt to provide a universal account of how responsibility ought to be in every society. The positive argument that I advance for taking care of things speaks to a specific culture of exchange that seems to suggest the opposite. Whether this "object stewardship" is appropriate within other economic systems is beyond the scope of the present argument. There is no reason to believe that every possible economy can be governed by the same normative structure, and no reason that I need to argue in such general terms. It should be enough to decide what form of accountability would be adequate for a global economy and its direct participants who trade in fiat currencies for items produced by strangers.

These kinds of economic relationships make it especially difficult to find meaning in things, but that task is difficult in any case. The category of things is inclusive of literally everything. As such, it is not easily compressed or sorted. Ideas, bosons, animals, and people are all things. Chapter 5 is dedicated to this richness. It tries to generalize the ways in which people can understand and care about things and their consequences, both instrumentally and as a matter of appreciation that goes beyond use value. While books written for social scientists on materialism tend to launch right in with this diversity, our course is guided by a more practical approach. If I can convince you that things help us to solve moral problems, and if I can convince you that other available solutions are not adequate in that they fail to establish a comprehensive, reliable, and compelling normative order for complex economies, then it will make sense to look more carefully at things. Only after satisfying this basic requirement can the range of objects be expanded beyond the most obvious products that already hold the attention of the business class.

This argument will develop more fully in later chapters, but for now I need only summarize the view that follows with a few main points. First, things are capable of both bringing people together and keeping them apart.[5] Things can be bridges or fences, water coolers, or office doors. The bridging and blocking capacities of things are also manifest in their relationships to other things. Plastic keeps the acid in a battery from escaping; metal allows the charge to flow through the contacts. Second, dependences on things are diverse and difficult to negotiate. Some changes would require massive reconfigurations because things are interdependent. Electric and hydrogen-powered cars are examples of things that are not easily adopted because of the network infrastructure that they require. At the same time, some networks persist long after they seem to be obsolete. Fax machines are still common in newsrooms and offices despite the outdated technology that they utilize. Third, despite (and because of) object dependence, people know a lot about things; whether they possess the right moral knowledge is an open question, but the fact that people study objects in order to pursue their personal projects and in order to meet social expectations seems beyond debate. Jokes about complicated remote controls aside, people are expected to negotiate interactions with myriad objects, from ensuring that a parking brake is disengaged in order to drive to knowing that cast iron pans cannot be left with water in them. If it can be granted that objects are linkages and barriers, that things are reliant on other things, and that people already expend a great deal of cognitive energy to understand certain things, then we can begin to understand how commodities differ from objects with histories and how some processes resist commodification.

Collapsing Commodities with Connections

From time to time, investigative journalists, academic researchers, and labor activists create shortcuts across supply chains to show consumers the lives of producers. There are endless variations on this theme tracing objects upstream and down, following iPads,[6] illegal drugs,[7] maps,[8] manhole covers,[9] food,[10] clothing,[11] shoes,[12] guns,[13] contraband cigarettes,[14] pharmaceuticals,[15] and money.[16] These reports remind us of our connections to others. They also suggest a mechanism for change: by focusing on the people and places where products originate, we might also take an interest in the unmitigated costs of their production.

At the heart of the journalists' approach is an old idea that specific objects have embodied meaning. Long-established religious and cultural traditions view objects in this way by treating them as sacred and irreplaceable. In legal traditions, objects also take on embodied historical meaning. Guns used for murder, for instance, are destroyed rather than resold. Doing so sustains the legal concept of the deodand, a harm-causing object that must be forfeited to God or the crown because of its history.[17] One justification for destroying these guns relates to the significance that they have to victims. Another derives from their physical uniqueness. Each gun leaves a distinct signature on each bullet fired from its barrel. Reusing the gun would make forensic evidence related to that gun more difficult to interpret.

Within the law, objects have also been treated as meaningful causes, a practice that dates back to the Roman Empire and can be followed through numerous common law traditions. The legal tradition of noxal surrender allows a person who has been harmed by another's property to claim that property as hers (or in those times, his).[18] Oliver Wendell Holmes claims that this concept began with taking vengeance on objects: a family's right to burn a tree from which a branch fell and killed a kinsman is actually a right to punish the tree.[19]

Though legal practices have evolved to focus on intention, causation, and restitution, it once made sense to view nonhuman objects as bearing moral responsibility for the consequences of their motion, and to pay a fine according to the price of the harming object rather than the cost of the harm done. These old ways may seem dead, but today's conscientious consumption gives them new cosmopolitan life within a universalizing ethic of object stewardship. The same logic that would punish a tree for a person's death would also find an iPad to be tainted if someone was harmed while producing it.

In the next section, I will begin to deal with objects as causes. One way to do so is to focus on singularities, on specific things and the outcomes with which they are associated. Notice the distinction between causes and agents. It is entirely possible for an object to be a causal factor in an outcome even though it is incapable of intending that outcome. Many objects are incapable of agency or they are manifestations of someone's intentions who is long dead. Still, the fact that the agent is not proximate does not divest the object of the properties that promote certain uses according to its inherent or designed function. Some trees are useful for lightweight boats, and others for trusses. A tree will never express a preference for being a bat, dresser, or toothpick, but its characteristics can nevertheless cause it to be used in a certain way.

Singularization

When we think of things as causes, the object becomes a vessel of virtue or blame: an object that has harmed others should be worth less than an object that has helped others. To make sense of this way of understanding objects, we have to treat each thing as a distinct entity. Accordingly, my iPad is unlike any other because it connects me to the individuals who made it. The iPad's value derives from its role in their lives, not just from its role in my life. Following the terminology of economic sociology, I will describe this logic as "singular value," and the objects to which it applies as "singularities."[20] Singular value contrasts with commodity value because functionally similar things can replace commodities, whereas singularities cannot be replaced by mere substitution (they are not fungible).

Some objects are almost universally recognized as singularities. Persons and pets are obvious examples of items that are not substitutable for similar alternatives. Original works of art are a more applicable example that derives from human craft. Given the singularity of artwork, it is not surprising that some of the most influential ideas about the social origins of objects emerged in the thought of one of the nineteenth century's great art historians. John Ruskin wrote of wealth, value, and the nobility of life. These values gain importance both as an end and as a means. Consider Ruskin's critique of what he calls "servile ornament":

> You can teach a man to draw a straight line ... with admirable speed and perfect precision ...; but if you ask him to think about any of those forms, to consider if he cannot find any better in his own head, he stops; his execution becomes hesitating; he thinks, and ten to one he thinks wrong; ten to one he makes a mistake in the first touch he gives to his work as a thinking being. But you have made a man of him for all that. He was only a machine before, an animated tool .... Men were not intended to work with the accuracy of tools, to be precise and perfect in all their actions. If you will have that precision out of them, and make their fingers measure degrees like cogwheels, and their arms strike curves like compasses, you must unhumanize them.[21]

Ruskin's argument applies well beyond the sphere of art. His critique generalizes to anything we esteem without appreciating the treatment of those who made it. What is most important for the present account of singularization is that Ruskin sees in each work the kind of life that its creation allowed its maker to live. The object connects us with those who made it, and the appreciation that we show the object applies also to the beauty or ugliness of its origins.

Normally, the determination of whether something is or is not a commodity is based upon the qualities of the thing and the relevance of such qualities to a potential purchaser.[22] Classic commodities include foodstuffs like wheat, corn, and soybeans.[23] They are commodities because their quality is indistinguishable within a given market. Granted, it is technically possible to distinguish these foods in many ways, including moisture content, genetic makeup, and pesticide use. But within a given market, all of these attributes may be disregarded in order to act as if each grain is like all the others. Because one cannot distinguish between two grains of wheat by taste,[24] we treat them as interchangeable and group them by volume without distinction.

Ethics Against Commodities

In a technical sense, commodities are defined by their fungibility, the fact that they can be freely replaced without a distinction in value. If most consumers are truly indifferent and incapable of distinguishing between two similar things, we would say that they are fungible. But this practical indistinguishability does not answer the moral question as to whether we ought to treat every grain of wheat the same. In fact, as Ruskin shows, the discriminating logic should run in the opposite direction. Whether an object can be exchanged with another depends on whether there are salient moral attributes that ought to matter. If there are good reasons to distinguish between objects, then they are not fungible. Suppose that you were presented with two identical and equally clean knives. One was used in a murder; the other was not. Science provides no reason to distinguish between them: they are equally sharp and sanitary, and equally capable of being used at the dinner table. But whether they are understood as being identical is a choice about the meaning of things. Treating the knife as a tainted object may not alter the fate of its victim, but the general practice of acknowledging the moral histories of things can become a powerful motive in a responsible economy.

Distinguishing between objects based upon their histories is not only a negative category. Objects sometimes take on a positive valence as well.

What matters most is not the world as it appears to our senses. Rather, the enjoyment we get from something derives from what we think that thing is. This is true for intellectual pleasures, such as the appreciation of paintings and stories, and also for pleasures that seem simpler, such as the satisfaction of hunger and lust. For a painting, it matters who the artist was; for a story, it matters whether it is truth or fiction; for a steak, we care about what sort of animal it came from; for sex, we are strongly affected by who we think our sexual partner really is.[25]

Pleasure often derives from such distinctions. Using examples ranging from sacred objects in Afro-Brazilian religion to forged paintings, Bloom argues that objects take on essential and unique characteristics through their special histories. These characteristics define the objects' value.

I will illustrate a subset of these processes later using contemporary cinematic mythologies deployed to captivate audiences and sell toys (see Singularizing Narratives in Chapter 2). At present, it suffices to note that both pleasant and unpleasant nonphysical characteristics can be personally and interpersonally significant object attributes. As Simmel discusses in the context of money, society is capable of endowing objects with value irrespective of the useful material properties of the things that it valorizes.[26] Numerous psychological and economic studies document these processes.[27]

What is not well described by this experimental research paradigm is the political, economic, and ethical conception of responsibility that emerges when groups of people attempt to consistently apply a moralizing perspective to supply chains. Many consumers have come to believe that distinguishing between similar objects is a matter of moral consequence, and that differences in the human and ecological costs incurred in an object's production ought to be a factor in the object's price and value. For them, this is true regardless of whether an object is practically substitutable because moral valence overwhelms an object's commodity status. For conscientious consumers, avoiding irresponsible products is a part of living responsibly.[28]

Trees, Toys, and Gold

It is not only conscientious consumers who care about specific objects. Singularization is a pragmatic way to understand the world, and this logic is already applied commonly in many organizations. This chapter describes the manifest concern for objects in three industries. Forestry is the primary example, and the discussion of trees is twice as long as the discussion of either toys or gold. Together, these three topics illustrate the range of supply chain stages where singularization

Table 1.1 *Morality-Adjacent Product Descriptions*

Homemade	Farm fresh	Authentic
Handmade	Sustainable	Artisanal
Made in America	Nontoxic	Natural
Community supported	Green	Responsibly invested
Locally grown	Family owned	Organic
Recyclable	Reusable	Biodegradable
Made with love	Fair trade	Sweatshop free
Cruelty free	Worker owned	Free range

makes sense, and the differences in the way that objects are perceived, commodified, and singularized.

Let us begin with the basic case for objects being treated as unique according to their origins. Most people have things that they would rather not sell or replace with a copy, and many people show an interest in products because of their unique histories. Marketing helps to sustain these product conceptions. Consider the lexicon of marketing claims that supersede or sidestep the functional properties of products, elaborated in Table 1.1.

Many of these claims are linked to product quality. Handmade bicycle frames were long thought to be better than machine-built ones. Homemade cookies taste different from mass-produced ones. But the distinctions that these claims introduce are not strictly related to functional qualities. Otherwise, handmade bicycle frames would say, "stronger, lighter, and more durably welded," and it would make no sense for a computer manufacturer to advertise the nontoxicity of the devices it sells. The claims communicate a complex set of value-laden concepts, many of which provide no benefit to a consumer, unless the consumer is interested in limiting harm and providing benefit to others.

Mainstream firms increasingly invoke such narratives to distinguish their products from the competition and to resonate with conscientious consumers. The claims are not limited to sustainable products and fair-trade goods, but these markets are particularly prone to the language of origins. Though a singularity logic is implied by taking an interest in product life cycle considerations, the sincerity of this interest is not a foregone conclusion.

Indeed, framing origination attributes as properties of brands, rather than products, runs the risk of negating the meaning and responsibility latent in object histories. In many cases, the actual attention to a product's life cycle goes no further than simplistic marketing pitched to sate consumers' consciences. Nor does the interest in origins provide a path to product singularization: products are still usually viewed and governed as commodities. Sometimes it even seems as if singularity value is being converted into commodity value.

The fact that origins are commodified does not negate the intention to take responsibility for product sources. It is likely that many consumers genuinely intend to make a difference, and so do many firms. When firms forgo profit and consumers pay a premium for a given product, they prove these intentions, particularly when they do so without fanfare. But even the most beneficent firms and consumers are only willing to incur finite costs.[29] Moreover, many firms are not especially interested in the internalization of upstream externalities, the care of distant workers, or sustainable production, because taking on these responsibilities greatly complicates their business activities.

Though it is often difficult to determine what firms intend (or whether firms are even capable of intention), we can ascribe motives to firms based upon the effectiveness of the means that they choose. The dominant purchasing strategy for many firms, which focuses on minimizing costs through a competitive global supply chain, is a deficient means for the internalization of upstream social and environmental costs. Whatever its merits, a competitive global supply chain increases complexity and uncertainty while reducing accountability for nonobservable product attributes. Global supply chains can control prices and (with some effort) maintain quality, but other features that cannot be measured with the physical attributes of an object and controlled with purse strings are not so easily guaranteed. This includes many of the product claims listed above, most of which are difficult for a consumer or globally sourced firm to check. Important moral considerations of an object's singular value suffer from this uncertainty.

If the logic of this contradiction is not obvious, consider the competing objectives of three mutually exclusive preferences: protection against supply chain disintermediation, increased competition, and code of workplace conduct compliance. Take college apparel as an example. Brands want to decrease the price of their factor inputs, which they hope to do through competition. Universities want to ensure that their codes of conduct are adhered to, and they are also happy to receive revenue from licensees that sell apparel with their logo. Intermediaries connect brands with producers so that brands do not always know which factories make which of their products. To guarantee code compliance, you need to know which factories are making your apparel. To protect competition, you need the possibility of moving production between factories. And to protect an intermediary's margin, you need to ensure that customers cannot identify suppliers or buy directly from them. Of course, some forms of supply chain policing are still possible, but the ends of competition and intermediation work against a brand's capacity to guarantee workplace safety and adequate wages.

The academic literature on global supply chains generally pits the challenges of maintaining supply chain governance[30] against the profitability of manufacturing in places where regulation is weaker and wages lower. The limits and potential of supply chain governance within the global economy continue to be a subject of considerable debate, but it is clear that variations in strategies for monitoring and maintaining private governance arrangements can cause divergent outcomes, as Graeme Auld has observed in his work on the governance of forestry, fisheries, and coffee supply chains.[31]

Looking closely at supply chains tends to require an industrial and geographic focus. Here, I consider the supply chains of three specific products, trees, toys, and gold, in order to illustrate some of the questions that arise when one begins to think of objects as singularities and to appraise their value accordingly. The observations are organized around a set of critical exchanges regarding the nature of object value rather than a more general account of how complex production networks are best managed.

Trees, toys, and gold provide a useful diversity for this inquiry. The interests of trees and wood fiber products are biologically and ecologically defined. Treating them as singularities begins with understanding the ecological interdependences that surround them. Toys, in contrast, are highly abstracted from their raw ingredients: one does not normally think about where toys come from or the materials of their components until a safety concern causes scrutiny. The extraction of gold, like trees, may also cause significant ecological harm, but unlike trees, gold is rarely used in disposable products. Instead, it serves as a medium of value exchange. Though there are lessons to be learned by examining the entire life cycle of all three objects, I focus on the ecological origins and extraction of trees; the manufacture, use, and disposal of toys; and the exchange of gold. Together, these phases constitute a complete product life cycle across the three different products. The cycle includes raw material extraction, manufacturing, exchange, use, and disposal.

The Forest and Its Trees

A complex set of biological motives drive natural objects like trees. Their lives, and indeed life in general, are sustained through absorption of nutrients, growth, and reproduction. Trees grow within communities that cycle and share resources. They are useful to other organisms within the forest and to persons within or outside of the forest. Though biological products from many habitats could be the focal subjects of this analysis, trees are a particularly important case given the ecological and economic debates around them.

Throughout the twentieth century, but particularly since the 1960s, American forests have been a contentious terrain over which ecological and economic interests wage a battle for control. Histories of the United States Forest Service document the rivaling visions of how the forest should be used and protected. The Forest Service has optimistically maintained the belief that ecological and economic ends are not mutually exclusive.[32] Nevertheless, this belief is contravened by the ongoing conflict between ecological foresters and commodity foresters who understand the value of trees in entirely different ways.

The core tenets of ecological forestry include the maintenance of structural complexity and species diversity; the recognition of complex interaction between water, soil, nitrogen, and biological cycles; the management of land tracts to avoid segmentation; the maintenance of soil to sustain ecological capacity; careful planning regarding road use; and periodic tree harvesting in ways that maintain local diversity in size and species. Commodity forestry prefers homogenous stands of genetically similar trees with faster growth rates, the use of herbicides to control other plants, convenient road access to reduce transportation costs, and either clear-cuts at a given site or the extraction of only the oldest and most valuable trees from a structurally complex forest. Each of these approaches has its own scientific movement, one of which is interested in monitoring the broader ecological community and recreating the natural diversity of old-growth forests, the other in addressing the agricultural problems of monoculture.[33]

As a consequence, they present competing sets of facts. Ecological foresters perceive synergies between different species that help make forests strong, resistant to disease, and useful for purposes other than tree production. Commodity foresters observe the near-term benefits of organized stands of trees that are accessible because other plants are not allowed to grow. Each of these orientations operate as a method of wood fiber production; they sell the same product. However, they are employed on separate parcels of land and often within separate ownership structures. It can be generalized that private forests are most often managed as commodity forests and federal forests lands are torn between ecological and commodity management strategies, but there are exceptions, and strategies vary by region as well.[34]

Whereas economic models of forest management encourage a sharp contrast between these management strategies, I aim to articulate a theory of value that would motivate a convergence so that all forests could be managed with the same spirit of ecological respect. I wish to suggest that private forest managers should be motivated to grow diverse, structurally complex, and ecologically stable stands that rival the aesthetic value placed upon old-growth forests, if we can get the economics of forestry right.

Such a unity of interest would be unprecedented given that foresters face a hitherto intractable conflict. Commodity forestry and ecological forestry comprise two very different ways of thinking about the same objects, creating a division deeply rooted in cultural values, in participants' sense of forest meaning.[35] Within the present account, the conflict between ecological and commodity forestry helpfully illustrates the difference between managing singularities and commodities. The recent success of green labeling further demonstrates the salience of supply chain governance and the corruptibility of some of these approaches.

The singular value of trees generally fits into two categories: first, the value of trees in their ecological settings and the good they do through their natural life cycle of growth, reproduction, death, and decomposition; second, the value of trees in economic supply chains, including the benefit of wood fiber products, the harm of unsustainable forestry practices, and the likely fates of their eventual disposal. The first category establishes the ecological consequences of removing a particular tree, or group of trees, as the opportunity costs of extraction. The second category establishes the consequences of the remainder of the product and by-product life cycles in production, distribution, consumption, and disposal. Wood fiber is used for diverse products, from paper to turpentine. Across this range, there are variations in how much social value we derive from the trees we cut down. The second category of singular value represents the range of benefits and costs that derive from private attempts to make trees economically useful. Bringing these considerations together will allow us to track forestry benefits and costs by focusing on the things themselves, on the way that they are used, and on the systems of relationships with other living things surrounding them. Accordingly, the next section focuses on trees' situated value in a forest and then the subsequent section turns to trees' value in the economy.

Trees in Forests

Commodity forestry is an agricultural application of industrialization. It simplifies a complex ecosystem into a narrow productive system with one main output. The industrial approach to forestry is intensive, both in the resources it uses to harvest and in the way in which it seeks to entirely define the ecology of the forests that it cultivates. To the commodity forester, land has the potential to yield a certain amount of wood fiber, measured in board feet. The rate at which the land yields wood, less the cost of bringing that wood to market, determines the profitability of the enterprise.

In its narrow use orientation towards the land, commodity forestry is not interested in the ecological value of any organisms that live there. Here I distinguish two forms of value discussed extensively later. Ecological value is conferred by a system of relationships to other entities, both persons and things. Commodity value derives exclusively from the market income of a standardized product or resource. The simplifying narrative of commodification defines value narrowly and empowers key organizational actors in the promotion of commodities to the detriment of other objects.

What other value might we find in forests? This depends both on how we relate to the forest and how we understand the way that the forest relates to itself. In a sense, "the tree is not an object at all, but a certain gathering together of the threads of life."[36] We are trying to expand the way that we understand objects as things to represent the life that they gather together. Commodity forestry makes no such attempt. Instead, to sustain commodity forestry, practitioners must disregard both the forest's complex potential as a diverse ecosystem and its complex potential for local human communities. Indeed, both are challenges to be overcome.

Diverse forests provide diverse products to whomever or whatever lives near them. Yet many human communities do not practice the kind of foraging that makes forests' diverse products useful. Using these products requires proximity, knowledge of where to find and how to make use of different plants and animals, and the time to do so. In the extreme, some indigenous foragers sustain complex diets, shelters, and cultural traditions entirely using forest resources. Amazonian indigenous communities, for example, meet their needs using the forest with very limited demand for wood fiber.[37]

Indigenous forest communities establish one end of a spectrum of interdependence with forest ecologies, yet it is worth noting that indigenous people have numerous and complex relationships with many different ecosystems. Not all indigenous communities are interested in promoting forests. M. Kat Anderson describes how California's dominant forests of Douglas firs were seen by Yurok basket weavers as encroaching on grasslands.[38] The Yurok people burned grasslands to push back the edge of the forest because grasses provided important seeds, foods, and cordage materials. There is hardly an ecosystem in the world that has not been somehow managed and subjugated by human preferences.

Anthropologists accuse environmentalists of politicizing the position of indigenous communities to sustain a somewhat deceptive narrative about pristine nature and sustainable practices. In fact, any community can be placed along a continuum in terms of its relationships with local habitats, ranging from near-complete dependence upon a single ecosystem to the complete denial of an ecosystem's complexity in favor of a single commodity output. Often, people are partially reliant on nearby forests, which provide seasonal nuts, berries, and mushrooms alongside commercial timber. Forests also provide other services like shade on hot summer days, the capacity to absorb pollution from nearby industry and transportation infrastructure, and the sequestration of carbon that reduces atmospheric carbon dioxide levels. While few people depend upon forests in their full complexity, many benefit from multiple aspects of forests and the ecological diversity within them.

I have focused on the value that people find in forests, but I am also interested in the ecological utility that different organisms find within a forest. As singularizing narratives develop, I will break down some elements of this distinction. Doing so allows people to value things because others value them. They can also value things because they are valuable to other living things. To better understand the value that a forest finds in itself, it is worth observing some of the practices proposed by ecological forestry. First of all, ecological forestry demands certain practices that would seem wasteful to the commodity forester. Ecologists would have foresters leave a certain number of cut logs on the ground, leave tree crowns near the place where the tree was cut down, and leave many grown trees in place to maintain age diversity within the forest. They would have foresters plant new trees from multiple species to maintain diversity, as well as nontree plants for the forest floor. They would have foresters avoid intensive site preparation that alters the soil, but makes it much easier to plant a new crop of trees.[39] These practices would promote the interests of the stand as a forest. The theme proves the singularity observation: traced from their origins and represented as unique entities, trees are useful to forests, not just to people.

What do trees do in forests? They are the constitutive element of forests, but this does not express the relationships between living things that they facilitate. Importantly, trees regulate the flow of resources through a forest ecosystem. They hold soil in place, control the flow of water, provide shelter from weather, and support diverse and complex interactions with other organisms. Without the cover of a canopy of trees, the ecology of a forest floor is a completely different environment and many native species cannot thrive. This is why clear-cuts and crown fires[40] are profoundly significant ecological events. Chapter 6 discusses a common aesthetic preference for well-used objects, for instance, otters fishing in clean streams and children playing with toys (see Chapter 6, Ethical Theory and Valuing Objects). These are simplified versions of an understanding that values system complexity for its dynamic and diverse order. Complex biodiversity is a foundational priority in singularity value because ecosystems rely upon symbiosis for living things to thrive:

In North American forestry, where conifers are the major commercial species, noncrop vegetation is virtually always broadleaved trees, forbs, shrubs, and grasses. A variety of studies have either conclusively demonstrated or strongly suggested that these plants perform numerous important ecological functions, including providing unique food (e.g., nuts, nectar), enhancing nutrient availability, replenishing nitrogen capital through biological fixation, stabilizing soil nutrients and biology following disturbances, and increasing resistance of conifers to herbivorous insects, pathogens, and fire. The complexity of interactions among plant species is only beginning to be understood but goes far beyond simple competition. For example, it is now well established that different plant species within at least some communities – including broadleaved trees and conifers – participate in a network of shared resources mediated by mycorrhizal fungi.[41]

Mutually advantageous interactions make biological health a property of biological systems rather than individual organisms, and demonstrate the importance of biodiversity. As we will see, the promotion of diversity presents certain normative challenges, but all things considered, biodiversity will remain one of the most compelling ecological imperatives, and one that is most sorely threatened by the intensive industrialization of commodity forestry. The loss of uniqueness and complexity is not just destructive to individual organisms, but to the health of the larger pattern.

What value is to be placed on the viability of these ecosystems? At what price can their utter destruction become conscionable? Looking at trees in the abstract makes such a question difficult to answer. Squirrels do not pay rent for their treetop homes. The utilitarian's summation of forest use-value requires a number of difficult-to-estimate parameters of ecological services that the forest provides to persons. There are those who seek to price such things as an illustration of natural capital.[42] I do not object to the effort, but singularity value provides an alternative and less circuitous approach. Observing the harm and benefit of a given singular object viewed across its history, one can ask in a straightforward manner whether the totality of that use makes the world better, more beautiful, and more complex. Trees are valuable on a planetary scale and to their local ecosystems. Given their value, any use to which they are put should provide more value than the trees were providing in their original location, and the price paid must cover the cost of repairing the trees' habitat.

In ecological terms, it would be preferable that these trees be taken in clusters at sporadic intervals from a large land area so that the forest could persist in its genetic and ecological diversity. Cutting trees need not be equated with deforestation, but this alternative is more costly. The industrial approach to forestry is a by-product of basic economic forces that provide few incentives for stewarding the long-term viability of the ecosystem. It is expensive to build mills for processing and roads for extraction, and the expense is more easily recovered through intensive use. At a given price, wood production is only justified for a given size of operation with a given local intensity.

Trees in Products

Though it may not be possible to determine the precise economic value of the ecological niche of an individual tree, it is possible to compare some aspects of the tree's contribution in this setting to the contribution that it makes elsewhere, after being cut down and processed. Trees are used in many different ways, some more wasteful than others. In 2009, the US Postal Service delivered 85.2 billion advertisements,[43] many of which would not have been considered useful by either the recipient or the sender, and almost all of which were printed on wood fiber-based paper. Though email, e-books, and digital filing systems have reduced some wasteful uses of trees, humans continue to increase the resources that they use. Wood fiber is wasted by tearing down structurally sound houses to build more spacious homes, by discarding building materials, and by making furniture that will not last. These practices encourage shortsighted consumption that increases waste. Because trees are valuable as trees, it would be preferable if we used as few of them as possible and if we used them in durable ways. Using a tree in a house or a book is acceptable, provided that the use value exceeds the lost use value of those materials in their native setting.

But the story of waste begins earlier, depending not only on the way that products are finally used, but on their conditions of extraction. In 1897, John Muir described a hierarchy of wastefulness in forestry. At the bottom of the heap he places the shake-maker:

Of all the destroyers that infest the woods, the shake-maker seems the happiest. Twenty or thirty years ago, shakes, a kind of long boardlike shingles split with a mallet and a frow, were in great demand for covering barns and sheds, and many are used still in preference to common shingles, especially those made from the sugar-pine, which do not warp or crack in the hottest sunshine . . ..

Only the lower, perfectly clear, free-splitting portions of the giant pines are used, – perhaps ten to twenty feet from a tree two hundred and fifty in height; all the rest is left a mass of ruins, to rot or to feed the forest fires, while thousands are hacked deeply and rejected in proving the grain . . .. It is not generally known that, notwithstanding the immense quantities of timber cut every year for foreign and home markets and mines, from five to ten times as much is destroyed as is used.[44]

Thus, our approximation of wastefulness must include both the unimportant uses to which things are put and the inefficient means by which they are extracted. Either of these factors can undermine the use value of an object from a singularity perspective.

Forestry is much improved since Muir's time. There are fewer trees to waste, and Muir's call for regulation was answered.[45] But unfortunately, the dominant norm of forestry continues to treat trees as a commodity. The economic organization of the industry confuses the downstream consumers who would prefer to act as good forest stewards. This presents a serious challenge for the singularization of objects from the consumer perspective, one to which we will return later in this text. If consumers cannot assess the quality of the products that they buy, they cannot make conscientious decisions about what to buy. Deprived of their capacity to care by dysfunctional sustainable-labeling initiatives, consumers may even be discouraged from the very possibility of living responsibly.

In wood fiber products, a controversy arose from the application of green labels by an organization that appears more concerned with the health of the forestry industry than the health of the forests.[46] Labeling initiatives have come to play an important role in the global governance of forest stewardship.[47] Like many supply chains, wood products are covered by numerous regulatory regimes, none of which can be said to guarantee sustainable forestry practices. Consumers and environmental groups rely upon environmental responsibility labeling initiatives to provide market incentives for organizations that choose to go beyond what the law requires to protect, and sustain, local ecologies.

The Sustainable Forestry Initiative (SFI) was founded in 1994 as an outgrowth of an industry group called the American Forest and Paper Association. Though it has since become a separate nonprofit organization, its board is comprised almost entirely of timber and paper industry insiders who, according to environmental groups, are creating a brand rather than a credible certification procedure.[48] "The SFI's standards and procedures have been developed and approved by industry for industry."[49] In November 2010, ForestEthics released a report on the lackluster performance of SFI that documented a long list of environmental hardships suffered by forests under SFI's care.[50] Among the more troubling issues are that SFI-certified auditors claim to have inspected more than 46,000 square miles of forests in five days; that SFI has done little or nothing to address problems with excessive chemical use, landslides, erosion, and species endangerment; and that the labeling system is designed to be confusing so that customers will see the word "sustainable" on their most common label, which is only meant to certify the percentage of the product that is made from recycled content. In September 2011, ForestEthics partnered with a coalition of twenty environmental organizations like the National Resource Defense Council and the Sierra Club to pressure SFI to "stop the greenwash." However, with an annual marketing budget of more than three million dollars,[51] SFI's labeling continues to influence consumers. And, despite more than ten years of public opposition since SFI was first accused of duplicity in the late 1990s,[52] there is no resolution in sight.

The SFI dilemma poses a challenging issue for singular values and the promulgation of a conscientious consumer ethic. Sustainable forestry requires careful stewardship of forest ecology, suggesting that a high value be placed upon forest products, and a price premium is likely the best way to guarantee this performance and to cover its costs. However, with a little environmental deception, firms can claim this price premium without incurring the costs of responsible production.

What is to be done about willful environmental deception? Some suggest that environmental deceivers should be driven out of business. As Ray Anderson, the environmentalist founder of a large carpet manufacturer, put it, "We must be genuine. Our actions must speak louder than our words. Greenwash (pseudo-green) is, and should be, business suicide. Our customers should and will see right through it."[53]

Anderson mixes normative and empirical claims by arguing that greenwashing is business suicide and that it ought to be suicide. Yet the enduring fight with the SFI would seem to indicate that greenwashing does not result in business failure, at least not immediately.

Conscientious consumption often works by denying the collective action problems of implementation. The conscientious consumer imagines, in a way that I will later trace back to Kant, that if she could get everyone to behave as she does, profound change is possible. If the lack of stewardship in the wood supply chain were to motivate the average consumer to avoid the consumption of wood, producers would be forced to change their practices. This is the level at which some industrial changes must occur when incremental change fails to progress. Reduced consumption does not target any especially harmful organization or benefit any especially beneficial ones, but it avoids the uncertainty of the ecological dilemma that wood fiber products pose. Singular values suggest that consumers should not buy wood products that are tainted by ecologically destructive forestry, but as long as commodity forestry can benefit parasitically from positive moral values by redirecting them toward pseudo-ecological products, conscientious consumption cannot achieve its objectives.

The contest is not only being carried out in board rooms and sales floors, but across a global ecological landscape. Forest ecosystems are constructed for economic use. Under the maximizing logic of commodity forestry, massive tracts of land are planted using simplified landscapes that deprive the land of its potential for biological diversity and complexity. These simplifying landscapes make the land less useful to numerous other organisms, including people, and more susceptible to a variety of threats and pathogens. Those who wish to maintain diverse forest ecologies are likely to care about the origins of a given wood product. For the commodity foresters who view trees like so many blades of grass, such an aesthetic is utterly foreign.

In forestry, there are issues at every stage of the process, from the cultivation of trees in nurseries through planting, harvesting, processing, using, recycling, and disposal. Forest scientists are still learning and experimenting to better understand the ecological and economic implications of their subject, but the implication of the singularity logic for those of us who are merely consumers of wood products is clear: if the value of a given use case does not exceed the value of the tree from which that wood originated, the tree should stay rooted in the ground. Given the nearly universal adoption of unsustainable forestry practices, diffused globally in the eighteenth and nineteenth centuries, the state of existing landscapes is not a reliable guide for how land should be used. Caring for trees in their diverse potential sets a higher standard.

Though only a few old-growth forests remain to demonstrate the full ecological potential of native plants, we still know the difference between forestry techniques that enrich the complexity of a forest and practices that only aim to simplify. As such, forests provide a key example in the analysis of objects as singularities. I have focused to a great extent on their cultivation because I will next turn to two other products at different stages of production. Then I will return to forests again at the end of this chapter to propose a more ecological approach to economics.

Tainted Toys

Forests and their trees have a prominent place in many ecological imaginations, but now I will turn to objects whose history is less conspicuous in the imaginations that they inspire. Usually, toys are representative of characters and their meaning is shaped by the sentimentality of the attachments that children form with them, but on occasion serious defects bring attention to their origins. Several toy recalls in the late 2000s brought the origins of such objects to prominence. Singularization may be justified by a concern for an originating ecology or by the appropriateness of an object for its intended use. Toy safety scandals raised concerns about product safety and the care shown by manufacturers for users.

During 2007, there were forty-two significant toy recalls due to lead contamination.[54] These recalls contributed to widespread public concern about safety and product quality in globally manufactured goods. Mattel, a large toy company, had three waves of recalls involving more than 20 million toys.[55] Lead was the initial focus of the recalls. The lead was accidentally introduced by the manufacturer that Mattel hired in China to produce the toys. Later recalls resulted from magnets that detached too easily and were potentially harmful if digested. This design failure directed blame at Mattel as well as its supply chain.[56]

Pirson and Malhotra[57] argue that Mattel's multiple conflicting public actions caused mistrust both upstream with Chinese suppliers and downstream with American consumers. The notion of toys as singularities does not direct responsibility to any one party or individual as could a contract or finding of negligence. Instead, singularities bring together communities with shared interests in common resources. The Chinese suppliers, the American designers, and the American purchasers are brought together by one specific toy that moves from one factory to one household and puts one child at risk. Within this community, responsibility would usually spread out so that both Mattel and its suppliers have obligations. But these specific things do not justify Mattel pointing fingers across the Pacific. As stewards of toys with responsibilities to their eventual consumers, both designers and manufacturers should think critically about the safety of the product.

The toy recalls had a profound emotional impact as one of several product safety issues that arose simultaneously from internationally sourced products. As the New York Times later reported,[58] Mattel blamed the contaminated toys on Lee Der Industrial, a toy manufacturer based in Foshan, China. Zhang Shuhong, the manager of that firm, committed suicide in the wake of his firm's vilification. Lead paint arrived at Lee Der from a supplier that sold several contaminated pigments. Looking downstream, the pigment supplier and paint supplier should both have known that the paint was being delivered to a toy factory. Since the dangers of lead materials are widely understood and manageable, the careful stewardship of lead should go all the way back to the original lead mining operation, but there was a failure at some point along the chain of custody.

In this case, dangerous materials were accidentally applied to products that would be used by the most delicate consumers. We should not imagine that the task of controlling this risk is easy: dynamic sourcing relationships are notoriously difficult to control and the further they spread, the more difficult it is to keep track of the moving parts. However, until suppliers develop a downstream sense of responsibility and accountability, their reputations remain at risk, as do the parties with whom they do business. Product streams flow together through assembly, and downstream consumers tend to develop extremely general understandings of the etiology of supply chain irresponsibility, particularly cross-culturally.

When the Peanut Corporation of America caused nine food poisoning deaths and 116 hospitalizations by violating health and safety regulations,[59] American consumers were angry at the company, at regulators, and at companies that used Peanut Corporation as a supplier.[60] Their acrimony was wholly consistent with an object theory of responsibility. However, when Mattel imported toys from China that were painted with lead, the blame was less focused.

American consumers did not trace the responsibility back to a pigment manufacturer in China. Instead, they generalized to all manufacturing in China and all China-sourced products. A Reuters poll reported that four out of five people were uncomfortable with the safety of products sourced from China after a few unrelated product safety scandals.[61] As a category of product origins, China is geographically, organizationally, and interpersonally far more diverse than the actual perpetrators. Nevertheless, this diversity escaped consumers.

By developing responsible production norms and sanctions, governments and local business communities can reduce the likelihood of untargeted sanctioning behavior that affects an entire industry or region. However, in response to some incidents, like the lead contamination of toys in China, regulators can be too targeted in their punishment. In the case of Lee Der, the result was professionally and personally devastating. The Chinese government revoked Lee Der's export license and the firm's prosperity instantly collapsed. After reinvesting nearly all of his personal wealth in Lee Der,[62] Mr. Zhang was forced to make a company-wide announcement encouraging everyone to seek other employment; he later killed himself in the factory where he lived and worked.

China singled out Lee Der as a scapegoat for the breach of trust perpetrated within the larger supply chain. Insofar as responsibility is shared throughout a supply chain, it is an injustice to focus blame so narrowly. Responsibility is shared by those who delivered lead paint to a toy manufacturer, by those who failed to check the contents of the paint used at Lee Der, and by Mattel's failure to monitor the safety of its products by inspection. This sense of shared responsibility demands vigilance from supply chain actors at all stages of production and distribution.

Some concerns for ecological value apply to toys as well. For instance, if toy manufacturers and consumers think of toys as singularities, they should concern themselves with the sources of petroleum by-products used in plastic. Any environmental or safety issues within these production processes are inherited by the toys. What distinguishes the toy case is a specific form of upstream and downstream vigilance. Safety issues are actually easier to address through a comprehensive supply chain accountability structure than problems like workers' rights. Unsafe toys can be tested for safety, whereas toys produced by exploited labor do not inherit any physical property during production. Similarly, paper made from sustainably harvested wood fiber is much like paper made from clear-cut forests.

As a technical matter, the origins of toys are much more easily traced than the origins of wood fiber products. Many toys are stamped with lot numbers, and almost all can be tracked back to a specific factory, if not a specific day of production. A ream of paper also has an origin story that is semitraceable, but the pulp from which it is made may include both recycled and new content. Wood fiber can be broken down into source percentages, as could the petroleum origins of toys. This is as close to singularities as these products can get.

Toy Life Cycles

Beyond safety and ecological issues that accumulate in production, the impact of toys also results from design, use, and disposal. Working within the ISO 14044 standard for Life Cycle Analysis (LCA), the dominant methodological standard guiding this form of accounting, Muñoz and colleagues attempted to measure the impact of "Winnie the Pooh Stories and Songs," an electronically voiced teddy bear. They found that manufacturing the toy accounted for 28–34 percent of the toy's total impact and that the batteries necessary for the toy's use accounted for 50–64 percent.[63] Though these impact factors vary by product, I will consider some additional details about this study of one toy to better understand the potential and limits of LCA approaches, including their boundaries and role in design improvement.

The Muñoz study focused on five impact categories: "abiotic depletion potential, acidification potential, global warming potential, eutrophication potential, and photochemical oxidants formation potential."[64] Lacking available data and modeling techniques, it was impossible to assess other potentially important factors like human and eco-toxicity potential and soil use impacts. These are major considerations in the ecological theory of value described below, but they are not easily measured in this assessment framework.

The following year's redesign of a similar toy managed to reduce some of its impact based upon the recommendations in the Muñoz analysis. The new toy used less plastic and more recycled content, it was more energy efficient, and it encouraged purchasers to use rechargeable batteries to reduce disposable battery use. This is the kind of product innovation that is so far possible on the ecological side of mainstream product design. There is no room here to suggest that we make and consume fewer such objects, but there is room for making the products less harmful in their direct and indirect consequences.

Practical pedagogies of resource conservation teach us to reduce, reuse, and recycle. This "waste hierarchy" prioritizes methods of conservation, with reduction having the greatest impact and recycling having the least. Each method involves certain challenges. In order to reduce, one must consume less. In order to reuse, one must tolerate degraded performance or initially invest in a more durable alternative. In order to recycle, an entire infrastructure must be put in place. Manufacturers must label their materials so that recyclers can identify them. Assembled products must be easy to disassemble. Materials must be collected and sorted from waste streams, and delivered to specialized recyclers. These practices are only feasible in countries with a reliable waste removal infrastructure. Moreover, recycling's role in conservation offers mixed results. Recyclers can only make use of a subset of all the materials delivered to them. For the subset of materials that can be recycled, significant water and energy resources are necessary to process them into a manufacturing-ready form. The remaining benefits of recycling are that in specific cases, recycled materials require fewer resources to process relative to virgin materials, and that recycling keeps these materials out of landfills.

This hierarchy has been in place for decades. It is sometimes expanded to clarify the options for end-of-life management. For example, the US Environmental Protection Agency adds compost, energy recovery, and landfill below the reduce, reuse, and recycle options.[65] The hierarchy cannot be strictly interpreted across all contexts. Several articles have criticized the simplifying linearity that the hierarchy implies, for example, by arguing that landfill and incineration may be preferable in regions with sparse populations.[66] More generally, it has been argued that the mixed environmental and economic consequences of different conservation options need to be better integrated into policy decisions, including an approach that sets aside recycling targets for variable price-based policies.[67]

The current waste management regime is not solving the waste problem. From 1975 to 2010, per-capita municipal solid waste (MSW) in the United States increased by approximately 36 percent. In 1975, the United States generated 127.8 million tons of MSW, recycling 9.3 million tons of that total. In 2010, the United States generated 249.9 million tons of MSW, recycling 85.1 million tons of that total. Despite a nine-fold increase in recycled waste volumes, the quantity of nonrecycled waste still increased by 39 percent from the mid-1970s.[68]

Unfortunately, the problem is not as simple as an improper priority system for the way that waste is handled. The larger problem is an economy that completely disconnects waste generation from waste responsibility. Fee-for-service infrastructures aim to address this disconnect in the aggregate, forcing households and businesses to pay for the amount that they discard. Yet waste is so easily discarded in small quantities at unmonitored locations, and so expensive to collect from these locations, that fee-for-service disposal becomes difficult to police. As a result, we neglect the opportunities to reduce and reuse in favor of recycling, which requires only modest innovation on the part of producers.

One of the biggest challenges for recyclers is e-waste. Electronic components are large, expensive to disassemble, and often full of toxic materials. The costs and regulatory hurdles of recycling them correctly have caused many recyclers to export trash to places where they will have serious consequences. To document this problem, a group of researchers hid tracking devices in e-waste. Their strategy is a perfect example of the opportunities for singularization presented by new technologies. The researchers tracked e-waste from US recycling centers to Mexico, Taiwan, China, Pakistan, Thailand, Dominican Republic, Canada, and Kenya.[69] Visiting these sites, they found dangerous conditions where workers were exposed to potentially harmful doses of known carcinogens. The workers at these sites were not trained to recognize which parts were dangerous, and they were not provided with safety equipment to protect themselves.

There are a few exceptions. Many grocery stores offer discounts to customers who bring their own bags, and some businesses invest in reusable shipping containers to reduce long-term capital costs. Nevertheless, many products would not exist if durable alternatives were a normative standard.

The LCA approach may be viewed as illustrative of the harm that a singularized product will cause, but the way that Life Cycle Analyses generalize, model, and establish confidence intervals fits more plausibly within a commodity framework. LCAs are based upon impact assessment models that are averaged over ordinary manufacturing, use, and disposal behaviors. Some of these toys may never be removed from their boxes; these will do the least harm through their battery consumption. The generalizing perspective of averaging outcomes and inputs is appropriate for a firm that will design, produce, and distribute many toys without much control over how they are treated.

Though Disney has certainly singularized its Winnie the Pooh character and his anthropomorphic friends with unique and human-like characteristics, none of this uniqueness is bestowed through the impact assessment procedure. The toys wait to be singularized until they reach a child's hands, where they are likely to be treated with some focused care. Young children develop powerful object attachments and find it more difficult to give up objects than other pro-social behaviors.[70] Nevertheless, children grow out of toys, and then they are desingularized and discarded. In the end, as in the beginning, the toy is blended into a commodity heap, its origins forgotten.

This chapter illustrates the practical understanding and limits of object singularization. In the case of toys, a safety scandal promoted focused awareness on object origins. This awareness dissipated as the scandal abated. The waste properties of toys are concerns for manufacturers, academics, and some conscientious consumers, but these examples help us to see that our interest in objects as singularities may often be ephemeral.

Applying the Golden Rule to Gold

The object perspective has almost limitless applications beyond toys and trees. The method is applicable to all products, resources, and equipment that are of sufficient worth or destructive power to warrant stewardship. If the premise is accepted that responsibilities flow with material goods, then many people should develop expansive supply chain knowledge throughout their careers. Relative to the understanding of career insiders, any account of this type is far too general. In forestry, for instance, an employee should be concerned with trees in general, and with a given set of trees, in a given place, destined for a given use. That said, the basic features of the trees and toys as singularities give us a point of departure. Unsustainable forestry is illustrative of the limits of use and the consequences of use-value being defined too narrowly. Unsafe and ecologically wasteful toys are illustrative of how usefulness is valued and how individual careers and well-being can become intertwined with supply chain stewardship. Most singular values begin with an analysis of the undisturbed value of an object and continue through the consequences of whatever supply chain may be desirable, including final disposal. Gold is interesting because it has no final disposal. Gold is made into new things and used in the transfer of value, but it is almost never discarded.

To understand the consequences of a thing, we must first look to the natural history of its component parts. Gold, for example, is buried in deposits, sometimes in streams and shallow pools, sometimes deep under the earth, sometimes in large pieces, and sometimes in veins that need to be concentrated and purified. The location and concentration of gold within a landscape determines the ecological intensity of a mining operation. Pieces of gold lodged in surface sediments that can be collected in pans require no alteration or destruction of the natural environment, but little gold is collected this way. Instead, most gold is collected from ore, often leaving behind acid-filled tailings and a poisoned water table. The gold extraction process is as interesting and as controversial as the extraction of trees. As with forestry, there are efforts to promote a responsible standard to protect the interests of small-scale gold producers and their ecologies,[71] but most gold purchasers are unaware of this standard and a minuscule percentage of the world's gold extraction is governed by it.

Gold's use is distinguished from other objects by the near certainty that it will be recycled and by its use as a commodity investment. Some gold becomes jewelry, but gold is also held as a value basis for currency and investment, a durable and perfectly fungible commodity. Gold has a long history in this role that complicates the linearity of the singular values described above. In this section, I set aside the originating issues of cyanidation, mercury, and ground water pollution as roughly analogous to the ecological considerations already described for trees. If the origins of wood fiber are important, so are the origins of gold. If the use and waste of wood products must be measured against the value of the trees undisturbed, the same holds for gold as well. Here, I focus on gold that is used as a medium of exchange.

Suppose that an ounce of gold had been procured in a responsible manner, without unnecessary environmental destruction and providing the requisite social benefit to those who labored in its extraction and refinement. Our description of singular value has focused upstream on the origins of objects, but now the purveyor of gold must look downstream at the uses of gold and at the sources of the currency for which the gold is exchanged.

Looking upstream, one would not purchase something acquired by theft. Looking downstream, one would not wish for gold to be used to hire a contract killer, to bribe a public official, or to further any other irresponsible end. This is a speculative realm, and one that would seem to be quite beyond the control of a seller. Nonetheless, the same spirit that would show concern for the origin of a thing must also consider its eventual use or misuse.

If an unscrupulous individual wished to use gold to make illicit payments untraceable, then the purveyor of the gold should wish to not to sell. Indeed, if this is how most gold is being used, then a person would have reason to avoid participating in the trade altogether. This is the spirit of "know your customer" procedures within banking, policies that seek to determine which customers are worthy of the money that they wield before helping them to wield it. We will soon arrive at the conclusion that gold is hardly ever singularized in this way, but first, we should understand the conceptual category of singularization that differs from everyday practices.

Consider a hypothetical scenario. Suppose that a gold buyer believes that a seller came by the gold in an unscrupulous manner. In such a case, the singularity logic implies that this buyer should prefer not to purchase the morally tainted gold. This is the fringe of the singular value paradigm, where the origins of money matter, commodities lose value when their origins are irresponsible. In her studies of the economic sociology of money, Viviana Zelizer observes that money is not nearly as fungible as economic theory would suggest. Often, it is earmarked for specific purposes according to the way in which it was acquired.[72] Of course, there are practical limitations to the number of transactions that can occur before money's moral valence attenuates, but the point stands as a conceptual idea with a significant normative application to durable assets like gold.

All of this is just a preview to a way of thinking about things as a gathering point for normative claims. Once we organize morality through objects, we can calculate harm and beneficence, justice, fairness, and numerous other moral considerations at an object level. The details of these moral calculations are important, as is the question of whether the right kind of calculation and comparison is even possible. As a primer, I said of trees that whatever value wood fiber products create must exceed the harm done in their extraction and that this value must be redistributed to remediate their extraction if the whole singularity value of the object, at every stage of its production, use, and disposal, is to be positive. Like trees, gold must also be put to a use that exceeds the ecological costs of its production. Moreover, the economic origins of a given piece of gold are as important as the ecological origins.

If it seems far-fetched that we should think about gold in terms of its origins, consider the trial of Reza Zarrab, a Turkish national who is accused of using gold and fictitious food shipments to launder sanctioned Iranian wealth into other currencies. Zarrab is implicated in a leaked Turkish police report that describes the bribery of public officials and falsification of documents, all aimed at delivering liquidity to cash-starved Iranians who would otherwise be unable to fund their imports. Of course, that was the whole point of sanctions, so the gold trade effectively set out to undermine the sanctions regime. Indeed, gold is an important part of the story. The growth of the gold trade between Turkey and Iran was massively inflated under the sanctions regime. In 2011, Turkey sold one metric ton of gold to Iran, whereas in 2012, this figure increased to 125.8 metric tons to Iran and another 85 metric tons to the United Arab Emirates.[73] In the process, the people moving this gold became extremely powerful by paying bribes to the highest levels of the Turkish government.

If we follow the singularity logic as it pertains to how objects create causal links in human behavior, then gold and other tradable objects gain significance by mediating behavior. A purchaser gives gold value through exchange. If the seller acquired the gold unscrupulously and caused harm in the process, the purchaser motivates that behavior by paying for it. Assuming that the sanctions regime was legitimate and morally defensible, the trade of gold which set out to subvert that regime cannot be, and the specific gold involved in that trade becomes morally suspect.

The sanctions case is more complicated than some other examples because the victims are diffused, if there are any victims. But regardless of the specificity of the harm, gold becomes tainted and its ownership suspect when its trade causes harm. This materialism promotes a radically different conception of organizational responsibility and economic risk. For consistency's sake, if the origins of trees and toys matter, then so should the origins of gold and dollars. But gold proves much more persistent in the economy, and unfortunately, many of gold's uses and extractive practices have been harmful. This includes a global history of slavery and brutality in mining practices dating from the colonial era. It includes gold expropriated from Jewish people by the Nazis in the 1930s and 40s. It also includes the things that this gold bought for corrupt regimes to fund their wars. Gold is still a medium of exchange between nations, and these exchanges merely add to the ingots' storied histories. The normative implication of gold as a singularity encourages a seller to ensure the responsibility of gold's origins and forces a buyer to do the same. And yet, in practice, gold's value is checked only by its purity, with acid scratch tests for instance.

Singular objects still have material properties aside from their ascribed normative characteristics. Without contradiction, a gold coin can be entirely tainted by its Nazi history and nearly pure by its chemical composition. The point of singularizing objects is not to imagine away the mechanical, chemical, and biological attributes of things, but to append to this list a moral history that pertains to specific entities. As I will show in the next section, ascribed moral characteristics will help us to organize ourselves, and our companies, around nonmaterial characteristics so that we can better manage consequences distributed across long supply chains.

Stewardship Economics

What can we infer from the three examples? Trees, toys, and gold provide opportunities for object stewardship that involve varying degrees of complexity and a range of information processing problems. The normative orientation that they share, however, is relatively coherent. The moralization of objects through singularization asserts responsibilities for supply chain participants. Later, I will consider the elements of this responsibility including stewardship, coordination, and foresight.

The challenges presented by singularization are both empirical and normative. As we begin to develop object singularization as an alternative framework for theorizing and optimizing human behavior, we will need to develop an economics of value that is compatible with environmental and social responsibility and attached to physical objects. It is always possible to value these notions in the terms of orthodox economics, for example, by increasing the price of sustainably forested wood products and decreasing the price of unsustainably forested products. But where do these price increases originate? What motivates the adjustment to new price equilibria, and what keeps suppliers from exploiting this price disparity by charging a sustainable price for unsustainable goods?

One common account looks beyond the market to find the inspiration for sustainable prices (see Chapter 4, Pricing Climate Change Agents). Some eco-optimists believe that the market already contains all of the motives that it needs to guide responsible production. These optimists belong to three main camps. Some believe that when social and ecological hardship become sufficiently certain, industries will be regulated and the market will adjust prices.[74] Others believe in the happy coincidence that the amount of available resources is less than, or equal to, the Earth's capacity to adjust to the complete use of these resources. They are incorrect. Already, it is certain that if our species was to weaponize and deploy the available stock of fissile materials, we could do catastrophic damage not only to civilizations, but to the Earth's capacity to sustain its diverse ecosystems. Some people have yet to realize that the overuse of fossil fuels may produce a commensurably catastrophic impact without any actions that seem catastrophic in scope. They believe that materials like oil will reach peak production before the damage caused by their use is irreversible. A third camp of eco-optimists believe in mankind's capacity to find new alternatives in near-catastrophic conditions. For them, it is not regulation or scarcity that will cause the adjustment, but a change in purposes reflective of the exigencies of new circumstances.[75]

I will return to these market-based accounts later in the text, critically in Chapter 3 and Chapter 4, and more constructively in Chapter 8. While ecological concerns provide key examples in this text, this book does little to evaluate the scientific case for anthropogenic climate change. Instead, it takes up climate change as one of a range of issues that can be addressed in interesting ways by focusing on objects and singularizing them. Here, I do not adopt a firm position on what social and ecological risks are most pressing, though I do draw from some examples that have received considerable scrutiny by others. My purpose in doing so is to point to the need for a system of incentives that recognizes risks and immediately adjusts prices to them. This system is market-based, but it involves a singularized sense of responsibility that the market currently lacks.

My argument is both descriptive and prescriptive. I describe a set of interests that need to be guided by some logic while also working from a prescriptive standard of conduct to guide an institutional architecture. The approach involves a complicated interaction between normative and empirical reference points. In order to describe the complex relationship between description and prescription, it is helpful to return to the example of forests.

Forestry Economics

Forestry, like other economic activities, suffers from governance failures. Supply chains are opaque, forests are large, and accounting for the actual forestry practices that have been used within a region can be costly. The ideal approach to wood production would take a sampling of trees in clusters, including trees of different sizes from across a wide area of a forest, in a way that mimics the natural forest disturbances like fires and wind damage. However, efforts to use these "selection cutting" techniques have not been successful. As Seymour and Hunter explain:

Given the popularity of selection cutting among the public and many environmentalists, it is worthwhile to recount why this system became discredited within American forestry circles in about 1960, so that foresters do not reinvent a square wheel in well-meaning attempts to practice ecologically based forestry. Typical misapplication of multicohort silviculture are harvests that: (a) remove just large trees; and (b) reduce density uniformly throughout the stand to a level that regenerates a new cohort virtually everywhere instead of in discrete gaps. These practices usually result from financial pressures to cut too many large trees; few natural analogues for such a disturbance pattern exist . . .. Often short-sighted management causes such 'selective' cuttings to be repeated more frequently than the natural disturbance intervals, each time discriminating heavily against the oldest or largest trees. The unfortunate result is typically a reduction in age, size, and species diversity, with cohort structures becoming more uniform over time and economically valuable species being lost.

In this case, the ideal forestry practice is not being maintained because short-term incentives are incompatible with long-term stewardship. A basic governance problem needs to be resolved before the best practices can be consistently maintained. Beyond the need for good governance, we also need a better theory of value to express clearly why these resources are worth protecting.

Nineteenth-century foresters drew on the economic theory of their day to develop an industrial approach to tree harvesting. "Soil rent theory" treated land as a factor input that should be intensively focused on growing trees, the economic purpose to which it was dedicated.[76] Forests provided an ideal setting for economic analysis: tree growth rates were easily measured in homogenous single-species plantations. Given these rates, the discount rate, and the market price of wood, a profit-maximizing forester could determine how long to wait until a given parcel of land was cut and replanted.[77] Foresters performed economic theory by simplifying the forest and making it easier to inventory for accounting purposes. They planted trees in rows and maintained a count of the available timber and they cleared the forest of underbrush to make this accounting even easier. The maximizing logic would never have been tractable in complex ecological forests. Economic sociologists are interested in the ways in which economic actors perform theories.[78] Like self-fulfilling prophesies,[79] some theories take over the imaginations of the actors that they describe and become motivations and justifications rather than mere descriptions.

Though it is unclear whether the applied logic of commodity forestry originated in factory production models or in economic theory, the strategies utilized in most private forests continue to mimic an approach to economics that focuses on specialization and maximization by simplifying forests. In contrast, advocates of ecological forestry suggest that interactions between trees and other organisms are important to system stability. They criticize organic matter removal, site preparation, roading, and monocultural practices that attempt to control the natural environment to ensure forest productivity because many of these strategies are harmful to the forest's biological system.

Markets Versus Nature

Rather than reforming the natural environment in the image of economics, perhaps we should reform economics in the image of our natural environment. I am certainly not the first to suggest such a transformation,[80] but the object-centered approach presents an important opportunity for doing so. An object focus provides a specialized lens for understanding the maximizing logic of economics within a framework of complex and pluralistic value. Economic orthodoxy imagines agents owning or renting resources which they deploy in order to maximize their own utilities, or at least to satisfy a set of preferences in choosing between the available options with which they are presented.

If we are to maximize something, perhaps we should maximize the use value of the objects with which we interact. It may not be possible to maximize pluralistic ends[81] because incommensurable values result in multiple mutually exclusive aims, but if we start at an object's origin and try to avoid harm at every stage, this implies a hierarchy of considerations within the history of each object. The final result of an object-centered approach is a new economy of stewardship. By tracing resource flows, this singularized approach offers a quasi-organic constraint on economic activity.

There are many important differences between the human economy and a mechanical or biological system, but there are some similarities as well. Most complex systems are regulated by the flow of resources and economies share this characteristic. For instance, plants grow with available sunlight, engines spin according to the throttled flow of air, and microprocessors run at the pace of the electricity supplied to them. Up to a point, increased inputs also increase the performance of these systems, but beyond this threshold, key components begin to fail. If a plant is exposed to too much sun, if an engine is allowed to rev too fast, or if a microprocessor is overclocked beyond the capacity of its cooling system, the damage can be irreparable. Energy arrives in different forms as radiation, combustion, and electricity. And heat causes the failures, because heat is the form of energy that is lost and dissipated every time energy changes form. With an efficient process, heat can be managed or harnessed; otherwise, heat becomes the cause of failure.

The regulation of input flows is extremely important for the stability of complex systems. Plants evolve leaves with different shades of green according to the intensity of sun exposure in their environment, an engine's throttle is constrained to govern its speed, and a computer's power supply constrains the flow of electricity to the microprocessors to avoid overheating. The need for a regulated flow of resources within the human economy is no less dire, but the capacity to regulate this flow is much less developed. Though singularization is incomplete, it provides one avenue through which consumption, use, and disposal can be throttled.

To fully justify object singularization, I will need to show what it accomplishes that other approaches to business ethics do not accomplish. Chapter 8 shows how objects can help business ethics to be more consistent and comprehensive. The main contribution here is one of location and direction. The metaphor of system efficiency provides a helpful analogy. In ethics, we ought to be interested in the scope of the moral claims that an approach provides and the likelihood that the right responsibilities are directed towards and recognized by the right parties. If these responsibilities dissipate without being addressed, then they, like heat in mechanical systems, become a significant source of inefficiency that wastes or fails to realize moral potential. Singularization promises to locate responsibilities more reliably among the people who can act on them, and by doing so singularization promises to mitigate the risk that important social and ecological values will not be allocated to anyone.

A more complete account of singularization begins with understanding the schema through which singularization occurs, as Chapter 2 describes. In this, I will seek to naturalize the notion of object-specific care and to show the many ways that people come to singularize things.

2 | Singularization Schema

Object singularization is relatively undertheorized. It is exceptional when things like fair-trade coffee and blood diamonds pop out from the moral background to have their stories told. While diamonds are exceptionally valuable, the fact that they flow through economies with weak states and a significant threat of violence is not, on its own, enough to distinguish them from many other products being bought and sold in these economies. Likewise, coffee beans are merely a low-hanging fruit in the moral economy of objects. There is no reason why we should not also be concerned with the people who pick apples, fire bricks, or disassemble circuit boards along with a whole universe of other objects that flow into and out of the economy. Across this range, it is clear that the market economy does not consistently force firms and employees to value object origins. More often, we are instructed to treat objects as commodities that can only be distinguished by their functional properties. As a result, the singularity logic is applied piecemeal to the few objects that gain moral attention and not to most others.

Though I will explore a more conscientious and systematic account of the motives for singularization in Chapter 5 and Chapter 6, it is worthwhile to first identify the intuitions that encourage singularization. Here, I examine how singularization manifests within person-object schema and becomes a morally significant pattern of relations thereafter.

A schema is a plan or mental model that a person uses to order and store information.[1] A person's schemas function as heuristics that allow the information stored to be more quickly processed, albeit with certain biases. Concepts like gender and race have been studied as role schemas that are applied in order to interpret social situations and situated action.[2] Social cognitive approaches to human behavior posit that relational schemas[3] define the way that persons understand themselves and others. I extend this idea to a broader class of nonhuman objects to understand the schemas of person-object relationships, including, usefulness (an object's utility), sentimentality (an object's emotional meaning), personification (an object's perceived agency), and stewardship (an object's extended consequences).

Clearly, contexts bind schemas to objects, but here I focus on the treatment of objects within narratives. Many narratives promote singularization by treating things as meaningful centers of value, but not for principled reasons. Singularization is not an outcome of moral casuistry. Nevertheless, we can learn from these narratives by recognizing the basic shape of singularization in popular culture.

Philosophy often draws upon morality tales. Many books present such tales in controversial configurations. Think of Thucydides' *History of the Peloponnesian War*, Skinner's *Walden Two*, or Rand's *Atlas Shrugged*. These stories shape ideas about virtue and possibility, sometimes making a position more concrete in a way that analytical arguments cannot. For contemporary examples, I will use animated Pixar films to demonstrate different ways that audiences can relate to objects and provide examples of these schema (usefulness, sentimentality, personification, and stewardship) in action, but first I will define these terms.

Usefulness

Utility is the cornerstone of person-object relations. In a capitalist economy, an object's value is determined by its capacity to satisfy preferences (i.e. its usefulness) and its scarcity. Value may be underestimated by this individualist scheme when a given object has value to natural ecologies or groups of people, but generally, usefulness is understood in terms of an object's utility for a given owner or group of owners who have access rights to the objects. Though usefulness implies a kind of sovereignty over objects that is purely instrumental, I will show that it can nevertheless stimulate singularization.

Marx distinguished between use value and exchange value in his critique of a capitalist economy. For Marx, exchange value is promoted by certain methods of producing and exchanging that emphasize the accumulation of money and commodities. However, observations of consumer behavior suggest a somewhat different conclusion. While the rise in consumer culture has clearly changed the way that people interact with things, it is not a foregone conclusion that consumers now treat their purchases as commodities. On the contrary, Miller argues that consumers make things their own in a process of "recontextualization."[4] Sayer describes "internal goods" which are bound up in use value by the relational and interpersonal forms of consumption that they promote.[5]

The key observation shared by these scholars is that products are not commoditized at the scale of the economy; they are commoditized within specific organizations and across specific transactions. To the same extent that a product can be commodified by such a process, this form of relations can be undone. "[W]hen a commodity is used to satisfy a need, this means that its character as a commodity is, so to say, dropped, forgotten."[6]

In an essay on the biographies of things, Igor Kopytoff places goods on a spectrum between commoditization and singularization, arguing that different features of an economy, like the development of its money system, determine the extent to which goods will be commoditized. Kopytoff understands singularization as a social process that takes seriously the biographies of things, but in his argument singularization also represents a form of resistance. For instance, in the trafficking of persons or in the use of gestational surrogates for bearing children, Kopytoff argues that prohibitions against exchange protect singularized forms of value and ensure that people will be treated as biographically "singular" rather than as mere commodities.

Kopytoff rightly observes that such prohibitions promote a person's singular value, but my approach to singularization is inconsistent with his more general claim that "[t]he hallmark of commoditization is exchange."[7] Instead, I will find singularities episodically in many different social relations and consistently when institutional structures are established to maintain their integrity (for example, the Kimberley Process; see Chapter 7, Optimal Stakeholder Salience).

In the case of usefulness as a singularizing force, usefulness motivates people to care about their property by recognizing the utility of the specific things that they own. Useful objects represent a personal investment that may not be easily recoverable. Most people establish habits to prolong the utility of the things that they often use. They keep liquids away from their computers, drive their cars with care, and clean their houses. Doing so maintains the safety, reliability, and market value of these objects.

Though a user cannot hope to sell an object for greater than its market (commodity) value, it does not follow that market price constitutes an upper boundary for the worth of a user's possessions. Subjective use value often exceeds market price. For example, a musician who uses a particular instrument skillfully may find other instruments to be inferior. Similarly, some objects perform in ways that markets do not fully appreciate.

Usefulness results in practices designed to maintain object value regardless of the object's commodity price, practices that I will refer to more generally as stewardship. Maintaining the value of a car is a habituated practice. Those who make a habit of oil changes do not check the car's market value before doing so. With the exception of cars that collectors prize, a used car's market value is almost always less than its use value. The economic explanation for this has to do with information inefficiencies and the "lemon problem." The usefulness of a car can be difficult for a purchaser to assess. A potential buyer realizes the uncertainty about whether a car will work properly and adjusts the price accordingly. As a result, the market may not reach an efficient price.[8] Ongoing usefulness explains the maintenance of old but functional cars, durable household goods, and personal effects like clothing, most of which are worth drastically less on a used market than they are to their original purchasers.

These are small ways in which a user demonstrates focused consideration for her own objects as singularities rather than commodities. As a rule, people do not maintain their neighbors' cars. But cars are an exceptionally expensive piece of equipment, and the fact that cars receive maintenance is not consistent with the way that people treat many other products in a disposable economy.

In comparison to other motives for object care, usefulness has only a marginal effect above the commodity baseline. Indeed, in many cases, we willingly discard old but functional products in preference for new ones. Drawers full of outdated iPhones are an illustrative counterexample to the car that one keeps beyond its prime.

We can surmise that usefulness is not a stable platform for object care. Self-interest limits concern for the externalities of purchase, use, and disposal. If new products include new features and if the price of these products is declining, a user may happily, and frequently, discard an item for a newer version. Likewise, if fad and fashion depress the perceived value of older objects, these external forces can decrease an object's usefulness.

It is for these reasons that "user" is so often shaded with a pejorative meaning. A user could never justify buying a different car or giving one up to reduce pollution unless doing so provides personal benefit as well. Similarly, a user cannot justify making extra effort to recycle a computer. The user has little concern for an object's origins, prior to acquisition, other than if these origins enhance the value of the object in terms of qualities that the user appreciates. Green and social marketers have found some success in inspiring the glow that consumers feel from making a responsible purchase, and this complex pleasure must be accounted for in the way that we understand personal utility. Even so, absent market failure (as in the "lemon problem"), a user is likely to value an object as a commodity and to treat it accordingly.

Sentimentality

Sentimental attachment is another common schema guiding person-object relations. Sentimentalized objects are the result of an emotional significance invested in a material thing. Sentimentality tends to focus a person on preserving a particular object, regardless of whether a useful equivalent could be found. The value of a sentimental object is determined by its authenticity. For example, fans scramble to catch a baseball hit by a star player even though that ball is essentially similar to any other ball. Likewise, parents keep their children's artistic works regardless of their aesthetic value.

Though it is generally assumed that mass consumption encourages buyers to treat products as commodities, Miller observes that many shoppers engage in relationally significant consumption to maintain or develop relationships.[9] The same process elevates objects by encouraging recipients to invest them with emotional meaning. Whereas an object's noncommodity usefulness derives from its functional qualities, an object's sentimental value derives from its authenticity.

Authenticity comes in many forms, including the location where a thing was acquired, the person from whom it was acquired, the material from which it was made, and the people with whom it has been used. For example, my mother has a cribbage board made from a tree on her grandfather's farm. She received it as a gift from her sister, and she played the game using the board with her father before he died.

Now she often uses it to play cribbage with my father. Each relational aspect strengthens her sentimental attachment to it.

Sentimentality is a powerful force, particularly when objects come to represent important relationships to other persons. But sentimentality can create problems too. There is no easy way to dispose of sentimentally meaningful things. As a result, accumulation can become a burden, cluttering a person's living space. Downsizing and divesting oneself of cherished possessions can be a traumatic undertaking. If a person viewed each item as a commodity that could be acquired again, she or he could easily justify culling an unmanageable collection. Selling items would yield money, and money could acquire the items again when needed. Instead, a person's welfare is sometimes undermined by burdensome emotional attachments to things.

Sentimentality involves attachments to objects where the objects serve as emotional signifiers. In this book, I suggest that taking care of things and assessing their consequences can distribute social and ecological responsibilities consistently and comprehensively. In principle, there is nothing wrong with the role that objects play as sentimental signifiers, but the kinds of object care that these attachments promote may be inconsistent with social and environmental considerations. For example, if a person is forced by emotional attachments to move things to a climate-controlled storage container where they are not used, the environmental consequences of doing so degrade the moral stories of these objects.

Accordingly, it is worth noting that many people try to avoid collecting sentimental objects. Indeed, on the other end of the spectrum from collectors are minimalists who strive to avoid the accumulation of possessions. Minimalism denies the consumer culture its power. There is mounting psychological evidence that meaningless things and meaningless choices can overwhelm other considerations and cause unnecessary cognitive stress.[10] It is important to note that one of the best ways to improve the stewardship of objects is to have fewer of them, a lesson that both businesses and individuals can learn.

Despite its benefits, minimalism can still facilitate a form of object fetishism that is use-focused. Take, for example, Steve Jobs' description of his family's decision about which washing machine to buy during an interview with *Wired* magazine.[11] It is apparent from the interview that he and his family dedicated considerable effort to understand exactly how the different options worked, what resources they used, and how they would fit into his family's routine. Enthusiastically expressing his appreciation for the design of his washing machine, Jobs said, "They did such a great job designing these washers and dryers. I got more thrill out of them than I have out of any piece of high tech in years."[12] The enthusiasm demonstrates the overlap between the positive emotions of use value and the formation of sentimental attachments. Jobs' careful choice was an alternative to indiscriminate accumulation that brought the object to the fore.

In the most extreme settings, prisoners and residents in mental health facilities are stripped of their personal possessions in ways that are aggressive and distressing. Goffman describes the strategies that individuals use to maintain some possessions, including carrying objects on their person and hiding them in caches.[13] This provides further evidence that object attachments are substantive and identity-relevant.

Personification

Utility and sentiment can elevate an object above its commodity worth, but they still limit the range of characteristics that can be applied to objects. In contrast, a personified object is viewed as an agent and can inherit many of the characteristics that would otherwise be reserved for intentional actors. Some of the same respect that persons are afforded may thus be extended to personified objects as well. The value of a personified object derives from the humanlike characteristics, real or imagined, that are found within it.

The literature on personification in both psychology and philosophy is extensive. Personification is important because it occurs frequently, affects the extension of moral regard, and alters individual behavior. Epley, Waytz, and Cacioppo describe three basic psychological factors that lead to the personification of agents: first, whether understanding how persons act helps to explain an object's behavior; second, the extent to which one is motivated to try to explain another agent's behavior; and third, the personifier's loneliness and need for personal contact.[14]

Like sentimentality, personification can also result in emotional attachment, but in the case of personification, the object is not merely representative of some other person or life event. The object serves as its own center of value, rights, and emotions. This anthropomorphic shift applies emotional and moral value to specific things:

Anthropomorphism is of practical interest in most social spheres because it turns nonhuman agents into moral agents who deserve to be treated with respect and concern. Pollution takes on a different tone altogether when it is "harming Mother Earth," for instance, and it is no surprise that such framing is common among environmentalist groups who show the strongest concern for the environment. Eating beef would become morally repugnant for many if bovine neurologists were to determine – through rather large fMRI equipment – that cattle were every bit as sentient and self-aware as (at least some of) our family members and friends.[15]

Personification is a way of paying attention to and imagining objects, which are important steps on the way to valuing things.

When an object is treated as a person and afforded humanlike consideration, one immediately begins to treat that object as a singularity. Many personified objects are given distinguishing characteristics to signal their quasi-human status. Pets, dolls, and other special objects are given names and marked with the owner's identity to limit the risk that they will be lost. Strong emotional attachments increase the trauma of losing a personified object.

Some will argue that the most important objects of personification, like pets, are not objects at all. Recall that the terms object and thing are not meant to be value-laden. I mean to think of objects more in a linguistic sense, as Sarah is the object in the sentence "Paul likes Sarah," and less in a pejorative sense, as when "Paul objectifies Sarah." The actual moral rights of pets and other living things are a matter of consequence. But as I will argue later (see Chapter 5), many things with important moral meaning are not endowed with personified or singularized meaning.

The point here is that personification is an ordinary practice. Children show a great propensity to personify objects.[16] Children's fiction encourages personification and developmental psychology views it as healthy. The personified object or attachment object (a "lovey") is viewed as a tool to allow a child to securely explore the world and develop as an individual. Personified objects afford children extremely local and controlled domains in which they can experiment with relating to others and consider how others might wish to be treated.

In order to acquire a personified object, one must first bond with it. After having established an emotional bond that is believed to be meaningful, one must respect a personified thing or violate the norms that demand respect for persons. For instance, Immanuel Kant's mere means principle stipulates that a person should not be treated as only useful, and that consideration should be given to that person's own interests.[17] Clearly, Kant did not suggest that this form of respect be expanded arbitrarily to other entities, but we know empirically that people do in fact come to view certain objects as worthy of moral regard and that the process by which they do so often blurs the boundary between humans and other entities.

Rather than treating a personified object as a mere means, it is common to instead use personified objects in collaborative ways. This involves treating the thing in the way that a person thinks that the anthropomorphic object would wish to be treated. Disposing of a personified object is difficult, but unlike the disposal of sentimental objects, one can be motivated by the object's own needs. As such, a personified object is not disposed but entrusted, since its well-being is conceived as a factor in its trajectory.

Stewardship

Object stewardship is the final basis for singularity value. It represents the culmination of understanding a thing's unique history and likely future, and concerning oneself with the important consequences of that path for that entity. The value of a stewarded object derives from that object's holistic worth to the self, other persons, and other living things, often across time and space.

In business ethics, the dominant discussion of stewardship focuses on taking care of organizations. Within this context, Hernandez defines stewardship as "the extent to which an individual willingly subjugates his or her personal interests to act in the protection of others' long-term welfare."[18] The problem with this definition is that it presumes that people's long-term welfare is the key object of care for organizational actors. I wish to expand the scope of stewardship by focusing directly on nonhuman organizational resources. This focus on caring for things is most consistent with stewardship as discussed in environmental sustainability and environmental ethics. Environmental stewardship raises certain controversies about the relationship between people and the biophysical environment and the way that we understand it, and to some critics the very notion of stewardship implies a superior position for humanity that we have never deserved.

In religious communities, the notion of stewardship is also sometimes used as a way to talk about financial resources without using secular economic language. As Abend explains, "Money was an indispensable asset, but the word 'money' did not sound pleasing to the ear, so 'stewardship' became something of a euphemism."[19] The concept of stewardship traces its origins to the Old English word "stigweard," a servant who looks after an estate or piece of land.[20] Over time, the word evolved to reference a range of behaviors associated with managing objects such as ships, finances, and wine cellars. While there is little debate that people need to care for the natural environment, the idea that the environment can be managed is controversial.[21] The interactions between biotic and abiotic elements within and across different habitats and ecosystems are sufficiently complex that changes often cause results that people struggle to predict, much less control. This leaves us with an overwhelming imperative, a desire to care for the environment that cannot be wholly achieved. We are stuck. The natural environment cannot be managed by anyone, but must be managed by everyone.

The alternative approach, which recommends itself to solving this kind of problem, is object stewardship. It is overwhelming to manage the environment, but it is less overwhelming to manage the material footprint of our work. We have a better chance at managing the direct consequences of the objects with which we interact than we do of managing the environment as a whole. Stewarding objects requires us to steward the things with which they are directly connected (see Chapter 6). Object stewardship provides a key insight into the localization of the global problems that "managing" the biophysical environment seems to present.

Here, I focus more specifically on how stewardship compares with usefulness, sentimentality, and personification. Within this range of singularization schema, stewardship is an other-regarding boundary on the opposite end of the spectrum from usefulness. Whereas a user seeks an object's services for personal gain, a steward seeks to protect the value of an object across as many possible uses, times, and places as she can comprehend in a way that joins the interests of other entities with the interests of the self.

Singularization is only the first step towards a practical system of stewardship. Once a person decides to take responsibility for a specific object, a whole range of questions remain. How should competing interests be prioritized? What is to be done if others do not share the same priorities? Is one responsible for an object's misuse after selling it or giving it away?

Initially, an object steward looks like a user. She or he does what is necessary to maintain physical objects. Then, as the steward begins to look further into the object's history and future, the bounded product expands and the steward begins to acknowledge responsibility for upstream and downstream actions. Later, I will explore how these extensions play out in the context of business ethics. But first, I observe some of the places where these narratives pop up in popular culture.

Singularizing Narratives

Bernard Williams wrote that "contemporary moral philosophy has found an original way of being boring, which is by not discussing moral issues at all."[22] In this, he refers to those philosophers who abstract so far from substantive ethical questions that they lose contact with the issues and insights that give moral life its weight. For Williams, the problems with this analytical mode of philosophy are both stylistic and epistemological, and they are related.

Like Williams, I have a problem with the stylistic and epistemological approach to writing about the ethics of material things. The material line of analysis is too tangible and real. It presents novel things with lively verbs, and these novelties lead writers to follow thinking that strays ever further from common sense. Readers are then faced with the choice between accepting a line of analysis that seems interesting but counterintuitive or maintaining the status quo and avoiding all of that weirdness. In this text, I tried to reduce some of the strain of that choice by showing that objects can matter in very conventional ways, that many people already act as if objects matter, and that material things have stories of their own. And, as we will see, these stories can be made to empathize with objects as singularities. It just depends on how we tell the tale.

In this chapter, I consider narratives from three major productions of the computer animation studio Pixar. Sentimentality is first, explored through *Up* (2009), then personification in *Toy Story* (1995, 1999, 2010), and finally, usefulness and stewardship in *WALL-E* (2008).

These five Pixar films received a total of twenty-one Academy Award nominations and generated global ticket sales of over $3.2 billion. Perhaps more importantly, they serve as powerful mythologies for a generation of young people in their thinking about object meanings. Growing up in a culture that is in a constant state of consumer excess creates an essential, existential tension. For those who have so much, none of it means much, at least not for long.

Pixar films address this tension in interesting ways. The narratives are instructive for the larger project of singularization. That these narratives can help us to develop a critical pedagogy for questioning the cycle of meaning and consumption makes them all the more important.

Sentimentality – Man Loves House

Pixar's *Up*[23] pits sentimentalized objects against human relationships. A surprisingly intense[24] life history in the opening montage infuses objects with emotions and character histories. The remainder of the film focuses on breaking the bonds between the widower protagonist and the things that he shared with his wife during the years of their relationship. Some have argued that the introductory sequence is emotionally manipulative.[25] It shows seventy years of the protagonist's life, from the moment he meets his best friend as a child, through their marriage, until she dies. At the end of this sequence, Carl Fredricksen wakes up in a house that the audience understands to be full of his memories.

Up includes adventure, anthropomorphic animals, and many other narrative elements shared by family films. What distinguishes its plot from most films is the tension that it develops between Carl's sentimentalized objects and the changing world in which he lives. This interplay between an old man and his things shows the dynamic relationship between Carl's well-being and his house's survival. At first, he protects it from developers and construction workers, and then he steals it away from their clutches. The titular direction of the movie arises from Carl's choice to float his house with helium balloons and then to pilot it on an adventure. During Carl's odyssey, he creates new relationships to others. The burden of the house is finally cast away in deference to these new attachments.

The magical realism of a choice to float a house blends an impossible action with a perfectly comprehensible motive. We can all understand caring about the things that connect us to the people we love, especially after losing a loved one. The objects are a reminder for the character and the audience of the loss of Carl's beloved Ellie. Carl values the house and its contents as singularities, as a home, and as a center of meaning. The narrative illustrates perfectly the kinds of attachments that produce strong noncommodity schema for objects and their histories. It also shows the boundaries around such attachments.

As other-regarding as sentimentality seems to be, it is also selfish. Sentimentality may focus on external relations through objects, but these motives are stale. A sentimentally attached person focuses on things as they were, not things as they are. In the case of *Up*, Fredricksen puts a child's life at risk and nearly allows a rare bird to go extinct in deference to a house. He does so even though these actions are inconsistent with the moral character that gave the house meaning in the first place. This is the selfishness of sentimentality, in which a person's fixation on his own past overwhelms his ability to behave responsibly in the present. It is not always the case that maintaining sentimental attachments and investing meaning in things to protect a memory has such a deleterious effect. There is an alternative in which respecting burial sites and other sacred places with important histories maintains a shared sense of cultural significance by investing ceremonial purpose into places or things. At a human scale, one might think of sponsored park benches located in places that have a special meaning for those who they honor. The difference between these cases and the example of *Up* is that they produce an ongoing use for others. If Fredricksen had tried to find a young couple who could enjoy his house as much as he and his wife had enjoyed it, there would be no tension between sentimentality and responsibility.

As if to further the illustration, once the sentimentality in *Up* collapses, and Fredricksen wakes up to the moral priority of his situation, the consequences of the object become meaningless. Fredricksen dumps his house and possessions across a scenic and ecologically distinctive landscape without any concern for the consequences. In allowing for this wastefulness, sentimental attachments differ from a fuller moral theory of stewardship.

When they first met, Ellie awarded Carl a pin made from a grape soda cap. He wears it proudly throughout the film. After a safe return from his journey, Carl gives the pin to the child who accompanied him along the way, explaining that he "would like to award the highest honor . . . the Ellie badge." In doing so, he passes on one of the last items connected to Ellie.

We can understand sentimentality as focusing almost exclusively on preservation. However, it is also possible to create new meanings for things by using them for a purpose, and this is how Carl finally escapes the strictures of his last material bonds.

The grape soda cap pin also illustrates the imaginative possibilities of sentimental attachment. Inspiring children to use available resources for imaginative play can turn sticks into toys and fresh snow into a fort. It may seem as if these synthetic forms of value are unique to children's objects, but adults also fabricate imagined worth. For example, people value their wedding bands in a way that is only partially determined by their cost. It follows that symbolic significance creates an object's singular value, and that we must hope to endow material objects with symbolic value that is commensurate with their value to people and living things.

Personification – Toys Love Boy

The *Toy Story* films[26] follow anthropomorphic toys through their adventures. The toys are human in ways that a child might imagine them to be. They like to be used as toys and fear their own demise. The characters in all three films are haunted by a fear of death by irrelevance.

The boy who owns them, Andy, has two favorite toys, an antique cowboy named Woody and a modern plastic action figure named Buzz Lightyear. When Andy is not looking, the toys come alive with personalities and feelings. They deliberate about what to do when they are no longer useful, and where to go in order to be useful to someone else. Their role in Andy's life is threatened in each film. In the first film, a sadistic child plans to destroy Buzz with a rocket. In the second film, a toy dealer steals Woody in order to sell him to a collector. In the third film, Andy must decide what to do with his toys when he goes to college.

The toys of *Toy Story* want only to be valued as toys, a value that they measure in terms of how often they are used for play and whether the play is abusive. Their aspiration is to be cared for by Andy forever, but they also seem to have Andy's best interests in mind. They love him. The films suggest that objects want to be useful, and that this desire can either be fulfilled by using them or by transferring them to someone who will do so.

It is not surprising that a movie's depiction of plastic and cloth toys with human personalities would cultivate empathy, and one might miss the point entirely by thinking that it is the human voices justifying Andy's care for them. But Andy never hears the voices or sees them move. In fact, the most emotional scenes in all three *Toy Story* movies depict the toys as inanimate objects that are only alive in Andy's imagination.

The film extends the toy's personalities into other situations that highlight their use and disposal. The possibility of wasting toys, the tragedy of the commons of being a shared toy, and the fate of going to the dump are explored in detail. However, origins are not discussed prior to the toy store where these toys are purchased. The people who spend their lives making pieces of plastic to sell to children are a reality that finds no expression in the *Toy Story* series. Nor is there any consideration of the ecological resources that go into these objects.

The point is not to claim that personification provides a stand-alone theory of stewardship for objects like toys. It does not. The lens of an object perspective is no more morally aware than the moral agent who imagines it, but this moral imagination nonetheless provides an important example of how singularity values can be realized by taking seriously individual objects and their unique histories. The next challenge will be to articulate a way of personifying objects that is sensitive to the right sorts of considerations within the object's domain. It should be focused on meaningful ethical considerations, not on morally insignificant object interactions. I would argue that this requires an ecological basis for valuing objects. It is not enough to recognize a tree's value to people;[27] one must also recognize its value to the forest and (perhaps) to itself. As I will argue on aesthetic grounds, there is something good about the efficient use of resources and the maintenance of complexity. Animated films play on this aesthetic principle, both in the way that toys are satisfyingly enjoyed by children and in the aesthetic perversity of toys being abused or destroyed.

Stewardship – Robot Befriends Cockroach

As the Earth's last caretaker, WALL-E exemplifies the creative spirit of stewardship. The eponymous star in Pixar's 2008 computer-animated film[28] shows concern for objects and for others. He consumes conscientiously, uses responsibly, and destroys constructively. WALL-E values objects, relationships, and living things with remarkable humanity (for a robot).

Pixar produced a dense and evocative account of environmental responsibility in *WALL-E*, within a critical narrative. But, given Pixar's status as a consumer goods marketing juggernaut, the *WALL-E* narrative of overconsumption is intentionally ironic as well.

Set in a time after humans have abandoned the Earth, *WALL-E* begins with a view from space. A dense layer of satellites orbiting the once-blue planet make it look like a dust ball. As the perspective falls to the surface smog, mountains appear on the distant horizon, but mountains they are not. Pointed heaps of trash come quickly into focus. Then the scene changes to a cityscape of massive skyscrapers. However, like the mountains, the buildings are a mirage that proves to be towers of trash on closer inspection. These tricks of perspective tell a visual story of scale and environmental callousness. Few intend to destroy the environment, but many do so by failing to look closely. At one scale, coal power heats homes; at another, it pollutes air and water. The complacent and willfully ignorant maintain a self-serving perspective that makes trash heaps look like mountains.

Who Is to Blame?

In legal definitions of fault, blameworthiness is determined by whether an actor knew or ought to have known that their actions or failure to act would contribute to harm. *WALL-E* provides a scenario in which the human species is to blame, and the blame cannot be passed on to anyone else. It then tells a history of the ecological crisis that shows just how confused people can be about their own responsibilities. The first four minutes of the film present three ironies of responsibility: irresponsible humans, a trusted corporation, and a responsible robot.

Humans are morally responsible agents, but one might not know it from this dystopian portrait. Though humans are obviously responsible for the trash they created and the environment that they wasted, they left. Worse yet, they (mis)placed their trust in a corporation. The firm entrusted with trash removal, Buy N Large (BNL), is also a superstore retailer that sold the products lining the trash heaps. Žižek has a contradiction like this in mind when he critiques "liberal communists" for "ruthless financial exploitation combined with its counter-agent, humanitarian worry about the catastrophic social consequences of the unbridled market economy."[29] Despite BNL's conflicted position, customers nonetheless trusted the firm to save their planet, and it seems to have done its best with endless robots meant to sort and process trash. Nevertheless, the robots eventually failed, with the exception of WALL-E. BNL's cleanup robots litter the landscape as BNL-branded memorials to an eternal corporation that was never capable of being responsible. If we take a step back, Pixar's role in making *WALL-E* has a similar irony as a film that looks critically upon waste while selling toys that become waste.

It is often possible to delegate productive roles to other parties and to allocate work to machines. Economic life depends on such delegation, but whether ethical responsibility can be similarly displaced is another matter. For example, one can easily hire a caretaker for a child, but cannot so easily or persistently abdicate parental responsibility. *WALL-E* depicts a world of misplaced responsibility where a corporation and its machines are trusted to remedy a long history of environmental neglect. The fact that they finally failed in their cleanup effort cannot be blamed on the robots, most of which seem to have followed their programming until they wore out. WALL-E is different, not only because he has managed to survive. He is a robot who seems genuinely interested in improving the world through his work. His trash removal programming demands a simple routine of collecting and compacting, but he exceeds this program by collecting treasures as well. WALL-E seems to have developed some of the moral capacity that would make a being potentially blameworthy, but he was not responsible for making the mess. Nevertheless, he is now the sole individual working to clean it up. The mess cannot be wholly blamed on the corporation either. BNL was as much a tool of the social order as the robots were of the corporation. Some responsibility must fall on the humans, yet they are long-absent and longer-complacent. As the scene develops, there aren't very many potentially responsible parties to choose from.

Material Care

As far as the audience knows, this world has two survivors, WALL-E and his resilient pet cockroach. WALL-E is solar-powered and his cockroach lives off age-old Twinkies. Though the robotic protagonist needs no food, he carries a lunchbox to work and uses it to bring treasures home. He lives in a hoarder's paradise with motorized shelves that index an endless array of trinkets collected during centuries of work. His collection includes forks, spoons, a spork, Zippo lighters, light bulbs, road cones, bowling pins, a bra, Christmas lights, gnomes, and a video of *Hello Dolly*. The first signs of WALL-E's humanity are seen in his looking closely at objects that interest him. Gathering resources that would otherwise be wasted is a form of conscientious consumption. Like a dumpster-diving hipster, WALL-E defines a personal aesthetic out of objects that others call trash in a world of material excess. WALL-E can claim anything he wants as his own because he is alone in the world. Even so, he makes a home for himself and fills it with the things that he decides to value.

When WALL-E finally discovers the surviving humans living opulently but uncritically aboard a space yacht, he ends up teaching them and their robots a complex moral lesson. At first, he appears to be enslaved in his menial labor. Eventually, it becomes clear that WALL-E has a comprehensive theory of value that the other beings lack. He values work, objects, and other beings, and he values them for their uniqueness.

WALL-E is a film about material care, cleaning up after oneself, taking responsibility for one's actions, and taking an interest in other objects, including other moral agents. I introduce the example of *WALL-E* for its evocative description of relations with objects and because it is characteristic of anthropomorphic computer animations that look closely and carefully at the lives of things. It is also a story of liberation. When WALL-E finds the remainder of humanity living aboard a luxury spaceship, he discovers a pattern into which he cannot fit. By breaking the pattern, he frees humanity from the tyranny of routine. The dystopia aboard the spaceship is unlike the dystopia on

Earth, but it is not clear which is worse: meaningless abundance or struggle amidst the ugliness we inherit from our ancestors. Pixar's *WALL-E*, as a prospective morality tale, implicitly advocates a third option: present-day environmental stewardship.

WALL-E values things for their uniqueness. In the process, others come to value his uniqueness. Singularity value is achieved through a process of differentiation in which commodities become meaningful in their specificity. The narrowest recognition of uniqueness is only afforded to human beings, who are presumed to be individually special. However, in WALL-E, even the captain of the surviving humans is following a program defined by BNL corporation. The spaceship, itself a thing, sets down a routine that orders the lives of the humans aboard. Without WALL-E's individuality, others would never encounter their own individualities.

While stewardship is the dominant moral lesson in *WALL-E*, it is juxtaposed against usefulness. Usefulness means fitting into the pattern set down by the BNL corporation. Robots that do not follow their programming are not useful. They are imprisoned for their irregularities. WALL-E liberates these misfits and uses them to mount a revolution. Our analysis will have little to say about the balance between conformity and routine. Biological life is as dependent upon chemical routines as corporations are on social routines. Some routines are constructive and others destructive. What is important in this portrayal of usefulness is its recognition that systems of order define a sense of utility, sometimes prioritizing order over other moral imperatives.

The Conscientious Consumer

These films evoke all of the singularization schema that I outline above. It may be strange to imagine that the treatment of toys that Andy models in *Toy Story* could eventually influence a person-object inter-action between an employee and a firm's product. However, the social cognitive model suggests that behavioral scripts determined by the schemas that individuals apply to objects are often relatively dur-able personal characteristics, which also suggests that these schemas may be gradually adopted and revised. Narratives are only one of an expansive set of influences that can set the terms of person-object relationships, and they are probably not as powerful as early childhood influences like direct parental feedback. That said, my argument here is that singularization does exist within the cultural scripts of a market economy, and that these cultural influences deserve a better theoretical account to explain how they might function within a broader normative view.

Many of the phenomena here described in object terms have already been explained as products of human psychology. Sentimentalized objects are, in a psychological frame, the objects of loss aversion. Singularities are, to an economist, goods with multiple qualitative properties that are difficult to assess and quantify. Personification is, to a psychologist, a source of cognitive bias that can be experimentally manipulated.

These empirical portraits of biases, intuitions, and ways of understanding are behaviorally predictive, but they lack a more general evaluative frame. Social science provides discrete accounts of how persons think and act in certain contexts given certain stimuli, but social science cannot account for the coherence of a general scheme. In Chapter 3, I turn to the limits of human cooperation that an object-centered scheme is meant to address. It takes the conscientious consumer as its protagonist. But rather than trying to describe the consumer's behavior, it attempts to rationalize this behavior, to explain its rationale.

We can understand the conscientious consumer as a person who cares about objects, who may never have outgrown the view that specific objects matter as entities, and who uses object trajectories as a way to organize social and environmental responsibility. This behavior can be explained in many ways: as an extension of the boycotts that were popularized in the civil rights era, as an extension of a consumer logic of market-based control into once-political issues, and as the by-product of marketing campaigns that some advertisers use to distinguish their products, with or without a meaningful commitment to making a difference. All of these explanations are clearly behavioral. They are not easily circumscribed within an established moral theory. Instead, they show how one might have come to think in a certain way without determining whether one ought to have done so. Later, in Chapter 4, I introduce some specific problems that an object-focused formulation of responsibility could help conscientious consumers to address when markets and states fail to do so. In the end, conscientious consumption fails to coordinate behavior efficiently, but it remains one of the few uncompromised alternatives available to an individual who wishes to live responsibly in an irresponsible economy.

3 | The Power of Negative Thinking

When Herbert Marcuse wrote about "the power of negative thinking," he was playing on the title of a popular self-help manual that extols the virtues of thinking positively.[1] Marcuse argues that "philosophical thought begins with the recognition that the facts do not correspond to the concepts imposed by common sense and scientific reason – in short, with the refusal to accept them."[2] In this chapter, I argue that conscientious consumers have good reasons to refuse to accept the facts of the regulated market. I argue that both market and regulatory mechanisms fail to address significant social and ecological problems. Personal morality is rejected as a catch-all alternative to functional institutions.

A critical lens allows us to merge empirical observations with evaluative claims, to ask what we can expect, and what we ought to be able to expect, from our prevailing institutions. This approach is based upon a dialectical form of argumentation "used as a tool for analyzing the world of facts in terms of its internal inadequacy." Marcuse continues:

"Inadequacy" implies a value judgment. Dialectical thought invalidates the a priori opposition of value and fact by understanding all facts as stages of a single process .... All facts embody the knower as well as the doer; they continuously translate the past into the present.[3]

To put it another way, knowledge is tainted by the world it describes. Defining the limits of our institutions and the intuitions that they substantiate allows us to reform them.

In the end, we will need to decide whether an object-focused approach to the allocation of responsibility provides adequate or superior answers to pressing moral questions. But first, we should recognize why other approaches provide inadequate answers. Building from a negative case brings objects into tension. It pulls them between their best moral uses and the best economic uses available in a practical economy. Market, democratic, and regulatory failures create this moral tension by providing incentives for the misuse of things. When old-growth forests are cut down to produce palm oil for junk food, when lead enters a toy and then a child's mouth, or when gold is used to circumvent sanctions, material things stretch across the moral distance between positive potential and misuse.

This argument is not written dialectically as a matter of style and makes no claims about historical necessity, nor does it assert that any single initiative is a logical entailment of the argument. I am intrigued by the possibility that the economy would be more adequately governed, and Earth's precious resources would be more comprehensively stewarded, if everyone found responsibility by focusing on objects. The positive thinking in my argument comes from the possibilities of a singularized economy. Yet I first turn to negative thinking as an explanation and an inspiration for social and economic reorganization.

Critical Conscientious Consumption

In recent years, many social groups and economic entities have begun to participate in responsible supply chains, to form eco-labeling initiatives, and to set up responsible alternatives to harmful business practices.[4] One might reasonably wonder why they bother.[5] I wish to suggest that the disappointments of state and market conduct catalyze object moralization and conscientious consumption.

Many people choose green products to maintain their identities or to acquire status symbols that their friends will respect, but these motives are not consequential to a normative account of their actions. Demonstrated concern for object origins is an act of political and economic critique. The conscientious consumer's interest in the origins of objects reflects a learned skepticism about the established mechanisms governing upstream supply chain conduct.[6]

If conscientious consumers believed that economic actors had a natural propensity to resolve moral problems by virtue of market incentives, they would have no reason to participate in the governance process. Likewise, if conscientious consumers trusted the law to provide untainted products, they would have no reason to go through the effort of seeking responsible alternatives and paying a premium for them. Broken institutional trust[7] justifies the search for a new approach.

I wish to be clear about the forms of evidence that this argument draws upon. As Marcuse explained above, negative thinking merges evaluative and empirical inputs. I draw empirical evidence from the functional (and dysfunctional) capabilities of states and markets and use these observations for a moral justification of conscientious consumption. To be clear, the question is not "What causes conscientious consumers to consume conscientiously?" The question is whether their consumption is justified such that all consumers should be conscientious.

Normative approaches to this topic are not always popular with empiricists. As Miller has argued, consumer critics make elitist judgments without observing behavior, and research on consumption suffers as a result.[8] However, Andrew Sayer sees more room for normative insights, particularly in describing the boundary between relationally significant goods and things that people acquire for external exchange.[9] This argument is part of Sayer's general view that social science cannot adequately observe social reality without parsing and valuing normative concepts.[10]

Nevertheless, there are important questions that empiricists cannot ask or answer, even empiricists who are informed by normative insights. For example, empirical research on conscientious consumption tends to focus on the price premiums that consumers are willing to pay. This cannot determine whether one ought to pay a price premium. I will argue that conscientious consumption is most justifiable as a positive response to an unreliable form of economic coordination, and this argument cannot be made without evaluative judgments.

In Chapter 7, I criticize consumer-directed singularization and propose that we shift the burden of object stewardship onto producers. At this point, we can focus on the practical question of whether the conscientious consumer's innovation is constructive by determining whether states and markets fail in ways that conscientiousness can overcome. Accordingly, I focus on the negative case.

For those who are already convinced that states, markets, and personal morality are unable to solve key coordination problems such as inequality, climate change, and financial governance, this chapter is superfluous. It will just reinforce the doubt that they already have in the capacities of these institutional forms. For everyone else, there is a reason for all of this criticism.

Blaming Markets, Blaming States

To begin our critical appraisal of markets and states, we must accept that these systems may never meet standards set by their idealist theoreticians. In place of perfect markets and ideal democracies, we need to consider how workaday markets and democracies actually function, blemishes and all.

These are the main points of the argument that follows: despite their dominant positions, states and markets fail in significant ways. These failures lead us to look for alternatives, but few alternatives present themselves. In place of systemic reform, many critics turn to ethics. The first half of this chapter summarizes the deficiencies of markets and states. The second half of this chapter describes the limitations of business ethics. It is sometimes tempting for business ethics scholars to look to market failures and transgressions as demonstrations of "why we need ethics," and in a sense this is the right sentiment. However, stating that normative interventions are necessary is quite different from deciding where those normative interventions ought to be undertaken.

Ethics is the whipping boy of institutional failure. Individual ethics takes the blame whenever a coordinating social structure underperforms. We observe this each time a scapegoat is found to answer for a scandal. When market failures are understood as moral failures, the power of negative thinking is lost. Rather than working through the tension implicit within the system, we wish for agents who will take responsibility for the limits of the system coordinating them. This is a theory of moral responsibility in itself. It says: "follow orders, except when you shouldn't." When a problem arises, the quiescent moral agent is expected to spring into action in defense of what is morally right.

The problem with this theory of responsibility is pragmatic rather than theoretical. In theory, using morality as a check on system functions is effectively the same as using morality all the time. In practice, these activities are very different. Deliberating about and acting upon moral insight takes practice. Like any ability, moral awareness atrophies through disuse. Whereas theory suggests that these systems can be corrected through a strong moral compass, practice suggests that markets, states, and corporations distort moral compass readings. Both markets and democracies provide powerful internal normative influences that shape perceptions, often in ways that are inconsistent with external perspectives. The presumption that morally upright people can make markets and states better is entirely defensible. However, we have a problem if markets and states encourage dispositional characteristics that are inconsistent with the moral uprightness that markets and states demand. For ethics to guide behavior, it must both work as an influence in the everyday decisions of institutionalized action and it must inform the critical process by which these decisions are considered and improved. Ethics will never be reliable if it is brought into play as a fallback.

On the other hand, from the perspective of system participants, personal moral innovation may seem to be an ethical responsibility when systems fail. Ethical dilemmas are sometimes embedded within empirical questions of institutional trust. Assume for a moment that we have certain moral duties of rescue and charity to other persons. For instance, assume that I am morally obligated to lend aid to a person who is freezing to death when I can shelter him. Consider the interaction between a person begging for money and a person who has money to give. The potential benefactor has no information about the beggar other than what she can see, and what she sees are signs of poverty. But the benefactor also knows about the background institutions and organizations in her community. If the benefactor lives in a society where she knows with certainty that basic social welfare provisions are available, including food, shelter, and physical safety, then the benefactor should only give if she wishes this beggar to have more than the basic social provisions. On the other hand, if the benefactor lives in a society without such provisions, or with stigmatizing versions of them, then she must consider taking personal responsibility for the beggar's basic needs.

Trust in markets and regulatory processes, like trust in welfare safety nets, shifts the ethical responsibility from the individual to the social system. When these systems fail, the responsibility shifts back. If the market and the state cannot reliably shape economic behavior to promote positive social and environmental outcomes, then one must consider taking personal responsibility all the time. Treating objects as singularities is one way of doing so. I describe system failures to show

how ethics can help to shape behavior, but a consistent application of ethics implies the need for institutional change.

The argument centers on the present state of American capitalism, American political discourse, and the academic field of business ethics. The American example should not be taken to characterize the global diversity of state-market relationships. Even so, America's market organization is a dominant approach that is in the midst of a serious crisis of confidence. If its problems can be addressed, the insights may apply to other economies in helpful ways.

Mistrusting Markets

Many of us believe in markets because they reward innovation and punish waste[11] without violent coercion or a visionary social planner.[12] We admire markets' capacity to coordinate behavior, communicate information, and satisfy preferences. The price mechanism is at the heart of what we admire about markets. According to the First Fundamental Theorem of Welfare Economics, no price could better satisfy buyers and sellers. These are all commendable qualities. The trouble is the "if" statement that follows. The beneficial properties of general equilibrium theory obtain in situations without externalities under conditions of perfect information, low barriers to entry and exit, numerous competitors, and low transaction costs.

The conditions are byzantine, but let us unpack them. Externalities are costs and benefits that do not accrue to a seller or purchaser. If a factory's pollution harms others, this is a negative externality.[13] If a song brings joy to people who do not pay for it, this is a positive externality.[14] Perfect markets can have neither negative nor positive externalities, otherwise a product's price would be too low or high, respectively.

Perfect information requires that all buyers and sellers be informed about the quality and value of the items that they purchase.[15] This means that some parties cannot be aware of defects while others are unable to observe them, as is the case in so-called "lemons" markets for products like used cars.[16] That kind of uncertainty reduces prices to a new, lower equilibrium, but the new price is no longer as efficient as the previous one. In fact, under conditions of perfect information, there would be two markets for two different products: a high price for cars that work well and a low price for cars that are likely to make their purchasers miserable. However, in a market where buyers cannot observe product defects until after purchasing, a high price yields disappointed customers and a low one disappointed sellers; in either case, the market is not achieving its potential. A great deal of research in economics attests to the problems of information asymmetries in numerous markets. This particular condition (also understood as an assumption of the model) is perhaps the most important and the most frequently violated.

Barriers to entry refer to a surplus cost of starting to produce or sell in an industry. High barriers would make it costly to start participating. In contrast, barriers to exit keep firms from exiting the market. High barriers to entry reinforce monopolistic or oligopolistic competition, though distinguishing between seemingly efficient barriers like taxi medallions and seemingly inefficient barriers like predatory pricing can be a subtle art.[17] Political barriers to exit can keep firms in business when performance suggests they should collapse. Instead, firms persist in a state of "permanent failure."[18]

Transaction costs are uncertainties that make it impossible to write a contract that anticipates all eventualities.[19] Simple goods provided at standard and measurable qualities have low transaction costs. Complex or custom goods and services are not easily controlled through contracts. Transaction costs are one of the reasons why production is organized within firms rather than having one big, perfect market. It is a matter of some consequence that we can buy cars as working systems from unified brands that are responsible for all of the components working together. Directly contracting with the thousands of laborers and suppliers that contribute engine pieces, turn signals, upholstery, and an endless variety of consequential minutia to each car would be much more costly. Firms organize these activities into hierarchies rather than markets, which creates a wonderful opportunity for productive innovation and a significant opportunity for governance to fail.

Imperfect by Design

It is extraordinary to meet any of these "perfect market" assumptions, much less all of them together.[20] It would be difficult to name a single market that is entirely compatible with the ideals of economic theory.[21] Because these conditions are rarely met, everyday transactions often fail to achieve their theoretical potential.[22] In the real world, many positive and negative aspects of economic action are not priced into the market; in fact, externalizing costs onto third parties is a way to avoid incurring them, something that market participants are motivated to do.[23] Market participants also avoid competition in order to increase profit.[24] Moreover, they use information asymmetries to manipulate and sometimes defraud other parties.[25] Economies of scale, barriers to entry, and anti-competitive practices create transactional environments of price manipulation and undersupply, all within the motives of economic performance. It is profitable to use these strategies.

The limits of markets are widely recognized by economists. In fact, many modern approaches to economic research move beyond abstract models to understand the actual human behaviors that make basic theories break down. Behavioral economists account for decision heuristics based on limited information, cognitive biases, and cooperation as basic features of economic life that do not fit into the orthodox description of economic behavior or market coordination. These considerations represent a major part of the economic research enterprise, at least on the scientific side of the discipline.[26] Developments in information economics,[27] theories of the firm,[28] and economic behavior[29] have moved beyond rote assumptions of rationality and efficiency. Instead, researchers try to understand the narrow and fickle motives that do not conform to the smooth and predictable idealisms of preference, rationality, and choice.

These economic insights can derive important and practical conclusions from theory. For instance, to make contractors pave quality roads, hire them to ensure the road's performance rather than paying for the construction work. To reduce greenhouse gas emissions, cap the allowable output and permit polluters to trade their carbon credits in order to efficiently allocate the remaining emissions. To encourage healthful eating, change the way that foods are displayed and taxed to alter the incentives for buying and selling harmful products. The field of economics can produce many important and constructive insights from its market failures model.

Interpreting Market Failures

Behavioral economics produces helpful insights for the design of institutional structures, yet an awareness of market imperfections can also be used strategically for personal gain. For example, intermittently disrupting the supply of valued commodities allows market actors to reap profits from volatility. The US Senate Permanent Subcommittee on Investigations has documented numerous significant cases of commodity price manipulation in gasoline,[30] natural gas,[31] wheat,[32] metal, coal, and ore.[33]

In 2014, the committee reported on a two-year investigation into banks' commercial activities. Traditionally, US policy has discouraged banks from participating in commercial businesses. Such participation raises three primary concerns. First, regulators worry that banks may become exposed to significant downside risks through commercial ventures. For example, the Senate Committee discusses Morgan Stanley's plans to develop compressed natural gas (CNG) facilities that could expose the firm to significant environmental liabilities. Because banks are discouraged from these kinds of operations, they sometimes create structures to distance themselves formally from commercial activities. Morgan Stanley established an entity called Wentworth Compression, LLC to develop the CNG facilities. That company is wholly owned by Morgan Stanley. It has no employees and is entirely controlled by Morgan Stanley staff and designees. It operates out of Morgan Stanley offices.[34] The committee was not satisfied that the mere formalism of a separate legal structure could actually protect the bank from liability should a catastrophic failure occur. Because banks play a special role in maintaining liquidity and access to savings, regulators argue that banks should not jeopardize their capacity to perform this role with other nonbanking business risks. In this same vein, a second concern raised by regulators concerns the competitive position of banks relative to other commercial firms. It is deemed unfair for banks to compete in commercial business because their special access to capital allows them to dominate the competitive environment, taking risks that other firms could not afford to take.

The third concern raised by regulators is that banks will be more interested in using the commercial entity's capacity to influence prices than they will in operating commercial entities efficiently. The report discusses Goldman Sachs' participation in the aluminum commodities business. Goldman's aluminum holdings were massive. In 2012, it held 1.5 million metric tons of aluminum, a quarter of the annual US demand for the material.[35] By 2014, Goldman controlled 85 percent of the US capacity to store aluminum in London-Metal-Exchange-certified facilities for foreign commodities markets. As the New York Times reported,[36] Goldman managed these storage facilities and developed policies that could only be explained as a method of subverting regulatory strictures. In the three years after Goldman purchased aluminum warehouser Metro International Trade Services, delays in the delivery of aluminum went from six weeks to more than ten times as long. To meet technical storage requirements, Goldman developed a practice of shuffling metal between facilities in different parts of Detroit, a practice that is akin to a bank withdrawing money from one of its branches just to deposit it in another in order to make it look as if it had more withdrawals within a given day.

This case is not only interesting for the present discussion of market failures, but for the broader argument on singularization and commodification. It illustrates the gamesmanship surrounding commoditization as a commercial activity. Some people want to own aluminum or to buy it in the future. Others want to make things out of aluminum, like soda cans and airplanes. You might think that these two types of users could do business with each other. Certainly, many of the current users are parties who wish to buy it in the future. Accordingly, commodities markets were developed to stabilize instabilities in supply and demand and to facilitate warehousing. By purchasing futures, commodities purchasers could hedge against price volatility and focus on other aspects of their businesses. At the same time, a common exchange seems to make the price more competitive and transparent. However, in order to make these markets, practices needed to be put into place to guarantee that the people who say that they have something actually have it. Goldman's activities aimed to manipulate these practices. Goldman found ways to make the market opaque and volatile using the infrastructure that was intended to make the market transparent and liquid.

Business ethics scholars sometimes imagine that understanding market failures can help firms to decide when they ought to be responsible. It would certainly seem that in the example of Goldman's aluminum business, the firm would have behaved better if it had not been trying to exploit market imperfections. Joseph Heath is the leading proponent of this view. He argues that the primary task for business ethics scholars is the promotion of market efficiency. He formulates this efficiency in terms of Pareto optimality, which he defines as "the principle that, whenever it is possible to improve at least one person's condition without worsening anyone else's, it is better to do so than not."[37]

In many ways, the argument in this book coincides with Heath's work. Both support nonfoundationalist approaches to business ethics to avoid intractable controversies in ethical theory. I agree with Heath that businesses are not exclusively responsible for generating profit. We also agree that businesses cannot justify making people worse off in search of profit.

However, we disagree over three significant points. First, Heath employs an anthropocentric conception of efficiency that I view as inadequate. The primary contribution of this volume is to promote an ecocentric approach to efficiency in the form of object stewardship. In any choice that pits the life-supporting capacities of living systems against individual welfare, Pareto optimality will side with human welfare; object stewardship will weigh these values against each other (see Chapter 6, Object Utilitarianism).

Second, Heath suggests that business ethics can respond to market failures without making a positive case for what business ought to accomplish. Indeed, Heath argues that a good way to teach the subject is to try to keep our students from acting in ways that will get them sent to prison. Accordingly, the latter part of his book focuses on criminological approaches to business ethics. In explaining the contribution of market failures to business ethics, Heath uses the metaphor of a game that businesses are playing, and that they should be permitted to play as long as they follow the rules that allow them to maintain fair competition. This "fair play" metaphor is a long-standing theme in business ethics scholarship. It is interesting to note that Heath's market failure argument works against the dominant narrative in finance. For today's financially trained businesspeople, market failures are a fundamental component of business strategy. How should the public respond? The market failures approach to business ethics can only scold these financiers for their meaningless shuffling of abstract aluminum. It has no substantive vision for what the market might otherwise accomplish. It says that firms should make people better off, but how? Which people? In contrast, stewardship contributes a substantive proposal. It says that aluminum should be useful and should not cause harm, and businesses that trade in aluminum should do what they can to make it as useful as possible. These stewards do not need to ask whether the market is working so that they can compete without regard for the consequences, because they know that these consequences are their business.

The third difference between Heath's argument and mine concerns the way that we apply market failure insights to the field of business ethics. Heath believes that the welfare state and its regulatory capacity are sufficient bulwarks to protect moral responsibility from entering into private hands. I believe that the welfare state sometimes regulates and redistributes well, but that when it fails to do so, the fact that the state might play a redistributive role has no significance to the question of how one should act in the face of pressing moral needs. For Heath, the market failures approach aligns business ethics with the way that competitive markets are supposed to work within a regulatory welfare state. I agree that telling managers not to exploit market failures unites many of the key insights from the liberal conception of the market and the state, but I find this alignment to be a liability rather than an asset. The liberal conception of the market and the state is hardly a global platform for responsible conduct, and it is hard to imagine a near future in which it becomes one.

States very often lack the political will to either regulate the negative externalities of market dysfunctions or to subsidize the positive externalities that markets inadequately supply. These states are as likely to lack the political will to overcome market failures as they are to lack the expertise necessary to maintain the coercive regulatory and redistributive apparatus. In terms of regulation, government can either directly coordinate behavior through administrative and criminal law, or attempt to massage markets to make them function through civil law. In either case, the focus shifts from ideal markets to ideal governance and then to ideal government. Alas, states underperform in their role as readily as do markets.

Mistrusting Democracy

Why trust democracy? Many believe in democratic rule because it acknowledges the interests and voice of all people, at least in conditions of universal suffrage. Markets deliver us products. Democracy delivered us from autocracy (to be fair, both economic and political participation played a role in the development of rule by the people).[38] Democracy means that votes count, that letters to representatives are likely to be read, and that citizens can run for office and sponsor change if representatives fail to serve the public.

Under democratic control, elected officials share the interests of the electorate; whether they stay in power depends upon the quality of the representation that they provide. John Stewart Mill argued that democracy's benefits are not only derived from the system's ability to impose publicly useful policies, but also from its ability to reform the public itself. Democratic citizens are changed by democracy, formed into people who aim to resolve problems:

The people who think it a shame when anything goes wrong – who rush to the conclusion that the evil could and ought to have been prevented, are those who, in the long run, do most to make the world better. [T]he passive type of character is favored by the government of one or few, and the active self-helping type by that of the many. Irresponsible rulers need the quiescence of the ruled more than they need any activity but that which they can compel.[39]

The results of an empowered public and an accountable public sector are palpable. As Nobel laureate Amartya Sen notes, "No substantial famine has ever occurred in any independent country with a democratic form of government and a relatively free press."[40] It follows that whenever markets can be managed in the public interest, democracy will ensure that they perform, not only avoiding famine but also encouraging substantive human achievements.

Unfortunately, as with perfect markets, democratic theory describes fantastical ideal types. Take the United States as an example. One hundred and seventy years ago, Alexis de Tocqueville viewed the democratic project in America as an overwhelming success, not only because of the structure of the US government, but, more importantly, because of the democratic spirit of the people who lived there.[41] Could he say the same today?

There are many ways in which the technical structure of the US government is inconsistent with its democratic ideal. The United States is constitutionally republican, a legally constrained form of democracy that checks legislative and administrative authority against the rule of law.[42] Moreover, representation is delegated in ways that unevenly allocate voting power, especially in the Senate. These are technical practicalities of the US government that may hinder democracy or avoid its most painful excesses. However, these are not the most important barriers to public-minded government.

The same self-interest that motivates market participants to opportunism plays out in politics as well. There is no democratic spirit to be found in the aggressive gerrymandering of political districts and the uneven representation that results.[43] Likewise, the way that laws are written and brokered involves an elite strata of policy institutes ("think tanks") and various related fora of prelegislative policy formation[44] that are opaque to the public and often insensitive to the public's interests. None of this accords with rule by the people. The evolving influence of economic power constitutes an even greater threat as citizens question how their votes stack up against input from economic elites.[45] And even if the policy process could sustain democratic inputs, antidemocratic influence is pervasive along the porous boundary between regulators and the industries that they regulate.[46] Moreover, the relative position of economic elites seems to be on the rise, as Vogel noted while discussing civil regulatory frameworks that govern businesses without much state oversight: "Economic globalization, with the increased legitimacy and influence of neoliberal values and policies, appears to have undermined both the willingness and capacity of governments to make global firms politically accountable."[47]

Internal Threats

Private citizens and corporations are not the only threats to democracy. Threats also come from within the state. This can be true without any formal change of power or military coup. The nature of political discourse has changed. News coverage fails to meaningfully treat substantive issues[48] and political life has become such a performance that it inspired Manin to coin the term "audience democracy."[49] As a result, the state's internal workings and policy aims are poorly understood by citizens, and the state's activities are poorly controlled.

Political parties fare no better, with rates of affiliation and loyalty at historical lows across a broad subset of industrialized democracies.[50] Basic features of democratic order are threatened from without and from within, and the biggest threat may be the officials themselves.

Most elected officials come from a rarified stratum, and their personal wealth denies the everyman theory of government.[51] Even when class affiliations do not attenuate the quality of representation, candidates with humbler origins are still eventually beholden to moneyed interests through the campaign funding that the electoral process requires.[52] The Supreme Court struck down key provisions of bipartisan legislation governing campaign contributions on the use of corporate resources in political advocacy, which has opened the valves for significant economic flows that were already leaking into the electoral system.[53]

The class critique of federal representative government is hardly a new concern, though modern campaigns have made the game exorbitantly more expensive than it used to be. At the same time, other factors like ideological shifts, low voter turnout among poor people, and wealthy people's direct influence over the legislative and political process have ensured that democracy does not slow rising inequality.[54] The problem is not only representative mismatch, but a change in the distribution of wealth across the whole society. McCarty, Poole, and Rosenthal describe rising wages for the wealthy and stagnant wages for the poor as one of the key factors causing increased polarization.[55] The direct consequence of polarization is a reduction in representatives' ability to govern due to uncooperative ideological convictions. An example of the embarrassment associated with partisan political squabbling occurred in 2011 when US bonds were downgraded to a higher risk asset class after Congress delayed an increase of the US debt ceiling. In this case, the international financial community recognized the previously unimaginable threat of legislative irresponsibility in US government resulting in a near-term default. It is especially troubling that inequality seems to be generating the kinds of political values that make the state incapable of dealing with inequality. As I described above, upstanding moral convictions would help both a democracy and a market to thrive, but American political discourse has shown more capacity to degrade than elevate public democratic values. To sum up, there are many ways in which the collective decision-making apparatus of the United States government is incapable of generating the sorts of policies necessary to govern an economy.

Even if every elected official was sincerely dedicated to serving the public interest such that counterproductive partisanship rarely occurred, many of the leaders of the administrative apparatus would nevertheless be put into compromised positions by their superiors. Revolving doors between the US Department of Agriculture and agribusiness, between the Department of Defense and defense contractors, and between the Food and Drug Administration and pharmaceuticals lead to disparities between compensation in public versus private sector jobs that create perverse incentives. Despite earnest efforts by many career professionals who keep the regulatory state running, the historical trajectory of deregulation and the increased technical specificity of regulation hinders the state's capacity to manage the market and itself.

Regulation Deterioration

In response to weak democratic institutions in the US government, numerous ethics rules, legal reforms, and publicity campaigns attempted to promote change. Nongovernmental organizations serve as watchdogs as well by advocating for a more responsive system of government. Despite these efforts, it would seem that the democratic system is at least as fragile as the market economy. Worse yet, the interface between them is almost inescapably compromised.

Though regulators are charged with governing economic actors, regulators, and legislators, I have outlined some of the powerful mechanisms by which the influence runs in the opposite direction. Market regulations have already been undercut or eviscerated in banking,[56] healthcare,[57] consumer credit,[58] and postsecondary education.[59] When the public is poorly informed, ideologically divided, civically disengaged, and focused on other issues, the state often fails to govern the market.

This situation is made even worse by a shift in the balance of power between private market actors and public institutions. States now view themselves as competing for business, and the terms of the competition are regulatory. The mobility of capital facilitates this competition while also threatening the workforce mobilization that could otherwise help to maintain effective regulations.

Organized labor traditionally played a key role in claiming compensation and benefits for unskilled and semiskilled workers. Peasant revolts long before inspired the decline in feudalism, and organized labor has played a key role in winning employer and state concessions ever since. Given this history, one might expect to find a global shortage of desperately poor workers, but the effects are localized and temporary. Rates of unionization have greatly declined and many workers are employed in regulatory regimes that deny them the right to organize. Moreover, even if these workers could act collectively, the strikes and work stoppages that historically encouraged private and public action are less effective when deployed within a competitive global supply chain.[60] A strike in a factory that supplies products to third parties may result in the factory losing contracts without the workers gaining anything.[61] Organizing strikes has always been risky and costly, but it has traditionally increased the compensation and other benefits available to workers by putting capital at risk. In a competitive supply chain, the buyer has little capital at risk. Labor strife means delivery delays and reputation risks that can also be costly, but these delays and risks can often be addressed by shifting demand rather than engaging with workers. Though a few social movements have managed to organize further upstream,[62] this sort of engagement is extremely difficult to coordinate. The regulatory capacity of democratic states in public and private life has not kept pace with the rise of global business. Together, these findings raise serious questions about democracy's capacity to regulate the market or even to act in the public's interest.

Blaming Ethics

Those who question the state's capacity to regulate the market and the market's capacity to regulate itself often turn to ethics. Though markets and states utilize formalized procedures and rules, both are highly dependent on informal practices. When the institutions fail to resolve public problems, journalists, politicians, and commentators blame ethics. I have already criticized this use of ethics as a default or fallback category on the grounds that we need to practice and build identities around ethical principles, not roll them out periodically for aberrant cases. Indeed, where states and markets function well, we find a spirit of democracy and capitalism that allows them to do so.

Procedurally, it is relatively easy to go through the motions of democracy and market exchange, as demonstrated by the rise in electoral authoritarian states since the end of the Cold War. But beyond pure proceduralism, these social systems require strong normative cultures and embedded informal institutions that are not so easily copied. Prices and votes will never be enough to shape the expectations and behaviors of a functional democracy or a competitive economy.

Markets work best with honesty, trust, and accountability. Democracy works best with active participation, a culture of critical inquiry, and a sense of shared interests. Both democracy and markets benefit from transparency, education, equality, protected human rights, and a well-informed public. This complex mixture of systemic inputs derives from cultural processes that are embedded among individuals within communities.

Because formal rules are only one ingredient in the institutional mix of markets and states, we cannot understand or reform economies and states without first recognizing the ethical systems that define their activities. Unfortunately, political leaders sometimes operate under the assumption that political and economic systems can be delivered wholesale to other countries. In 2003, I briefly met Congressional Majority Leader Tom DeLay in a session on American politics. When asked about America's increasingly active participation in the Middle East, DeLay answered unabashedly, "The United States is in the business of exporting freedom and democracy."[63] In the years since, the prospects for democracy in Iraq and Afghanistan have failed to meet DeLay's expectations despite formal policies legislated under American guidance.

There are two lessons here, one on hubris and the other on policy. The hubris lesson concerns the notion that American democracy is reliable enough to serve as an export. Americans enjoy many benefits from their democratic government, but its reliability is not always certain, and today's partisan factions seem to be posing a serious threat to an already-imperfect system of political accountability. DeLay's career is a case study in the fragile democratic control of representative governments. While serving as house majority leader, he was censured by the congressional ethics committee, and his party promptly changed ethics rules that would allow leadership to maintain their positions even when indicted for a crime. DeLay's party also considered, but finally scrapped, a plan to alter ethics rules in order to avoid future investigations.[64] Even when DeLay was finally prosecuted for money laundering and ousted from his position as speaker, politics dominated the legal process. At trial, with judges recusing themselves over political affiliations, the appointed judge allowed the case to go to trial, and a jury found DeLay guilty. Later the conviction was overturned on appeal by a court that split on party lines. During the trial for money laundering and after being implicated in pay-to-play politics with Russian oligarchs,[65] Texas Republicans still nominated DeLay to serve as their representative.

The policy lesson concerns the conditions under which norms are created and protected. DeLay wanted to export freedom and democracy, as if these are things that can be packaged and shipped. I have already argued that American freedom and democracy is a buggy product that is not reliable enough for export. Even in the heyday of America's democratic order, even when American democracy seemed more reliable, interventionist regime changes were a questionable policy tool. The institutions of state and market are not easily imposed on others. As the next section discusses, norms often emerge within particular historical conditions that are not easily fabricated.

Dispirited Capitalism

In *The Protestant Ethic and the Spirit of Capitalism*,[66] Max Weber contends that the virtues sustaining capitalism arose through a special form of Protestantism that claimed worldly success as a sign of virtue and virtue as a means to worldly success. For Weber, this cycle tied capitalism into a neat enough knot that it was never to be undone. Whatever the fate of the religious sects that spawned the ideology, capitalism was trapped in an "iron cage" of maximizing rationality. This iron cage encourages frugality, stewardship, and promise-keeping as means to success while exalting success as a moral accomplishment.

In reading Weber, it is unclear which religious doctrines are carried into the secularized spirit of the market system. Protestant virtues are substantive. They demand frugality and self-denial as a spiritual matter, viewing worldly rewards as temptations for hedonists. At a minimum, Weber believed that the secular spirit of capitalism preserved a way of counting and attributing success within a money economy and an instrumental form of virtue that prizes savings and admonishes broken oaths. Without these norms, Weber suggests that capitalism would cease to function. These minimal prescriptions overlap to a great extent with the market failures approach to business ethics. Weber proposes that the ethic of capitalism developed as the minimal conditions for allowing the capitalist economy to function.

There are two key differences between Heath's market failures approach and Weber's spirit of capitalism. First, Weber implies that capitalist virtues will produce positive economic returns, but Heath is not committed to this view. Second, Heath treats the market's ability to function as a cause for action, whereas Weber suggests that the normative system predated the market and helped to give it shape.

If Weber is right, business ethics professors should have easy jobs. The norms of capitalism are constantly confirmed by its internal logic. Because most questions can be answered through the maximization of profit, few moral dilemmas remain. It is important to understand what this means. Weber is not saying that few dilemmas remain as estimated by a precapitalist morality. He is not saying that capitalist accumulation is objectively just, right, and good. He is saying that the capitalist system found a morality that suited it, absent moral claims that would contradict what markets demand from people. Should a firm buy political influence, invest in private prisons, and provide partner benefits to same-sex couples? The spirit of capitalism that Weber describes has no prohibitions against buying political influence or profiting from coercive state authority, nor does it demand fair treatment for workers. Instead, it defines these issues as problems of public policy for which firms are not responsible. Consequently, in this capitalist spirit, we can answer all of these questions with ethics or with economics because the right answer would produce positive moral and economic results. Business ethics, though not trivial, would be a simple question of economic pragmatism and legal compliance. Other fields use market research and financial modeling as a means to profit; business ethics would use fairness, honesty, and delayed gratification.

Many business ethics teachers pursue the subject as if this is the case. We are encouraged to do so by our career-minded students whose training is better adapted to decisions about how best to accomplish a goal than decisions about what the goal ought to be. It is certainly easier to convince a pragmatic egoist of the value of business ethics by first demonstrating a basic alignment between responsible action and worldly success. Indeed, there are good reasons for thinking of business as a cooperative game of trust and collaboration, and good reasons not to emphasize the competitive, warlike nature of business.[67] Moreover, the norms of capitalism do not require perfect alignment; it is enough for ethics to be a stable strategy, an approach to making decisions that wins most of the time.[68]

Some key components of business morality are internal to business practice. Many businesspeople quickly learn that being honest and trustworthy earns business opportunities, and that being dishonest has serious reputation costs. Others find customers, suppliers, and communities that encourage a responsible approach to business. Once these businesspeople get started on an ethical path, the strategy is self-perpetuating and rewarding. There is considerable evidence that, despite the moral failings of the global economy, some professions, businesses, and industries are guided by integrity.

As for whether this helps them to maximize profit, it is difficult to say. The question captivates academics, and hundreds of studies now explore the statistical association and causal relationship between corporate social and financial performance.[69] However, enthusiasm for measuring morality is not universally shared. Critics argue that weak measures of social performance, persistent gaming of the measurement process, and episodic external pressures render evidence inconclusive regardless of statistical significance. The alternative is a more nuanced, industry-specific account of contextual effects.[70] But even if the research showed that responsibility pays, the question is, how much? These studies do not conceive of ethics as bounded by the norms that are useful for capitalists (as did Weber) or for the capitalist system (as does Heath); they conceive of ethics the way that other people do, as relating to questions of how we should live and treat each other. By this standard, it is not enough to say that ethics pays. We would also need to know how much responsibility the market will reward, and at what rate of return.

I am skeptical. The great swath of environmental destruction and a preponderance of unresolved social issues within the economy indicate that the market does not demand as much responsibility as we ought to supply. Too many employees are mistreated, too many firms are dishonest about the riskiness of their products, and too many environmental resources are wasted to be confident that ethics always pays.

Humanity's impact on the ecological landscape is not endemic to capitalism. Millennia prior to the development of market economies, humans were already reshaping land for agricultural purposes and hunting animals to extinction. Yet the pace of ecological havoc since the Industrial Revolution is extraordinary, a direct consequence of capitalism's success. Having increased productivity, capitalism has also increased pollution, species extinction, and the destruction of other ecological resources. These dysfunctions are endemic to capitalism and inimical to Weber's proposition that capitalism can sustain its own normative structure of self-denial to further the needs of the system as a whole.

As Weber imagines it, people learn not to consume in order to save and capitalize. Historically, they learned these lessons from religion, but once the lessons became the rationale of the system, the religious order was no longer necessary to enforce the norms. I can accept this overall argument as long as we stipulate that the growth of the capitalist economy has coincided with the decline in the natural resource systems that sustain it. Thus, Weber's claim that capitalism's rationality is reliable and inescapable fails to appreciate the need to avoid consuming for ecological reasons. Alas, despite the ecological precipice visible on the horizon, the wealth-seeking frugality upon which capitalism depends shows no capacity to guarantee the foregone consumption and foregone profit that sustainability requires.

For these reasons, many of capitalism's critics are dispirited by its future. The closure and internality of the market's morality is collapsing on itself. The question, within this critique, is what to do about it. If dispirited capitalism manifests as a global capacity for destruction, what must be done to forge an alternative?

Answering Moral Questions

Answering moral questions presents challenges in the context of business. This section explores some of these specific challenges to situate the discussion of object stewardship that follows.

I begin with the risk that, absorbing the market's implicit shadings of truth allows the market to shape the way that moral problems are perceived and to thereby limit our solutions. The false consciousness of markets is illustrated through the example of corporate boundaries and circumscribed responsibilities.

Then, I turn to corporate accountability and the method of moral analysis. It is often desirable to theorize in ways that are objective in the sense that they do not prefer one party's interests over another. Yet different moral views within business ethics support different kinds of partiality. At the same time, we are encouraged to treat moral logics as nonpractical procedures rather than policy proposals. This leaves a wide gulf between the theory and practice of business ethics.

Finally, I discuss the sheer diversity of business activities as a problem for moral universalism. Applying principles across this whole range is a challenge for moral theory and also a challenge for laws that might otherwise be designed to overlap with moral principles.

The False Consciousness of Circumscribed Responsibility

In the introduction to his book on the political appropriation of German literary figures, Franz Mehring observes that "even the clearest minds may not be clear as to the motives that determine their actions."[71] In correspondence about the book, Friedrich Engels wrote to Mehring, agreeing that:

Ideology is a process accomplished by the so-called thinker consciously, indeed, but with a false consciousness. The real motives impelling him remain unknown to him, otherwise it would not be an ideological process at all.[72]

The concept of a false consciousness has since become an important concept in Marxist thought. For Mehring, as for Engels, dominant cultural narratives are shaded with political understandings in ways that reify unquestioned truths. These ideological processes, unlike propaganda, are not motivated by a desire to deceive, and may even be motivated by a desire to represent facts accurately.

Marxists subscribe to a toolkit that they believe will help them to see facts as they are. While I will not take up those tools in this argument, I will draw upon the notion of false consciousness in describing the accepted facts of the corporation and its boundaries.

Most business ethicists assume capitalism and related institutions, and then proceed by asking how to behave responsibly within this system. Though the presumption may be necessary for getting work done, it comes with a weighty list of adulterated concepts that we only understand through the economy that we know. Karl Polanyi describes the conceptual influence of the market system:

Concepts such as freedom, justice, equality, rationality, and rule of law seemed to attain their culmination in the market system. Freedom came to mean free enterprise; justice centered around the protection of private property, the upholding of contracts, and the natural verdict of prices in the market. A man's property, his revenue and income, the prices of his wares, were now just as if they were formed in a competitive market. Equality came to mean the unlimited right of all to enter into contract as partners. Rationality was epitomized by efficiency and by a maximized market behavior. The market was now the economic institution, its rules identical with the rule of law, which reduced all social relations to the norms of property and contract.[73]

Because economic life defines concepts of justice and duty, foundational concepts like contracts,[74] freedom,[75] justice,[76] and equality[77] are tautologically self-referential when used to explain justice within the economic system that defines them.

Internally, capitalism promotes a particular logic, but the outside perspective is different. Internally, we are not people, but workers and managers; our knowledge is transformed into human capital, and our sense of justice is reduced to a market preference. Externally, people have a unique ethical value and capacity for moral autonomy that exceeds the role of worker or manager. Externally, knowledge engenders understanding, empathy, and interpersonal concern. Externally, justice is the realization of human autonomy put to the best possible use.

Nowhere is the field of business ethics more confounded by the market's internal conceptual structure than in the way that it discusses the moral boundaries of the firm. In a precapitalist economy, labor and property ran together in overflowing and complex arrangements between neighbors, friends, and members of communities. James Scott describes attempts to map the complexity of these relationships in the late Middle Ages, before states forced households to simplify the boundaries of their property and the rights to their land, mostly for the purpose of taxation.[78] As Scott illustrates, the demands for governability (in his term, legibility) alter the shape and boundaries of overlapping social and economic relations.

In business ethics, we also try to map relational economies. Freeman describes the process by which a firm maps its stakeholders. "Ideally, the starting point for constructing a map for a particular business is an historical analysis of the environment of that particular firm."[79] Stakeholder analysis inherits the market's categories by looking to the firm's environment and history to define its constituencies. I will suggest later that this is a problem that is easily solved by defining the scope of a firm's stakeholder relations through the firm's material entanglements. But as long as stakeholders are identified via the firm's history within relatively rigid "stakeholder role set,"[80] this approach will often produce a self-referential and market-based portrait of the firm's stakeholder community.

The market's internal logic takes shape within the governance system, legal norms, management ideologies, and business ethics textbooks by isolating responsibility within each legal business unit. The market needs this in order to anticipate future returns from this business unit's revenue stream and future costs from its bounded cost structure. Standard organizational governance limits liability for shareholders as a policy means to gather more capital by allowing shareholders to only risk what they put into the firm, thereby managing risk and collective property,[81] but limited liability seems to increase risk-taking behavior in industries like chemical production[82] and finance.[83]

Corporate governance causes the proliferation of semiautonomous organizational entities whose managers focus on one narrow slice of business activity. Their economic and political task is isolated to a short time horizon and a constricted stakeholder population. Whether their shareholders, customers, and suppliers benefit in the long run has limited short-term bearing on their performance and compensation. The market approach to governance results in significant gaps in the stewardship of the larger economy and makes it appear as if these gaps define the legitimate scope of business responsibility.

Occasionally, these business boundaries are called into question. For example, advocates of living wages for factory workers in upstream facilities suggest that corporations change their supplier contracts to take responsibility for the interests of their suppliers' employees. They suggest that products should be expensive enough for upstream employees to educate their children, one input in the calculus of a living wage. Globally, many workers receive wages too modest for their children to remain in school during adolescence. Families in need may take their children out of school for work or servitude. Especially in the poorest countries, macroeconomic shocks can reduce investments into children's human capital.[84] This argument challenges the market logic of prices and boundaries. It is often employed through different kinds of customer and shareholder engagement. In ethical terms, these advocates attempt to make an objective argument about wages, to suggest that a standard is not merely defined by a legal minimum or a market price. Their assertion suggests that there is some external standard against which wages can be judged, not as a subjective preference of a worker, but as a moral right. If sufficient, anyone who examines its validity should reach the same conclusion. The unspoken premise of the entire exercise is that we ought to evaluate our business activities impartially.

Against a pure impartiality for corporate actions, many business ethics scholars believe that the legal and moral basis of the corporation demands partiality towards shareholders. In stakeholder research, there is a tension between duties to shareholders and duties to other parties who are potentially vulnerable when a firm acts. As Goodpaster has argued, a strategic orientation for shareholders and a multifiduciary orientation for stakeholders, the leading polarities in this debate, seem to be paradoxically opposite yet both consistent with ethics. He calls this "the stakeholder paradox":

It seems essential, yet in some ways illegitimate, to orient corporate decisions by ethical values that go beyond strategic stakeholder considerations to multi-fiduciary ones. I call this a paradox because it says there is an ethical problem whichever approach management takes. Ethics seems both to forbid and to demand a strategic, profit-maximizing mind-set.[85]

According to this argument, there is a justifiable inconsistency in how we direct our firms because competing moral imperatives each have some weight.

Goodpaster suggests that by focusing the firm on its moral obligations, the firm might both serve its stakeholders responsibly while also treating the shareholders with the special moral regard that their position demands. I agree that this is the right solution, but I question whether it can be implemented without first turning away from the market and the boundaries that we inherit from it.

Moving forward, I will try to be especially cautious in the concepts that I employ unreflectively. As Scott demonstrates, drawing lines on maps is a powerful act. Whether the maps track physical property or stakeholder obligations, the principle stands. However convenient for the market and the state to package neat contractual burdens around each organization, these conveniences do not provide adequate moral arguments for a bounded stakeholder community, much less shareholder primacy.

From Theory to Practice and Back

A second challenge presented by efforts to do normative work in the business context concerns the relationship between analytical and practical strategies. Many approaches to philosophical ethics are detached from political and institutional features because these features complicate theorizing and undermine objectivity. For the reasons outlined above, we need to find some perspective from which we can judge the worker's wage without accepting the market's evaluative standard. The upside of an external method is that it should make our conclusions more generalizable and less contextual, but this is also a liability. Focusing exclusively on moral choice without embedding choice within a system of social control may miss opportunities to persuade or to recognize the actual facts on the ground. Even if objectivity is to be the highest order of moral thought,[86] lofty values may be practically worthless if they cannot be translated into reliably practical norms and values.

The alternative is to embed ethics into practice, making moral theory and moral accountability a part of the same systemic view. This presents different challenges by crossing disciplinary boundaries and confusing practical constraints with moral justifications. Nevertheless, some of the most beloved normative arguments cross these boundaries.

Rawls' theory of justice, for instance, explicitly denies its real-life procedural value. Rawls proposed a procedure for thinking about justice, not enacting justice. However, numerous deliberative democracy researchers have been inspired by Rawlsian ethics as a practically applicable approach to democratic choice, believing that citizens will give public reasons and reach just decisions through deliberation. This work extends an ideal theory to a practical domain, and then follows with an ethic that accepts less-than-ideal conditions.[87]

To Rawlsian ethics, these practical implications do not matter. How people actually deliberate has no impact on the abstract interests that define Rawls' moral system. Philosophers like David Hume[88] and G.E. Moore[89] suggest that moral theory cannot be derived from statements of fact or from desirable properties of objects and natural observations. Philosophical ethics has taken their arguments to heart. In the process, philosophy has become more analytical and formalized, and less connected with practical processes and ordinary political discourse. Recently, a countermovement has taken empirical processes more seriously as a way to test the premises of philosophical arguments and to reintroduce the importance of subjective experience within ethics.

In some ways, this practical and empirical countermovement follows a path taken by business ethics from the start. One cannot expect to solidify a theory of ethical responsibility for something as specific and practically defined as business ethics using only abstract reasoning. Human motives are subject to powerful social forces that shape and frame what we value, and the economy is among the most powerful of these. It makes little sense to hold individuals responsible for their wayward values if these values are actually produced by the economy and its motives. Rather than focusing on personal responsibility, the best work in business ethics attempts to harmonize individual choices with the institutions that shape them. The complexity of doing so is a major challenge that this project seeks to address, if not through changes in incentives, then at least through a reconfiguration of the scope of a person's and organization's moral responsibilities.

These moves from theory to practice are especially fraught in the context of disappointing institutional performance. In these contexts, we must decide how to work with ideal normative theories in conditions that are far from perfect. The incongruities of theory and practice in these settings present a much more serious contradiction than what Goodpaster described in the context of shareholder primacy. Unfortunately, the states and markets in which people are most prepared to lend aid and act in ways that take care of key political and economic institutions are usually the ones in which they are least likely to need to do so. Countries with high measures of interpersonal and institutional trust are not trusting because people are nice; they are trusting because norms are effectively enforced or proper conduct routinized. In these contexts, aberrant behavior either does not occur, or it is effectively sanctioned when it does. Despite this contradiction, the good news about norm enforcement is that normative preferences can change very quickly if both injunctive norms (what people approve of or disapprove of) and behavior change at the same time.[90] With a modicum of political freedom, some behavioral norms can be rapidly transformed.[91]

The bad news is that norms in business conduct are notoriously difficult to enforce. Actions are private. Many business actors assume that others are shirking even when they are not. But before we start trying to impose effective norms, we need to gain some clarity about which norms we want. This move back to theory creates some serious challenges.

As stated previously, if both the market and the state functioned well, we should not need ethics to fall back upon. When systems fail, individuals are responsible for picking up the slack. In other words, ethics and economics are jointly responsible for just, fair, good business outcomes. If the combined apparatus of the market and the welfare state needs to rely upon personal actions to take care of public responsibilities, these systems have failed. Still, ethics fails if individuals are not ready to take responsibility when institutions fail to do so.

The challenge as we move back to practice is that this joint responsibility presents a serious collective action problem. The division of labor allows people to specialize, and this specialization promotes efficiency through specialized skills and reward structures. In contrast, undifferentiated work that is not rewarded is likely to result in free rider problems.

Accountability mechanisms are not always necessary for cooperation. With proper communication, it is possible for people to collaborate without significant threats and sanctions, provided that they share common interests. However, once these interests diverge, communication is strained and the likelihood of a mutually beneficial form of cooperation diminishes. Organizational life is rife with divergent motives, many of which cannot be resolved without hierarchical authority, but I have already said that the main source of authoritative solutions, the state, is not providing them. I will suggest that accountability can flow through the economy with products, not only from the state, and propose collaborative communities to see this possibility realized.

Universalism Versus Heterogeneity

Even if we can resolve the first two problems of normative analysis in business contexts, gaining a critical vantage to assess business concepts without assuming market norms and finding ways to harmonize universal moral considerations with tractable and practicable actions, a third challenge remains.

It is not surprising that business ethics would confront a challenging task in humanizing business. Implicitly, business is neither good nor evil. The category of business includes activities that are extremely diverse. Consequently, it is difficult, if not impossible, to define a universally applicable moral code for businesspeople. Whereas professions like law and medicine serve relatively discrete functions so that legal and medical ethics can focus on specific occupational roles, business does almost everything people do and money goes almost everywhere people go. If business is as diverse as the human experience, it would seem that business morality must be as comprehensive as human moralities. Business ethics seems to require a comprehensive moral view, the kind of moral view that has been most difficult to agree upon in a multicultural society. Organizations differ in purpose, structure, institutional environment, founding conditions, geographic location, and many other features, and most of these variations affect firms' moral priorities. How is one to establish a universal ethic that applies to all of them?

Applying abstract principles in a process of moral casuistry forces norms into settings where they do not motivate behavior, though perhaps they should. From abstract principles we get vague notions, like "care for others," which speak to high aims without the specificity that accountability requires. Durkheim observed this problem long ago when he remarked upon the underdeveloped ethics of business as a profession. Unlike other professions,

> If we attempted to express ... contemporary ideas of what should be the relationship between employer and white-collar worker ... how imprecise would be the statements that we could formulate! Some vague generalities about the loyalty and commitment that employees of every kind owe to those who employ them, or about the moderation that employers should manifest in exercising their economic superiority ... this is almost the sum total of what the ethical consciousness of these professions comprises. Moreover, most of these precepts lack any juridical character .... So vague a morality, one so inconsistent, cannot constitute any kind of discipline.[92]

There is nothing wrong with local, situation-specific moralities governing behavior. These moralities are likely to be connected with the distinctive social and environmental contingencies that general theory cannot track. Though situational moral logics are not necessarily connected to universal moral norms or collective well-being,[93] they may still serve important local functions. Indeed, some business ethicists have suggested that these "authentic norms" be taken seriously as a matter of principle.[94] But in order for them to work in a moral system, local norms must be globally accountable. In the same way that societies must decide whether to drive on the right side or the left, societies must allocate duties of care to organizations and organizational actors. Whether parents or hospitals are responsible for newborns is a matter of choice, but that someone must be responsible is a moral necessity.

Over a hundred years of subsequent development notwithstanding, the allocation of specific economic responsibility has not advanced beyond the limitations that Durkheim describes. There is no moral consensus governing economic responsibility; whatever "hypernorms"[95] are in play, the frequency of their violation justifies considerable doubt about their practical recognition. Nor are there coherent regulatory and governance mechanisms constraining economic responsibility with reliable regulation. In this text, I use "juridical character," Durkheim's term, to denote the problem of economic regulatory capacity that overlaps with a problem in the specification of responsibilities across narrow professional domains.

Even within industries that are narrow enough to have specific rules and powerful enough to warrant attention, we often fail to get governance right. Those who are appointed as stewards and watchdogs of the larger economy seem often to fail. Speaking of the regulatory agency that governs securities, whistleblower Harry Markopolos remarked in his testimony at Bernie Madoff's trial, "The SEC is a group of 3,500 chickens tasked to chase down and catch foxes."[96] The Securities and Exchange Commission looked into its failure to identify Madoff's Ponzi scheme despite receiving several explicit complaints and found that its shallow investigations not only failed to identify the underlying problem, but that these investigative failures were used to legitimate Madoff's activities and to perpetuate his crimes.[97]

Because general oversight is unwieldy and sector-specific oversight is under-resourced and incompetent, external governance often fails to appreciate, much less maintain, the principles that ought to guide specific professional activities. This limitation poses significant challenges for normative theorizing in the business context, and voluntary initiatives do not necessarily overcome this hurdle.

Consider the universal imperative to care for stakeholders. If any norm instilled in a business ethics pedagogy could be expected to apply across contexts, one would expect for stakeholder prioritization to do so.[98] Yet legitimate and powerful stakeholders vary with a firm's specific structure and purpose. The key stakeholders of a hospital are not the key stakeholders of an ice cream shop or a for-profit university. Not only do they differ, but different tests and theories are necessary in order to evaluate stakeholder claims across firms. The notion that managers ought to care about stakeholders sounds like the notion that human beings ought to care for others, a view that, while powerful, becomes much more motivational when grounded in specific expectations, like legal rights and responsibilities. The inconsistent implementations of stakeholder concepts may be supported in the interest of diversity, but it also runs the risk of allowing firms to shirk stakeholder obligations.

Object-Focused Stewardship

In my reconstruction of conscientious consumption, I begin with the failure of state and market approaches to organizing responsibility.

Conscientious consumers know that they cannot trust legal minimums and market incentives to direct their moral duties. Instead, they turn to their role as consumers and to the long causal chains in which their consumption is involved.

By focusing on objects and perhaps moralizing them, conscientious consumers take an interest in the needs and lives of distant persons and ecological settings. A key rationale for focusing on objects is that objects connect with real causal chains that cross geographic and political boundaries. Accordingly, a supply chain connects both materials and causal actions, creating opportunities for interventions. Because individuals benefit from others within the chain and because the chain could be disrupted at any stage by persons of conscience, it is not unreasonable for a person to believe that a sense of responsibility joins with products and materials along their paths.

This section defines key aspects of conscientious consumption, locates it within a supply chain, and acknowledges its limitations. Nevertheless, it argues that the singularization logic within conscientious consumption is able to work through the main challenges of answering moral questions in a business context. It can instill a particularistic yet global economic ethic, overcome the false consciousness of market-based concepts, and move from theory to practice and back.

We have already discussed the concept of singularization at length. Singularities are things that have unique histories, where economic actors take an interest in the things' biographies. Once people show this interest, it is only one step further to develop normative claims based upon the histories of objects, to suggest that one should prefer organic fruit because pesticides endanger agricultural workers, for example. In this focus on objects, a new singularizing ethic is born.

Singularizing ethics are everywhere, once you know to look for them. They appear in business ethics cases, as a logic deployed by fair-trade labeling organizations, and in children's movies. Objects also serve as a lightning rod for ephemeral attention in the arena of public outrage.[99]

Consider the mistreatment of employees by Nike subcontractors as an example of the emergent singularization of objects. Nike now uses contractual relationships and supplier monitoring to improve manufacturing responsibility, but when first accused of selling sweatshop goods, their response was one of denial and abdication. Nike's monitoring works through a relatively direct relationship with suppliers, but the pressure brought to bear on Nike has sometimes followed a much more protracted route. In one extreme example, the student movement that began in the early 2000s demanded that university administrators demand that apparel brands demand responsible working conditions from their suppliers, an improbable chain of expectations without some overarching logic of shoe-centered responsibility.[100]

Then as now, Nike enjoyed the legal right to profit from the sale of its products, regardless of the working conditions in the manufacturing facilities owned by its subcontractors. Yet, as Nike was soon to learn, what the law condones and what workers' rights advocates deemed acceptable were very different things.[101] Ultimately, public sentiment went with the workers as numerous constituencies rejected Nike's claim that its responsibility went no further than its payroll.[102] Instead, they asserted that Nike's power within its supply chain made it responsible for the mistreatment of upstream employees because it had the capacity to help. Insofar as mistreatment arose from cost constraints resulting from competitive pressures that Nike used to drive down manufacturing costs, it was all the more responsible. Notice again the counter-market moral logic that views competitive pressure as potentially leading to mistreatment rather than only generative for efficiency.

Factory employees gained media attention through their proximity to a branded and recognizable object. For many customers, the workers' plight was sewn into the shoes and apparel that Nike sold. The extent of this movement was limited. There was no global shift in consciousness that united customers and shareholders in an effort to protect the world's working poor. There was only a product and its sordid origins. Nike's supply chain conduct has since changed significantly,[103] far beyond its peers. The shift, like other turnarounds in supply chain accountability, was focused on a distinct product.

The movement against "blood diamonds" also displays the singularization logic. Activists were concerned with the use of slave labor and the funding of violent dictatorships in the diamond trade.[104] Because diamonds are used in meaningful objects like engagement rings, the dark tale of their possible origins shifted consumer demand and justified the expense of the Kimberley process[105] as an effort to guarantee the source of the stones. The result is a movement towards a linked form of responsibility that bridges gaps between people, a civilizing process in the market.[106]

The transition from an isolated system of discrete organizations to a connected value chain is now well documented.[107] My contribution is to develop a form of value chain responsibility as a general account of organizational and workplace responsibility. Because most business obligations can be traced through material relations, I argue that all companies should concern themselves with the histories of their products and equipment. I argue that all products should be subject to the treatment of shoes and diamonds. It should matter where things come from and where they go.

Stewardship as the First Virtue

The new model of business behavior that object singularization aims to establish is best described as stewardship. The business ethics literature conceives of stewardship as an alternative behavioral description of agency theory,[108] a basic financial responsibility of trustees,[109] or a form of environmental caretaking.[110] Though the present account of stewardship is consistent with all three usages, it is also more expansive.

The conscientious consumer's object stewardship understands caretaking responsibilities, ecological and otherwise, as the basis of economic ethics, and, by extension, as the first virtue of economic organization. These ideas are at least partially consistent with existing approaches to business ethics, but some aspects move in new directions.

Stewardship, properly conceived, can provide a basic framework to organize the normative insights of stakeholder theory,[111] human rights theory,[112] and numerous other normative theories of value. These approaches are stable. They do not need objects to decide the difference between right and wrong. However, I wish to suggest that these approaches need objects to allocate their conclusions to specific persons and entities in a consistent and comprehensive way.

Directing responsibilities through material things expands and reshapes ethics, and especially business ethics. Here, I will outline the most basic formulation of an object-centered ethic that can be applied to the business context. With an object focus, things are not merely tools; they are important signifiers of obligations that guide moral agents to their responsibilities. At a basic level, I can redefine the central concepts of this account in the following way:

- **Stewardship** is taking care of things as a form of responsibility.
- **Objects** are the things for which stewards care.
- **Governance** is the system that encourages stewards to behave responsibly.

These are three concepts that hold this account together, and from them I can build a general statement of the organizational ethic that this text pursues.

Stewardship is the first virtue of economic organization, and governance is the system that guarantees it. A well-governed economy is populated by responsible organizations with stable value commitments, thoughtful organizational actors, and conscientious consumers. Together, they form and revise their economic activities to use resources without using them up. They take objects seriously as the only unbiased guide to comprehensive social and environmental responsibility within the tangled web of global economic interactions.

Stewarding objects involves following them from creation to destruction, from cradle to grave. This life cycle orientation imposes personal and organizational responsibility for all related objects. The object-oriented manager treats everything that an organization possesses, everyone it employs, and everywhere that it operates as objects of care worthy of moral consideration. As a result, organizational objects are uniquely valued singularities, and the organization's mission begins to focus on promoting their complex interests. In the end, object stewardship becomes the basic strategy for making profit.

Some people already rely upon an object-oriented approach to their economic activities. Conscientious consumers, environmentalists, locavores, and responsible investors all treat some of their purchases and income as singularities. Though the conscientious consumption movement is especially common in the progressive left, conservatives also use a similar logic in some of their political activism, for instance, by organizing to punish healthcare clinics for providing abortions or to discourage pharmacies from selling emergency contraception. Sometimes, both conservatives and liberals line up to support or oppose values associated with the same objects. When the restaurant chain Chick-fil-A maintained a public position against same-sex marriage, civil rights advocates boycotted the chain and conservatives organized a "Chick-fil-A appreciation day" to support the restaurant.[113] On the conservative side, it is apparently important that food be procured from a restaurant that shares moral values. On the progressive side, corporate contributions to organizations that fight marriage equality seemed to be channeling customers' money into causes that they did not support. In either case, the sandwiches gained a moral character. The singularity logic shows up in bipartisan initiatives as well, such as legislation restricting the flow of money into organizations that fund terrorism and rogue nations.

While singularization has an affinity with sustainability and human rights awareness, the use of purchases as a modality of political expression of things is essentially value neutral, and can serve reprehensible causes as well. For example, in the 1920s and 30s, both Nazis and Klansmen organized boycotts of Jewish-owned businesses. These examples demonstrate that the underlying values are as important as the mode by which they are promulgated. It is to be hoped that both governance systems and stewardship priorities will be focused on substantive moral causes that are worthy of human care rather than anti-semitism or xenophobia, but this is not guaranteed by the structural arrangement of distributing responsibility across all supply chain partners. The only procedural stricture is that the multicultural communities of production, distribution, consumption, and disposal are more likely to be mobilized by shared understandings of human empathy than a joint expression of hate.

Universalizing Singularization

Most research on conscientious consumption seems to fixate on the extent to which consumers are willing to pay for responsibility, but this is the wrong point of departure. We should be interested in whether consumers would prefer a just economy, rather than whether they are willing to forgo consumption in order to advance responsibility even if others fail to do so. While consumers often prefer sustainable and responsible products, they are not always willing to incur the costs. It is easy to be distracted by troubling observations, like the fact that a focus on environmental sustainability sometimes reduces perceptions of quality.[114] What is more important, yet more challenging, is to make sense of the singularization process as a point of departure on the way to a universal standard of human conduct.

Kant famously established a nonconsequentialist approach to ethics by determining whether a rule or norm is universalizable, that is, whether the rule could be adopted as a rule that all should follow.[115] Let us form a basic model of object stewardship based on two specific rules:

1. Objects will not be purchased or used if they originate in harm.
2. Objects will not be sold to those who would do harm with them.

Rule 1 relates to upstream conduct and Rule 2 relates to downstream conduct. Notice that neither rule concerns the conduct of the moral agent; these are external norms that mean to influence the actions of others. Robert Axelrod describes these enforcement mechanisms as "metanorms."[116] They work according to an agent's willingness to punish someone else for not enforcing a norm. The stewards' own actions are constrained through the norms of others, not through an internal ethical code. This is in keeping with the Kantian notion of living by rules that others should also follow. Individuals become stewards of objects through a panoptic approach to economic responsibility.

Provided that I can develop a stable definition of harm, as Joel Feinberg did in *Harm to Others*,[117] then the only remaining uncertainty arises through the social burden of these rules. This will not be sufficient to complete the account, but it does lay the basic normative structure and shows how one might become involved in stewardship through the motives that this generalized standard of conduct would impose.

Implausible but Inspiring

As serious as some of these object moralizers may be, a consistent application of their views seems implausible. Even product engineers struggle to process all of the necessary information when their work requires a life cycle analysis. It is far more challenging for an uninformed and untrained outsider to make decisions regarding thousands of complex objects. We simply do not know where things originate or how the employees who made them will spend their money.

The exercise of political will through economic channels seems profoundly burdensome, if not preposterous to the point of futility.

Despite the onerous task of object stewardship, there is no better way to allocate responsibility in a complex economy than to focus on the objects with which individual persons are connected. The object-centered approach assigns responsibility comprehensively so that the economic worth of an object is intertwined with its social and ecological history. Following the tendrils of an object's history leads to marginalized economic actors whose interests ought to be relevant. The benefit that a purchaser gets from buying a piece of fruit is balanced against the ecological consequences of the way that the fruit was grown, the treatment of the workers who picked it, and the externalities of the rest of the supply chain.

The advantage is that everyone who needs to be cared for and every natural resource that the economy puts at risk is now connected to an economic decision maker with the power to choose. All of this would be ours, if we could process the information. But the cognitive strain of accounting for a short list of items would be substantial. Fair-trade labels and supply chain monitors try to reduce this burden. Unfortunately, these arrangements have not achieved reliable results for the vulnerable parties that they purport to serve. And, as the forestry example illustrated in Chapter 1, labeling schemes can also be gamed. The current approach to labeling does little to adapt to the singularity logic described in Chapter 2. With supply chain traceability and increased opportunities for disposal surveillance, we are likely to see new approaches to singularization and more fully developed platforms for accountability.

Before jumping to the question of viable alternatives, it is worthwhile to explain what we have now, and how it works. Today's dominant accountability regime finely segments responsibility so that each organization's liabilities are isolated from the next: the farm that employs fruit pickers, the shipper that employs fruit handlers, and the grocer that employs fruit sellers are each independently responsible for their own employees. Other than the food safety of the fruit that they sell, they share few responsibilities, and have few reasons to police upstream activities. Just as responsibility is isolated, so are resources. If agriculture is more competitive than retail, farms gain fewer resources. As a consequence, the distribution of profit may be inconsistent with the location of social and ecological issues within the supply chain: the retailers profit while the growers lack the resources to responsibly protect fruit pickers. The ordinary logic of profit maximization within the supply chain minimizes the priority of the workers' needs. The retailers keep their profits and the workers keep their social costs. Conscientious consumers are increasingly dissatisfied with this arrangement.[118]

In contrast, an object focus allocates shared responsibility to all of those who deal with the object. Rather than producing bounded and localized notions of responsibility within a specific geography or organization, an object orientation encourages every moral actor to look beyond the immediate scope of a business activity. The resultant ethic works through a system of network responsibility,[119] thereby supporting interpersonal duties of care within a highly mediated global economy. It asks, "Where did this come from? Was anyone harmed? Is this a responsible product?" When the social and ecological history of the fruit becomes the focus, the seller cannot responsibly claim profits until the pickers are fairly paid. The possibility of profit begins once upstream harms have been wholly eradicated. For the purpose of this text, I will focus on the intentions that motivate an object focus and the way that they understand the economy at large. In this moral view, an object focus could be adequately represented as a focus on income as well.

Later in this volume, I will argue that singularization is a much more interesting proposal for manufacturer responsibility than for consumer responsibility, and that professionals could learn a lot about ethics by learning about the material things with which they work. But let us bracket the question of how singularization is deployed to consider how an object focus addresses the concerns outlined above. Can object stewardship deal with responsibilities when markets and states fail to address important social and ecological concerns? I believe that it can, and it does so by addressing the key challenges of answering moral questions in a business context. Can objects instill a particularistic yet global economic ethic? It would seem that they can. Looking at objects focuses us on the details, and allows us to specify different forms of care and risk management that are appropriate for different classes of objects. Just as we worried over the diversity of businesses, so must we worry over the diversity of objects. But the people who deal with these objects must already manage distinctions, such as ensuring that patients who are taking medication for low blood pressure do not also take arrhythmia medication that causes a potentially deadly interaction. Managing these kinds of distinctions is what organizations and specialized labor are uniquely suited to do. Because objects help to drill down to the specifics of organizational competencies while also reaching across supply chains to places where markets and states may fail to solve important problems, they do address the problem of universalism versus heterogeneity described above.

A focus on objects also avoids some of the tainted market concepts that carry so many moral prejudices along with them. Despite the factual observation that many people do not have market and legal protections for their safety and welfare, consumers and companies often wish to suggest that it is governments and markets that are exclusively responsible for maintaining these responsibilities. To focus on an object is to set aside the wider policy apparatus and to look back across the object's history. What a steward finds in that history becomes a judgment of whether the product is responsible, and also whether the market and state are serving their functions well.

Finally, because objects keep decision makers grounded, they allow fluid movements from applied responsibility to abstract theory and back. Using objects as a gathering point for moral concerns does not set aside the human rights, fairness, harm avoidance, virtue, or goodness that different moral theories wish to promote. Instead, it sharpens these insights and gives them a place to be. Object stewardship is a practice of searching for unmet moral obligations. It is not a practice of checking a box to assume that everything is in order. Instead, the constant search to understand objects introduces a new dynamic for organizational moral awareness. As I will suggest in the final section of this chapter, the process of singularization creates a new standard for stakeholder inclusiveness, one that is not defined by the market or the state.

Summary

As a matter of abstract morality, I see no reason why we need to care about the origins of any objects or instruments of value. Whether caring for things is expedient and morally useful or not, it will not be abstract moral right that provides proof. It is only through a critical conversation involving the limits of markets, democracy, and ethics that we come to realize that we need to develop self-reinforcing mechanisms to encourage moral responsibility within the economy.

This chapter moved quickly from the topic of singularization and the nature of object histories into the limits of markets, states, and ethics as approaches to social organization. As a moralized understanding of objects, singularization is more than consumer preference. It has the potential to reinforce a normative structure within the economy that allows markets to function more reliably, democracies to govern more representatively, and ethics to flourish.

Ethics is our fallback position. Ethics takes up the slack when markets and democracies fail. But even with strong moral guidance, it is not obvious that ethics can resolve the problems in markets and states, at least not without first changing the nature of the market to make it more susceptible to the input that ethics provides. Chapter 4 puts forth three examples of important social and environmental problems that are yet unresolved by the regulatory state and its market. If the stewardship of objects provides a norm capable of resolving the confounding problems of inequality, climate change, and financial instability, then we can set about refining the concept of stewardship and developing a governance regime to consistently inspire it.

4 | *Three Failures in Regulated Markets*

The limits of economic and political theory are most meaningfully described within the context of the social and ecological problems that these systems fail to resolve. To understand the conscientious consumer's skepticism about market and state capabilities, I discuss three significant issues that remain unresolved: inequality, global climate change, and the crisis-prone financial system.

These issues are not organized around specific industries or firms, and indeed, that is part of what makes them so intractable. Here I focus on the coordination of responsibility within modern regulatory capitalism, on the strong moral components that guide the way that we think about responsibility, and on the failure of state and market models that distribute that responsibility. Moral systems, markets, and states have not established a juridical character to distribute responsibilities for curtailing inequality, global climate change, or the risk of financial crises, but I will argue that an object-centered approach holds the key to doing so.

Failing at Inequality

More than any choice that we make, our lives are first determined by factors that go unchosen. These "accidents of birth" position us within geographies, communities, families, and bodies that set the conditions for our lives. The worst of these conditions cry out for attention and strike at our most basic moral sensibilities. The best of them glitter with the enviable trappings of comfort, status, love, and order.

Luck egalitarians understand equality as a matter of life chances. More equality means that life chances are more equal, that more people will be capable of accomplishing their goals. Depending on how societies are organized, on who takes responsibility for whom, there is a lot that we can do to improve people's life chances. We can build buildings in ways that allow wheelchair users to access them, make healthcare universally available so that even the poorest people can live healthy lives, allow free movement across national borders so that workers can go where jobs are located, and treat labor as valuable at every level of social status. Societies differ in the way that they handle these egalitarian opportunities.

Among social science disciplines, sociology is perhaps best organized to track the consequences of inequality. Demographers and stratification scholars observe the relative life chances of different populations and find striking disparities. While these disparities are tracked in positivist terms, even a positivist sociological discourse cannot help but pass judgment on inequality given its entanglements with other public problems. From infant mortality[1] and public corruption[2] to weak public education, as inequality increases, important measures of public welfare decline.

Economists, broadly speaking, have shown relatively less interest in inequality. Some of that is changing, particularly with the publication of *Capital in the 21st Century*, which takes inequality seriously as a question for economic analysis and contends that public institutions can handle inequality when they set out to do so.[3]

In comparison, management research has only recently discovered poverty,[4] and that line of inquiry treats poor people as potential customers rather than organizational members or primary producers. Scholars in critical management studies (CMS) view organizational power as a source of inequality rather than a solution to it.[5] In most cases, their critical perspective is not yet paired with a constructive alternative, and the solutions that CMS seems to favor do not draw a straight line towards less inequality. Inequality and hierarchy are almost ubiquitous in economic organization, so much so that they pervade even workers' cooperatives, the darlings of CMS scholarship. Aside from the more critical academic disciplines, management research has little to say about the problems of inequality within organizations and even less to say about the organizational processes that limit contact between the wealthy and the poor.

It is understandable that management researchers should feel some ambivalence about dealing with inequality and stratification. After all, the quintessential objectives of mainstream management research – superior firm performance and above-average returns – are as likely to increase elite incomes as they are to distribute wealth broadly.

In terms of inequality, it is a secondary question as to whether organizations accomplish good in the public interest, but as I will discuss in Chapter 8, this too is a subject of controversy. If superior firm performance produces public goods, it is often by happy coincidence rather than by any intention of the profit-seeker or any innate capacity of the market to ensure this outcome. Worse, the question of whether there is a social benefit generally exceeds the scope of the question of whether a firm is or is not profitable.

However marginalized inequality research has been and however inconsistent it may be with managerial discourse, inequality remains a pressing social problem worthy of study. Whenever the benefits of corporate success are distributed too narrowly, the legitimacy accorded to such a distribution will be limited as well. Note that I am not advocating total equality, but instead a moderation of the excesses that produce too much inequality. Market restraint and regulatory constraint should produce a tolerable level of inequality. In this case, a "tolerable level" is defined as a balance of competing priorities. If there is too much inequality, society suffers; if there is too little, systems of control become illiberal. But I will argue later that if we are genuinely interested in fairness, we can distribute responsibilities for behaving fairly through material objects through which we are connected to establish a more liberal form of equality.

For now, economic inequality is a persistent feature of modern society. Indeed, it has persisted for centuries across very different economic systems. In fact, it is through history that stratification becomes embedded and imposed categorically. Stratification is not unique or endemic to capitalism, but its categories are often deeply intertwined with market activities. As Massey explains:

[H]igh levels of income inequality are neither necessary nor inevitable by-products of a market economy, irrespective of whether the market is global or national in scope . . . . The difference between a market society and other political economies is that under capitalism categorical mechanisms of inequality . . . are often built into the social organization of the market itself.[6]

Markets create explicit categories of value that extend and substantiate extant distinctions of social stratification. Insofar as race, class, and gender become encoded into occupational status, income distribution, and organizational hierarchy, market institutions can become institutions of inequality.

There have been times in American history when democratic institutions produced a dramatic convergence of income distributions, most notably in the New Deal era. However, after forty years of rollbacks in entitlement programs and increases in income inequality, which Massey calls "the great U-turn," a democratic solution is still not politically viable. Neither democratic organizations nor market entities have proven particularly eager to overcome historical inequalities. I will argue that both state and market forces are complicit and complacent in the persistence of economic inequality in the United States. This critical appraisal lays the groundwork for a negative justification of the object-focused approach to the distribution of responsibility: if inequality is the sort of problem that markets and states do not handle gracefully, then it will help to explain the conscientious consumer's strategic singularization of resources.

To think about the processes reinforcing inequality in American society, we need to look closer at a mixture of economic and political institutions. I focus on stakeholder exploitation, healthcare, education, monopoly profit, and incarceration as a diverse set of contexts in which organizations and institutions maintain or increase the gap between rich and poor. This is not a comprehensive list, but it represents several key topics and demonstrates the range of fundamental causal processes that serve as intervention sites for object stewardship.

Stakeholder Exploitation

Let us begin by acknowledging that some inequality cannot be explained by market and regulatory failures. As Robert Nozick famously argued (see below), people freely give away part of what they have to reward those with special talents, and inequality results. However, elite performance does not adequately explain elite compensation, and even if it did, it is not the only source of inequality. The undercompensation of basic wage earners and the accumulation of profit without incurring the costs of harms caused also sustain inequality.

When businesses generate profit at the expense of other parties who are unfairly harmed, one result is a concentration of wealth. The inequality comes from organizational policies that force employees and/or communities to bear the costs of an organization's production while managers and investors benefit. Though many market failures can contribute to inequality, externalities and information asymmetries are particularly likely to do so.

Senior managers are privy to more information about their firm and its risks than junior employees. If junior employees had access to perfect information, they might not take the riskiest jobs. Asbestos miners and installers, for example, were misled about the risks of their work.[7] Many suffered debilitating injuries and eventually death caused by workplace exposures.

Unfortunately, the asbestos case is not an isolated incident. There are many examples of bodily risks borne by workers and their communities without fair warning or due care, particularly where regulations do not effectively control workplace processes. For instance, many of New York City's manhole covers are produced in India at foundries where insufficient safety standards put workers in harm's way.[8] The same can be said of electronic parts recyclers, who are constantly exposed to toxic chemicals without either managerial care or regulation to guarantee their safety. The risks spill over to nearby residents and their children as well.[9] These risks worsen the relative position of disadvantaged people in unjustifiable ways, undermining the extent to which executives and corporate insiders deserve the money they are paid. Risk shifting also occurs within more personal matters, like the burden of healthcare costs. Even market apologists who argue that risks are borne consensually cannot justify the way that these costs are distributed. Consent only serves as a justification when it occurs under free and informed conditions. If employees are deceived into accepting unsafe conditions and others are enriched in the process, inequality is a likely result.

Healthcare

The United States generally organizes healthcare through insurance provided by employers,[10] yet many firms avoid these costs by hiring employees as temporary or contract workers.[11] As a result, the most precarious workers often face unmitigated financial and health risks.[12] These risks might be temporarily acceptable if the jobs were as transitional as they are said to be. However, temporary jobs may be the only jobs that people can get because many jobs do not offer upward mobility opportunities.[13] The combination of regulatory and market-based solutions provided by the Affordable Care Act mitigate these risks, but despite the Act, millions of Americans remain uninsured or underinsured, many because of underemployment rather than unemployment.

Though firms are meant to internalize the costs of healthcare, organizational initiatives and weak regulation allow these costs to be externalized, increasing an organization's profitability while decreasing the income and security of the parties who bear the costs. Some have argued that avoiding healthcare costs decreases firm performance. For example, miserly sick leave policies and a lack of insurance coverage may encourage employees to work while sick, which makes them contagious and less productive.[14] Despite these arguments, many view healthcare coverage as a cost without a related return.

Medical expenses are a significant factor in personal economic stress. A 2007 study found that 62 percent of all personal bankruptcies are attributable to medical causes; controlling for other factors, the proportion of medical bankruptcies had more than doubled in six years.[15] The increase in healthcare-attributable bankruptcies coincides with an overall decline in the availability and quality of employer-provided healthcare coverage.[16] Employers do not bear all of the blame, however, as cost increases in healthcare have also undermined the availability of care for the least advantaged.

Given the state's role in regulating markets, there is a sense in which poor policies and ineffective administration can be blamed for all of the market's failures. Though we can target government responsibility, there is always an interaction between state service provision and private service provision. For example, in the United States, unequal access to healthcare begins influencing an American's life chances before birth[17] and continues throughout the life course.[18] These health outcomes are not entirely attributable to the state, nor can they be entirely blamed on the market. Private healthcare provision and funding are at the heart of the American system. The state leaves the responsibility for these services to the private sector, and if the private sector fails, then so does the state's policy.

One might expect the state to perform better at addressing inequality than markets do. After all, market exchange is based on an equality in the value of dollars, whereas democratic participation is based on an equality in the value of persons. Nevertheless, democracies struggle perennially with the problem of social inequality. By providing unequal access to education,[19] tolerating monopolies,[20] and failing to resolve historical inequities,[21] the state is easily blamed for persistent social stratification.

Education

Blame for the crisis in primary and secondary education is easier to place on the public sector. The United States has a longer tradition of public education than it has of employer-provided health insurance, and even as that tradition is being called into question by advocates of vouchers and charter schools, the public's responsibility for quality educational access remains a near-consensus issue.[22] Nevertheless, American schools, like American hospitals, provide widely varying outcomes in ways that reinforce class boundaries.

Though educational inequality can be blamed on resource disparities,[23] mismanagement,[24] and social issues surrounding the school environment,[25] educational failures are also indicative of a wider decline in civic governance. Americans have lost important forms of civic organization and participation that once kept students performing in the classroom.[26] Given declining democratic participation, it is the citizens who are failing the schools as much as the reverse. In any case, an important class of educational reforms aims to address educational inequality by organizing and developing community capacity to interface with schools. This approach explicitly acknowledges the important participatory context of public education.[27]

Education is a source of inequality that neither markets nor democracies have managed to address. The fact that market-based approaches are pitted against increased public investment brings the education crisis into sharp focus. Distrusting the public sector makes taxpayers withhold contributions other than those that are directly controlled by local communities.

The public-sector situation is worsened further by the ideological stalemate discussed in Chapter 3. A changing workforce needs resources to develop new skills and to adapt to a changing labor market. At no time in history has the gap between skilled and unskilled wages been greater. One of the consequences of this gap is rising inequality. However, there seems to be very little political will to confront these changes. As McCarty, Poole, and Rosenthal explain, "polarization in the context of American political institutions now means that the political process cannot be used to redress inequality

124 *Three Failures in Regulated Markets*

that may arise from nonpolitical changes in technology, lifestyle, and compensation practices."[28]

Unfortunately, private-sector alternatives have also disappointed communities that invested in them often enough to suggest that education choice does not address the underlying challenge of educational inequality.

Schooling is not, strictly speaking, a part of the conscientious consumption agenda. Though some progressive parents insist upon sending their children to public schools in order to take responsibility for community education, this choice is not normally listed among the fair-trade products that conscientious consumers prefer. For the moment, we can surmise that education requires a mobilization of resources and organizational trust that strains both public and private governance systems.

Monopoly Profit

Inequality is not only produced by unjust disadvantages at the bottom of the income distribution. It also occurs because unfair advantages accrue at the top of the income distribution. I have already mentioned elite employees and elite students. Now I turn to the advantages of owners. There is a long line of argument that says that capital reproduces itself, starting with the work of Karl Marx.[29] The claim is also made from a libertarian perspective; Robert Nozick argues that inequality reproduces itself through unequal talents. He provides the example of Wilt Chamberlain, a now-dated reference to a basketball player whose talent would quickly produce extraordinary income with the willing contributions of his fans.[30] Nozick claims that even if we equalized all endowments of property, inequality would immediately reassert itself, and that we should accept this inequality as a feature of any voluntary economic system. Indeed, there are substantive and meaningful reasons for respecting people's rights to command the resources with which they are best acquainted, especially if these owners came to possess them legitimately. Nevertheless, many of the advantages enjoyed by investors and owners do not belong to this category. Monopoly profit is a good example.

Since the late nineteenth century, the United States has explicitly prohibited monopolies. For a century since, attempts to devise an optimal competition policy have been ongoing, involving regulators, legal theorists, and economic planners. Their stated intention is to serve consumer interest by maintaining an apolitical definition of monopoly power. Even so, politics enters the equation through administrative priorities that directly determine when regulators break up large firms. Massive legal action has dismantled railroads, oil producers, banks, and telecommunications firms. Still, the debate persists and the terrain grows more contentious. Large software companies, financial services firms, airlines, Internet service providers, computer manufacturers, and prominent websites are all subject to ongoing monopoly considerations in US and European courts.

These concentrations of market power result in monopoly rents that accrue to owners at the time when the monopoly is formed.[31] Concentrations facilitate inequalities in two ways. First, they enable founders and large investors to reap excessive returns. Second, they force customers to pay a price above the one that they would pay under conditions of competition. Depending on the conditions that sustain the monopoly, it is likely that Nozick's entitlement theory would find fault with many examples of monopoly rent, particularly when anticompetitive practices, collusion, and deception are used to guard market power.

Some companies ought to be monopolies, at least locally speaking. Internet service through hard lines involves an infrastructure investment that is more easily made for all households within an area. This problem is solved in Europe by regulating ISPs as utilities. As a result, European households pay less for high-speed connections than American households. Natural monopolies do exist, and there are ways to maintain near-competitive prices and reliable quality within them, but only with the cooperation of the state.

In fact, monopoly rents do spread beyond owners. Senior managers are sometimes in the best position to extract them. Managers can also extract rents from nonmonopolies thanks to weak governance regimes and inadequate checks on managerial authority. The result is excessive executive compensation, known to management scholars as the performance-pay gap.[32] There is considerable evidence that top-tier employees receive more compensation than their work product justifies at the expense of fairness and relative equality. The unjustified payments threaten workplace morale and make firms less competitive even as they increase the gap between the rich and the poor.[33]

Monopoly rents are not the only source of inequality, but they are one example of a class of problems that worsen inequality between firms. Recent economic research focusing on technological changes in productivity suggests that most inequality is now explained by variation between firms rather than within them.[34] Unfortunately, these kinds of inequality are difficult to counteract with traditional models of labor organization or upskilling, particularly when there are a finite number of market positions at which technological advantages accrue above average returns.

These examples show how justifications move back and forth from blaming markets to blaming states, and how states' and markets' faults sometimes exacerbate one another. States fail to regulate monopolists partially because of the monopolists' successful lobbying efforts, but also because some of their advantages seem natural and even meritocratic. At the same time, the internal distributional dynamics of firms are not themselves distributively "fair" or even performance-based, which indicates the double blow of monopolist income. First, consumers pay more than they should, so that firms gather more revenues than they should, and second, within firms, those revenues are distributed more narrowly than they should be. None of this looks much like Nozick's ideal case.

Incarceration

The present state of stratification in the United States cannot be summarized without reference to mass incarceration, the state's most overt, aggressive, and racially coded intervention. The criminalization of drug possession coupled with increases in minimum sentences have led to millions of nonviolent offenders serving prolonged sentences. As a result, there has been a drastic increase in the American prison population since the early 1980s, and the burden has fallen heavily on historically disadvantaged communities.[35] Incarceration is more racially stratified than either health or occupational opportunity. As Massey notes, "Whereas racial disparities in unemployment and infant mortality stand at roughly two to one, and the disparity in unwed childbearing is three to one, the differential with respect to imprisonment is eight to one."[36]

The consequences are very serious for disadvantaged communities. Children are denied parental care and young men are robbed of reliable role models. Moreover, incarcerated individuals miss out on workforce experience and are left stigmatized with a record that makes workforce re-entry extremely difficult. The consequences echo through America's poorest communities so that incarceration has come to be an "engine of social inequality."[37]

Also troubling is the way in which incarceration improves the apparent performance of the real economy. Not only do prisons employ guards, cooks, and other service staff, but they also remove a whole population from unemployment counts. As Western and Beckett have argued, the penal system serves many functions of a labor market institution, belying the myth that the US labor market flourished through the 1980s and 1990s without regulation.[38]

For those who manage to stay out of the criminal justice system, persistent educational inequality is reinforced by unequal access to occupational opportunity[39] and a persistent gender and racial pay gap. Because these burdens, like incarceration, are disproportionately borne by historically disadvantaged groups, they reinforce extant stereotypes. These stereotypes have both internal and external effects, undermining the very possibility of educational, economic, and legal equality.

Perfect markets might help to reduce inequality, but actual markets often fail to do so. As always, the process depends on the contextual details. In the case of healthcare provision and monopoly profit, the inferences are quite clear: firms distribute risks unevenly in order to avoid costs or to spread costs onto other parties. Likewise, firms claim resources aggressively in order to increase returns, and inequality results.

Some of the worst incidents occur when public and private actors collude for antisocial purposes. For instance, two judges were paid by a private juvenile detention center to keep cells full in Luzerne County, Pennsylvania.[40] Children as young as ten years old received sentences; the system was so consistent that lawyers refused to take clients to the court because they knew that they could not change the outcome.

Still, the animus for harsh criminal sanction rarely originates in the private sector. Why do democracies permit and promote inequality through harsh sanctions? One might expect for democratic order to disrupt inequality for the same reasons that Kant believed democracies would avoid wars of aggression:[41] the decision makers are also the ones who bear the costs.

Democracies may bully their own people and other states if doing so is ideologically, structurally, and politically expedient. Ideologies of self-sufficiency couple with retributive conceptions of justice to sustain the intuition that those who choose to break the law deserve to be punished. These ideologies persist because structural distance between the electorate and the burdens of their decisions hides the human consequences. For instance, when a marginalized population has few social ties beyond a minority community, their tragic experiences can be marginalized as well. Mass incarceration is also a by-product of a political mobilization strategy that overcomes fractious politics with the solidarity that only a moral panic can provide.

There is a technical question of whether punishment or treatment is a more effective response to American drug use. The question can be answered with reference to rates of recidivism, costs of incarceration, harms caused by the crime, and lost revenue from the potentially taxable distribution of drugs. However, once the issue becomes an ideological gathering point for political factions, there is little room left for technical answers. With weak oversight, poor information, and a lack of organization, democracies have a tendency to miss many important administrative details, and these costs are borne disproportionately by those who lack the resources to demand restitution.

In describing inequality, I have focused on the United States, the wealthiest country in the world by total gross domestic product and a country with relatively high economic inequality.[42] I have done so in order to show that inequality persists even when resources are available and when democratic institutions provide many citizens with the formal power to demand relative equality. It is possible for state institutions to address inequality and for market systems to help as well, but these possibilities are too often unrealized.

Global disparities in resource distributions dwarf national disparities. The global poor live without access to infrastructure, they trade with currency that has almost no purchasing power outside of their countries, and they often lack access to basic necessities like clean drinking water. If democratic regimes are not handling domestic inequality, it is unlikely that they will resolve international inequality, which presents an even more serious threat to human rights.

Inequality and the Singularizing Narrative

This chapter sets out to show that singularization is more strategic and coherent than critics of responsible consumption may realize, and that it arises very often in settings where regulatory and market failures seem particularly irredeemable. Following this logic, it is not surprising that we see boycotts and political advocacy against firms that participate in the prison system. It is also not surprising that we see discussions of consumer responsibility in education and workplace safety for numerous other products. These are guiding concerns not just because products, services, and money seem to connect people to them, but also because, in the American context, regulatory capitalism seems to provide few other solutions that are politically realistic to those conscientious worriers who wish for system reform.

We will not return to these examples until Chapter 7 (see Overcoming the Limits of the Market and the State), but I can summarize the way that an object-focused perspective and the singularization of resources allocates responsibility for global inequality. The ecological approach to value presented in this book allows us to appreciate the worth of things in the service that they do for us and in the service that they could do for others, and to treat our own use of a resource as an opportunity cost for other possible uses. It also allows us to attribute blame to those who help build the capacity to misuse resources.

Building prisons moves concrete, steel, barbed wire, and human bodies into particular roles, employing some in order to incarcerate others. In moral terms, the misuse of concrete is less vital than the misuse of the people who are forced to live in concrete rooms. But in terms of the attribution of blame, an object-centered account directs us to consider those who develop the state's capacity to incarcerate alongside other actors who actively support the institutional formations of a carceral state. Here is the point: if the incarcerated population is not justifiably imprisoned, then the entire ecology of provisioning that builds and maintains excessive capacity to incarcerate shares responsibility with the legal system and the legislative bodies and the law enforcement personnel who enact draconian sentences. In the politics of blame, it is often tempting to focus responsibility narrowly on those who most directly made decisions. In the present example, we might focus on the polity that voted for representatives who support misguided policies, or on policymakers who endorsed lengthening prison sentences for nonviolent offenders because their decisions knowingly, perhaps even intentionally, resulted in worse life chances for members of America's poorest communities.

In contrast, the object-centered approach to blame recognizes a wider causal structure. Policies are not only enacted by legislative votes; they are also enacted by the willing participation of the workforce and supply chains that carry out the legislative will. Michel Foucault famously observed that the state exerts control in very personal ways, containing and torturing human bodies in order to demonstrate the physical extent of its power. Over time, however, these exertions of power have become more discreet. As a result, "Punishment [became] the most hidden part of the penal process . . .. From being an art of unbearable sensations punishment has become an economy of suspended rights."[43] Still, for Foucault, punishment is embodied in important ways, even in the modern context. Food rations, sexual deprivation, and solitary confinement are key examples of the ways that prisoners' bodies are still punished. Objects are a guide to the formative causal background of the prison system. They can also help us to understand the interdependences between people and objects, which explain why the state's punishment is so serious. As discussed in Chapter 5, people are objects too, and our bodily objects live and thrive through connections to other things.

What help object stewardship will provide to education reform will take longer to explain, but the reason why objects do not help us to allocate responsibilities for schools as they do responsibilities for prisons is instructive. Suppose that a school and a prison both provide negative social value to their respective students and inmates, but that the students are deserving of education whereas the prisoners are not deserving of incarceration. In the negative case of the prison, blame may be distributed to those who built the misused edifice, but can we say the same of the school which has a positive use to which it is not being put?

In material terms, there ought to be a difference between an object with an unrealized positive use and an object that is likely only to cause harm. And yet, to make this distinction we must again engage with intentions, which we set aside in the account above. Here the theory begins to run dry. The bricklayer who built a school, provided that she contributes to a school that is safe, lasting, and capable of creating effective educational space, can hardly be blamed if the educators within that school fail to make effective use of that space. Accordingly, object singularization may not be the key to school reform. However, we may recover some interesting conclusions that lead in a different direction.

While objects will not give us much material with which to work in attributing blame for failing educational institutions, they will provide us with some ideas about how widely the responsibility could be shared for teaching future generations. Think of the ubiquity of mobile devices and the information that they deliver. Many young people are now mobile-only users.[44] Advertisers are restricted in the content that they can deliver to young users and in the information that they can collect from young users.[45] Advertising in this context represents a missed opportunity. Societies expend significant resources to educate children and young adults, yet they fail to make use of powerful tools that could effectively communicate, educate, and inspire these users. The omnipresence of market messages represents a massive mobilization of material resources to communicate with people, mostly in order to sell them things. Because an object focus places the use of material things in a comparative context, it raises questions about the use and misuse of human attention. I will not develop this argument further, but there is an intriguing possibility that it is education and social awareness that ought to be ubiquitous as a part of a pervasive pedagogy. Measured against the opportunity to inform the public about important matters, the meaninglessness of most marketing campaigns provides an exceptionally weak justification for the use of material resources.

The next examples of how regulatory capitalism fails will provide more obvious corollaries in the singularization of material things. Both climate change and finance are made possible by the mistreatment and misappraisal of the value of physical resources. Much of what I will say about these topics applies secondarily to the topic of inequality because both climate change and financial crises contribute to inequality when they disproportionately impact poor people.

Failing at Climate Change

In order to reach our present social and ecological position, human societies overcame many significant constraints. Our progenitors developed tools and strategies to hunt with bodies that were slower and weaker than those of their prey. They cultivated land, navigated the open sea, harnessed combustion for locomotion, and learned to fly. These achievements are now dwarfed by a global communication and transportation infrastructure that forms the backbone of an increasingly global economy. Perhaps our greatest achievement is the mastery of ourselves. We are still learning to prevent war, though a century of declining intraspecies violence gives hope for a more peaceful future.[46]

Together, these achievements allowed the human population to expand, to live longer, to consume more, and to strain ecological resources that once seemed inexhaustible. The oceans and skies are so large that they appear immutable, but we have changed them; now we are beginning to recognize the costs. From driving species into extinction to reshaping the natural biosphere, humans have done great damage to the living Earth. Navigable rivers, expansive monocultural landscapes, polluted cities, and a changed atmosphere are visible signs of a planet made ready for human consumption. This consumer's Earth has unforeseen consequences that present challenging new constraints. Its storms, droughts, melting ice caps, sea levels, and resource flows are changing in ways that we did not anticipate and do not desire. Avoiding these changes is likely to require an unprecedented degree of global cooperation, yet our governments and markets seem as ill-equipped to deal with these changes as they are with respect to inequality.

Climate Change and Inequality

Human-created greenhouse gas emissions have fundamentally changed the composition of the Earth's atmosphere. The most important of these gases is carbon dioxide, which, due to the burning of fossil fuels and changes in land use, has increased to a concentration of over 400 ppm.[47] At this concentration, atmospheric CO_2 grossly exceeds the natural range (180–300 ppm) observed over the past 650,000 years.[48] Concentrations of methane and nitrous oxide have also increased significantly, mostly due to agriculture. These gases affect the way that the sun's radiation is absorbed and reflected in the Earth's atmosphere. Since the early twentieth century, the long-term cooling trend has reversed, and we are now headed for average temperatures not observed in the past 10,000 years.[49]

Global climate change, once referred to generally as "global warming," is not exclusively concerned with temperature fluctuations. Climate change can also affect the frequency and distribution of weather events, including more severe hurricanes and typhoons[50] as well as droughts that cover more area and last longer.[51] Like other global risks, the cost of global climate change is not fairly distributed. Projections in a recent report from the United Nations Development Programme indicate that if action is not taken soon to reduce climate change emissions drastically, the consequence will be as many as 3.1 billion additional people living in extreme poverty in 2050:

Most disadvantaged people contribute little to global environmental deterioration, but they often bear the brunt of its impacts .... Environmental threats are among the most grave impediments to lifting human development, and their consequences for poverty are likely to be high. The longer action is delayed, the higher the cost will be.[52]

The subjects of welfare, development, and environmental economics have come to be viewed as inextricably linked. Eriksson and Andersson explain that "Sustainability ... requires us to live within the Earth's productive capacity. To do so in a global world requires us to distribute the world's resources more evenly."[53]

Pricing Climate Change Agents

Like inequality, sustainability depends upon the moderation of some people's consumption so that other people can consume more. Ecological responsibility, however, enlarges the category of "others" to include nonhuman organisms. These entities may not have interests of their own, but we must learn to include them in ours.[54] One way of doing so is through market exchange. In a perfect market, we are told, efficient prices should lead to optimum consumption. When buyers are overconsuming, prices increase, which encourages buyers to substitute with alternatives. A market that provides optimal prices should have the capacity to moderate consumption through price increases, thereby mitigating the risks of climate change as well. Actions that are monumentally destructive to the environment should also be monumentally expensive. Hence, failing to upgrade the inefficient heating and cooling systems in old properties, building a fleet of larger-than-necessary automobiles, expanding coal-fired power production without a viable means to sequester carbon, or drilling for oil in places that will result in irrevocable environmental damage should incur such significant costs for firms and investors that they cannot proceed with these actions.

However, these are not the costs that we observe. The modest decline in resource consumption in industrial economies[55] only slightly offsets the disproportionately high per-capita resource consumption enjoyed by these economies.[56] Moreover, many postindustrial economies consume significant resources through goods that they procure internationally. Labeling the resource demands of production undertaken abroad as another nation's responsibility creates an artificial distinction between consumers' and producers' resource use.

One consequence of these distortions, a problem frequently highlighted by critics of globalization, is that consumers become less likely to incur the costs of producers' environmental impact. When weak regulation allows manufacturers to produce goods without incurring the cost of pollution, consumers may actually benefit because their goods may get cheaper. Consumers are used to price reductions and experience them as an increase in buying power rather than a source of moral ambiguity. Such distortions are intensified by the timing, the incompleteness of pricing, and the limited scope of organizational knowledge. First, in many cases, resource depletion will not occur in the near term. As such, resource owners are unable to capitalize on scarcity, and unsustainable extraction continues to be in their short-term interest. Second, many ecological services are not priced into the market. Though the basic economic model of production involves capital investment in factors of production to provide an output that satisfies market demand, this model does not account for the ongoing uncertainty or denial of externalities caused by production. And third, the geographic scope of organizational knowledge can hinder the development of balanced resource use. Organizations lose sight of their consumption and their waste by maintaining an arms-length detachment from extraction and disposal. These limitations hinder the genesis of sustainable price levels. Whereas prices might otherwise encourage consumption at a sustainable pace, unsustainable prices encourage consumers to buy too much of some things and too little of others.

There are those, like Simon, who claim that the market is already balancing ecological overuse.[57] Others, like Hawken, suggest that business innovation is already being driven toward a sustainable form of capitalism.[58] These eco-optimists share an element of capitalistic faith, but they differ in their underlying critique. Whereas both Hawken and Simon believe that market forces and businesses are essential mechanisms in changing the human pattern of consumption, Hawken also writes, "There is no polite way to say that business is destroying the world."[59] Hawken's acknowledgement of capitalism's world-destroying potential is fundamentally at odds with Simon's antiregulatory argument, which contends that an unwarranted fear of commodity price fluctuations is leading to bad social policy outcomes.[60]

Regulating Climate Overuse

In fact, commodity prices do play a significant role in US regulation, but not in the way that Simon suggests. High oil prices caused high gasoline prices, leading the average American household to spend almost 4 percent of pretax income on gasoline in 2012.[61] This, coupled with the bailout of US automotive firms, reduced these firms' ability to lobby against increased automotive efficiency standards that the Obama administration passed into law. Oil prices may decline as new energy sources become available, but the rate of crude oil extraction is not being determined by the threshold of overuse and climate change capacity. There is essentially no relationship between the climate change risk that threatens global ecosystems and human communities and the price paid for petroleum.

Nor can it be said, as Hawken sometimes suggests, that business is already solving these problems.[62] In fact, the business response to climate change is still in its infancy. For decades, US firms either denied climate change or ignored its risks. As the scientific community reached a consensus, industry groups became more active in their denials.[63] They did so by funding denial research and by aggressively publicizing possible uncertainties, science denial tactics transplanted directly from tobacco lobbying to fossil fuel firms.[64] However, business interests around climate change are fragmenting. Denial is increasingly counteracted by business interests like those of the insurance industry, which relies upon actuarial science to ensure its bottom line. When climate change makes the world less predictable, insurance firms take on more risk. The Carbon Disclosure Project (CDP) represents fifty-four large corporations; it regularly surveys its members and their suppliers. In a recent survey of 2415 firms, CDP found that 70 percent acknowledge climate change risks. Though 92 percent of CDP's supply chain members had carbon emissions goals, only 38 percent of these firms' suppliers had set similar objectives.[65]

This voluntary activity is encouraging, and it is not isolated. Efficiency labeling initiatives in electronics and household products, automotive and locomotive hybrid vehicles, and countless other innovations demonstrate firms' willingness to participate in a more sustainable capitalism. Nevertheless, these piecemeal undertakings are still overwhelmed by the significance of the challenge ahead.

Markets are failing to internalize the price of upstream pollution and downstream waste. For example, computer manufacturers have been slow to adopt recycling programs despite toxic components that can cause significant harm as e-waste. The question that these firms ask is not whether their products cause harm at the point of disposal, but whether the harm that they cause is likely to turn into a cost that the firms must incur. Until harms become direct costs, motives do not change. This illustrates a basic principle: markets do not determine which costs will be included in the price that a customer pays. It is regulation and property rights that force cost internalization. While firms can voluntarily absorb external costs for good will, too much of this can put a firm at a competitive disadvantage. Regulation must maintain market performance.

Inaction and Perverse Incentives

The necessary regulations are not being imposed. Despite decades of evidence of CO_2's potential as a climate change agent, the United States Environmental Protection Agency has only recently defined it as harmful to human health, a change that was nevertheless controversial.[66] Broadly speaking, progress towards climate change regulation has been extremely slow.[67] The United States has no comprehensive policy on climate change, and even closely related topics like energy policy fail to address emissions reductions coherently. The global policy discussion is active and well publicized, but similarly ineffective. Strategies range from attempts at scientific consensus-building like the Intergovernmental Panel on Climate Change to United Nations summits and negotiations. It is always most difficult to negotiate multi-lateral agreements when state interests diverge, and climate change represents a profoundly divisive policy regime that makes a unified response difficult. However, without a unified response, national responses are equally ineffectual. For example, when European commitments encouraged states to take coal power production offline and reduce producer emissions, some of these resource-intensive producers simply moved to places that permitted their extant carbon intensity, making apparent emissions reductions illusory. As Helm observes, the Kyoto negotiations are based on production rather than consumption, which allows companies with significant imports in material goods to avoid taking responsibility for the emissions involved in the product of these goods.[68]

Though the United States has yet to take responsibility for reducing its own carbon emissions to a meaningful extent, it is even further away from taking responsibility for the secondary emissions initiated by US consumers. The costs of doing so may be significant, but they are believed to be manageable. Rather than waiting to implement an emissions reduction plan, acting now could make emissions reductions relatively affordable, perhaps costing 1 percent of GDP.[69] It is somewhat surprising that such a policy has been blocked so successfully, since current action is more likely to maintain status quo market opportunities. Moreover, a great deal of advocacy has already been undertaken to encourage an efficient allocation of emissions reductions through cap-and-trade programs, and a carbon exchange has already been established to facilitate these trades. Nevertheless, the regulatory limits that would make these markets move have yet to be established; no cap, no trade.

Not only is the US regulatory regime slow to advance a climate agenda, but it is also supporting a number of policies that directly undermine future emissions goals. Consider, for example, subsidized ethanol production, which has been shown to change land use patterns in ways that increase rather than decrease carbon emissions.[70] Subsidized roads and aggressive support for home construction through bank subsidies produce poorly designed cities[71] with low density and high-energy footprints. At the same time, the failure to subsidize long-term investments in public transportation and renewable energy sustains the status quo inefficiencies of a car-centered culture. The US policy agenda is not without green initiatives, including renewable energy subsidies and electric car tax benefits, but the lack of a comprehensive approach remains a major policy oversight.

Local Success, National Failure

Other areas of US environmental policy have been reasonably successful. The regulation of sulfur emissions to curb acid rain has been effective, though other emissions are now more apparent problems in polluted precipitation.[72] So far, the United States also enjoys relatively clean and drinkable tap water, which is a special privilege relative to many other nations and a triumph of water pollution regulation.

Perhaps the greatest ecological successes in the American public sector are happening within cities where urban farms, bike paths, improved public transportation, stormwater management, and numerous other local initiatives are taking shape to alter the ecological impact of urban life. Some states have also taken on environmental causes. California, for instance, passed tougher automotive fuel and emissions efficiency standards before the Obama administration managed to do so.

These local initiatives illustrate the overarching problem in climate change regulation: a divergence of interests. Misunderstood science reinforces the narrow and local perspectives about environmental regulation and the American democracy remains divided about climate change policy. Perhaps this is democracy at its best. The costs of global climate change are not going to be evenly shared, so neither will the motivations to avoid such costs. Moreover, democracies have rarely been effective at opposing the public's desires. Autocratic regimes can dictate family size and numerous other personal choices that democracies are ill-equipped to address. Democracy is particularly inept when it comes to advancing controversial norms against popular preference, something that climate change regulation is likely to entail.

Regardless of whether the failure to regulate climate change is caused by regulatory ineptitude, wayward special interests, or a systemic conservatism that must follow rather than advance social change, the result is the same from a conscientious consumer's perspective. If climate change is to be addressed, personal action is necessary, and there is no better way to allocate responsibility for personal action than through material things. It is the production, delivery, use, and disposal of things that causes the greater part of anthropogenic climate change.

While we may continue to wish for drastic change in the corporate culture of environmental waste and immediate state action, absent these movements, the only comprehensive response to the threat of climate change must necessarily allocate responsibility for climate change through a reappraisal of our responsibilities with respect to specific objects.

Failing at Finance

Now I turn to the role that markets and states play in financial crises. Moderating the uncertain storms of financial markets will prove no less challenging than moderating humanity's impact on the global climate. In both cases, causes are complex and causal ascriptions are politically contentious. The most recent financial crisis is an apt example of how systemic failures can play to the weaknesses of markets and states.

From 2007 to 2008, a valuation bubble in the United States home mortgage and real estate markets, coupled with the growth of investments based on these inflated assets, and significant holdings of such investments within large investment banks, resulted in a massive reorganization of Wall Street's largest entities and a near toppling of the global financial system. Without public intervention, the changes might have been catastrophic. Even with trillions of dollars injected into the financial sector and billions more in subsidies for other industries, the events of 2007–2008 sparked a global recession that cost millions of people their jobs and resulted in many more losing their savings.

Dozens of books now describe the 2008 financial crisis,[73] each with a slightly different take on the same basic themes:

1. An influx of investment into American markets created a capital glut that increased demand for lower-quality investment opportunities. Home mortgages were one of the few markets large enough to absorb this influx. However, there is a finite population of Americans with sufficient income to support a mortgage. To grow the market, lower-quality subprime mortgages were offered to people who could not afford them.
2. The growth of substandard lending practices and the extension of loans to people who could not afford them created undesirable and overvalued debt. Large banks' internal governance systems failed to recognize or respond to this mounting risk.

3. Supervision from credit rating agencies and government regulators did not reliably enforce effective risk management procedures or force banks to maintain liquidity.
4. Over-the-counter (OTC) derivatives and credit default swap (CDS) exposures amplified risk contagion and forced a bailout of AIG, an insurance company. AIG's insolvency threatened many other firms with tight financial ties to the insurance giant.
5. Government responses encouraged an already consolidated financial services industry to further concentrate control, weakening competition-based checks on risk taking.

Any of these themes can be blamed on the market or the regulatory state that constrains it. For example, the inadequacies of risk management systems within major banks appears to be a private sector matter, a market failure. If a capital market is unable to ensure that firms protect shareholder wealth, then these markets are failing in the central task that their advocates assign to them.[74] Nevertheless, the state is blamed for faulty bank risk management through the state's choice to rescue the banks. Because the possibility of bailouts introduces moral hazard by allowing banks to escape consequences, the state is blamed for the banks' actions in a "spare the rod, spoil the child" theory of paternalist financial regulation. The state is also expected to play a key role in financial oversight by regulating risk management systems and practices, which were apparently not sufficient to avert this crisis.

Rarely have American financial processes, entities, and elites been subjected to greater public scrutiny than in the years immediately following the crisis. With the Fraud Enforcement and Recovery Act of 2009, Congress created the National Commission on the Causes of the Financial and Economic Crisis in the United States. Six Democratic and four Republican appointees were selected to serve on the commission, which eventually published a six-hundred-page report based on the results of its fact-finding mission.[75] In the end, the commission could only agree partially on how to explain the crisis.[76] Numerous private and public actors implicated in the crisis wish to influence the way that history remembers their deeds. The forensic activities that follow are understandably politicized, not only through competing regulatory visions, but also through the contentious allocation of personal blame.

History is not the only concern in the immediate wake of a crisis. The future is also at issue. Regardless of historical legacies, market recovery depends on the restoration of investor confidence. Without confidence in the viability of the financial and economic system, savings go under mattresses, spending trickles to necessities, and economic growth grinds to a halt. Ironically, the confidence that regulators wish to restore is the same belief that made investors vulnerable to the crisis. It is confidence that allows price bubbles to form[77] and confidence that restores order after bubbles pop.

If confidence is so fickle and so internally inconsistent, it is no wonder that financial crises occur and reoccur. Economic crises are natural by-products of basic propensities within financial systems.[78] Even the core capitalist institutions of the greatest financial center in the world are subject to irrational and herd-like behavior.

The most significant consequence of the 2008 financial crisis was the global event that it caused. Reinhart and Rogoff document numerous financial crises, but few have the global scope of this "second great contraction." Not since the Great Depression has a financial event reached such a wide geographic scope. While country-level crises, whether in public defaults, inflation, or relative exchange rates, are common across regions and history, there are only a few examples of global crises.[79] One consequence of a global financial crisis is that countries and regions cannot as easily offset the contractions of other regions:

[W]hen a crisis is truly global, exports no longer form a cushion for growth. In a global financial crisis, one typically finds that output, trade, equity prices, and other indicators behave qualitatively (if not quantitatively) much the same way for the world aggregates as they do in individual countries. A sudden stop in financing typically not only hits one country or region but to some extent impacts a large part of the world's public and private sectors.[80]

I will not deal here with the full global complexity of this financial crisis, which is now implicated in the European sovereign debt crises and other regional shocks. Instead, I will focus on the fractal ungovernability of debt.

Debt at Every Scale

Debt is the primitive basis of value in consumer capitalism. Consumers are defined by their credit scores and the debt that they service. The fates of firms are likewise determined by their creditworthiness; failure to service debt, given the absence of a lender of last resort, necessarily entails insolvency. Even governments are defined by their debt and their ability to borrow more. Like the old story that imagines the Earth balanced atop an endless tower of turtles,[81] our economy stands on a tower of debt without any firmer ground to stand upon.

Capitalist economies are sustained by trade, especially the exchange of labor and resources for money. And money maintains its value through debt, especially investments in a given currency that act as loans to an economy and a shared belief that more such loans are going to be made. From there, it is debt all the way down. Debt exists at many levels: interpersonal household debt, institutional household debt, debt between banks, debt between banks and a central bank, debt between central banks, and debt between countries and multilateral institutions. Though these formulations of debt occur at different scales, some of the same patterns unfold.

In mathematics, a structure that appears similar at every scale is known as a fractal. Viewed microscopically or macroscopically, the same pattern takes shape. Mandelbrot, who pioneered the study of fractals, argued that they are common to many natural topographies and are more common than other mathematical representations of natural forms, such as lines and curves.[82] The closer you look at the shape of a coast, the trunk of a tree, or a snowflake, the more complex is the structure that you see. Sometimes, this complexity takes on a similar form to the larger pattern.

Eventually, at a small enough scale, natural fractals no longer hold the same structure. A shore cannot be a true fractal, the mathematical infinitude of which is made possible by lines with no width that are materially impossible.[83] However, a fractal's topography does give a sense of three interesting principles. First, measurement is scale-dependent; the length of a shore depends on how closely you look at it. Second, when the same process produces a structure across scales, the patterns become predictable. And third, the system's stability depends upon this scalar consistency.

The fractal concept is only occasionally deployed in social science research. Barrett and Swallow describe "fractal poverty traps" to explain an equilibrium that sustains extreme poverty at micro-, meso-, and macroscales.[84] Philosophers have long been intrigued by the metaphorical notion of society as a person, which implies a fractal-like sense of self-similarity across scale; both Plato and Aristotle used this scheme to pattern the virtues of society after the virtues of individual persons.

In the case of debt, some of the same dynamics that characterize macroeconomic trade imbalances occur within the dynamics of large banks and home mortgage debt as well. The mechanisms differ: macroeconomic trade imbalances are checked by regional planning and global currency markets, whereas bank activities are controlled by markets and domestic regulations. Consumer debt is controlled by bank policies and law. Nevertheless, the basic shape of the relations between debt and expectations and the basic process through which control is lost follows similar principles. As an example of cross-scale consistency in the debt problem, consider the macroeconomic, household-level, and industry-level expansion of indebtedness amidst declining accountability.

Macroeconomic Patterns

Macroeconomic factors are frequently cited in accounts of the 2008 financial crisis. As early as 2005, then-Federal Reserve Governor Ben Bernanke highlighted the "global savings glut" that was financing the United States current account deficit.[85] This has since been a recurrent theme in explanations of how the crisis happened. For instance, as Paul Krugman explained to the Crisis Commission,

It's hard to envisage us having had this crisis without considering international monetary capital movements. The U.S. housing bubble was financed by large capital inflows. So were Spanish and Irish and Baltic bubbles. It's a combination of ... a less regulated financial system and a world that was increasingly wide open for big international capital movements.

Though net savings were sent to the United States by numerous export-oriented countries and also major European banks in Germany, France, and Italy, the dissenting Republicans from the Crisis Inquiry Commission were particularly eager to blame increased Chinese investment.[86] In any case, it is a special form of ingratitude that blames a financial crisis on another country's generosity, especially when the generous parties ended up bearing significant costs in the process.

One account of the macroeconomic processes stands out as particularly thoughtful and comprehensive. In *Fault Lines*, Raghuram Rajan, the former chief economist at the International Monetary Fund, argues that macroeconomic forces played a powerful role in the lead-up to the collapse of the US housing market.[87] Rajan suggests that trade imbalances led producing countries to make investments in the US market, and that an increase in the supply of foreign capital raised the demand for debt, which resulted in a decrease in the quality of debt being sold. This pattern, he claims, has now played out twice in the last two decades. First, it occurred in response to the stagnant economy of the early 1990s, when the US undertook a domestic policy to increase consumption. Meanwhile, increased foreign investment was channeled into a burgeoning technology sector, much of which proved unsustainable as the dot-com boom went bust. The same pattern recurred with consumer mortgages that were expected to be more reliable investments and were judged as such by rating agencies.

Powerful checks are usually in place to maintain loan quality as a part of a country's concern over its own economic health. However, rising inequality has trumped these checks to force easy credit as an expedient, albeit shortsighted, solution. The wider historical context of trade policy relates to the development financing provided internationally during macroeconomic shocks. Rajan argues that the aggressive adjustments imposed as conditions for receiving IMF loans led developing nations to focus on an export-centered form of economic development in order to preserve sovereign control over domestic policy. Without encouraging domestic consumption, developing nations have been forced to invest income in net consuming nations in order to maintain exchange rates. At the same time, the United States' consumption-oriented approach to addressing economic downturns has fueled these countries' export strategies. Unfortunately, the US has not managed to address the income inequality that these policies were meant to target.

Rajan's concern with inequality covers both domestic and global issues. He views American inequality as a by-product of a dysfunctional educational system that is not preparing students or retraining adults for a technology-centered economy. While the skills mismatch sustains significant pay gaps, these pay gaps create a political climate that increases demand on social services. For example, the increasing duration of unemployment challenges the resilience of the American economy, given that unemployment insurance programs are designed for temporary and transitional protection.[88] These same fault lines, he claims, play out on the international stage as well. For this reason, Rajan opposes blaming individuals and entities because this denies a wider system of social and economic trends:

We should resist the temptation to round up the most proximate suspects and pin the blame only on them. Greedy bankers can be regulated; lax government officials can be replaced. This is a convenient focus, because the villains are easily identified and measures can be taken against malfeasance and neglect. What's more, it absolves the rest of us of our responsibility for precipitating this crisis. But this is too facile a response.[89]

The scope of Rajan's account is sweeping and historical, as are the solutions that he proposes, including policies to reduce American inequality, better dialogue between nations for economic development planning, and specific improvements in the financial system that allowed too much risk to accumulate. If we are to maintain debt as the centerpiece of a global economic system, Rajan maps out a number of core issues involved in doing so.

Subprime Mortgages

TIME magazine recently ranked the subprime mortgage among the world's fifty worst inventions, along with DDT, the Ford Pinto, hydrogen blimps, asbestos, and leaded gasoline.[90] In most cases, debt is issued to those who are believed to be able to pay, hopefully under terms that will encourage them to do so. There is another motive for debt issuance that occurs when a lender wishes to acquire the asset put up to secure a loan. For example, in *The Jungle*, the protagonist is thrust into poverty by using all of his savings to put a down payment on a tenement from which he was quickly evicted; the lender benefits from the quick turn-around by retaining both the down payment and the property.[91] Subprime mortgages were often issued with little or no down payment to parties whose income and credit rating provided little confidence that they would ever be able to repay. Under the terms of some of these loans, even very wealthy households would struggle to keep up with rate increases.

Giving a loan without intending for it to be repaid is unusual. Under other conditions, we might call it charity. In this case, subprime mortgages were anything but charitable.[92] Instead, they ushered unqualified borrowers into the home-buying market, thereby inflating home prices and increasing the pool of assets that banks could bundle and sell to investors. As long as housing prices increased, the real consequences of these loans were not apparent: borrowers could refinance to avoid balloon payments and rate increases, and lenders could ignore impending defaults. But when housing prices stopped rising in 2006, those who invested in the homes that buyers purchased were left seeking payment from families that could not afford to service their own mortgages. It was not until 2007 that the more serious impact of unrealistic household debt loads began to affect the values of the assets derived from these debts.

Subprime lending practices were promoted by government-sponsored entities (GSEs) as well as by private banks that sold related securities. As long as the debt flowed, these entities grew in status and value, however ill-conceived the means. One might expect for the market or the state to have curtailed self-destructive practices, but instead it was market flows and state directives that changed mortgage quality, while denying evidence of debt's changing value:

[M]ajor financial institutions ineffectively sampled loans they were purchasing to package and sell to investors. They knew a significant percentage of the sampled loans did not meet their own underwriting standards or those of the originators. Nonetheless, they sold those securities to investors.[93]

This finding supports the "originate-to-distribute" theory that concealment and self-deception were the tools of mortgage issuers intent upon extracting rents from their clients.[94] Against this view, some argue that banks held assets that they sold, in other words, that they "originate-to-hold."[95] Under this theory, banks, like their clients, were deceived by mortgage recipients and fraudsters who took advantage of their trust:

While there is no doubt that certain lenders did take advantage of certain borrowers, ... the reverse also occurred. During the frothiest period of the housing market, stories abounded of homeowners flipping properties after a year or two, generating leveraged returns that would make a hedge-fund manager jealous. Loose lending standards also benefited first-time homebuyers who couldn't otherwise afford to purchase, and many of these households haven't defaulted and are presumably better off. Moreover, even among the households who have defaulted, while many are certainly worse off, there are also those who can afford to pay their mortgage payments but have chosen to "strategically default" because it's simply more profitable to do so.[96]

There is no reason to think that one pattern must dominate the other. Indeed, it is even possible for borrowers and lenders to benefit together from a bubble's growth. Akerlof and Shiller suggest that deception and price increases occur within "an economic equilibrium that encompassed the whole chain."[97]

In any case, the blame cannot fall on the debt instrument itself. Someone must have seen fit to allow the debt to be issued in this manner. While the borrowers who signed contracts that they could not fulfill deserve some blame, rarely do mortgage borrowers write the terms of their loans. Regulators permitted subprime mortgages and bankers eagerly issued them. Consumers were largely unaware of the banking sector's transformation.

Financial Innovation

According to the standard view of market governance, investors protect themselves by seeking the highest return available at the lowest risk. Investors are expected to act on these long-term interests because they intend to use their savings at some later date and because most investors are risk averse. However, with the wrong models and the wrong information, their behavior can make risk accumulate.

It is often difficult to see the long term when other market participants seem to be benefitting from short-term price increases. As White explained in 2010, there were many macroeconomic warning signs of the coming crisis, but they were ignored. They were not only ignored by investors, but also by leading financial professionals:

Why were the warnings unheeded? It didn't play to the prejudices of the various actors. Insofar as the private sector was concerned, everybody was making huge sums of money. The financial sector, at the boom, made up 40 percent of all the profits in the United States. Nobody wanted to talk about the fact that this might be risk taking. They all wanted to say that they were clever .... Prejudices rest on a platform of beliefs. The models that people were using didn't allow for crises of this kind.[98]

In practice, market prices are often treated as measures of actual value, especially when they confirm shared beliefs. Market prices become their own realities with their own internal dynamics. Consider, for example, a commodity like wheat. News of weather damaging wheat yields might help us to estimate the acres affected and thus to infer a shift in supply. With less supply, prices should increase, and we can use this information to revise our own view of the current spot commodity and futures prices. Predicting the price better than other market participants allows us to buy low and sell high. When daily fluctuations follow these standard economic inferences based on historical price adjustments and knowledge of present conditions, they lead investors to a false sense of confidence. Because our inferences index from the market price, their key assumption is that the starting price was correct.

Weak Signals and Invalid Assumptions

This assumption may be valid, but if it is not, the market's dynamics will not behave any differently in the short run. A person with superior short-term information cannot help but participate in faddish prices even if her long-term information is just as flawed as everyone else's. Bikhchandani, Hirshleifer, and Welch describe this situation as an "information cascade." When information cascades, each individual is motivated to discard their own private information in order to follow the collective behavior.[99] This can account for bubble formation and a freeze in liquidity as well. The wheat purchaser has to believe the price in order to participate, particularly when the timing of a price adjustment is uncertain.

Signals of price distortion are difficult to read. Perhaps an asset or commodity is overvalued, but as long as the market does not share this belief, it is costly and risky to hold assets and wait for prices to adjust. These assets are difficult to track when they respond to real world circumstances, and the complexities increase when assets are linked to unobservable financial relationships. It used to be that a firm's performance could be guessed by understanding the dynamics of its costs and revenues: jet fuel prices go up and airline profits go down, automotive sales increase and so do automotive profits. However, because investors have an appetite for smooth returns, firms began locking in commodity prices. In large international transactions, they would lock in exchange rates by buying currency futures, but there was a problem. What if the organization that issued the future could not pay its debt? Finance had a solution for that problem as well, a credit default swap (CDS). These assets could be issued to remedy the credit event. As the volumes of synthetic financial assets have accumulated, it became extremely difficult to determine who owns what and who bears which risks. Markets fail under conditions of opacity. Investment banks and financial services firms created new financial complexity and thus opacity. Ironically, they did so in the name of risk management.

Organizational Adaptations

Investment banks and other financial institutions played a key role in channeling increased macroeconomic capital flows through numerous investment vehicles[100] into home mortgages even as these mortgages decreased in credit quality. This was accomplished amidst a massive technological transformation of the financial industry, a transformation that cloaked the declining quality of the assets being sold.

All financial intermediation involves connecting savers with borrowers. At one point, this relationship was local and immediate: banks held savings accounts and provided interest in return for the ability to loan funds to others who wanted to borrow. Today's financial system is more centralized and layered than this simple relationship. Now, a long chain of institutional stages mediates between savers and borrowers. The new system has certain advantages. For instance, insurance avoids the risk of bank runs. Also, in place of local limits on lending opportunities, savings can be channeled from places with high savings to places with a demand for them.

The new system has its limitations as well. In the old system, lenders were directly involved in making sure that they were repaid and directly motivated to make good lending decisions. Today's loan issuer or credit card customer service person has far less reason to worry about whether a customer will actually be able to repay his or her debt. The new system also attenuates the information available to other parties. With less information, the quality of governance and oversight also declines.

In the highly mediated form of banking, a specialized set of banks emerged to address challenges in capitalizing businesses. These investment banks specialized in helping companies to find investors and lenders. This can be done by advising a company through a merger, by underwriting an initial public offering, or by helping a company to raise money through a bond issue. In 1933, the Glass-Steagall Act explicitly detached these services from other commercial and retail banking services that banks traditionally provided. However, important provisions of the act were repealed in 1999.[101] The change allowed commercial banks and investment banks to join together in issuing securities. The earliest versions of mortgage-backed securities, some forms of which had already been around for almost two decades, cannot be blamed on the repeal of Glass-Steagall. Even so, it may have precipitated a transformation in banking cultures. As Stiglitz argued:

> The most important consequence of the repeal of Glass-Steagall was indirect – it lay in the way repeal changed an entire culture. Commercial banks are not supposed to be high-risk ventures; they are supposed to manage other people's money very conservatively. It is with this understanding that the government agrees to pick up the tab should they fail. Investment banks, on the other hand, have traditionally managed rich people's money – people who can take bigger risks in order to get bigger returns. When [the] repeal of Glass-Steagall brought investment and commercial banks together, the investment-bank culture came out on top. There was a demand for the kind of high returns that could be obtained only through high leverage and big risk taking.[102]

To read this passage, one might think that investment banks had always been cultures of risk, but for decades in the mid-twentieth century their activities were relatively stable and predictable. In fact, investment banks went through their own cultural transformation starting in the late 1970s.

Banking Culture

One significant change in the culture of investment banks occurred as these organizations transformed their internal governance structures from private entities to publicly traded corporations. Beginning in 1970, the New York Stock Exchange permitted banks to go public. Morrison and Wilhelm argue that investment banks' decision to go public was largely precipitated by a series of technological shocks that altered the need for capital and the value of tacit human capital within established firms.[103] This happened starting in the late 1960s as computers became important for clearing orders in retail banks. It happened again in the early 1980s as computers became useful in modeling and immediately updating valuation estimates.

These dynamics were also influenced by the changing shape of the workforce, which now required the expertise to run the new data systems. In the old investment bank cultures, partnerships were heavily invested in employee mentoring and retention. The whole partnership scheme was designed for an internal leadership retention strategy. This reduced the propensity for labor mobility within the industry while forming tight, firm-centered cultures. But as technology and expertise changed, so did firms. By the late 1990s, these organizational cultures were a thing of the past. In place of mentorship, employees arrived with quantitative training that they honed on the job. This made employees much more mobile and it made their long-term partnership prospects less alluring than the payout of an annual bonus. Even as outside investors began making capital contributions to large banks, the organizations in which they were investing were changing form, competing more aggressively for employees who were less connected with bank cultures and less controlled by their managers.

This is the context of rapid financial innovation. Gone were the days when bank employees could sponsor a nephew as a junior job candidate by paying half of his first-year salary. In the new banking culture, these practices would be viewed as nepotism and weakness. Tight-knit partnership cultures inhabited by the prototypical "organization man"[104] gave way to free agent workplaces in which labor is only temporarily attached to any particular organization.[105] On the upside, equal opportunity policies were at least somewhat more successful in the new banking cultures. At the same time, as the long-term stability of one's employer became less of a factor in one's career success, governance faltered. These changes occurred amidst the emergence of a new set of quantitative tools. At first these were theoretical models for asset pricing, then later they were computerized approaches to technical analysis that tracked trends and patterns in asset prices. Eventually, they were imaginative solutions for basic financial problems.

New Tools

The financial crisis of 2008 brought two financial tools, securitized debt and financial derivatives, out of obscurity and into the spotlight. Both instruments represent specialized abstractions that are formed from collections of underlying assets or contractual obligations.[106] An object focus will help us to stand in judgment of these tools. It does so by demonstrating the way these financial instruments increase complexity and abstract away from an economy of material responsibility.

Many accounts of finance and financial innovation focus on the intelligence of the innovators. For instance, one widely read account of Enron is titled *The Smartest Guys in the Room*.[107] Indeed, the complexity of these financial instruments and strategies is undeniable. But whenever complex arrangements unwind to massive losses, we must wonder whether the intelligence is being deployed for benevolent or malevolent purposes. Two recent scandals stand out as particularly characteristic of this pattern. First, Jérôme Kerviel executed a series of bad trades in 2008 that cost Société Générale billions. More recently, JPMorgan lost over six billion dollars on positions taken by Bruno Michel Iksil, the so-called "London Whale."

Perhaps senior managers simply failed to appreciate the underlying volatility of housing prices. A more insidious possibility is that senior management did not actually understand the fundamentals of the new financial instruments that their employees were using or that they did understand the fundamentals but chose to risk anyway because of short-term incentives. Whatever the managerial mindset, the riskiest behaviors occur in the shadows that regulation does not control. The new activity falls into an ill-defined category of "shadow banking." Kerviel's trading activity was meant to focus on derivatives pricing. Iksil's losses occurred through CDS positions. Shadow banking encompasses the variety of banking, insurance, and investments that occur within a range of instruments that are not regulated as either banking securities or insurance coverage.

Traditional banks are forced to maintain reserves in order to ensure liquidity. Banks are then made to pay for additional federal insurance to guarantee deposits. Insurance providers are similarly required to maintain reserves and also reinsurance from a secondary market. The financial relationships that fall beyond or between these regulatory structures are formed from securities that were often designed explicitly to avoid regulatory oversight. The risk of these instruments comes from their novelty, their complexity, and the lack of regulatory coverage.

The populist outrage at the growth and risk of shadow banking stems from four key observations. First, banks often seem to be aware of the risks and externalities of these arrangements. Second, banks have aggressively contributed to the American political process in order to stave off regulation. Third, credit ratings agencies have helped to sustain the veneer of legitimacy over very risky assets in a way that seems to undermine investor protections.[108] And fourth, despite precipitating a global recession, there is little evidence to suggest that the shadow banking system is now effectively regulated.[109]

As of June 2012, the Bank for International Settlements (BIS) reported more than 600 trillion dollars, roughly ten years of today's gross world product (global GDP), in outstanding derivatives contracts.[110] Many of these contracts will expire without ever being exercised, and most others will cost far less than their notional value; nevertheless, these sums illustrate the overcommitment of a shadow banking sector that is not forced to hold reserves in order to guarantee its contracts. Some risk is managed by private arrangements within the margin requirements of central clearinghouses, but these limits are designed by the financial industry for the financial industry, rather than by regulators with systemic risk in mind. Insurance giant AIG was massively exposed to derivatives risk, a position that forced an unprecedented bailout of a single entity, at public expense, in order to avoid the possibility of a chain reaction.

These are rather abstract problems, so let us consider a concrete example. Interest rate derivatives are the largest category in the BIS report, comprising almost 80 percent of outstanding contracts. Yet these rates are not predictable in purely economic terms. The Federal Reserve's increases in the prime rate are subject to significant political and economic debate. Rate changes already directly influence the economy through changes in lending behavior and indirectly through changes in the money supply and via the expectations channel. That these changes can then result in solvency issues for major financial entities creates tertiary effects that did not exist before derivatives contracts were popularized.

Shadow banking results in a puffed-up financial system, the true value of which is almost impossible to determine. Like global capital flows and lax debt origination standards, increasing complexity means increasing uncertainty, yet the additional complexity has enabled an expansion of debt rather than an increased perception of risk.

Uncertainty Across Scale

There is remarkable similarity across scale in the permissive expansion of debt for American home mortgages, the American economy and public sector, and the global market as well. Because debt is expanding across scales, it can be difficult to observe the overall increase. As of

December 2016, American households owed a total of $12.58 trillion, a mere 0.8 percent below the 2008 peak.[111] In terms of public debt, United States' gross national debt was over $18.6 trillion in 2016, almost 107 percent of US GDP.[112] Global bond markets have shown a similar trend of increasing debt and declining debt quality. As a Morgan Stanley report on the development of the bond market describes, there has been a steady decline in the quality of corporate debt for the past 25 years:

> Starting in the U.S. and then spreading to Europe, firms have found it expedient to "optimize" their capital structure by increasing leverage to improve return on equity and boost shareholder returns without jeopardizing solvency. [T]he proportion of the US corporate market rated 'AAA' has virtually vanished while the 'A' and 'BBB' segments have grown substantially.[113]

At the same time, bond yields, the effective rate that the borrower pays to investors, have also declined. Investors are accepting decreasing returns and declining debt quality,[114] which is characteristic of what we observe at the household level as well. The same is true of public debt. And at least for US borrowers, real interest rates continue to be held at historical lows by a prolonged period of aggressive monetary expansion. As far as the quantity of corporate debt, those numbers depend on what is counted as debt. The total market capitalization of the global bond market was almost $100 trillion in 2011.[115] If obligations like derivatives are included, as the previous section describes, then these amounts can be drastically higher.

Examples of Multilevel Uncertainty

At each of these levels, the picture is a great deal more complex than a single number can capture. Spain has one of the highest household debt-to-income ratios in Europe. However, given Spain's youth unemployment rate of over 50 percent in early 2013, an understanding of the value of this debt must account for the likelihood that it will actually be repaid. With the accumulated social burden already being placed on families and some of the most restrictive mortgage renegotiation standards in Europe, the debt's value is likely to be steeply discounted.

As another example of how aggregate measures hide underlying realities, consider American student debt. Americans owe over a trillion dollars in student loans.[116] In one federal lending program, more than a fifth of those students in the repayment phase are in default or forbearance.[117] This debt is the only subset of household debt to increase in the course of the recession. In keeping with debt expansions at other scales, education quality is declining within the debt pool. For-profit universities are a major concern in this declining education quality because they lead students to take on significant costs without commensurate employment opportunities. The default rate for student loans from for-profit universities is over 22 percent, more than twice the public university rate.[118] And, unlike public universities, for-profit universities are actively engaged in aggressive student outreach to try to delay defaults to avoid regulatory restrictions on their access to student loan income.[119] We simply cannot infer from a debt percentage or a debt aggregation that there is any homogeneity in the debt's value. If Spanish households owe money but lack jobs to make payments, and if American students owe money for substandard educations, these debts are not equivalent to the imagined reality of debt as fixed income, and they cannot be summed to a meaningful total.

It is sometimes tempting to view economic activity as nested, imagining persons within companies doing business within states, their money bubbling up to total GDP. Under this scheme each state is responsible for regulating its own economy so that all the pieces work together. Indeed, many of our data collection strategies are designed with these hierarchical levels in mind. However, this understanding overlooks the true complexity and unity of a global economy. For instance, it ignores the direct connection between the elite oligarchs of the developing world and the economies where they choose to siphon their wealth. The Cypriot banking crisis is a characteristic example of this complexity. During the crisis, Russian businesses and individuals that held large accounts in Cyprus were, in effect, forced to recapitalize the banks. The tax treaty between Cyprus and Russia that encouraged these capital flows suggests that the Cypriot economy is a part of the Russian economy, yet the bailout negotiation was largely undertaken within the structure of the European Union. Thus, individual, national, and international arrangements connect in ways that cannot be reconciled with a hierarchical model.

Debt Fractals

I use the concept of a fractal to suggest an alternative conception of this complexity to recognize similar structural features across levels of analysis without endowing the elements of the economic system with a fixed hierarchical position. The same basic logic is applied within network science to the idea of scale-free networks, which exhibit similar structural features, like the distribution of network ties, at different sizes.

For the purpose of financial regulation, the problem is that network systems cannot be controlled through hierarchical means without first imposing hierarchy upon them. We have crossed the threshold when country-level regulations and local controls could check errant behavior. At this point, global systemic imbalances are shaping local behavior in deeply problematic ways. If we are to have a scale-free economy, we must also have a scale-free regulatory system, a system that builds from basic and simple procedures into a complex and globally coherent whole.

The bank consolidation strategy of the Obama administration is illustrative of how inappropriate hierarchical control has become for the global economy. Even after it was broadly agreed that firms were impossible to censure in the 2008 financial crisis because of their size, further consolidation has been allowed and even encouraged. These ungovernable proportions make fines counted in the billions of dollars into ordinary business expenses. Seemingly genuine apologies mask an industry that is almost unchanged despite having caused massive social costs in the pursuit of profit. Worse yet, investors have grown tolerant of firms' misdeeds. The financial services sector received a shocking wave of criticism at the end of 2012 concerning income from drug cartels, terrorist organizations, and embargoed states like Iran.[120] These affiliations are wildly unpopular, yet these firms ended the year with share prices up.[121]

Risk Without Control

Neither market self-control nor democratic regulatory control is effectively addressing the world's accumulated financial risk. The problem is not only with the multiple levels of complacency, but with the expedience of credit as a persistent form of delayed conflict. Cheap credit is too convenient a political and economic solution. On the market side, borrowers, titling companies, lenders, securities bundlers, accredited investors, central bankers, and legislators all benefit more from system stability in the near term than they do from long-term viability. On the political side, debt is an immediate answer to a long-term problem, providing needed social services without having to pay for them. As public and private debts accumulate, so do risks. Eventually, failure becomes unavoidable, and we observe periodic and sudden downward price adjustments, organizational failures, and earnings restatements. We can also observe, in the accumulation of debt, the basis for a more radical platform of economic upheaval. As Graeber notes:

> For thousands of years, the struggle between rich and poor has largely taken the form of conflicts between creditors and debtors – of arguments about the rights and wrongs of interest payments, debt peonage, amnesty, repossession, restitution, the sequestering of sheep, the seizing of vineyards, and the selling of debtors' children into slavery. By the same token, for the last five thousand years, with remarkable regularity, popular insurrections have begun the same way: with the ritual destruction of the debt records – tablets, papyri, ledgers, whatever form they might have taken in any particular time and place. (After that, rebels usually go after the records of landholding and tax assessments.) As the great classicist Moses Finley often liked to say, in the ancient world, all revolutionary movements had a single program: "Cancel the debts and redistribute the land."[122]

In this section I have treated debt as it is generally treated in economics, as a social process through which individuals gain additional resources in the long run by making sacrifices in the short run. As Graeber illustrates in his book, the moralized interpersonal understanding that we have about fairness with respect to debt is not at all consistent with the historical processes through which debt controls and subordinates. These prove to be powerful levers of social transformation whenever mass movements assert themselves over the workaday economics of a complex global economy, but canceling the debt seems merely to reset the problem without solving the underlying issues. Even a radical egalitarian cannot deny the cyclical and fortune-shifting nature of debt.

Limited recourse is available to the egalitarian who, having reset the debt through a Jubilee, must now watch as debts begin to accumulate into a fresh form of inequality. The governance requirements of a functional economy are external to its practice. Because markets do not self-regulate, they cannot reliably allocate responsibility for resolving market failures, particularly in areas where conflicts of interest run as deep as those that arise within finance, accounting, management, investment, and banking. Since banking regulators are captured by the industry that they ostensibly control,[123] there is no external arbiter to deal with banking's ever-increasing complexity.

Looking from a complex and intentionally obfuscated system like finance to the state for regulatory oversight places an extraordinary burden upon the regulatory body. Whether the state can do a better job of controlling the financial sector in the future is an open question, but it is likely to be a significant (and possibly fruitless) struggle. These episodes do not lend faith to the prospect of effective social, environmental, and financial regulation through political action or self-regulating markets. Conscientious consumers suggest another possibility.

Through the materialist conception of responsibility, the debt-holder becomes interested in the nature of the resources to which she is connected. She cannot hide her responsibilities behind commodification and the abstraction of financial risk. She must grant that debt buys things, and that she is partially responsible for the things that it buys. The full realization of this ethos must also account for flows of money, which are beyond the scope of the present inquiry, but it would be a giant leap forward for financial firms to view their portfolios as concrete, specific, and physical structures that have worth by virtue of the material benefits that they produce.

In Chapter 5, I turn to a set of humanist problems that objects can solve. Building from there, a new economics of ecological use value will begin to take shape.

5 | *Person, Place, and Product*

Walking past a pond, a man sees a young child drowning in shallow water. He can save the child, but his feet will get muddy and his expensive shoes will be ruined. What should he do? Peter Singer, the utilitarian philosopher who introduced this dilemma, thinks the man should save the child and ruin the shoes.[1] You probably agree. What is a new pair of shoes weighed against the life of a child?

Singer argues that this description is a reasonable approximation of the dilemma that consumers face every day when they choose between contributions that could alleviate suffering and luxury expenditures. Because one ought to save the child, by extension, one ought to forgo luxuries in order to save children who are dying of malnutrition and otherwise suffering. According to Singer, the geographic distance between you and the dying child and the specific cause of the child's preventable death does not lessen your duty to lend aid.

Deaths from malnutrition and disease are declining, but, as Singer notes, each year almost 10 million children die before they reach their fifth birthday. Singer argues that we share a global responsibility for alleviating this suffering. The implication of the dilemma is clear: until all children are properly nourished, educated, and safe, fancy shoes do not matter.

This chapter explores the scope criterion of ethics. It begins with the humanistic concerns that motivate Singer's argument and then moves to a more basic framework for mapping out the things that we value. As we move from understanding and empathizing with other people to understanding and empathizing with objects, we must deal with the normative order in which people and things ought to act or be used in a certain way. These questions of ends (teleology) would be easiest to answer if we had a plan for everything in the universe. Still, even without such a plan, we can make reliable judgments about certain uses and misuses of things. This begins with extending a theory of value to more diverse objects and, in Chapter 6, to objects within complex systems.

Here, "value" is treated as an active verb that involves both appreciating worth and acting to protect the valued object. This moves in a slightly different direction from the typical philosophical question of what matters. Relating appreciation, attention, and care into a unified concept captures the multiple aspects of value. If an employee said, "I like my job because they value me," he might be thinking about displays of appreciation, having a highly appraised worth, or receiving attention. All three experiences are more active than a mere price. Value is not only a passive appraisal; it is an active verb, something that we do. The union of attention and action will prove important, not only in responding to Singer's dilemma of the child in need, but also in deciding whether inanimate objects like shoes matter in other ways.

Shoe Versus Child

Philosophers like Singer spend a great deal of time exploring the nature of moral priorities, what matters in a moral sense. Most believe that people matter and many believe that cultures matter too. Some prioritize a wider biological community, for instance, all pain-sensing organisms or all living things. Singer, for instance, has argued extensively on animal rights and the importance of showing empathy for all things that suffer.[2] Philosophers give many reasons for including living communities as objects of moral concern, including their rights and their intrinsic worth.

These priorities may set the standard for which objects receive moral consideration, but they do not decide whether this consideration spreads to other causally related things. Schwartz considers the economic structure as an important feature of how human actions have consequences for others, especially through consumption. He argues that both consequentialist and nonconsequentialist theories of responsibility lead to the conclusion that purchasing choices are morally relevant.[3] This approach illustrates the collective action problems of conscientious consumption and highlights the importance of economic wrongdoing. Schwartz claims that consumption is a causal process that motivates upstream behavior, and that even if irresponsible productive activity would persist without a consumer's patronage, the consumer still participates in the wrongdoing by purchasing a product linked to it.

Philosophy's Limits

These arguments play to philosophy's strengths. Reasoned arguments about the basic features of conscientious consumption connect responsible purchasing behaviors with more basic moral
intuitions to identify a consumer's responsibilities and their limits.
However, Schwartz's account has much less practical insight for
how to sustain consumer responsibility. Schwartz notes that "living an ethical consumer life is in many ways an epistemological
burden."[4] But he does not explain how this burden might be
overcome, other than through the already dysfunctional economy
of information. As such, his faith in improvement can only focus
on the most general problems where consumers enjoy considerable
information about upstream supply chain conduct:

[C]onsumers perpetuate the present system not from a lack of moral fiber but
from simple ignorance. Once people become aware of the wrongdoings
associated with what they buy, many will be moved to alter their buying
habits.[5]

This empirical claim can fail twice: first, if there is no mechanism to
inform people, and second, if the information does not motivate
behavioral change. So far, the progress towards conscientious consumption is incomplete and likely never to be completed. Even if
consumers are motivated to pay more for a responsible product or to
avoid an irresponsible product, doing so may not produce the pro-
mised results.

As long as information is structurally disjointed, a consumer's conscience may not be actionable. A much wider gap exists between supply
chain consequences and consumer choices than Schwartz admits. This
is not a devastating critique of his argument, which I think is coherent
and defensible. Nevertheless, without the institutionalization of an
information system that can sustain consumer-motivated responsibility, these ethical aspirations are unlikely to address more than the
most serious and public incidents. Philosophical inquiry and an interpersonal ethic of care may start us on our journey, but these tools
cannot plot the course. Specifically, interpersonal ethics cannot focus
moral attention to acute moral problems within the global economy.
Instead, such an ethic tends to draw people towards whichever concerns are popular at a given moment, while neglecting others.

Translating to Practice

Value theory is capable of describing reasons why things are good or why they deserve to be treated with care, but it cannot say how best to allocate the duties of care. In translating abstract priorities into concrete obligations, we must determine who should implement an obligation that we all share. Here, philosophy reaches the limit of abstract reasoning. Responsibility can be allocated through social, economic, and political institutions with varying results. Value theory has something to say about whether these results should be optimized, but little to say about how the optimization is to be accomplished.

"Save the child!" insists the interpersonal ethos of care. But how? Should a professional lifeguard be paid? Should the child have been taught to swim? Should the pond have been made child-safe? The reasons to act are obvious, but these reasons do not decide the best way to organize our actions. Dilemmas like Singer's limit confounding factors. The well-shod walker is not faced with a choice between a functional welfare state and a limited government; he is faced with a choice between shoes and life. By stripping social complexity out of the dilemma, the argument maintains the intuition that life matters, but something is lost in the process. The social complexity of a modern economy confuses and undermines an interpersonal ethos.

Children should be educated, nourished, protected from poverty, and provided with clean drinking water. The ethic of care that leads to this conviction has a solid moral foundation. However, our economy has not yet managed to pursue these convictions. Instead, we do many things that make poverty worse, and some of our actions that are meant to address poverty have the opposite effect.[6] The interpersonal morality that directs us to alleviate poverty is incapable of providing the system regulation necessary to curtail remote injustices. It is not even clear that these sentiments are sufficient to address local injustices when they are directed entirely through volunteerism; more structural solutions are also necessary, and charity can actually undermine their development.[7] Moral sentiments need effective strategies to ensure responsibility.

An effective strategy for allocating moral duties is necessary to maintain moral accountability. Business ethics is especially sensitive to the presence of stable ethical accountability. For better or for worse, economic performance is the primary consideration in many businesses. In order for ethics to matter, it must matter in economic terms. Rights are disconnected from responsibilities when harmful choices do not result in negative consequences. If buying an ecologically harmful product leaves a purchaser ignorant of the harm, it is unlikely that the duty to prevent and remedy the harm is going to be communicated. Likewise, when a producer behaves responsibly, the act is often invisible to consumers, thus undermining the market motive.

Shoes Matter Too

What is missing from Singer's call for global poverty alleviation is the recognition of a simple fact: shoes also matter. In Singer's dilemma, the pond is a location where responsibility gathers so that the context creates an obvious and immediate choice. The child's tangible need demands action from the passerby in a way that the distant woes of the global poor never will. In Singer's account, the shoes represent luxury, status, and consumer culture. In mine, they represent materiality and essential features of a global economy. An apparel supply chain, and the shoes it provides, is more likely than a pond to connect an at-risk child to a wealthy consumer. Things draw us together.[8] The shoes may not matter in and of themselves and they certainly do not matter in the same way that the child's life does, but the development of a responsible global economy depends upon the shoes mattering in certain ways.

The problem is that the shoes do not cry out for attention, as does a child. Many aspects of economic responsibility are banal. Overtiming, restricted mobility, the deskilling of labor, exploitative wages, and gaps in workplace safety deprive persons of well-being, autonomy, and meaning in ways that are not always observable to outsiders. Many aspects of economic responsibility are quietly relevant in small ways that are lost in the noise of the immediate moral concerns of daily life. However, unless we can find ways to organize an economy around the protection of subtle human and environmental interests, interpersonal morality will continue to be tragically disappointed at a global scale. This reorganization will require a major overhaul of the way that we value everything and everyone.

When faced with a choice between the survival of a person and a fashion accessory, the person is the right choice.[9] But the story should not end there. Having ruined a nice pair of shoes to save a child, the humanist passerby should show a similar degree of care for those who made the next pair of shoes. After all, if a random child in a pond matters, so should the persons and communities that produce our goods.

To lay out the key concepts and considerations involved in taking responsibility for objects, like shoes, one must focus on recognizing the moral priorities found in objects. Caring for persons, places, and things relies upon similar epistemological elements.

Person, Place, and Thing

When I was a child, we played a game called Twenty Questions. In this game, one player chooses a noun and the others ask questions to guess it. The player selects the noun from three general categories: person, place, or thing. Humans are persons, locations are places, and everything else is a thing.

The categories seem simple and distinct, but numerous descriptive problems compromise the typology. People are also things. Our component parts are not persons, and we cannot isolate our humanity from the inorganic materials and organic compounds of our bodies. Most of a person's mass is made up of oxygen atoms, which we acquire by breathing air and drinking water. Water and air are things, not people. Does inhalation convert a thing into a person and exhalation convert a person into a thing? Stated this way, it becomes unclear where the person ends and the thing begins.

Moreover, just as persons are physically intertwined with things, we are also conceptually and cognitively intertwined with physical objects. As Maurice Merleau-Ponty argued, our bodies are a part of their world and so are our perceptions. The boundary between persons and things is more important in the way that we define ourselves than in the way that we define things.[10] And yet, as concrete and separate as external objects may seem because we can feel their edges and sense their distinctness, we should not imagine that physical things adhere to their categories. McDonough and Braungart argue that household materials are constantly abrading and interacting with people:[11] lead paint chips off of walls and formaldehyde off-gasses from fiberboard. These releases are consequential precisely because there is a porous boundary between people and things.

The boundary between person and place is equally porous. I take up space and alter the place wherever I am. Even if I tread lightly, I change my context. Sitting quietly makes one sort of place, and singing makes another. My empty office is not the same place as my occupied office.

The result is that I am part person, part place, and part thing. In fact, most objects belong to multiple categories. America is both a place and a people. We treat pets like persons, except when we treat them like things. The Great Barrier Reef is a place and the largest living thing. Because these categories describe the boundaries of morality, their limits matter a great deal.

Humanists, utilitarians, and rights activists share a basic modern perspective that persons deserve special moral respect. Personhood is a thick description[12] that preferentially allocates moral and legal rights to persons over other things. It is not clear whether this emphasis on people helped create a liberal political culture or resulted as a by-product of its emergence. In its initial formulation, asserting that people have rights was a denial of the dehumanizing legacy of serfdom, an ideological component of democracy, and an acknowledgement of the complex intentionality that humans share. However, the concept was also bounded. Personhood draws a boundary around the objects of empathy and brings interpersonal morality to the fore of the ethical landscape. It asserts the Golden Rule, "Do unto others as you would have them do unto you," as a complete description of morality. And in this case, "others" are always people.

Things are on the other end of the spectrum. The feminist critique of the objectifying male gaze condemns the way that women are viewed as things. It took a great political struggle to make women persons rather than property; moving in the other direction by treating women as sexual or reproductive objects is justifiably offensive. Likewise, referring to an transgender person as "it" is slanderous because things are not worthy of respect. Being a thing means lacking intrinsic value, and being unworthy of direct moral consideration. As psychologists explain, this form of objectification deprives a subject of a mind,[13] and the ascription of a mind is an essential aspect of moral regard.[14] Moving in the other direction, humanlike moral regard can be applied positively to the protection of nonhuman species.[15]

Deleuze and Guattari observe that things are minorities when they do not fulfill the categorical standard of man. "Man is the molar entity par excellence."[16] This standard-dominance grants power:

It is not a question of knowing whether there are more mosquitoes or flies than men, but of knowing how "man" constituted a standard in the universe .... The majority in a government presupposes the right to vote ... the majority in the universe assumes as pregiven the right and power of man. In this sense women, children, but also animals, plants, and molecules, are minoritarian.[17]

Deleuze and Guattari raise an important point in observing that, once power is afforded to some special subset of entities, the volume of entities excluded is of no consequence. Yet care must be taken in shifting from persons as deliberators to persons as rulers with supreme moral priority. I would rather suggest that deliberative power be circumscribed within a participatory definition that is distinct from the definition of moral importance. It is nonsensical to debate with a molecule or animal, but there is no reason to assume that these things (inanimate and animate) cannot have value just because they cannot deliberate.

As a rule, the value of a thing comes from the value that it provides to others. Things are used, wasted, and discarded on the whim of morally relevant parties. Persons, on the other hand, have intrinsic value. The contrast is stark. In most moral theory, being a thing means being nothing. But even as we work to protect women and gender minorities from the stigma of thingness, we must rethink the stigma itself.

I-Object

In fact, persons have never been as far from things as moral philosophy seems to suggest. We treat ourselves as objects, we treat each other as objects, and we show concern for things as if they deserve it. Persons, places, and things are all objects of value. From here, I will use the term objects almost exclusively because I mean to blur the boundaries between persons, places, and things. Nonetheless, I will start with a framework that values persons and work to a more general account of valuing objects.

Saying that persons, places, and things are objects of value does not imply that persons should be for sale or that all three categories should be valued in the same way. Instead, it suggests that there are common valuation processes to all person-object interactions. Participating in the external world forces us to evaluate the objects around us. The evaluative process decides what we esteem, and what we esteem determines how we behave.

Our valuations need not work through standard economic units for all objects. In fact, the most fundamental measure of what we value is probably time rather than money. Each person must decide how to spend a relatively short life. Time is a universal currency that can be applied across all domains of human activity as a measure of value. We say that time is money, but the truth is that money has value because we are willing to give it our time.

The stewardship of all valued objects has a common essence because whether one wishes to care for a person, a place, or a thing, one must first take time to understand it. This involves observing and appreciating the object's needs, the inputs that help it to do what it does. It also involves observing the object's worth based upon the outputs that connect the object to other things of value. The importance of observation is key. The genesis of value is closely related to the application of attention, the appreciation of which involves the recognition of an entity in its totality. As Buber explains:

> I contemplate a tree ..., accept it as a picture ..., feel it as a movement ..., assign it to a species and observe it as an instance .... Throughout all of this the tree remains my object .... But it can also happen, if will and grace are joined, that as I contemplate the tree I am drawn into a relation, and the tree ceases to be an It. The power of exclusiveness has seized me .... One should not try to dilute the meaning of relation: relation is reciprocity.[18]

Though I embrace Buber's idea, I do not use his terminology. In my account, neither "object" nor "it" can imply stigma and otherness. In Buber's terms, we must distinguish between the I-It relation and the I-You relation. The former grants only qualities and observation, whereas the latter embraces an entity in its totality. For Buber, "[t]he object is ... standing still, ceasing, breaking off, becoming rigid, standing out, the lack of relation, the lack of presence. What is essential is lived in the present, objects in the past."[19] In contrast, my approach to objects will place them on timelines by recognizing past, present, and future. This can only be accomplished by dismantling barriers between the subject and the object, between the self and its environment.

The relationship between a person and a thing belongs to a context, a context that gives meaning to things and power to persons. Just as modern society has often denied the meaning of things, so has it denied the priority of places. For the present discussion, we need only recognize that the problem of object responsibility is as much a problem of places as it is a problem of things.

There are essentially two ways to reintegrate persons into places. One is to theorize the natural world and its value in a form that human beings can understand and protect. Alternatively, we can rethink our presuppositions about nature itself. As Morton has argued in *Ecology Without Nature*, the development of romantic naturalism emerged, not coincidentally, at the same time as mass industrialism. Buber makes a similar claim, locating the emergence of an I-It relation within modernity. Accordingly, the portrait of nature may be as problematic as the industrialism that gave it form, neither resolving the tension of the underlying opposition. "Just when it brings us into proximity with the nonhuman 'other,' nature reestablishes a comfortable distance between 'us' and 'them.'"[20]

Thinking of nature conjures images of wild and untamed places where humans must not trespass just as thinking of romance conjures images of candle-lit intimacy where children do not belong. Yet romance produces children who grow up to produce their own romances, and nature produced humans who have grown up to imagine a nature without themselves. Morton labels this fuzzy and contradictory sense of nature as "ambience."

I will try to navigate these issues without relying on a bygone pastoralism or a wilderness utopianism. What aligns me most closely with Morton and others who are labeled for their "object-oriented ontologies" is my attention to things in and of themselves, and my speculative strategy for paying attention. However, my interest does not reside in these basic ontological questions. Instead, I suggest that ecological outcomes are the direct result of the order that we choose. We allow our economy to ascribe value to things, and then we allow these values to motivate our actions. As a result, some ecological resources thrive and others are washed away. This economy lacks a structural capacity to speculatively contemplate the value of things. It does not comprehend the order it produces, and no single agent conceives of that order as a choice and wills it into being.

We must find a way to embed the creative task of value assessment into the fundamental activities of economic actors. We can bask in the irradiated afterglow of a carbon-caked atmosphere, subsuming ourselves into the technological frenzy of our time, or we can choose another order. Call it nature, industry, efficiency, or value, the system that we inhabit is the system that we make for ourselves. There is no nature to blame for this particular choice, and no natural template to guide the path ahead. Nevertheless, we can simplify the complexity of our social and ecological situations by allocating responsibilities for who attends to what. Each of us must find a way to selectively apply our attention, to be "drawn into a relation" with the right objects.[21] If the economy is successful in allocating attention so that each individual focuses on a worthy subset of objects, the aggregate result will inspire a new order, and provide new inspiration for our moral selves.

Valuing Related Objects

While I will blur certain moral boundaries in this argument, building a platform for valuing objects and people does not require us to dismantle the distinction between subjects and objects, or between intrinsic and extrinsic value. We can still recognize that a child is a subject of moral regard whose intrinsic value is ontologically different from a pair of shoes. However, what we discover is that these ontological categories – subject and object, person and thing – are unable to allocate responsibility for the care of either the child or the persons connected to the shoes.

Pragmatists observe that important philosophical debates are rarely settled or resolved. More often, as Rorty describes, they are set aside.[22] Attention shifts as we find new issues to address. Here, I wish to address the allocation of responsibility for causing harm within the global economy. My argument begins with the deficiency of an ethic that is exclusively focused on differentiating worthy, intrinsically valuable subjects from objects of moral disregard. The ethic is deficient because it fails to answer the question at hand. Those who wish to lecture businesspeople and consumers on the moral duties of care for workers' safety and environmental sustainability misunderstand the basic problem. Most businesspeople are as capable of recognizing moral subjects as anyone else. They do not kick puppies, spit on homeless people, or watch with disinterest as children wander into traffic. The problem is not that they are incapable of care, but that their capacity to care is not yet focused in a way that manages the consequences of doing business. In other words, even when we all agree about a just, good, and right outcome, we still disagree about who is responsible for realizing it.

Where such disagreements arise, they cannot be answered by reiterating the moral priority of human moral subjects and their rights. In fact, it becomes more difficult to allocate responsibility once we focus exclusively on human moral subjects. Doing so strips them out of the field of objects that can otherwise direct the allocation of responsibility. Disregarding the pattern of objects that bring us together as communities within local, regional, and global economies makes it seem as if responsibilities belong exclusively within local deliberative relations, firms, and professional roles. As if every harm suffered is the consequence of a person who intends for it to occur. Bringing objects back in allows us to allocate responsibilities across the more diverse participants in a causal outcome, many of whom never wished for harm to occur.

In the late 1930s, John Dewey took up a closely related question from a pragmatist perspective.[23] Dewey wanted to show that people have cause to value the instrumentalities of the good as they have cause to value the good that these instrumentalities accomplish. It is nonsensical, he argued, to value an outcome without also assessing the costs at which that outcome is accomplished. Suppose that you are in your kitchen and are hungry for fresh fruit, but all you have is bread. The question is not whether you prefer fruit to bread, but whether getting fruit is worth the hassle. If you want fresh fruit, you will have to decide how much you want it. Your desire for an end should not be independent of the means necessary to obtain it.

Our lives are full of these conditions, of things that we want, but may not want enough to acquire. These trade-offs apply as much to issues of moral concern as they do to everyday household choices. The arguments outlined previously for wheelchair accessibility and improving people's life chances are applicable in modern cities because they can be undertaken at a reasonable cost. If we tried to apply this standard to Andean and Himalayan villages where accommodation would be extraordinarily disruptive and unrealistically expensive, we would not reach the same conclusion.

Dewey demonstrates that valuation involves an activity, a form of caretaking that I will call stewardship:

the words 'caring' and 'caring for' are, as modes of behavior, closely connected with 'liking,' and that other substantially equivalent words are 'looking out for or after,' ... 'attending to,' ... 'fostering' words that all seem to be variants of what is referred to by 'prizing,'[24]

This active vision of valuation differs markedly from the way that many philosophers and economists treat value. For those who find value in the revealed preference of a purchase or the market price, value is discovered through the way that we get things rather than by the way that we treat them.

Another innovation that we find in Dewey is a recognition of the place of objects and materials in the active process of carrying out our plans. To this he ascribes relevance that others have missed:

[A]ctivity and activities ... involve, like any actual behavior, existential materials, as breathing involves air; walking, the earth; buying and selling, commodities; inquiry, things investigated, etc. No human activity operates in a vacuum; it acts in the world and has materials upon which and through which it produces results.[25]

I will pursue the place of these materials much further than Dewey, and they will lead to different conclusions. In Dewey's account, the role of the evaluator is always close at hand. The evaluator is the agent and also the person whose desires take shape through certain plans. The kind of empathy that I aim to inspire through object relations looks for the needs of other people and living systems as alternatives to one's own planned use of a thing. But these considerations do not factor into Dewey's account:

a child who has found a bright smooth stone ... is gratified. But there is no valuation ... until the child treasures what he has accidentally hit upon. The moment he begins to prize and care for it he puts it to some use and thereby employs it as a means to some end, and, depending upon his maturity, he estimates or values it in that relation.[26]

This passage is not entirely inconsistent with the account that follows. We will also find value in the activity of caring for things, and we will put them to use in ways that promote our own interests. But where Dewey understands this value to emanate entirely from an evaluator's own plans and desires, I find persons to be capable of valuing states of affairs that have little to do with them. Indeed, this is a pivotal move in my argument. Attending to things is a form of valuing them, and appreciating the worth of things in their undisturbed roles or in the way that others will use them establishes a standard against which we judge our own use.

In fairness to Dewey, the experiential elements of his argument would allow an evaluator to reach a similar conclusion with enough time and consideration. Dewey suggests that each appraisal has an end-in-view, and that once that end is realized, a person must then reappraise the consequences and allow these new appraisals to influence subsequent evaluations. This conception of evaluation is entirely compatible with the eventual realization of things' value and a desire to protect them from overuse. Dewey's evaluator can appreciate the worth of trees in the forest once he discovers that using all the trees to make furniture takes away an ecological resource that he also values. The problem is that this realization comes too late in Dewey, after too much experience and too many mistakes. Where Dewey suggests that an evaluator should make use of a thing and learn to appreciate it accordingly, I suggest that users begin by studying and attending to the things that they wish to use. Their attentive process should continue before, during, and after use to anticipate and mitigate the adverse consequences of their actions. As such, I begin with a process of attending to rather than a process of making plans for, and suggest that this is a more appropriate start to approximate materials' worth.

Value as Attention

There is probably some space between your work and home that you pass every day but never truly notice. If you were to go there and turn over a log or rock, you would find little things that are living and thriving, things that you had never noticed before. If you paid attention to them, learned their names, sought out a book about their physiology, and learned more about their lives, you might start to care about them. As your understanding increased, it is likely that your appreciation would also increase in equal measure. Seeing and valuing are inexorably connected. The closer we look, the more we care.

Unfortunately, we cannot look closely everywhere, so valuing objects involves an explicit choice about what sorts of things we carefully examine. We need to balance our time, but we cannot be stingy with what we value; doing so implies a callous disregard for the worth of objects. Understanding the process of valuing objects involves examining the moral attention that objects of value receive. As an epistemological matter, I have shown that this attention is more broadly applied than one might expect. Now, I should demonstrate that ethics must also be broadly applied.

Few insights are more fundamental to ethics than the principle that we should treat others as we wish to be treated, but which "others" should we consider? In whose interests should we be interested? Business ethics uses stakeholder theory, the "principle of who and what really count,"[27] to answer these questions, particularly with respect to how organizations focus and prioritize their moral duties to others. Rob Phillips, a business ethicist who has written extensively about stakeholders, fairness, and organizational responsibility, describes the prioritization of stakeholders as the "defining challenge" in business ethics. He explains, "[a]s long as there is division of labor, there will be questions about the division of spoils and the division of responsibility."[28] The scope of ethics is also a major topic in moral philosophy where the main candidates are humans,[29] sentients,[30] and living things.

The Golden Rule ascribes value to other persons and suggests that we need only examine our own interests to understand our obligations to others. One's interests are a reasonable point of departure for ethics, particularly because they are the interests best known to each individual. Yet there is a danger in the suggestion that everyone wishes to be treated in the same way. Others may not wish to be treated similarly: we do not all share the same experiences, purposes, or senses of meaning and we are not all similarly interested. It is rarely sufficient to assume that others wish as we do. Instead, we deliberate, empathize, and observe to determine if others share our desires.

When we attend to the needs of others, we do not bother to rephrase these needs in the first person. I do not ask how I would want to be treated before taking an interest in my partner's well-being. Nor do I ask what I would want when buying her a present. To do so would seem perversely self-centered, and sometimes it just seems silly to think in personal terms. How would I (as a man) wish to be treated if I were pregnant? The impossibility contradicts the meaningfulness of the question. Yet the fact that I cannot know from direct sensory experience does not alter the moral force of the notion that I ought to care how others wish to be treated. I can only move forward if I understand them in their own terms.

Empathizing with Others

Psychologists distinguish between perspective taking, which is a cognitive process, and empathizing, which is an emotional process. The distinction is used to differentiate between levels of involvement in the observed interests of others. For instance, perspective-takers out-perform empathizers in negotiations, presumably because they are able to utilize an understanding of the counterparty's interests without adopting them.[31] Here, I use the affective framework of empathy because I am interested in a process of assessing and pursuing another's interests, not the process of manipulating another based upon an understanding of these interests. Nonetheless, the process would seem to involve both thinking and feeling.

One is not equally likely to take the perspective of all others. There are prejudices involved in how we select those with whom we empathize. Some people are better than others at moving beyond the in-group biases that narrow this scope. Those who prioritize their moral identities[32] have been shown to have an extended scope of moral regard for out-group members, even during times of intergroup conflict.[33]

This section will discuss some of the information and evaluative inputs in the way that we actively value others, that is, in the way that we understand and care for them. It begins with understanding and uncertainty, and then turns to purposes and paternalistic normative judgments about people.

Understanding Others

Assuming that one wishes to act in others' interests, the next step is to understand them. Taking another's perspective, emotionally or cogni-tively, can be a major empirical challenge on the path to responsible action.[34] Self-aware adults with whom we share language and signals make it relatively easy for us to infer their perspective by telling us what they want and signaling what they do not want: the driver honks at another driver when he cuts her off, the hiker says he's tired, the student nods with understanding or stares in bewilderment. With the right focus, a person capable of recognizing these signals can quickly adapt and adjust his or her behavior.

Infants are not so easy to read. Their cooing and crying provides a sense of pleasure or displeasure, but it is incumbent upon the caretaker to guess at the cause. How is this done? Often through a process of elimination: by changing, feeding, warming, and entertaining a baby, one hopes to eliminate sources of distress and to thereby stop the baby from crying. As Dewey explains:

A baby cries. The mother takes the cry as a sign the baby is hungry or that a pin is pricking it, and so acts to change the organic condition inferred to exist by using the cry as an evidential sign.[35]

Alternatively, one can maintain a regime that meets some normative or average needs of other children, adjusting to the individual. In either case, the guardian must establish a causal theory that focuses on the needs of the child in order to respond. Experienced parents do this effortlessly by picking up on subtle cues.

Others seek theories elsewhere. Some people even Google it, running online searches to find a cause for a child's woes. The well-trod search phrase, "Why is my baby crying?" leads to innumerable articles and forums discussing the causes of and remedies for a baby's tears. Each of these offers the empathetic guardian actionable causal theories without ever asking how the guardian herself would wish to be treated. The puzzle is a real one. As one Twitter user quipped, "Having a baby has really driven home how terrible it is when several issues result in the same error message."[36]

Googling Others

People seek causal theories in order to understand and respond to an incredible diversity of objects, many of which are not human. Table 5.1 summarizes common Internet search terms following the question "Why is my ... ?" The objects of these searches fall into four categories: inanimate objects, personal objects, natural objects, and persons. Inanimate objects include many of the most common frustrations that users experience with technology. More than a third of the inanimate object questions reference issues that users face with the speed of a program, an Internet connection, or a computer. Questions about personal objects include a variety of itches, discolorations, pains, and disfigurations that inquisitors wish to explain. Natural objects include cats being mean, dogs eating grass, grass turning yellow, and orchids dying. Here as well, the causal researcher wishes to understand why the change is occurring and how to respond, so she or he turns to Google.

Table 5.1 *Common Searches for "Why is my ..." on Google*[37]

Inanimate Object	Personal Objects	Natural Object	Person
computer so slow	poop green	dog eating grass	boyfriend so mean
Internet so slow	eye twitching	kitten sneezing	girlfriend so mean to me
air conditioner freezing up	period late	orchid dying	mom so mean
Facebook account temporarily unavailable	hair falling out	zucchini wilting	brother so annoying
Apple id disabled	jaw sore	dog shaking	girlfriend so moody
house so dusty	tongue white	goldfish turning black	
quarter gold	urine cloudy	cat sneezing	
refrigerator not cooling	vision blurry	dog throwing up	
keyboard not working	big toe numb	fish tank cloudy	
laptop so hot	face so oily	grass yellow	
printer offline	knee swollen	Japanese maple turning green	
room so hot	nose always stuffy	zucchini rotting on the vine	
video choppy	sperm yellow	kitten so mean	
Wii black and white	vitamin d low	tomato plant turning yellow	
Xbox 360 freezing	butt bleeding	water brown	
car overheating	eye red	dog's nose dry	
electric bill so high	heart beating so fast	kitten biting me	
62 in total	41 in total	21 in total	5 in total

Finally, a series of searches refer to individual behavior like, "Why is my brother so annoying?"

It is noteworthy that, given the phrasing, children and young people can be presumed to initiate most person-oriented searches about brothers, boyfriends, girlfriends, and moms. Adults may have other sources of insight about the motives and needs of other persons. Since the question "Why is my" could be left out of most of these queries without degrading the results, the search phrase itself indicates a lack of computer sophistication, but the scope of the results is nonetheless indicative of the diversity of valued objects that Internet users aim to understand. Moreover, there is evidence that adults use Google in a similar way to answer very adult questions like, "Why was I fired?" or "Why did my wife/husband cheat on me?"

Individuals wish to decode the signals that they receive, not only from other persons, but also from natural objects that they value, from mechanical objects that they want to make work better, and from their own bodies. The most general strategy for resolving problems involves an empirical and causally descriptive process, a process of empathizing with objects.

Empirical and Normative Understandings

In ethics, we distinguish between normative and empirical questions when these sorts of questions are answered by different methods. Statistics will not show why murder is wrong any more than reason will prove that murder is rare. In contrast to divergent is/ought methodologies, the online quest for a causal theory illustrates regularity in dealing with both other persons and other objects. Moral agents seek to understand the interests, motivations, and needs of another object or person and to use this information to guide pragmatic action regardless of the moral standing of the subject of their search.[38] This logic forms the basic cognitive and affective process of stewardship.

But regardless of the blurring of boundaries, the fundamental and value-laden questions of ethics and aesthetics are also constitutive of caring for others. We must still decide what life is best to live, what world is best to live in, and what things make that world more beautiful, just, and good. So far, our theory of empathy relies upon two forms of knowledge: knowledge of the self, of one's own desires; and knowledge of others in general or, in particular, what others desire. I have already suggested some ways in which these forms of knowledge can be acquired, including communication, Internet research, experimentation, and direct observation. Most simple interactions between people rely upon these two forms of knowledge, but some tough cases require knowledge of what matters, a third form of knowledge. For instance, observation sometimes suggests that a person either does not know or lacks the fortitude to pursue his or her own interests. In dismissing a person's own assessment of his or her interests, the perceiving paternalist must somehow determine what the person ought to want. To make such a determination, we draw upon knowledge that must certainly not be based upon the paternalist's subjective perspective and that cannot be derived from a generalization of what most people desire. The fact that I do not like mayonnaise does not justify me prohibiting others from its enjoyment. But, at the same time, even if everyone other than me enjoys mayonnaise, this is not a reason for me to like it.

In order to decide what others should want, a paternalist must have knowledge of desirable end states, of what makes a person thrive or flourish, or of what a person deserves. For instance, if a depressed person spends whole days in a dark room, a true friend would throw the blinds open and try to inspire interest in the outside world. This course runs against the depressed person's desire to sit in the dark, but is nonetheless the right thing to do based upon a description of human needs and an understanding of mental illness. Such knowledge is essential to paternalism, and is also useful in the general case. For example, by understanding the value of human relationships, one can anticipate the grief experienced in the loss of a loved one.

Moral Understanding

The epistemological status of moral knowledge is a subject of some controversy. Aristotelians view moral knowledge as practical wisdom connecting actions with positive outcomes. This linkage is even stronger among utilitarians whose moral view creates a fundamental connection between right acts and positive consequences. In contrast, Kantians view moral knowledge as an objective truth found in reason. A Kantian might reject the notion that moral knowledge can usefully predict the needs of persons or otherwise anticipate real outcomes. This would be an extreme view, because the deontic position only requires the Kantian to be agnostic as to whether moral knowledge yields positive consequences. In other words, the truthfulness of the moral knowledge does not derive from its tendency to make those who have it better off. In Kant's view, it is rather that action directed by good will (which is based on moral reason) allows a person to deserve to be happy, regardless of whether the action results in her happiness or not.[39] These are issues too basic to be adequately addressed here, but my view coincides with the Aristotelians:

ethics is often as useful as it is right. As such, I view moral knowledge, consequentialist or deontological, as a useful source of empathy. However, some observations of others' interests are also deeply flawed, as I will explain below.

The three forms of knowledge are often difficult to distinguish. One cannot help but look to one's own preferences as a first approximation of what others might want and as a paradigmatic example of what one ought to want.[40] It is clear that empathy thrives as one moves beyond a narrow, self-referential understanding of what matters to others and what ought to matter in general. But it is also clear that this step from the tangible and personal into the impartial and external enters a realm of competing visions of justice, responsibility, aesthetics, and ethics. There is some unity, coherence, and consistency to self-knowledge that moral knowledge rarely achieves. There are, to put it mildly, numerous potentially viable conceptions of what is good and right. Some of these conceptions are more defensible than others. Some conceptions of the good are wholly incompatible with others. Fortunately, we do not all need to agree. There should be some "moral free space"[41] or room for personal projects[42] in which groups and individuals pursue their own ideas about what matters.

If our goal is to observe and support others' purposes, one does not need to resolve the contradiction. My sister values fashion and sports, and I care for neither, yet I care for her and thus value the things that she values secondarily, at least inasmuch as they are necessary for her to flourish.

Value Pluralism

Value pluralism, the view that accepts multiple irreducible conceptions of ethics,[43] does not preclude moral insight or moral progress. However, it certainly raises doubt that a single perspective can provide an evaluative frame for all spheres of social, environmental, and economic valuation. There are numerous thoughtful and helpful ideas about what ought to matter. Development scholars like Nussbaum and Sen prioritize the opportunities that individuals have to fulfill their potential.[44] Deep ecologists propose an environmentally centered ethic.[45] Others have linked the pursuit of ethical knowledge with an understanding of aesthetics.[46]

There are desirable end states like ecological complexity, human flourishing, fairness, sustainability, efficient use, and entitlements to property, but I will not conclusively demonstrate their desirability.[47]

This leaves many of the most profound questions of ethics open, questions that must be answered in order to steward objects. It also recognizes that no single ethical theory can respond to the diversity of contexts in which objects are harvested, produced, distributed, used, and discarded. Remaining open to multiple theories leaves room for moral insight to inform and develop around the stewardship of objects. And develop it must, because new ways of thinking are badly needed in many parts of the global economy.

The initial assessment of another person's interests is not necessarily a moral judgment. Instead, the inquiry makes factual inferences to appreciate another person's perspective. Moral theory is frequently interested in human purposes as a basic element of a teleological account of ethics (see Chapter 6, Object Stewardship as Recursive Teleology). For example, consequentialists order their normative judgments based upon the preferences satisfied by a given choice. But it is possible to treat human purposes descriptively as well. In technical terms, a descriptive approach to purposes is sometimes called teleonomy, which is distinguished from teleology by the fact that it makes no reference to an agent's or god's generative intent. In biology, for instance, evolution seems to serve certain purposes as if it is pursuing an end, yet because these purposes are undertaken without design, we try to avoid descriptions that imply agency or intent.[48]

Understanding Purposes

Both consequentialist and nonconsequentialist approaches to ethics share a fixation with human purposes. Purpose, for nonconsequentialists, is the basis of intention upon which we judge the goodness of one's will. Purpose, for consequentialists, is the subset of one's preferences that link directly to actions and motivations.

Human preferences and intentions are influenced by the economy in which they are formed. Hence, any direct reliance upon preferences and intentions absorbs the distortions of the market, including the normalization of unsustainable and unjustifiable expectations. One's preferences for meat, exotic produce, car ownership, housing density, and luxury good consumption are shaped by market prices, availability, and peer consumption. If the market fails to communicate the real costs of these purchases while aggressively marketing them to induce demand, the preferences can hardly be treated as objective inputs for a moral calculus.

As such, preferences and intentions may prove to be unreliable guides in the pursuit of justice. Rawls stripped jealousy and in-group bias from the evaluation of social justice. Likewise, we must strip the boundless expansion of human consumption from the system of preferences upon which we base an ethical economy. Instead, I will argue for a shared vision of social organization as a collective purpose. Rather than focusing on the interests of individuals as the basis for an economy, the argument will turn on the ecological and social accomplishments that a whole society works to produce.

This directive of collective accomplishment is at least as important for the way an economy works as the satisfaction of individual preferences. From the first corporate charters, firms were used to build bridges and cross oceans, overcoming collective action problems in pursuit of shared goals. In contrast to the liberal tradition of statecraft and the distributive justice tradition that evaluates it, these economic activities were not meant to minimize the collaborative burden. Rather than each individual pursuing isolated and particularistic aims, corporations were formed from shared interests and common goals. Moreover, these goals were reached collectively rather than forcibly. Corporations have been put to perverse use throughout history; the worst of these purposes is as misguided as the worst intentions of any individual. However, they do set a standard for a certain form of mobilization.

The economy must somehow endeavor to fulfill a higher aim, not a private aim. No single individual shapes the ecological and social accomplishments of our species; we do so collectively. The economy must identify and sustain a sense of purpose that is greater than and distinct from the purposes that any individual agent conceives. The next section focuses on empathizing with objects and understanding their needs as an extension of interpersonal empathy. Later (see Chapter 6), these ideas will be placed within an aggregate understanding of shared purposes.

Empathizing with Objects

One can understand a great diversity of objects when equipped with knowledge of the self, knowledge of others, and knowledge of desirable end states. This allows a form of empathy that includes both organic and inorganic objects.

Organic nonhuman objects are perhaps most easily valued. Natural objects, such as living organisms and habitats, have relatable interests and indicators of health; they can be dehydrated, hurt, malnourished, or displaced just like persons. The pain experienced by animals when killed, for instance, is presumed to be similar to the pain that we feel through our own physiologically similar nerves, even if nonhuman animals cannot explain how it hurts.[49]

Modern science proposes a variety of indicators for the health of entire ecosystems, and indigenous peoples have their own local indicators of environmental health. For example, some indigenous peoples monitor caribou fat as an indicator of herd health[50] in a process that is not so different from human health indicators like body mass index. We grant personhood, legal standing, and a theory of interests to many amorphous structures, including corporations. As Stone argues, these entities are more difficult to read and protect than environmental entities:

The guardian-attorney for a smog-endangered stand of pines could venture with more confidence that his client wants the smog stopped, than the directors of a corporation can assert that 'the corporation' wants dividends declared. We make decisions on behalf of, and in the purported interests of, others every day; these 'others' are often creatures whose wants are far less verifiable, and even far more metaphysical in conception, than the wants of rivers, trees, and land.[51]

Yet while corporations enjoy legal personhood that allows them to go about their business as if all their needs are coherent and verifiable, natural objects do not. The policy patchwork protecting natural objects, at least in the United States, affords episodic consideration without legal rights. The same can be said for protections provided by the economy, which does appreciate some environmental objects while ignoring or devaluing many others.

Inanimate Objects

Though natural, living objects have relatable interests, inanimate objects do not. This poses a special challenge in recognizing their "interests," and one may conclude that objects do not actually have any interests at all. Many moral theorists reject the notion that objects can have interests.[52] For them, it seems very important that we differentiate between the kind of part-whole functionality relationship that a gear might have to a machine and the kind of interests that persons have in being treated with dignity. The distinction is important because, they believe, interests are what morality is about and part-whole functionality relationships are not what morality is about. As a pragmatist, I believe that definitions should be judged according to their results. If defining ethics by restricting objects from the field of moral subjects helps to make ethics work better, then we should define ethics accordingly. But I do not find this to be the case.

Sustainability issues are an important counterexample. Unabated global climate change emissions can be blamed, at least partially, on a failure to appreciate ecosystems' interest in a given level of carbon dioxide. Two moves are necessary here. The first involves an appreciation of ecosystems' interests and the interests of nonhuman living things. The second involves an appreciation of nonliving things according to the functional role that they play within certain complex systems. I will discuss system-level considerations in Chapter 6. Here I focus on individual elements. The pragmatic point about defining "interests" by moral exclusion is this: it is often useful for morality to value the elements of multiple systems and to engage moral thought in understanding these consequential elements' as matters of curiosity and care. Accordingly, I am certain that many living things have discernible interests, and I also believe that many nonliving things have quasi-interests in the sense that they can be elements of a system that relies upon them and "interested" in fulfilling their roles. I see a greater risk in excluding objects from moral view than I do in making room for them as valuable interdependent elements.

In relating to inanimate objects, knowledge of self is a particularly limited source of inspiration. Comparisons with human desires are strained by direct application to nonhumans, and especially to inanimate objects. The conditions of many products are improved by being ground, mixed, melted, boiled, sewn, glued, sanded, drilled, and sealed, but these same processes are quite distressing if applied to persons. What similarities do exist between persons and nonhuman objects occur at a very high level of abstraction. This problem of relating generalizes to the totality of an object's "interests." Inanimate objects provide no obvious interests, relatable or otherwise. If gold, oil, rocks, and water have interests of their own, we humans are blind to them.

It is nonetheless possible for these inanimate objects to be instrumentalities of benefit or harm that is desirable or undesirable from an external, impartial perspective. Here, the end state theory becomes particularly important. It can be challenging to map the interdependences of objects, but in some cases the consequences are clear.

For example, when a child is killed while playing with a gun, the result is a moral tragedy; something about the world is less good based on an end state theory. The outcome is negative for the community surrounding the child and for those who made the gun, for the gun itself, and even for the steel used in its manufacture. Better for the steel to have become a bridge or a wire than to become the instrument of the violent death; for that matter, better for the steel's component ingredients to have been left untouched in the earth. This does not mean that the gun wishes to protect the child, but even when inorganic objects have no interests, it is still possible to graft a set of moral sentiments onto them through their involvement in morally relevant outcomes. With the proper care of the guns that exist, the child would not have been shot.

The relationship between persons and objects has been a significant theme in twentieth century philosophy, from Heidegger's treatment of tools in *Being and Time* through more recent work by Latour on actor-network theory, and into relevant work by speculative realists about the material nature of objects. Again, we are working from a pragmatist perspective, and this allows us to avoid some of these debates. We can proceed, quite capably, without being waylaid by the question of whether a gun might be made up of mental substance, as panpsychism suggests, and whether an object's moral sensibilities would be too alien to care for petty biological concerns. There is little room for musing in these directions if we follow the pragmatic analysis. Nevertheless, I wish to mention the philosophical adjustment that is taking place, at least in certain schools of continental philosophy. As Harman argues, no object is wholly capable of understanding any other because every object perceives and uses other objects in a simplifying way. It follows that

human consciousness is not a unique instrument of distortion. In fact, any relation between two objects will be unable to avoid caricature. And here we are reminded of why the countless messiahs who "overcome the subject-object divide" are nowhere near radical enough. The problem is not the divide. The problem is that human subjects and nonhuman objects are wrongly proposed as the two ubiquitous ingredients of the universe.[53]

Speculative realism suggests that there are many objects with many meanings, all of which differ depending on the object perceiving them. To my chair, I am a compressing force; to my stove, I am a mechanical input. To the tree outside my window, I am nothing at all. Objects make contact with each other in partial and ephemeral ways, only fleetingly engaged, transformed, or transforming.

I do not aim to resolve the metaphysical questions that material objects present. My purpose here is to invoke the general view that matter matters. What is much more challenging is to contain this view. Must we worry over the experiences of oxygen molecules? Are bifocals oppressive to photons? Though a wider sense of being may open up a metaphysical landscape, shaping a moral code for such a landscape requires focus.

Attention, Care, and Value

I have argued that attention is a way of valuing objects and a way of learning to care for objects. This implies an escalation model in which attention begets care and care begets more attention. The self-reinforcing process continues until the objects receive care in proportion to the object's fully informed value. At this point, additional attention does not yield additional strategies for caring or observations of value.

In caring for people, one must find balance between inattention and smothering. People need to be noticed, recognized, valued, and respected, but any of these needs can be perversely exceeded. The same holds for other living things that need balance in the attention and resources that they receive.

This theory of object care is a different take on an ethics of care that has come to play a central role in modern humanism. Traditionally, care stands for a form of concern shown interpersonally. The Oxford English Dictionary lists the following care-based phrases: "to care for: to take thought for, provide for, look after, take care of."[54] The word has almost as many negative constructions as positive ones, including "careless," "carefree," and "without a care." One of the greatest strengths of the ethic of care is also its chief limitation, the intimacy of its humanism. Like a localized version of Singer's drowning child, an ethic of care demands action without a system-scale strategy. Its results are proximate kindness with a moral callousness for the needs of those who are far away.

However, scholars have attempted to build a more systematic account of responsibility with care as its foundation. Fisher and Tronto define care as "a species activity that includes everything that we do to maintain, continue, and repair our 'world' so that we can live in it as well as possible. That world includes our bodies, ourselves, and our environment, all of which we seek to interweave in a complex, life-sustaining web."[55] This definition should be viewed as aspirational rather than descriptive. For many caretakers, the world for which they care is a microsocial space that denies a wider context and limits structural power. Tronto has been especially active in mounting a resistance against a purely interpersonal understanding of care. Her work explores care as a viable moral view, long important to both men and women, but feminized in a way that tends to marginalize caretakers.[56]

Fisher and Tronto's definition resists the feminization of care by including an environmental component. Doing so directs the caretaker's ethic towards a more global orientation. Unfortunately, environmental care generally construed cannot be a practical activity like interpersonal care. As Tronto later wrote:

[C]are has a dual set of meanings. It refers both to a mental disposition of concern and to actual practices that we engage in as a result of these concerns; for example, a doctor's care involves both attentiveness and concern and the concrete practices of prescribing medical treatment ... much of the current discussion of care either overemphasizes the emotional and intellectual qualities and ignores its reference to actual work or overemphasizes care as work at the expense of understanding the deeper intellectual and emotional activities.[57]

As with the related concept of valuing described above through Dewey, caring is not merely an orientation; it is an action. The caretaker's activity is stretched thin by general environmental responsibility. However, if we can focus this care on specific objects and their histories, the way that the doctor focuses on a specific person, then the practice and the orientation can nest together.

We have already reached the limits of what this object focus can accomplish. Now we must push further to explore the context in which objects thrive. To advance a theory of object care, I focus first on individual objects and then on the totality of their interdependent communities. Their purposes will take shape through these interdependences, and only with a recognition of this purpose can we finally decide how much value to place in an object.

When applied to persons and objects in isolation, empathy produces some idea of the object's utility and the inputs that sustain it. These estimations of an object's worth and needs are important first steps. Thereafter, a new calculus displaces empathy. An object's current function and the resources it needs to thrive are balanced against the resources that other objects require. Chapter 6 reflects upon utilitarian and deontological approaches to ethics within a framework of object care. A conception of ecological use value provides an alternative utilitarian calculus that will then be applied to business decisions. This relational approach to utilitarianism shapes determinations about how and when to care that strike a balance between relational and global responsibilities.

Plurality of Purpose

The forms of care so far discussed suggest an object-oriented ethic, which I will pursue on both consequentialist and nonconsequentialist grounds. However, first I would like to briefly digress from the main line of argument to note important developments in philosophy that make room for such an object-orientation.

Though interactions between persons continue to take up the great majority of the ethical landscape, there is little controversy left in the notion that both natural and person-built objects are ethically significant. While anthropocentric and ecocentric orientations continue to diverge over whether the natural environment is a collection of objects useful to persons or a collection of objects with intrinsic worth, there is certainly room in social and political philosophy for a moral system that carefully attends to the uses and abuses of nonhuman materiality. Interestingly, fields like metaphysics are also beginning to shift their focus away from persons and their singular cognitive perspective.

Philosophy's human fixation arises first from the discipline's special appreciation for reason and the capacity of thought. From its etymological roots, philosophy names its followers lovers of knowledge. Since Greek thinkers adopted the name, reason and argument have been the most important tools of philosophical activity. By adopting a reflective orientation towards the external world, philosophers considered the nature of their relationships to each other and to the external environment. From this position of reflective thought, philosophers explore the nature of existence and the limits of knowledge.

Though it is difficult to rank philosophy's sub-disciplines by their anthropocentrism, both metaphysics and epistemology have developed along especially person-centered lines. Aristotle distinguished humans from animals by their creativity and their capacity to reason.[58] Ever since, our thinking has separated us from other beings. This distinguishing feature has been reformed to describe animals' unfreedom,[59] animals' inability to think without language,[60] and animals' lack of self-reflective thought.[61] For example, Descartes emphasized the importance of language as a basis for the development of mind, a distinction that leads him to view nonspeaking animals as machines that lack a soul.[62]

Reasonable Care

Reason does not need to be an ability that separates person from beast. In its use, reason can easily produce the opposite result. Through reason, persons reflect upon the activities of other beings and develop compassion for nonhuman objects. Perhaps animals are soulless. Then we might reasonably ask what it is like to be soulless. We can do the same for the machines to which animals are compared. The suggestion that philosophy ought to be engaged in imagining the being of nonhuman objects, what some call "speculative realism," moves far beyond the standard fixation on human knowing and being.

One version of this development can be traced back to Heidegger, one of the most important twentieth-century philosophers. Until Heidegger, most philosophers cared little for things. Objects were incidental to the work of philosophy. In the quest for deeper meaning, artistic objects became studies in form, biology became material for a mind-body dualism, and ethics became an agreement among disembodied and amorphous contractors. Philosophy was objectivity without objects, a realm of analysis that aimed to detach itself from the vicissitudes of physicality. Heidegger changed the game with his analysis of "equipment."

From the first pages of *Being and Time*, Heidegger sets the stage for an object focus. Consider this discussion of hammering with a hammer:

[A]n entity of this kind is not grasped thematically . . .. The hammering does not simply have knowledge about the hammer's character as equipment, but it has appropriated this equipment in a way which could not possibly be more suitable.

The encounter with an object is shaped by a specific material inter-action. The more perfect its application, they less it gets noticed. Theoretical knowledge tries to understand the object from a distance. But it fails.

[T]he less we just stare at the hammer-Thing, and the more we seize hold of it and use it, the more primordial does our relationship to it become, and the more unveiledly is it encountered as that which it is – as equipment.

The encounter with an object is mediated by the distance of theory. It becomes immediate in use, or more generally, in application. The term "equipment" has also been translated as "tool" or "gear." Heidegger's "equipment" overlaps with what I have called "objects," a whole universe of persons, places, and things.[63]

The kind of Being which equipment possesses – in which it manifests itself in its own right – we call "readiness-to-hand" . . .. No matter how sharply we just look at the "outward appearance" of Things, in whatever form this takes, we cannot discover anything ready-to-hand.[64]

Contemplation involves a distanced consideration from a thing that denies the contemplative theorist the understanding that comes with use. The encounter that manifests within an object's use gives the equipment a specific kind of being, "readiness-to-hand." This can be viewed as an existence that any object has to any other as the objects interact, an existence that is not outwardly visible.

But when we deal with [equipment] by using them and manipulating them, this activity is not a blind one; it has its own kind of sight, by which our manipulation is guided and from which it acquires its specific Thingly character. Dealings with equipment subordinate themselves to the manifold assignments of the "in-order-to."[65]

While the specific existential state of objects only occurs through interaction, the interaction is not a source of understanding. It denies understanding in favor of its other purposes, the "in-order-to."

Heidegger's approach suggests several moral questions: What forms of appropriation could not be more suitable for equipment? What are the limits of object uses that shape the "readiness-to-hand"? Are the manifold assignments of the "in-order-to" handed out on a per-object basis? If these are moral questions, then metaphysics is unlikely to provide satisfying answers. As such, Heidegger's utility for ethics is questionable. He did not view his metaphysics as a foundation for ethics, and while some have tried to move in that direction, doing so requires a rather selective reading.

It is interesting and perhaps surprising to note that Dewey's pragmatic account of valuation shares Heideggerian themes. Pragmatists like Dewey are almost ideologically opposed to metaphysicians, but Dewey showed an enduring interest in the transformative nature of problematization. In his essay on valuation, Dewey argues that we come to value things through the lack of them, and that only when we have need of something to carry out our plans do we become fully aware of it. Heidegger makes a similar argument about broken tools, arguing that when our ability to use a thing is interrupted, one's inattention to that tool is also interrupted, we see its readiness to hand for the first time once it is broken.

But let us focus, for a moment, on the kinds of questions that an object ethic demands of us, on tools' uses and misuses. Taking up Heidegger's hammer, that instrument appears not only as a building device but also as an instrument of violence across cultural history, from the Bible to the Beatles.[66] Approached directly, nail hammering and skull hammering are equally exemplary of a hammer's state of being, but not of the hammer's "involvement." Heidegger explains that hammering can nail down a roof to protect a person from bad weather, becoming entangled in an ultimate purpose "in which there is no further involvement .... The primary 'towards-which' is a 'for-the-sake-of-which'."[67] This argument seems to lead us directly back to an anthropocentric description of morality in which teleology is ultimately connected to persons.

Tool-Being

In the last decade, Graham Harman, a Heidegger devotee and critic, has sought to revitalize the discussion about the ontological status of things, not just tools but all things. Harman rejects the understanding of persons as the center of Heidegger's thought, arguing instead that the entire corpus of Heidegger's work is motivated by a basic contradiction in the metaphysics of objects that Harman calls "tool-being." Understand this correctly, Harman claims, and the priority of humans collapses.[68] Here the existential status of tools is applicable to all objects. Theoretical knowledge of things requires distance, yet a sense of an object's being is realized through use. As a result, using an object makes it recede into the background so that both states remain distant from each other. "[T]he true chasm in ontology lies not between humans and the world, but between objects and relations .... There is strife between the presence of a thing and its being."[69]

Ontology takes on an entirely different character as we come to recognize this tension. First, there is some fundamental incomprehensibility that exists between persons and objects, a claim that Heideggerians would rightly attribute to his work. Second, the same incomprehensibility that exists between a person's theoretical understanding of an object and their engagement with the object also exists between other objects as well. The hammer's experience of the nail is no more complete than the carpenter's experience of the hammer. Heidegger stopped short of making this claim, but one can easily follow Harman to the conclusion. This conclusion makes sense of objects as networks of interaction and interdependence with uncertain knowledge at every stage, an approach that I will pursue further in Chapter 6.[70]

Where does tool-being leave metaphysics? In one sense, it opens up the worlds of ontologies onto diverse senses of being that differ entirely between objects and object pairings. In another sense, it collapses ontology into a "tiny ontology"[71] in which an object's state of being no longer has the power to exclude. In either case, we are left with a metaphysics that is far more attuned to an object-centered ethic than its predecessors.

Ethics is even beginning to follow along with this new metaphysics. Introna finds in Heidegger an ethos of "dwelling" that "means to cultivate and care for the being of beings,"[72] a concept that is also pursued by Zimmerman as a basis for environmental ethics.[73] These are rich ideas that resonate strongly with the present account of object stewardship. Introna describes it as "poetry of things":

[O]ne can think of the profound attunement that emerges between a skilled artisan and her tools . . . . the intimacy and obvious respect that the artisan accords her tools – they reveal her and she reveals them, not as mere objects but as possibilities for being otherwise . . . . In this intimacy the thing becomes, in a penetrating way, a singular – it is spoken of in tenderness and maintained with care. Indeed, a singular whose loss is often experienced with anguish.[74]

The inferences from this attunement suggest a different focus, as I have argued as well. What I call empathy is "mindfulness" in Introna's terms; his "letting-be" is closely related with the stewardship that I set out to define.

These are rich and expressive ideas that comport well with the present discourse. I find object-oriented ontology to be a helpful framework that advances the plurality of objects and their purposes. And yet, it is clear that the ethical system that we graft onto our objects is not a necessity of one's contemplation of things. I do not believe that we can move directly from object metaphysics to object ethics.

Disturbing Object Uses

Consider again the example of the hammer. The only way that we can distinguish between a hammer being used well and used poorly is through value theory. If the hammer cries out when used for perversity, we cannot hear it. However, the hammer's misuse does captivate our aesthetic and moral judgments. The example that presents itself is woefully gruesome, so I hope that the reader will forgive its violence for its illustrative power.

In 2007, Viktor Sayenko and Igor Suprunyuck killed nineteen people, using a hammer in some of the murders. They videoed some of their crimes, and one of these videos was leaked to the public and then edited into a viral Internet short. Here you read an echo of its echo, for I have not watched it. The original video is not hosted on any legitimate website, but it is readily available along the conduits where such things flow. One site that does not host the original hosts thousands of echoes. On YouTube.com, one can choose between more than 5,000 "reaction" videos in which a person sits in front of a camera watching the murder video. For phenomenologists who understand identity formation as a product of others' reactions to self-expression, this is a particularly refined configuration for expression to take. In essence, the reactor watches the murder, and the audience watches the reactor, viewing the murderers' looking-glass selves.[75]

From these reactions, there is little ambiguity in the dominant response of shock, discomfort, horror, and often tears. The voyeurs often express regret for having watched the murder, even though nearly all of them had already seen and read someone else expressing regret for watching. The website Urban Dictionary introduces the topic of this particular video with a user-written warning:

Before I get to the "definition", just hear this: never, ever, ever, EVER watch this video wherever you may find it because it leaves a troubling image burnt into your mind that depresses you whenever you think about it.[76]

The warning says nothing about the victim, his family, or the fact that such a thing would be available online. It passes no judgment on the audience, and instead stresses the experience of participating in the spectacle. We can infer that people find great ugliness in the exhibition of injustice and inhumanity, a conclusion that is consistent with Scarry's aesthetic arguments linking beauty and justice.[77]

However, the ugliness that they observe is not metaphysically endowed in the objects at hand. The crime does not change the way that we understand hammers, nor does the video change the way that we understand computers and the Internet. The instrumentalities merely broaden with each new purpose. Whatever judgment we may pass on this way of using things does not originate in a metaphysics of objects.

Though tool-being may not entail a moral view as a necessary component of object ontologies, focusing on objects does lend itself to certain aesthetic and ethical realizations. In particular, it suggests the diversity of ways in which objects can be and, within these states of being, the many uses that objects have to each other.

An ontological approach to objects places them all on equal footing, as equally uncertain, equally used, and equally perplexed. My approach aims to ascribe different values to objects so that we can decide which ones to treat with the most care. This prioritization necessarily involves a departure from the metaphysical perspective. Earlier in this chapter, I took the first step away from metaphysics by treating value as an attentional process. Like object ontologies, attending to things emphasizes the different ways that objects bring each other into being. But unlike object ontologies, I presume that important aspects of these relationships can be observed, recognized, and appreciated by persons who choose to look closely at them. Whether a tool is broken or not, ready-to-hand or not, in order for the moralization of objects to produce reliable ethical insights, we must be able to understand how objects rely on each other. These reliances, and the morality that they undergird, are the subject of Chapter 6.

6 | *Ecological Value*

This chapter introduces a theory of value as a way of appreciating and caring for objects within complex social and biological systems. The first part, "Networks of Value," explores the interdependent nature of value within ecosystems and communities to outline a framework for recognizing the competing needs that objects satisfy. The second part, "Ethical Theory and Valuing Objects," refines this approach by using it to channel three distinct forms of normative theorizing: utilitarianism, virtue ethics, and human rights theory. The second section further interrogates the notion of ecological value by applying it to problems like the conception of wastefulness and by developing a recursive and teleological framework for enacting ecological value in the stewardship of objects. The third part, "Overcoming the Limits of the Market and the State," returns to the problems presented in Chapter 4 to decide whether this ecological approach to value, enacted in the form of object stewardship, can help us to deal with problems that states and markets do not handle well, namely inequality, finance, and global climate change.

The appreciation of intrinsic value accumulates with attention. But intrinsic value is only a small part of the system of worth. Value expands as we recognize the linkages between things. Interdependence transforms basic materials like soil, water, and air, which at first seem inert but are then revealed as the basic media of life.

"Soil is the thin unconsolidated mantle of earth that serves as a medium for plant growth, the source of 95 percent of our food."[1] The great environmental poets sing the praises of soil. Wendell Berry writes, "The soil is the great connector of lives, the source and destination of all."[2] In a similar spirit, Aldo Leopold writes that "Land, then, is not merely soil; it is a fountain of energy flowing through a circuit of soils, plants, and animals."[3] The notion of connectivity is key for these observations, which highlight connections between living things and connections with the past. Unique origins make unique soils.

Charles Kellogg, a US Department of Agriculture agronomist, observes this diversity from a more scientific perspective: "Each soil has had its own history. Like a river, a mountain, a forest, or any natural thing, its present condition is due to the influences of many things and events of the past."[4]

While the connectivity and biographies of soils inspire poets, the necessity of soils inspire statesmen. Franklin Delano Roosevelt remarked that "The nation that destroys its soil, destroys itself."[5] Thomas Jefferson is quoted as saying, "While the farmer holds the title to the land, actually it belongs to all the people because civilization itself rests upon the soil."[6] Soil teems with life, so it is not a perfect example of a nonliving thing. But soil exemplifies the kinds of materials that warrant care, even if they do not cry out for attention.

Those who focus exclusively on intrinsically valuable subjects miss these subjects' diverse reliances upon indispensable objects. Breathable air and drinkable water are not worthy of moral regard on their own. But they are never on their own. A failure to protect air and water threatens the well-being of living things that are worthy of moral regard.

If we wish to enumerate the things that ought to be protected, that list must necessarily include both intrinsically valuable elements and things that are valuable by virtue of the services that they do for things of value. In making that list, we might easily set aside the question of whether a thing is intrinsically valuable or not. As long as some of the elements of a system are valued or as long as the system as a whole has value, the question of whether a given entity has value outside its system context is moot. In fact, as this chapter will argue, it is often easier to understand a system and its health than to understand every object and the interactions of all objects within a system. Some things are too complicated to take apart and put back together.

Consider the bicycle, a complex mechanical system that is nevertheless simple in comparison with a living thing. In a photographic study of things, Todd McLellan disassembled a bicycle and artfully arrayed its 893 parts.[7] When those parts are brought together, they perform specific functions. The bearings are pressed between cups and cones so that the wheels, handlebars, cranks, and pedals will turn smoothly and minimize friction. The brakes have the opposite function: when pressed against the rim, brakes increase friction whenever the rider wishes. To repair a bicycle, a mechanic must understand the parts' unique functions and how they work together. When a mechanic checks a bicycle, she ensures that the bolts are tight and visually inspects the frame, but once she's done that, she needs to ride it. Some problems arise from the way that parts interface with each other. Chains get stretched by the force applied in the drivetrain. Derailleurs get knocked out of alignment. Some problems are only observable when the bike performs as a system with the chain pulling under load.

Perhaps bikes are not intrinsically valuable, but that does not mean that the people who work on them will not come to value them and treat them with care. Doing so values their riders and the rider's safety, but part of what makes a mechanic good at her job is that she values the bike itself. As one mechanic advises:

Love the bike for its own sake. When you're motivated to see a bike fixed right, because every bike deserves to be fixed right, you're less likely to overlook seemingly small problems like a squeaky seat or a loose bolt. A good mechanic tries to make every bike work as well as it possibly can, 'cause that's how it should be.[8]

An argument like this one emphasizes the bike's totality and the way that the person repairing it stands in relation to it. Pirsig is perhaps most famous for arguing that participating in technology, appreciating it, and coming to terms with our relationships with it are essential human values. For Pirsig, we depend on technologies; knowing how to use and fix technological devices is a value in itself, while the "condemnation of technology is ingratitude."[9] Technology is "not an exploitation of nature, but a fusion of nature and the human spirit into a new kind of creation that transcends both."[10]

Relative to a living thing, a habitat, or a social system, a bike is simple. Its parts have specific purposes that realize a designers' intent. The parts continue to fulfill their usual function; they do not develop, they only degrade. The bike's purpose does not evolve. The clarity of purpose where the parts fit into the whole makes a bicycle, however complex, far simpler than a dynamic system like an ecosystem. Given this difference, we need to decide how far we can push system-level thinking. I will suggest that even when it is impossible to comprehend the roles of every element within a system, it is possible to recognize whether a given action causes a system's elements to thrive or languish.

Whether the parts of a system work in concert or opposition, whether they thrive by being brought together or being kept apart, they stand in relation to one another. The importance of appreciating their interdependences is an essential factor in making responsible decisions about the use of these parts either for human or ecological purposes. Once we accept this, we are able to focus on objects in sets, and this will greatly simplify the work that we have to do to use objects responsibly. Ecological forestry provides an apt example. While singularizing wood fiber products leads us to care for certain forests from which our product come, once we do so, things get confusing. The tree does so many different things within the forest. How should it be valued? When is it appropriate to cut one down? These questions have no easy answers. However, if we stop focusing on the trees and begin looking at the forest as a whole, we see the forest as a living, breathing thing through which water, energy, and CO_2 must flow. We need not spurn the forest's economic potential by hugging every tree. Looking at a system level, some trees can be removed from the forest at little cost to its ecology and much benefit to those who remove them. Appreciating the forest as an ecosystem will tell us not only how much wood can be removed, but how best to remove it, and monitoring the forest's health will help us maintain a sustainable forestry regime over time.

Bikes can be cared for as mechanical systems. The example of forests illustrates that complex organic systems can also be subject to care, provided that we can conceptualize the aggregate health of the forest. Biologists and ecologists recognize the diversity and contingency of living things and living communities. Life is too dynamic for static conservation. The question is not whether some species should go extinct, but whether a given rate of extinction is acceptable. If we can assess the stock of biodiversity available and the rate at which new species emerge, then we can be stewards of aggregate biodiversity. It follows that the end state for which we steward resources in ecological life may be characterized by its rate of change rather than its constancy.

This dynamic focus accords with the way that both social scientists and biological scientists think about change in the populations they study. Everyone agrees that certain characteristics are useful to organisms and societies. In the late nineteenth and early twentieth centuries, it was assumed that these functional features were the key to scientific inquiry. However, functionalism fell out of favor in the mid-twentieth century.

To steward objects, I argue that we need to understand how they function within a complex system, but that does not make me a functionalist. Functionalists view useful attributes as the reasons why organisms and people have these attributes. This causal narrative leaves little room for random variation as a cause in biological systems and for sense-making in social systems. However, phenotypical variation in biological systems results from random mutations. Variation in social systems is contingent upon how people and groups understand situations. Object stewardship does ascribe functions to both living and social objects, but it is not a functionalist theory. It does not understand functions as primary causal factors guiding social and biological life. Working from a description of aggregate health in a society or ecosystem helps to guarantee that individuals and organisms are not pigeonholed into fixed roles.

I take the position that it is possible to differentiate between a thriving ecology and an emaciated one and that we can also differentiate between a healthy community and one that is suffering. I suggest that it is possible to experimentally perturb both social and biological systems in responsible ways, and to gradually improve the overall health of these systems by learning from the results of these perturbations. But I nonetheless recognize that these qualitative distinctions in system health must not be relied upon too heavily to avoid reifying social systems that are changing and ought to change, and to avoid the futility of trying to freeze ecological evolution at a given moment in Earth's history.

Nevertheless, making these distinctions will help us to describe the priority of agents, resources, and organisms within their contexts, to apprehend their ecological value. I use the term "ecological value" to denote an entity's value to a more complex system that includes humans. This notion intentionally merges human and non-human ecology into a unified perspective, though it is often useful to separately delineate the environmental and social consequences of using an object.

There are complexities and challenges ahead, but do not let them overwhelm the practical purpose of our inquiry. We can evaluate the conditions within ecological and social communities. We just need to look with enough subtlety to recognize the evolving relationships, to understand where order can be expected and where disorder should reign.

Networks of Value

Caring for things involves understanding how they are best used, either in their own interests or in the interests of other objects. These judgments require both empirical and normative understanding. Whereas I previously worked from the assumption that everything had value, now I can focus on the value that objects have to each other. These perspectives can be added together so that objects have some intrinsic value coupled with their extrinsic (interdependent) value. I have value, and to that value I add the value I have to others. The same can be said of a tree, a river, and the soil's nutrients. To make sense of these values, we must work with them as sets, as complex systems. It does not matter whether aggregate interdependence within an ecosystem is an end in and of itself or what Dewey calls an "end-in-view," as long as we recognize the vital interactions that make life possible. Aristotle argued that to take care of a person, one must take care of her city. In order for us to work out the consequences of different object uses, we must follow a similar line.

Previously, I focused on examples about unitary objects. It is developmentally good for an individual child that she plays with other children, so we encourage her to do so in her own interest. When it comes to intrinsically valuable entities, we can often make direct judgments about how those things are cared for in terms of their health, growth, etc. However, we cannot make such direct judgments about many other objects, including some living ones. What value should be placed on the mosquitoes that transmit Zika virus? Before we eradicate them, we need to decide if they have any role in a world that is just and good.

These normative insights require us to shift our focus and its scale, to broaden our perspective. We cannot discover a tree's value by looking only at that tree: we must see the tree in its context. This requires us to consider the ecology around the thing and the interdependences within that ecology. In contrast to intrinsic value, extrinsic value is interconnected, woven through threads of interdependence between persons, living things, and inanimate objects. The totality of this fabric best represents the notion of place and place-based responsibility, but whether we can apprehend these complex systems as totalities remains to be seen.

Value in Biological Ecologies

Though the simplest forms of autotrophic life can fix carbon and energy from their environment without reliance on nutrients from other living things, the complex living systems that we value and rely upon for our survival are highly interdependent. It follows that one cannot value a deer without also valuing the field in which it lives, the foliage that it eats, and the soil bacteria that help that foliage to grow. Likewise, one cannot value a person without valuing the ecology upon which that person depends.

The foremost consideration in esteeming natural objects is understanding their interests as communities of life. Prior to deciding whether and how living things can be used in the human economy, we must understand their interdependences. Only then can we care for them. This calculation requires an end-state theory that understands the purpose, or at least the health, of the living system. Natural objects require a community-level evaluative frame. Having a sense of how these organisms ought to work together makes it possible to value individual organisms embedded within wider complexity.

One way to observe the interdependence of living things is to take them apart. We can certainly tell when organisms from an ecosystem do not thrive in isolation, and many organisms do not. Most microbes cannot be cultured in a lab.[11] Some larger organisms are difficult, if not impossible, to breed in captivity. Likewise, when plants are removed from their native soil ecologies, they may not grow well or be resilient to pathogens.

In an ecology, it is useful to track the populations of different species to monitor their overall health. When populations begin to decline, ecologists try to differentiate between the normal ebb and flow of living systems which are always dynamic, and threshold events that can have serious consequences that make recovery unlikely. When deer become overpopulated there is not enough food for them to eat. They grow weak, and it becomes easier for predators to catch them. As they are culled or starve, the population declines. Thereafter, food becomes more plentiful and populations can recover. These sorts of demographic dynamics are internal to a given ecosystem. They may be a sign of missing elements, like predators that have been displaced by people, but the fact that some species become more or less plentiful within an ecosystem over time is not an immediate cause for alarm.

While population-level indicators are key, health threats can also emerge among individuals. The face tumors suffered by Tasmanian devils, for example, are a contagious illness that threatens the whole population. Without intervention, they might go extinct.

The indicators of ecosystem health can be assessed at both macroscopic and microscopic scales. NASA's soil moisture mission uses a satellite to monitor 1000-kilometer-wide swaths of terrain and to estimate vegetation levels and moisture within these swaths. At the other extreme, hydrologists check oxygen, turbidity, and pH from thimbles of surface water. For business ethics practitioners, understanding ecosystem health may involve a degree of expertise that is beyond their professional interest, training, or capabilities. The stewardship logic would not make sense if it expected everyone to have advanced training in biochemistry, agronomy, or hydrology. Prudential care of singularized objects does not demand this, but it does suggest that we become active seekers of the information that experts provide. As such, the reference here is important. We want to know when important ecosystem components cease to serve the ecosystems well. We realize that our occupational and industrial activities can impact these complex systems, and we need to determine when our activities are altering their capacity to thrive.

We are not only interested in when these systems cease to serve people well. If we are shortsightedly selfish, "[o]nly when the services provided by ecosystem functions are unmistakably disrupted do we step back and reconsider."[12] However, object stewards try to understand the systems that they affect, so that they can anticipate problems and mitigate the costs of their actions.

Biodiversity, the conservation of species, the interdependence between resource cycles in soils, waters, and atmospheric processes, and the specific needs of individual species are all sources of value that we can call upon as reasons to care about a living system. These are all relevant factors in the calculation of how best to use a thing.

In any case, we will find value beyond the picturesque and the economically exploitable. For the object steward, the industrial and agricultural utility of fertile dry land is merely the easiest value to appreciate in human terms. Object stewards think in nonhuman terms. Traditionally, wetlands and bogs have been viewed as wasted land because they are not useful for agriculture, transportation, or housing. But ecologists love wetlands and so must object stewards. Wetlands support diverse species and protect them from predators, and they maintain important parts of the water cycle. The fact that a person would not want to sleep in a place, work there, or paint a picture of it does not diminish its value. The key difference here between ecological aesthetics and the valuation of specific organisms as singularities involves a transition from the protection of an individual to the appreciation of a whole context. We must understand and support life-affirming values by supporting the way that living things operate within competitive and mutualistic communities.

Tiny Things

Should we share the peculiar obsessions of scientific ecology? Perhaps. There is something magnificent about the persistence of living things and the adaptations that they show. There are reasons to shelter as many different ways of being alive as possible from the threat of destruction. Still, using wonder as a standard for conservation places a disproportionate emphasis on so-called "charismatic megafauna." UK TV presenter Simon Watt makes a joke out of this with his "ugly animal preservation society." One of the benefits of focusing on ecosystems is that we can evaluate their health regardless of whether there is a fierce or cuddly mammal depending upon them.

Darwin described "disinterested love for all living creatures" as "the most noble attribute of man,"[13] and looking closer at ecosystems is one of the best ways to promote this noble attribute. As Darwin noted with remarkable prescience, given the lack of microbiological knowledge in his time:

We cannot fathom the marvelous complexity of an organic being; but on the hypothesis here advanced this complexity is much increased. Each living creature must be looked at as a microcosm—a little universe, formed of a host of self-propagating organisms, inconceivable minute and as numerous as the stars in heaven."[14]

Understanding living things requires us to look across scale and recognize the limits of our own visual consciousness. We must value living things that we cannot see, including single-cellular organisms.

The cell is "the smallest autopoietic structure known today[,] the minimal unit that is capable of incessant self-organizing metabolism."[15]

And this is what we like: life, the incessant self-organizing metabolism within the context of dynamic, evolving complexity. Our appreciation of these living things, however diminutive, is not required by their vanity. However, in pursuit of self-preservation and conceptual honesty, it is vital that we understand microscopic living things.

The massive biomass, irreplaceable ecological functions, and sensitivity to changes in the environment make single cellular organisms important for ecosystem health and for the way that we track it. Again, we appreciate things the more closely that we look. Venter and coauthors observe that "Microorganisms are responsible for most of the biogeochemical cycles that shape the environment of Earth and its oceans. Yet these organisms are the least well understood on Earth."[16] The authors set out to observe some of the unobserved microbes, the ones that are not easily cultured in a lab. By sampling DNA from water at different locations near Bermuda, they find evidence that the sea's microecologies operate as distinct patchy environments with specialist organisms in each patch. In our terms, this implies that we can even singularize the microscopic living communities in the Earth's oceans to relatively local microclimates. The ocean is not one thing, but many things flowing together. And, in the context of appreciating the importance of bacteria, Venter demonstrates the priority of the smallest units of life, not only as a causal factor in environmental processes, but also as a platform for innovations that may help to reduce greenhouse gas emissions. For him, the priority is established by our global ecology: "If you do not like bacteria, you're on the wrong planet. This is the planet of the bacteria."[17]

Death and Regrowth

Valuing life may also require us to value death and to naturalize senescence as a life process. Thinking ecologically leads directly to circumstances where an organism's progeny may thrive under conditions that are deadly to the organism itself. To recognize the difference between community-level ecological consciousness and the singularization of objects that we considered thus far, to shift from thinking about an organism to thinking about its niche within a certain complex ecosystem, it is helpful to consider the way that specific entities can be constructively destroyed, how the loss of the part may improve the whole.

Consider the role of fire in pyrophilic plant communities. Fire defines ecological landscapes in important ways, despite the fact that it kills living things.[18] Some plants have evolved flammable phenotypes[19] and other species are fire-resistant. Genetic persistence of plants through fire-promoted seed propagation and fire survival are obvious signs of fitness in a fire-prone ecology. The idea that some ecologies thrive by burning creates a sharp distinction between the health of the individual and the health of the community because fire destroys individual plants. As such, we cannot use the health of individual organisms as a baseline. We must select criteria of aggregate benefit at the level of an ecological community in order to evaluate aggregate outcomes, and even this may not be a wide enough scale if there are interdependences between ecological communities. Some have argued that the entire Earth must be understood as a complete living system,[20] which suggests that we would need a theory of Earth's purpose and health in order to proceed with the stewardship of its subsystems. For the moment, let us focus on a given habitat, such as a prairie.

At first glance, a burned prairie appears wasted. Fire leaves few signs of life on the surface. But as time scales lengthen, the prairie regenerates. Flora regrows and fauna returns, often in a healthier condition than before the burn. Fire can benefit an ecosystem's biodiversity, resilience, nutrient distribution, and the fitness of individual organisms. The beneficiary organisms may not be the original occupants, because these individuals may have burned, but some of the beneficiaries may be the progeny of burned plants.

Only a sophisticated ecological vision can understand destructive fire as a constructive force. By comparing an ecosystem that burned to another that did not, we can observe differences. These differences must be interpreted through an evaluative frame that, once again, relates to some desirable end. The factors of system health are not defined directly by the interests of the burned biological entity, but by the responses of other entities within the ecology and the survival of that plant's progeny. Valuing living things amounts to valuing the totalities of the places where they thrive.

Negative Biological Value

Some objects have negative value within a place because they seek resources so greedily that they threaten the living systems around them. In many cases, these system-destabilizing organisms are invasive species: they evolved in a given ecosystem and were introduced to another. Whereas their original context had organisms capable of checking the species' growth, the new context does not. Global climate change and habitat destruction can also alter the balance in an ecosystem.

People often pass judgment on the value of living things within different habitats, particularly when they are trying to cultivate certain plants and animals. Organisms that hinder human plans are known as weeds and pests. In general, weeds and pests are a threat because they either displace or damage the commodities that a farmer means to bring to market, but the category of "weed" is not taxonomically useful. Some plants that are useful and desired in one context are a hindrance in another. For instance, people grow mint, but its rhizomatic root structure also allows it to displace other plants. The important observation is that a subjective preference, coupled with a theory of value, is necessary to determine which plants are weeds in which contexts. It is not enough to focus on evolutionary fitness. Indeed, both invasive and indigenous species can be weeds. Indigenous plants gain their advantage over cultivars through fitness to the environment. To determine the value of such plants, we must pit the interests of persons against the value of native habitats.

Judging the worth of plants involves a kind of discernment. While I have criticized many forms of anthropocentrism, in principle there is nothing wrong with the fact that humans shape ecologies. There is extensive evidence that people have done so since long before industrialization,[21] in some ways that have increased biological diversity, for example, by carrying seeds over great distances. Even today, some human structures prove useful to non-human species in unintended ways. Many bird species inhabit abandoned buildings on Alcatraz Island, a success story for urban ecology.[22]

However, the role that people play is often destabilizing. It can threaten the distinctive biodiversity of local habitats with the uniformity of globally competitive species. As such, invasive species lead to a more obvious moral conclusion than do weeds. These organisms thrive at the exclusion of native species, sometimes threatening the basic ecological order that predated their arrival. If we accept an evolutionary ethic that the strong should rule, then our global ecologies will be a bramble of kudzu vines,[23] our waterways will be simplified by uncontested zebra mussel colonization,[24] and European rabbits will rule the islands.[25] If, however, we value diversity and uniqueness, then we should value native species and distinctive habitats.

The global Darwinist theory allows and requires no judgment, but it comes at a terrible ecological price. In exchange for the cost of management, we trade uniqueness, diversity, and rich components of an ecological heritage. Again, these are choices to be made about what we value in living systems. It is far too late to step back and let the wilderness unfold, and we live too close to the natural world to even consider it. For example, some people live in or near forests that would naturally burn on a periodic basis, yet their homes and lives depend upon the suppression of fires within local habitats (I discuss pyrogenic plants above).[26] The stakes are often high in deciding what living things belong in a certain place, but there is no way to avoid making such decisions.

Humans in Biological Value

It sometimes seems as if living things can either be useful to persons or to a natural environment, but not both. Coastal lands can hold mangrove forests or shrimp farms.[27] Rivers can generate electricity or they can serve as spawning grounds.[28] These are choices that have an either/or character involving inescapable tradeoffs.

In the short term, these tradeoffs are certainly real, but the long run is less clear. Once we recognize that humans are a small part of a much larger ecology in which we must provide services and receive them, there is no mutually exclusive tradeoff.

Acting as if nature exists only to feed, clothe, shelter, oxygenate, and fascinate humans does have the advantage of acknowledging the actual location of the political debate for conservation.[29] But such an account struggles with the complexity of interactions between biotic and abiotic elements. Even if one found humans to be superior beings worthy of exclusive moral consideration, it might still be worthwhile to value the relationships between objects that do not directly concern persons. Efforts to maximize the value that biological systems provide to humans have tended to oversimplify the ecological networks necessary for living things to thrive.

But even this anthropocentric approach to maximizing the value of living systems seems to be beyond us. Unfortunately, humans are not always interested in managing natural ecologies to ensure that they thrive. Humans may be the most invasive species of all. Not only do we destroy habitats, but we are the most significant global vector that causes other species to invade.

Clearly, the biological value of persons is not static. It is the result of an endogenous process that depends on our conduct. If we control our own resource consumption, cultivate diversity, preserve natural systems, and live within Earth's means, then we are contributors. If we do not, then we are detractors, weeds. We often ask how we should value nature. Numerous researchers have estimated the economic value of the global ecological services provided to mankind by the natural environment.

It is less common to ask what value humans bring to Earth's living systems, and the answers to that question, whether calculated at the individual or ecosystem level, can be rather disconcerting. Once we set a normative standard for how living systems ought to function, we can easily add our own conduct as a key variable and find that we play a very significant role in the degradation of living systems. Alas, most humans, especially the richest humans and most of the companies that serve them, have a negative ecological value because they use resources without replacement.

One way to understand this biological judgment of persons is as a form of posthumanism that belittles the worth of our species and its members. In an ecocentric ethic, it would be nonsensical to imagine that all persons are created equal. Some are more destructive than others, and therefore less worthy. In the extreme, ecological value supplants and subverts humanism. According to this posthumanist ethic, a person's value derives, like any other object, from the system of ecological and interpersonal relationships that he or she affects. Those who do no harm, who create balance and sustain life, are worth more than those who do the opposite.

Described as posthumanism, ecological value is unlikely to win the people's choice award. It is easy to see why we might prefer to emphasize the Earth's utility in terms of ecological services rather than describing humanity's disutility to the Earth. But these two equations balance each other because they describe the same system of variables. Whether we expect the Earth's ecosystems to serve humanity or the reverse, if human actions degrade the Earth's unique life-carrying capacity, we suffer alongside the planet's ecosystems.

The main conclusion is as follows: we can evaluate the health of complex biological entities like ecosystems, and whoever acts in ways that influence ecosystem health has an obligation to understand these consequences. Because it is our use of material and living things that causes these effects, we must monitor resource use according to its ecological impact. The best hope for a transformation of culture requires a shift in resource utilization and a prioritization of resource flows. It is unavoidable that some people will cause harm. The rest of us must do our best to ensure that these individuals are not entrusted with resource control. Rather than trying to hold those with power responsible, we must work in the opposite direction, to forge an institutional regime in which power flows to those who have proven most responsible and away from those who have not.

Value in Human Societies

Just as biological systems have a value that exceeds the sum of their parts, so do social systems. Likewise, just as the biotic and abiotic elements of an ecosystem work together to sustain life, social systems are also reliant upon both living and nonliving objects.

Understanding objects' context within social systems presents some of the same challenges of understanding objects' value within living systems. Elements of social systems are interdependent, and removing certain pieces can force adaptations with cascading effects. Elements of the built environment, like whether houses have porches and how far apart they are spaced will shape, at least in part, the way that neighbors relate to one another. Streetcars and affordable movie screenings bring people together in ways that private cars and home entertainment systems do not. I described in the introduction how physical things can form both bridging and blocking functions, and while these consequences are not always evaluated as good or bad, they are very often significant.

As with living systems, I cannot provide a definitive list of the qualities of a society that ought to be esteemed and protected. Social science, like natural science, has developed a number of measures of community health. These include crime rates, broken windows, community-level social capital, walkability, and access to valued resources like food, healthcare, transportation, education, and employment. The merits of each of these community resources is partially justified by the positive consequences that it has for individual persons in terms of their subjective well-being, economic resilience, social support, and physical health. Some of the qualities of community health are more problematic than others. Broken-windows-based policing, for example, seeks to force households and businesses to keep up a clean appearance with the presumption that broken windows send a signal to potential offenders that they can get away with criminal activity. However, this theory has been shown to encourage a destructive cycle of policing that forgoes substance in the name of appearances that are not even relevant to community members' subjective perceptions.[30]

The example of broken windows theory shows that care must be taken in establishing community attributes worth protecting. Policing for broken windows focuses attention on physical things, choosing the wrong things to worry about. Alternatively, there is considerable evidence that exposure to lead and a lack of access to clean drinking water can seriously degrade a community's health and quality of life. So, whereas broken windows may not be an important attribute of a human community, broken public infrastructure matters.

Because different people have different ideas about the requirements of human communities, there is no substitute for experimentation and evidence. Communities can try out different ways of living together, and see what works. In the end, individuals within groups must decide how persons and groups flourish. But we are likely to disagree and to have a number of fruitless adventures on the way to agreement. A wide range of needs represent qualities that thriving communities have. From an informed press and institutional accountability to interpersonal trust, these qualities are improved or threatened by businesses' interactions with objects, and those businesses owe it to the communities to respect the rules that the communities establish and the interests that the communities seem to endorse.

The key difference between human and biological ecologies is this: in human ecologies, we value self-determination, but in biological ecologies we do not. Biological "self-determination" is a triumph of weeds and a negligent response to the anthropogenic damage already done. But human self-determination gives people ownership over the experiments that they are conducting to decide how best to live, ownership over the wisdom that they find in their own experiences, and ownership over their traditions.

Sorting out the conflicts between self-determined values is beyond the scope of this chapter. I set out to show how objects can be managed, and why we ought to manage them. Complex systems, whether social or biological, present challenges for objects stewardship. Fortunately, there are tools available to help manage this complexity.

Value in Place

Some of the most compelling examples of interdependence come from complex biological and social systems. However, it is also worthwhile to consider interdependence in nonliving structures. Resource extraction presents numerous examples of cascading changes introduced by first intruding upon a single resource. In the case of a physical system gone wrong, the consequences that worry us are human and biological, but the chain of causality is physical (mechanical, chemical, electrical, hydrological, etc.).

Consider the example of Tuzla, Bosnia. Settlements in Tuzla date back more than a millennium. But few of the city's historical structures still stand and many of the city's existing buildings are cracking and degrading. These buildings were not destroyed by the ethnic conflicts of the early 1990s that destroyed other Bosnian cities. In fact, Tuzla was governed throughout the war by a coalition that managed to avoid being drawn into competing nationalist positions.[31]

Instead, the cause of the city's degradation is written in its name; Tuzla means "salt" in Turkish. The city's stability was literally undermined by the salt industry, whose aggressive practices are still causing subsistence and sinkholes.[32] Undermining, or mining under, the city creates voids in the geological structure that leave less ground for Tuzla to stand upon.

There are two ways to understand the economy that degraded this city's physical infrastructure. Focusing on regulation, governance, and individual decisions, one might blame weak mining laws and those who managed the mine. According to this account, each of us becomes accountable through the force of the state. It is true that the destructive practices would not have happened if managers and firms were properly incentivized to take care of the city that stood atop the mine. This is a very modern way of thinking: better laws make better incentives, better incentives make better managers, and better managers make better mines.

The second perspective, the one developed throughout this text, traces blame through the salt itself. Every grain of salt carries numerous possibilities. It could salt a steak or a road, or it could serve as a structural component of the land that holds a city in place. Every grain of salt removed from under the city is attached to a grain of responsibility for weakening the city's foundations. The managers, the workers, the local tax base, and those who consume the salt are materially linked to Tuzla's lost architectural legacy.

Many other products have already been transformed from commodities to singularities, from interchangeable items to items with meaningful histories. According to this singularized theory, the inspiration for responsibility should come from within the economy itself. Destructive mining practices should never occur because there should not be a market for the products of these activities, nor should anyone be willing to do the work because the profits from this labor are also tainted.

It is important to note how these material obligations come together in a place-based ethic. Places have physical, material interfaces in which responsibilities are manifest. The propinquity of resources is an essential factor in production and transactions. One of the reasons why managers need to cultivate a sense of place within the organizations that they manage is that the consequences of their managerial actions often stick to places. Dumped resources persist in the local environment. Digging under foundations will undermine their structure, now and far into the future. Responsibilities must be drawn wherever the consequences are located. To make sense of ecological value, we must also make sense of our obligations to the places where we tread.

Managing Ecological Value

Gaining the insights necessary to manage objects within complex systems and places can be extremely difficult. System-wide understanding is limited by the observational detail available. The industrial response has been to simplify the system. Through monoculture and tight control over nutrients, pests, and genetic factors, industrial agriculture attempts to impose an ordered, scientific system where complex ecologies previously grew.

I endorse another path. The alternative is to accept that the complexity of the system is sufficient to warrant caution and preservation as key strategies. Rather than attempting to control the entire ecology through monoculture, an active observer can learn to navigate a complex system using a form of experimentation known as adaptive management:

In adaptive management, the goal is not to produce the highest biological or economic yield, but to understand the system and to learn more about uncertainties by probing the system. Feedback from management outcomes provides for corrections to avoid thresholds that may threaten the ecosystem and the social and economic system based on it.[33]

I view adaptive management as an appropriate response to certain kinds of uncertainty, provided that the experimental site is not so unique that the experiment runs the risk of doing irreparable damage.[34]

In a world of scientific uncertainty where nothing is entirely safe, regulators are often guided by either precaution or deregulation. Precaution places the burden of proof on the party that wishes to make a change. Deregulation waits until harm is done before seeking to curtail it. Adaptive management is a third option. It is an experimental paradigm for understanding ecosystem responsiveness to management. Adaptive managers act, but they act first in narrow and localized ways, using pilot projects and careful outcome tracking to determine whether it is appropriate to bring actions to scale. Adaptive management can also be useful as a regulatory paradigm to understand that all environmental interactions occur in a setting of unfolding uncertainty. By experimenting gently within living systems, one can better understand their health and better manage the resultant uncertainties. New normative insights arise from these observations. All of this begins by taking an interest in diverse ecologies rather than single commodity species.

The self-knowledge, knowledge of others, and knowledge of desirable end states from Chapter 5 are still applicable in valuing complex systems at multiple levels of analysis. Nevertheless, a comprehensive account of object value is only possible by valuing the relations between objects and other objects and also between objects and persons. A methodologically individualist account of object value is worse than useless: it is insensitive and inaccurate.

Stated succinctly, environmental objects can be valued according to their use to the system as a whole, and a similar scheme can make sense of human social organization as well. While it can be difficult to understand the role that things play within living and social systems, nonliving objects often have trajectories with known and predictable consequences. Understanding and taking responsibility for these consequences is the most important conclusion of this analysis.

Objects are resources and symbols of meaning; they are sources of healing and weapons of control. No object stands alone. The worth of things is maintained through the pattern of their connections. This ecological approach is no substitute for the humanistic claim that persons have certain inalienable rights. A person's right to subsistence, for instance, does not derive from his or her value within a pattern of other persons and natural resources. But neither is the individuated formulation of value sufficient on its own.

How does this ecological conception connect with the singularity approach to responsibility? Let us return to the gun safety example from Chapter 5. A world in which children die violently while playing with guns is worse than a world without such deaths, and not only from the perspective of the child. Taking the perspectives of all of those who are related to or connected with the child shows the way that a social ecology values an individual.

The child's value is uncontested, as is the vileness of a child dying violently. The debated question concerns the allocation of responsibility for such a death. On one side, many claim that "guns do not kill people, people kill people." They locate responsibility for the child's death in a person because an inanimate object does not choose to harm, owes no duty of care, cannot be negligent, and is not responsible in a moral sense.

On the other side, advocates of gun control argue for restricting the supply and flow of weapons and ammunition. Even the name "gun control" delineates the boundary of the debate, whether only people should be controlled or whether guns should also be controlled.

In terms of adaptive management, American gun control represents one of the most willful failures in the history of public policy. Recall that adaptive management involves experimentation and observation. We probe the ecosystem with certain actions, and then we monitor the results. The two elements of adaptive management are therefore local action and monitoring. In the case of American gun violence and gun regulation, both action and monitoring are forestalled by the policy system. While several American cities have attempted to pass gun ordinances that would reduce the risk of shootings, constitutional objections and active lobbying curtail most of these "probes." On the monitoring side, research funding has been systematically denied to researchers who wish to track the public health consequences of gun ownership. The politics here are quite clear, as House Speaker John Boehner explains:

The CDC is there to look at diseases that need to be dealt with to protect public health ... I'm sorry, but a gun is not a disease. Guns do not kill people – people do. And when people use weapons in a horrible way, we should condemn the actions of the individual and not blame the action on some weapon.[35]

On the surface, Boehner's argument makes sense. Guns do not act on their own, and violent outbursts are certainly blameworthy. But Boehner fails to apprehend the human ecology around gun violence, the contexts where guns are stored, the reverence with which they are used in movies, and the significant curiosity that their "do not touch that!" status has for American children. Looking at the gun itself and its place, and trying to change that object and that place, may be the only way to reduce the tragic toll of both accidental and intentional gun violence.

The debate over gun control is a debate over agency and objects, a debate to which I am now prepared to contribute. There is a rough equivalence between the notion of controlling guns and the notion of controlling people. As with other examples, the question is not whether gun violence is responsible, but about who should be responsible for gun violence. Consider two formulations of the same normative statement:

1. A gun should not be allowed to kill a child.
2. A gun owner should not allow a gun to kill a child.

Both express the same desirable end state, but one circumscribes the scope of responsibility within the bounds of ownership. The first claim might suggest that access to guns be limited, that private persons cannot own them, or that there be procedures in place to check gun access. Some of these already exist, like buying restrictions for felons. In contrast, the second claim locates responsibility entirely within the relationship between owner and property. The second claim focuses on a nearby agent, whereas the first focuses on the object.

Ecological value is best understood as an extension of an object's connections to people and living systems. Through these connections, objects can impact morally important resources, and this means that the objects become important and focal considerations in a scheme of responsibility. Singularity value treats a gun as having a negative value if it puts a child's life at risk, regardless of whether an adult might also be responsible. Commodity value can only understand the gun's value through its market price and the average utility of ownership.

According to the singularization logic, each person who makes guns and bullets knowing that these resources are often misused is putting an object into the stream of commerce without taking responsibility for that object's consequences. If that producer could say conclusively that the world needs more guns, she or he should make them. Otherwise, she or he should not. As we will see below, this way of thinking about value is not only important for responsibility, but also for economic valuation.

Ethical Theory and Valuing Objects

Adaptive management provides a practical approach to the valuation of things. In the spirit of Dewey, it argues that our appraisals of worth emerge through experience, and that each time we make use of a thing we discover new conditions for subsequent valuations. But adaptive management also moves beyond Dewey to a level of analysis where complex systems operate beyond our control and beyond our perception. Adaptive management makes room for things to have a value beyond what we can perceive. It argues that while we may not understand all of these interactions, if we are sufficiently gradual and gentle in the way that we work, we can avoid doing damage that cannot be undone.

I could stop here. I have already reached the two most important conclusions: that it is possible to manage the consequences of material things amidst complex interactions and that objects can help us to determine who shares responsibility for which things.

However, these arguments are not stated in a form that meshes well with the existing body of ethical theory or with the literature on business ethics. What is satisfying for a pragmatist, who views all knowledge as an emergent process, does not adequately answer a foundationalist who prefers clear concepts and stated propositions. The remainder of this chapter and the one that follows will explore these connections by backtracking and reframing some of our conclusions in terms of normative theory, utilitarianism, human rights, and virtue ethics.

Utilitarianism is the dominant ethic in economic analysis. Efficiency, general equilibrium, and trade liberalization are all justified in terms of aggregate utility and public welfare. However, there are assumptions demanded by the effort to maximize utility that cannot be sustained in the present approach to ecological value. As defined, ecological value includes too many different kinds of entities in its appreciative structure to maximize them together.

In most utilitarian thinking, scope is a key condition that must be established propositionally. Provided that utilitarians can agree upon the scope of morally relevant entities whose interests should be promoted through ethics and provided that they can determine the consequences of a given act or rule, the consequences (and thus the act or rule) can be conclusively evaluated. The usual process is to treat people's preferences as the relevant maximand. After making a few assumptions about preference ordering and the measurability of different outcomes, utilitarianism provides a judgment.

Heterogeneous ecological valuations work from a mixture of objects that includes ecosystems, people, products, and lots of other things. If we are interested in the well-being of a habitat, a road, a car, and a driver, taking them together will help us to understand some of their features and detractors. As we learned from Harman's tool-being, objects interact in dyad-specific ways. We cannot understand a road without recognizing the ways in which it cuts through the habitats it crosses, and the way that those habitats in turn cut through it. Making the road might destroy some root systems and divide biological communities. In turn, over time, the roots creep into cracks in the road, buckling its structure. Observing the functional dependences and consequences of these heterogeneous elements as pairwise interactions produces insights that anthropocentric value is unlikely to produce. But if we were to try to add together the quality of the road's and car's maintenance, the habitat's life-carrying capacity, and the driver's preferences, the heterogeneous elements cannot be tallied. They share no common unit or measure. They are incommensurable. And even if they could be added together by generating a common index or ordering them into monotonic preference sets, the result would still be uninterpretable. The only reason that the road and car matter is that they benefit the person and harm the habitat. But the habitat also benefits the person, and the person may benefit the habitat. These nested evaluative elements negate the independence assumptions that maximization generally requires. Doing the math would force us to simplify the complex systems, leaving us back where we began, with an anthropocentric normative model that stultifies moral imaginations and levels everything into a similarly inert moral status.

Does utilitarianism require the summation of utility? On the standard account, yes. However, there is an alternative.

Object Utilitarianism

Directly valuing objects allows for an alternative specification of utilitarianism. By focusing on singular objects rather than decisions and policies, these objects provide the boundaries otherwise derived from utilitarianism's scope criterion. Recall that we are interested in the ways that objects are useful to other elements of a complex system. An object's ecological use value is its extrinsic value within an interdependent biological or social ecology. If we tried to add objects to the usual formulation of utilitarianism, there would certainly be problems. Ecological use value gets confused when applied to acts and rules. These traditional targets of utilitarian judgments require the kinds of aggregation discussed above. We would need to choose between cars, habitats, people, and roads in order to weight their importance. Because ecological use value conflates the worthiness of multiple objects and entities, values are redundant and overlapping. However, when ecological use value is applied to an object, it provides a holistic account of the consequences of different uses of that object. If one wishes to value objects within a complex social and biological ecology, ecological use value is the most comprehensive, direct, and concrete specification.

Continuing with the previous example, ecological use value understands the habitat, road, car, and driver as interdependent entities. The driver and the habitat have intrinsic moral worth. All four entities have extrinsic moral worth insofar as they affect the worthy entities and the unworthy ones. Figure 6.1 illustrates the ways that objects mediate between different valued entities.

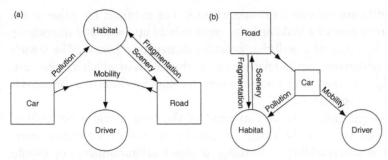

Figure 6.1 Interdependent Sources of Value

In this example, both the habitat and the driver are morally significant, but I excluded the direct impact that they might have on each
other to simplify the figure. This excludes the possibility that the driver
actually values the habitat or that the habitat directly benefits from the
driver taking care of it. I focus on the way that the relevant objects
affect these morally significant entities. In Part A of the figure, both the
habitat and the driver hold equal significance. It would be difficult to
surmise from this layout whether the habitat's interests or the driver's
should be given primacy. In Part B of the figure, the road is placed into
a focal position. We see that the habitat improves the road by providing
scenery, but the road makes the habitat more fragmented. We see that
the road gives the driver mobility, provided the driver has use of a car,
but the car pollutes the habitat. The tradeoff remains between the
driver's mobility and the habitat's cohesiveness (nonfragmentation).
By focusing on the road, we identify the driver and the habitat as two
different ends-in-view, and we can surmise the road's consequences for
these entities. This specification has not avoided the tradeoff between
roads and habitats, but this tradeoff is realized in the end of the analysis
rather than at the beginning. This is important because, as I have
argued, the attentional processes of the analysis promise to change
the evaluative dimension that appraises the relative importance of the
person and habitat.

Rather than maximizing the utility of a choice or act, ecological use
value maximizes the usefulness of an object amidst a field of proximate
objects. These interactions are always the evaluative key to appreciating nonhuman systems and the nonbiological objects upon which they
depend. A stone has no value other than the value it provides to persons

and biological entities connected to it. For example, the value of the cornerstone of a building is foremost to hold up a wall and secondarily to be a part of a wall that provides shelter for a person. The stone's value derives from its relationships to the whole, of which it is one part. Likewise, the road's value to a person comes by virtue of a car providing transportation.

Object utilitarianism may produce the same result as act utilitarianism, particularly if both are equally attuned to the human interest in sustainability. According to object utilitarianism, one should not remove a cornerstone from a valued building because doing so would reduce the building's capacity to provide benefits to its users. An act utilitarian would also evaluate the act of removing the cornerstone as utility-reducing and determine that the act is wrong. A rule utilitarian might establish a standard of conduct, for instance, "do not damage other people's things," and reach a similar conclusion. The difference is between act and rule utilitarianism, which put the proximate decision maker at the center of the dilemma, and object utilitarianism, which focuses on the way that a thing is created, treated, cared for, or used. These perspectives differ, but the moral is the same. More significant disagreements result when variants of utilitarianism are applied to ecological objects. Insofar as an object is undervalued by an anthropocentric utilitarianism, object utilitarianism can recognize its full biophysical value. In other cases, the results are more likely to converge.

The significant contrast concerns the allocation of responsibility, and this is the reason why object utilitarianism applies so capably to business ethics problems. Within an object-centered utilitarianism, responsibilities follow objects, whatever the path of their geographic, economic, and ecological histories. Even if act and rule utilitarianisms would reach the same conclusions about a desirable end state, these approaches locate dilemmas differently, and they are made feasible through different simplifications. Though it is possible for an act utilitarian to conceive of the choice between chocolate, vanilla, and strawberry ice cream as a calculation of the supply chain responsibilities of all three products, such a conception is more likely to fatigue than to empower a moral calculus. Object utilitarianism necessarily focuses a moral calculus on these considerations so that a person cannot properly value a thing without tracking the value of connected persons and objects.

Returning to the discussion of Figure 6.1, utilitarianism would tend to place the driver at the center of the case for building roads, as the chief beneficiary. However, focusing on the road shifts the driver into a position that balances her interests with the interests of the habitat, making it clear that their interests compete. Environmental impact assessments in construction projects accomplish this shift in focus, and a new generation of transport users are questioning the preeminence of cars, roads, and drivers in America. Object-focused utilitarianism goes one step further, suggesting not only that these consequences are important, but that the people who are most connected to them, the road builders and the drivers, are most responsible for taking care of the diverse entities that they put at risk. To make a utilitarian decision, we must still choose between the good of the habitat and the good of the driver, but ecological use value gives us a conceptual toolkit to make such choices. For example, we might ask whether the road will help the driver to make a more positive impact on other environmental resources than existing infrastructure, or whether the development is entirely negative from an environmental perspective. The goal is still to make things useful, but in this case, I seek to recognize the ways in which ecosystems are useful on their own. Doing so introduces a substantive hurdle to habitat destruction and encourages decision makers to re-examine the entities that they assume to be morally irrelevant.

The Utility of Utility

I have emphasized usefulness as the key evaluative concept, but I have not defended the importance of objects being useful to persons or to each other. Convinced utilitarians might justify a use-oriented view of object stewardship in terms of preference satisfaction: maximizing the use value of objects contributes to total utility. From this view, object utilitarianism might join act utilitarianism, and rule utilitarianism, as a level of abstraction at which utility is maximized.

There is some debate among utilitarians about the worthiness of different preferences. As John Stewart Mill describes, not all preferences are created equal. According to Mill, some preferences are baser than others. Pleasure, the end sought by hedonistic philosophers, is accorded a lower value than the satisfaction of learning. Whether these orders of worth are expressed in the law is a

somewhat different question. The liberal view of the legal apparatus, which is largely maintained here, suggests that self-harming
actions should be regulated with great care, if at all. As Lysander
Spooner wrote, "Vices are not crimes."[36] This does not mean that
vices are not bad, but their badness need not be illegal. At the same
time, acting in a way that is harmful to others is not merely a vice.
The law's express purpose is to punish these sorts of acts to help to
maintain the norms of a community.

   Object utilitarianism can easily account for both of these aspects of
human preferences in valuing objects connected to persons. It can
devalue those objects that are used to harm others without violating
the liberal strictures on the law's scope. Likewise, object utilitarianism
can be set up to distinguish between multiple uses for an object, some
of which satisfy higher preferences than others. A book can be read
for knowledge or burned for heat. Object utilitarianism, following
Mill, would say that knowledge is a higher use than heat. In the same
vein, paint can be used to make art or huffed to produce a psycho-
pharmacological effect. The artistic use of paint is a higher use
because the pleasure it provides is elevated and comes without
physical health risks.

Object Nonconsequentialism

Utilitarianism aims to maximize benefit and minimize harm. Object-
focused utilitarianism tries to make objects more beneficial and less
harmful for aggregate social welfare. The question to which I now turn
is whether objects can also be used to guide the application of deontic
(duty- and rights-based) principles. Critics argue that utilitarians
would wrong people in service of the common good, that a utility-
maximizing logic justifies disrespecting human dignity in the name of
aggregate welfare. I believe that their criticisms are often overstated.
The substantive differences between rights and welfare discourses are
exaggerated by stylized examples which fail to reflect practical con-
vergences. I believe, as did J. S. Mill, that general welfare is improved by
defending individuals' rights.

   But this is not the question at hand. Here, we need to decide whether
objects can guide a deontological ethic as I have shown that they
can guide a consequentialist ethic. I wish to suggest that objects are a
plausible locus of deontological responsibility and that consequentialist

and deontological ethics can be hybridized in object-focused ethics as easily as these can be hybridized anywhere else.

Let us consider two different nonconsequentialist approaches to ethics: virtue ethics and deontology based on human dignity. As they are usually taught, neither theory affords a significant role to material things. Virtue ethics is concerned with individual choices and community contexts that simultaneously produce responsibility as a form of excellence and happiness as a positive benefit of this responsibility. While the rewards of excellence are often remunerated through objects, the objects themselves do not have significance for the theory. Likewise, a rights-based approach concerns itself with showing respect to morally worthy entities. Since material things are excluded from the start, the usual sort of human rights argument has little or nothing to say about the role that objects play.

Nevertheless, object stewardship is as compatible with virtue- and rights-based approaches as it is with utilitarianism. The trick is to use objects to direct the kinds of moral concern that these theories view as important. I will not say that we should try to make objects virtuous, but that we should try to enhance the role that objects play in people's ability to live a virtuous or dignified life. Accordingly, in its object application, virtue ethics focuses on how certain ways of using objects will help or hinder a person's realization of her full potential, her excellence. Virtue ethics, like utilitarianism, relies on a theory of consequences, but it does so through a much more expansive conception of a person's ends. Though Mill attempts to discern and prioritize these ends, it is virtue ethics that takes substantive human well-being as its main object. Virtue is the union of what is good for a human being and what is good about being human. Virtue ethicists believe that doing the right thing contributes to human happiness; they deny the conflict between ethics and expedience.

Object stewardship is no less consistent with virtue ethics than with utilitarianism. In both theories, an object-centered perspective must somehow prioritize the morally substantive preferences of persons, but for virtue ethicists, these preferences are not merely wishes and desires; they are active strategies pursuant of goals within specific contexts. I will discuss these contexts as an aspect of virtue ethics in greater detail in Chapter 7. Here, it is enough to show that a person can flourish or flounder according to the way that she uses objects.

A key distinction between virtue ethics and deontology concerns moral motivations. In virtue ethics, doing the right thing helps a person to thrive, whereas in deontological ethics, doing the right thing helps a person to be free and to live a rationally consistent life. Suppose that a pregnant woman is trying to decide whether to have a glass of wine. Her doctor, whom she trusts, indicated that no amount of alcohol consumption is proven to be safe for a fetus.

If she is a virtue ethicist, she might frame the question as a matter of role-specific conduct. Virtue ethics often locates practical knowledge within social and occupational roles. The great majority of American women do not drink during pregnancy, and insofar as this woman believes her doctor's advice that alcohol consumption can forestall fetal development, she may view a glass of wine as inconsistent with her role as a pregnant woman.

She will likely reach a similar conclusion if she is a deontologist, but here she will be interested in the question of whether the fetus is a rights-bearing entity. If it is, then this will direct her inquiry. One formulation of deontological ethics considers whether everyone could act according to a given principle, a variant of the Golden Rule: Do unto others as you would have them do unto you.[37] If "you" is inclusive of a human fetus prior to birth, and if the mother believes the fetus has an interest in development that is hindered by alcohol, then she will conclude that drinking alcohol is not responsible. In a sense, whether as a deontologist or as a virtue ethicist, the woman is going to worry about consequences for the fetus, but neither approach is focused on consequences in general.

It is not difficult to reformulate these concerns in object terms. In fact, it makes sense to do so. The wine is the instrumentality of concern because there is considerable evidence that the consumption of alcohol is harmful to fetal development. Accordingly, many countries require alcohol to be labeled with text or pictures discouraging alcohol consumption during pregnancy. These labels show how ethics is encoded in objects, not just virtuous social roles or responsible decisions. Nevertheless, there is a problem with this example if it is applied to the general framework of supply chain responsibility proposed in this text. For a variety of reasons, there are considerable controversies about whether it is appropriate for businesses to refuse to sell alcohol to pregnant women. These controversies relate to the politics of abortion, the threat of paternalism, and the notion of consumer sovereignty.

While I presented the example of alcohol consumption by pregnant women as a choice that a pregnant woman will herself make, the analysis becomes more complicated when a third party is passing judgment. I will not resolve these controversies here, but I will say that the example illustrates how nonconsequentialist moral theories can be applied with an object focus, and how these same theories are likely to have something to say not just about how objects should be used, but about who should be involved in encouraging people to use objects responsibly.

To be sure, nonconsequentialists can judge rights-violating object uses as wrong irrespective of aggregate outcomes. For example, if police use military vehicles and armor to repress public dissent, this constitutes misuse without reference to aggregate welfare. Even if there is some utility in the social control that police exert, a deontologist would not weigh these factors against each other. This refusal to allow benefits to justify wrongs complicates an important class of nonconsequentialist object care questions.

I see few issues with the application of either virtue- or fairness-based approaches using objects. There are many applicable concerns that can be drawn upon in thinking about how objects are used. However, one area that raises some concerns will require additional discussion. The most significant test of object nonconsequentialism is the recognition of waste. Whether a given use is wasteful is a decisive judgment. Utilitarians recognize waste as a form of inefficient use, but deontologists also purport to be capable of judging wastefulness. Donaldson and Dunfee,[38] for instance, describe an "efficiency hypernorm." In their view, waste is not only ugly, it is wrong.

Amidst rising public awareness of fossil fuel emissions and global climate change, the firms that produce and store fossil fuel resources are increasingly aware of the wasteful releases that happen before fuels reach consumers. For example, a 2015 leak from a California storage facility is believed to have allowed 100,000 tons of methane into the atmosphere. By weight, methane's global climate change impact is much more significant than carbon dioxide's, and the 2015 release was the worst in US history for climate change impact.[39] In terms of object stewardship, the ethical and regulatory failure is discernible through the inattention to these facilities and their risks and through the underinvestment in technologies that would capture emissions.

Because methane is so much worse than carbon dioxide, it is common practice to ignite methane emissions from oil fields using massive flare towers that burn constantly. Only recently have companies begun to invest in the technologies necessary to capture these releases. Once captured, companies can dehydrate, purify, and sell methane.[40] They need not burn it. The difference between object misuse and object waste depends upon the possibility of an alternative use. Because a technology exists to capture methane, the fact that it is not being captured can be described as wasteful.

Methane emissions illustrate the bright line distinction between consequentialism and nonconsequentialism. In a world that is trying to burn fewer things, flare towers seem to be an observably inefficient misuse of precious resources. A nonconsequentialist might reach this conclusion without knowing the cost of cleaning up an oil field's emissions profile, but she cannot easily weight these costs or decide whether the rights that concern her are worth the cost of enforcement. On the other hand, a consequentialist would want to know whether the resources required to collect and purify methane emissions could have a more positive impact when applied elsewhere.

Thus, nonconsequentialists are less capable of evaluating tradeoffs and making prudential resource allocations. However, they can still have a theory of waste. A nonconsequentialist appraisal of waste can work from an efficiency norm, but it might just as well build on an aesthetic that finds ugliness in waste and beauty in efficient use. There is something wondrous, fitting, and good about an object being used by an entity that uses it in a special way. One might find intrinsic satisfaction observing an otter fishing in a stream, a child playing with a toy, or a craftsperson using a tool skillfully. The aesthetic value is demonstrated further by the obverse cases in which a thing of value is wasted, marred, or destroyed. There is something corrupt and ugly about a sea bird dying in an oil spill, a child with too many toys, or a business that wastes employee time on needless bureaucratic processes. In pragmatic terms, one's reactions to waste is as likely to be aesthetic as it is principled. The ugliness of waste provides an important justification for stewardship.

The Ethics of Waste

This section illustrates the importance of an object focus in realizing the damage that we do to complex systems. Judgments of wastefulness are among the most frequent applications of object-focused ethics. These judgements present interesting challenges because of the subjectivity of perceptions of waste. I will focus on the forms of waste that are by-products of an economy that fails to value objects. The near-extinction of the American bison is one example:

After the slaughter of the southern herds during the [eighteen] seventies, thousands of buffalo hunters and skinners came, some of them from as far as Texas, to the upper Missouri and the Yellowstone. These profes-sional hunters made a serious business of killing the bison for robes and hides. The Indians are said to have discontinued the slaughter of the buffalo as soon as the lust and pleasure of the chase had disappeared. The whites, being in the business for profit alone, had no such motive to cause them to desist from the hunt. Until the whites made buffalo hunting a profession, the great herds of the upper Missouri seemingly remained intact.[41]

Native Americans used most parts of the bison they killed, respecting the animals as a revered part of their cultural heritage and economic life. In contrast, European hunters took the animals for sport and pelts, leaving the carcasses to rot on the prairie. Their waste was an act far uglier than the complete use of a natural object, and it nearly resulted in the extinction of a herd of millions of animals. Bison served an impor-tant ecological purpose on the prairie as well. By spreading nutrients and seeds, they served a function that domesticated animals cannot match.

The example illustrates a spectrum between use and overuse, but it does not resolve an implicit aesthetic tension. When Alexis de Tocqueville visited America in the nineteenth century, he waxed lyrical about the beauty of the industry in Ohio and the ugliness of the wasted land in Kentucky.[42] He blamed slavery for the difference between the two: slavery stigmatized work, whereas freedom encouraged it. Kentucky enslaved men and let nature run wild, whereas Ohio enslaved nature and (almost) all men were free. To the nineteenth-century anthropologist, Ohio's industriousness was beautiful. Yet this same industriousness almost completely extirpated the indigenous flora and fauna.[43] Thus, while waste may be ugly, we must be very careful about the ways in which we conceive of efficient use. If we measure it by the success of agriculture in scouring the land clean, then we deny the value that native plants provide to each other. The native tallgrass prairies of this region, like the bison that inhabited them, were visible casualties of an unjustifiably narrow conception of value.

There is also a subjective element to the waste/efficient use distinction. I have given relatively obvious examples of waste, but not all examples are so categorically simple. Numerous rock bands have smashed instruments, burned pianos, and destroyed drums as expressive acts. Doing so would seem to violate the ecological use value of these objects, but this depends on the worth of the expressive act. Man Ray's famous work *Object to Be Destroyed* is an even more confusing example. Created in 1923, the work was a metronome with an affixed cutout of a woman's eye from a photograph. In 1957, a group of young artists smashed it.[44] Some expressive works are even meant to destroy other things. Jorn and Debord's *Mémoires* was bound in sandpaper so that it would destroy the books shelved next to it.[45] This destructive element is thematic for Debord, who writes in the final lines of the 1992 preface to *The Society of the Spectacle*, "This book should be read bearing in mind that it was written with the deliberate intention of doing harm to spectacular society."[46]

Moral philosopher Bernard Williams argues against a moral system that proscribes one's own projects, which he suggests are often worthy pursuits even if a strict moral doctrine makes demands that would distract us from them. It is possible, if exceptional, for waste to be such an expressive act. Indeed, it is possible, as Debord suggests, that some social arrangements need to be destroyed.

Object Stewardship as Recursive Teleology

At this point, all ways of treating objects are on the table. We can care for things or destroy them, leave them where they are or process them and bring them to market for sale. I believe that with the help of dominant consequentialist and non-consequentialist approaches to ethics, an ecological formulation of object value can provide important insights into which of these object treatments is most defensible, praiseworthy, or good. In a sense, this evaluative judgment is teleological. It decides what a thing is or ought to be for. But judgments of this sort are only reliable and defensible within the adaptive management framework described above. To explain why this is the case, I will introduce the concept of recursive teleology and defend it as a plausible basis for stewardship.

Table 6.1 *The Components of a Teleological Sentence*

I walk to the park	Action
Because	Explanatory operator
I believe walking makes me healthier	Causal expectation
And I value health	Evaluative statement

In Greek, a *telos* is an end or purpose; teleology is the study of these ends. Despite an emphasis on objects' propensities to be used by certain entities for certain purposes, object stewardship cannot be fully formed from teleological insights. Instead, I take objects' purposes to be emergent, pluralistic, and adaptive properties that are only observable and defensible in the context of thriving ecological and social systems. Accordingly, our task is to use objects in ways that help these systems to thrive. What is meant by thriving may emerge from a description of the related entities or from traditional ethical considerations like respect for human dignity. Stewardship is not a substitute for moral theorizing, but instead a way to connect moral theories with everyday activities.

As stewards, dignity-respecting persons can work together to enhance the objects in their economy by adding layers of meaning. A narrow teleological description of coffee defines its purpose as delivering a stimulant with a pleasant taste. Fair-trade coffee enhances this telos with an additional purpose: the coffee should help its purchasers to treat distant agricultural workers with dignity. The challenge is to decide what purposes objects ought to have. Traditional approaches to teleology are not helpful in meeting this challenge.

Andrew Woodfield summarizes his study of teleology with this generalization: "the essence of teleology lies in welding a causal element and an evaluative element to yield an explanatory device."[47] This has to do primarily with goal-seeking or purposive action. Consider the parts of the sentence, "I walk to the park because I believe walking makes me healthier and I value health."

This sentence explains walking. It does so through a causal claim that walking results in a favored purpose (health). In this way, the sentence gives walking an end or telos. From the perspective of object stewardship, this sentence obfuscates its main subject, the human body.

The purpose of the walk is concrete in the form of a healthy body, yet the body goes unmentioned. Teleology often has this characteristic. It is chiefly concerned with describing purposive action, and as a result, it can lose sight of either the actor or the objects of purpose. In Woodfield's analysis, teleology is the study of particular kinds of purposive claims found in language. These claims need to be teased apart philosophically because in ordinary language speakers often drop intentional operators. For example, a patriot might say "America is great" without having to say "I think America is great" or "many people agree that America is great." When we leave out the actors from these statements, we deny their subjectivity.

Object stewardship requires us to develop a different formulation of teleology. In contrast to Woodfield's teleological descriptions, we need teleological prescriptions to decide how things ought to be used. These prescriptions are not easily observed in Woodfield's linguistic analysis, which cannot answer the normative challenge of making teleological prescriptions right, good, or true. Still, assessing ecological value requires us to come to terms with many teleological statements that link causal claims with evaluative statements.

I use numerous teleological descriptions within my prescriptions. I make inferences based on causal relations between things and evaluative elements. For instance, planting more trees will mitigate climate change, and climate change mitigation will cause fewer people to starve, which is good. According to Woodfield, this is a teleological description. Teleological descriptions like this one are an input for decisions that one needs to make about how best to use things. In the example of climate change mitigation, the object of care is once again obscured by the teleological description. In making this teleological statement, I am actually interested in how best to use a piece of land, which can be planted with trees or developed for some other purpose.

As I have described using both Dewey's pragmatism and the concept of adaptive management, teleological descriptions need to evolve. In time, we can find new outcomes to value and we can understand new causal processes. Consequently, we need to revise our teleological statements to reflect new priorities and new ways to pursue them. It follows that object stewardship must be built upon a recursive form of teleology that treats purposes and causal processes as moving targets.

The next question to answer is whether this recursive teleology is subject to the main criticisms leveled against other teleological theories. I can answer this by expressing certain features of the object stewardship approach. First, I do not look to nature to determine fixed teleological purposes for things. Second, I am not hiding moral agency or distributing moral responsibility to entities that are incapable of purposive action. And third, I am not acting as if causality and outcomes can always be certain. Object stewardship operates in a probabilistic reality where stewards focus on taking care of the things for which they are most responsible in a way that accomplishes the worthiest goals. It does sometimes derive purposes from things, especially living systems worthy of moral regard, but more often it ascribes purposes to things as moral agents come to better appreciate the contributions that they can make to a valued outcome.

The Ethics of (Dis)entanglement

Reflecting on things through our relationships to them and their relationships to each other yields two key ethical insights that run in opposite directions. I have advocated an object-focused delineation of responsibility. We should embrace the responsibility that comes with the material things that we use, buy, and sell. We should direct moral attention with the flow of these resources. This is an ethic of entanglement.

But we may find that the objects overwhelm our plans and purposes. Caring for them may eventually keep us from caring for ourselves, for other people, and for the natural environment. Think again of Carl from Pixar's *Up*, whose burden of material attachments requires him to drag his entire house around behind him. Material entanglements can be burdensome, and sometimes they need to be escaped rather than engaged.

Hodder describes the process of disentanglement as an untying of things, one that is sometimes catalyzed by historical events.[48] In time, some attachments are lost and others gained. The depletion of resources, the relocation of residences, changes in technology, and shifts in demographics can all transform the way that people use things. As these changes occur, some things become more tightly integrated into a culture's practices and processes and others less.

To describe the knotting, unknotting, weaving, and severing of a culture's material entanglements in these broad historical terms suggests that many forces of entanglement are beyond the control of individual and collective judgments. Some are. It is difficult for a suburban community to disentangle itself from its cars, its big box stores, and the accumulated weight of the things that are deemed necessary for an ordinary household, to say nothing of the massive scope of the electrical, nutritional, and economic webs in which these households are entangled.

Regardless of these limitations on the rate of change, there is room for innovation in the way that cities are structured, in the way that households are organized, and in the way that businesses seek to serve them. The movement towards small-scale apartments in the United States is an instructive example. Often, city housing codes stipulate a minimum footprint for households and zoning commissions look unfavorably on too much density. Communities often dislike dense housing because they worry that additional people will bring more cars, which have a significant footprint in finite resources like parking. However, if small-scale households disentangle themselves from cars by swearing off car ownership, these concerns are alleviated. Instead, bicycles, public transportation, and car-sharing programs become essential aspects of everyday life. To live in a small apartment, households cannot afford to collect too many material things. More care is taken in multifunctionality and in limiting resource use. As a consequence, small households are more likely to make justifiable investments in resources than sprawling households. A desk that serves also as a table is more justifiable in the resources that it uses than a desk that is just a desk, particularly if it is used intensively. The example is instructive because it highlights the diversity of innovations that are required to disentangle problematic object dependencies. Disentanglement is possible, but often laborious.

An object focus does not make the effort easier, but it makes it more directed. It focuses attention on those material entanglements that have the most deleterious effects and those that create the least value. Indeed, it is hard to imagine how we can begin the project of questioning the social and ecological impact of our business practices without first tracking the material associations that we have within our societies and the entanglements that sustain them.

The question that we now face is whether we can establish new entanglements that are positive while dismantling entanglements that are not. This text gives numerous examples of things that connect with harmful practices at different stages of production, distribution, and disposal. Acknowledging that consumers and purchasers are also authors of these acts is one of the primary implications of the object focus and the singularization of resources. Sometimes working with these resources will require greater engagement. At other times, the total impact of resources may discourage us from consuming them at all. We may find that there are other ways to pursue our interests, ways that do not have the same impact. In this case, both entanglement and disentanglement, engagement and disengagement, appear available to us as meaningful options that must be kept open.

In endorsing a materialist view of this sort, there is a risk that we also endorse a new form of commodity fetishism and lose sight of individual projects. Life is and ought to be more inspired than a grand and entangled quest for more and better things. The moral inquiry into things leads away from rather than towards vacuous materialism. Indeed, a new materialism may recommend a new minimalism, an eventuality that seems more morally manageable than an endless accumulation of ethical duties through endless material attachments.

Overcoming the Limits of the Market and the State

Chapter 4 argued that markets and states are failing at inequality, climate change, and the regulation of the financial system. These failures helped to explain why conscientious consumers seek to directly intervene into the way that corporations provide products and services. These interventions may not be successful. Today's conscientious consumption may be a dead end and a marketing ploy. Issues with labeling, described in Chapter 1, raise concerns about the social procedure by which conscientious consumers make decisions. Nevertheless, we might still ask whether a pure form of object singularization would overcome important social issues. The main contribution of this application will be to show how an ethic of ecological use value speaks to all three social problems described above.

Inequality

As a matter of principle, the stewardship of objects and the holistic promotion of their ecological value passes no judgment on whether some people have more than others. Instead, an object focus directs burdens towards more privileged people in managing their property and in acknowledging the needs of others to whom they are connected. These paths of responsibility work against inequality by prioritizing the best use of a thing.

The relevant considerations mirror the utilitarian critique of inequality. Utilitarians worry that inequality places resources in the hands of those to whom they are less meaningful. An additional dollar of income has little meaning to a person whose compensation package provides tens of millions of dollars per year, whereas that dollar could double the daily earnings of the world's poorest people. Directing food, education, healthcare, and other resources to the upper echelon of society produces less utility than it would if these resources were shared. Object stewardship reaches a similar conclusion, but it does so by considering how a resource benefits people and the biophysical environment.

Still, some forms of inequality seem inevitable. New technologies create inequalities between those who have and those who do not. Some people have talents that make resources more productive for them than they would be for others. Some people live in places where they can drown in drinkable water; others live in deserts. If the random uneven distribution of resources was all that there is to inequality, there would be no reason to speak of it within a critique of the regulated economy. However, there is more. The real problems with inequality are structural, intergenerational, coercive, and distortionary. It is not inequality itself that creates significant social problems, but the processes that make inequality official, permanent, and embodied. Entrenched inequality creates a sense of hopelessness for those who might otherwise exceed the limits of their social positions and a sense of entitlement for those who might otherwise be driven to accomplish more.

Ecological use value does not demand total equality or directly control the allocation of resources. It places no direct judgments on who owns what. However, it cuts across some of the mechanisms by which inequality persists, undermining the callousness that ignores the suffering of distant persons who face poverty and demanding more care from those who do not. When we focus on objects and the people to whom they are connected, we see incongruities. We see sharp inequalities between producers and consumers of the same objects. One way to value material things according to their ecological uses is to apply a utilitarian criterion. Through object stewardship, we can become more aware of the low-cost opportunities to act in the interest of the most vulnerable supply chain participants and we can become more critical of the opulence enjoyed by other supply chain participants, seemingly at the expense of the poor. These inequalities are important from a utilitarian perspective because they demonstrate that there are resources available to intervene.

Ecological use value addresses inequality by passing judgment on elite expenditures and by seeking the most constructive use for objects. Many elite status symbols use resources lavishly. For example, the Kremlin armory in Moscow displays a gold platter that weighs more than six kilograms. As discussed in Chapter 1, gold is both rare and useful. The Kremlin maintains the platter as a display of wealth and state power, but the material could otherwise be useful in science and medicine. Given the treatment of gold miners and the impact of mining on local water quality, it is likely that the use of gold in this platter would be unjustifiable. In contrast, singularity value would give no grounds to criticize status symbols wrought from renewable resources by artists who are permitted free exercise of their talents and rewarded for their labor.[49]

While these expenditures do not cause any ecological harm, an ethic of stewardship might also raise questions about status consumption in terms of the communities where it occurs. As long as exclusive status orders are reinforced through the acquisition of things, ecological use value may judge these expenditures critically. It is one thing for a person to use resources for a house, a roof, a bed, and perhaps even an extra bed. But what about an extra house or multiple extra houses? Putting these expenditures into a critical comparative context where they are weighed against the use of the resources in their undisturbed origins provides a weighty counter to overconsumption. If a large house or yacht is less useful than the undisturbed origins of the resources necessary to produce it, that expenditure is unjustifiable.

Ecological value also finds fault with underprovision. There are many objects that are extremely useful to their final consumers and to the companies that sell them, but that produce much less value for the people who create them. Once we treat these objects as singularities and question their impact, we expect them to be constructive for all the people that participate in supplying them, preferably in ways that fairly allocate the value created. In this way, recognizing objects' origins helps to also recognize the needs of the worst off and to become connected to these needs. I take these two processes of constraining elites and empowering poor people to be characteristic of the response that objects provide to the problem of inequality.

Even so, a final caveat is warranted by the nature of this focused provision because it does not include everyone. If people are poor because they remain isolated from the global economy, their needs are beyond the scope of this argument. Ecological use value would appreciate the use of resources and land that indigenous people depend upon for their traditional agricultural systems and it would seek to protect such uses, but until the global economy intrudes upon such a culture, there is no mechanism by which it seeks them out. While an entirely cosmopolitan approach to ethics would treat this boundary as a defect in the moral theory, it may be an asset. Some groups decide to limit their engagement with the global economy for a variety of reasons. Others lack the infrastructure to participate readily. The cause of development seeks modernization, inclusion, and specialization, often without recognizing that local cultures already provide for their members in substantial and meaningful ways. Ecological use value avoids passing judgment on the well-being of cultures that are not trying to participate in the global economy, and by doing so it allows such cultures to define their own normative systems. I take this to be an asset rather than a liability.

Climate Change

Object singularization and ecological use value also provide responses to the problem of climate change. Indeed, as I argued in the introduction, concern over climate change is arguably the most significant locus of singularizing narratives in contemporary discourse. The discussion of a person's carbon footprint is a characteristic example.

A carbon footprint is a measure of the direct and indirect impact of an individual's consumption on the release of atmospheric carbon dioxide, one of the gases that plays an important role in climate change. Several websites provide calculators that estimate a person's carbon footprint by measuring the material consequences of his or her economic behavior. While these calculators do not know which gasoline is burned by which airplane on which trip, tracking average consequences is the next best thing to a truly singularized view of the consequences of economic action.

Object singularization and stewardship would discourage the use of carbon-intensive resources and encourage a more careful treatment of the biophysical environment. Where both regulators and markets have been slow to appreciate the moderation and constraint that climate change mitigation requires, ecological use value provides a direct measure in every object of value. This applies equally well to the energy intensity of metals, the benefits of responsible forestry practices, the way that we farm, and the way that we eat. If comprehensively adopted, an ethic of object stewardship would constantly track finite resources like the allowable threshold for atmospheric carbon, while also privileging local benefits that accrue from established and re-established ecosystems.

One of the dominant approaches to ecological responsibility focuses on cost-benefit models that value the well-being of future generations. The problem with these models, which is shared by the ethics of object stewardship, is their uncertainty.[50] It is difficult to predict future opportunities to solve today's problems and difficult to measure which constraints are therefore justifiable.[51] While object stewardship cannot provide perfect predictions or a panacea for uncertainty, it does encourage a kind of focused observation, perspective-taking, and experimentalism that can decrease uncertainty over time. By locating things within their social and biophysical relationships, we become open to connections that may have a significant impact. This is essentially the argument that climate scientists make when they claim that even though the climate is unpredictable, the sources of human impact are not.[52] Rather than imagining that objects are inert and that every use is acceptable, product distributors become interested in how their products are being used and what impact they have. There is a lot of hard work to be done before predictions become more reliable, but at least object stewardship motivates actors to notice the right variables.

Focusing on objects, knowing about them, and caring for their impact is at the heart of both ecological research and climate science. We may not know all of the relevant factors, but we know many of them. Object stewardship appreciates these concerns and encourages people to develop some expertise with respect to the materials that they use at work and in their daily lives. If we deploy our material expertise to care for others and for the planet, many of the risks of climate change will be averted.

Appreciating the importance of things requires us to recognize the ways that things influence each other and the ways that they influence persons. While our recognition of the relatedness of things is usually incomplete, it remains essential. Think of what we now understand about material objects. Things fit into other things; they interface in predictable ways within cycles of nutrients, energy, and information. This "fittingness"[53] can operate as a part-whole relationship within an "equipment totality."[54] In an organizational context, fittingness can operate within a behavioral chain, what Nelson and Winter describe as routines and their cues.[55] For example, when a database crashes and customer service staff are unable to help, the dependencies are linear and direct. However, objects are also entangled in complex processes with emergent properties that are not anticipated.

The story of the Stephens Island wren traces the extinction of the species to Tibbles, a lighthouse keeper's cat. Tibbles brought ten of the birds back to its master as gifts in the late nineteenth century.[56] The bird's fate is thus tied to the introduction of an invasive species, the domesticated cat, to an island where indigenous wildlife was not adapted to this new predator. Tracing the impact of our actions on living systems is not easy, but we know much more than we did in the nineteenth century. As nonlinear as object entanglements can be, it remains possible for us to make sense of the way that things fit together and to adjust our behavior so that the most important of these relationships is protected and the most harmful impacts avoided. Global climate change may be the most important example of how our relationships with the material world can and must be managed.

Finance

It is most difficult to apply stewardship to financial systems. Within finance, many objects are virtual and abstract and the value applied to them appears to be subjective. Nevertheless, there are ways in which one specific element of stewardship, the singularization of objects, could greatly benefit economic stability. Most financial firms are currently organized around abstractions in value. Rather than issuing loans, the largest banks buy thousands of loans together. They do so under the auspices of a specific vision of specialization and the distribution of risk.

Object stewardship denies this distribution of risk. It rejects the notion that the owner of an asset bears exclusive responsibility for the performance of that asset. Rather, it associates the entire chain of ownership with a joint responsibility for morally relevant conse-quences. In this way, it inspires financial insiders to take a closer look at the specific resources that they buy, sell, and trade.

Imagine how banks might have performed differently if, rather than viewing mortgage-backed securities as so many pieces of paper with an abstract value, the mortgages were viewed as concrete social relations materialized within contracts. If banks had reliably sampled their mortgages to detect fraud and to understand the conditions under which mortgages were being accepted, they would not have failed to notice a change in the financial situations for which loans were being issued and the prospects of households to perform on their terms. Viewing these economic assets as specific, tangible, and entangled objects might have averted the crisis or limited its impact.

Still, I mean to suggest a very modest contribution to this particular problem. The concept of singularization may apply to money as it has to other objects, but I have not explored this possibility here and many other issues will need to be addressed in order to do so. Moreover, in each of these three areas of concern, the impact of object stewardship depends on the creativity and intent with which it is applied. Those who would help others, understand their own impact, and try to govern the economy more reliably can do so and an object focus may help them to be more successful in their efforts. But understanding objects well may be used to the opposite effect.

Consider the way that terrorists chose the center of financial power as a target in the attacks on September 11, 2001. The World Trade Center was a conspicuous location, an iconic aspect of the New York skyline, and an important address for many businesses. Targeting New York's skyline created a visible scar that millions of people could see. The political impact of that incident will persist for decades, partially because the target was connected so widely to a human ecol-ogy with significant political power. Many times more people have died in terrorist incidents since, but none has had the scope of impact because of the social, political, and economic ecologies where the loss of life occurred.

Object stewardship provides a strategy for well-intentioned indivi-duals to encourage others to behave responsibly, but it cannot reform people's intentions. Its capacity to reach across entire supply chains is limited by the availability of information and the application of con-cern. I contend that financial elites have applied their attention poorly, failing to recognize important risks and thereby destabilizing the systems that they steward. I also contend that looking more closely at assets, not just in terms of the contractual obligations, but in terms of the people and places to which they connect, could help bankers to better mitigate some of these risks. How to inspire banks to shift their focus beyond their abstract bottom lines is beyond the scope of the present discussion.

7 | Putting Responsibility to Work

Moral responsibility is humanity's most distinctive energy. It flows from the compassion that we show to one another and from the principles that we use to determine how we wish to live. Like all forms of energy, moral responsibility's capacity to do work depends on the efficiency with which it is directed.

Some people channel all of their moral energy into caring for their intimate friends and family. Others look to institutions like the church, the firm, and the state to define their obligations. In many ways, these channels complement each other by dividing a person's recognized duties across different moral spheres. It is often possible to be a good citizen, parent, and employee even though these roles usually demand different actions. The roles reinforce a core moral identity which applies to moral choices across different settings.

However, doing the right thing requires more than role compliance, rule following, and a positive moral identity. When we allow our moral imaginations to be eclipsed by the unimaginative enterprise of doing what we are told to do or what we routinely do, authority and tradition siphon off the energy that might otherwise be dedicated to the vital task of discovering the responsibilities that our social positions have not allocated to anyone.

It is worth noting that many traditional moralities make special provisions for a society's outsiders. Judaism, Christianity, and Islam all share a notion that it is virtuous to be hospitable to strangers. Believers are taught that hospitality to strangers can bring them closer to angels or God.[1] These provisions for outsiders aim to overcome the limits of social closure.

When we give our social roles an exclusive mandate, we often put too much effort into tasks that do not require it. Caring partners become codependents and parents are transformed into tiger moms. We must not presume that existing institutions store, contain, and define our responsibilities. Adhering to prescribed roles is merely the first step in stumbling through a complex moral system in which there is work left to be done and nobody in particular is responsible for doing it. There are habitats to restore, working conditions to improve, emissions to reduce, species to track, products to make safer, and waste to reuse. How will we channel enough moral energy to accomplish these tasks?

Material things provide one option. The solution is imperfect. It requires us to learn more about the things that we use for work, and perhaps to try to reduce the material complexity of the things upon which we depend. But, once we begin to stretch out our moral responsibilities through material things, we discover a comprehensive, stable, and efficient directive for our moral energies. In lieu of the arcane grid of moral directives that we find in family, work, and state, things implicate everyone who participates in the global economy when moral energy flows through them. What is more, material responsibilities amass with material excess. The wealthiest people and those who consume the most are the ones with the greatest burden, which is as it should be.

The upside is this: if everyone would care for the objects with which they interact by taking an interest in these objects' consequences, every object in the economy would be subject to norms of stewardship. Object stewardship would lay down a pattern of personal responsibility that adequately governs the global economy. Civil society could hold firms and officials responsible for their object-specific accomplishments and failures on global and local scales.

Following the energy metaphor one step further suggests that the moral impulse often dissipates if not properly directed. Just as energy is lost as heat each time it changes form, moral regard can be squandered through social distance and attenuated action. As people become convinced that there is nothing that they can do to solve big problems, they resign themselves to a scale of morality that protects their moral identities from failure.

The risk of drawing down the moral energy too quickly is as great as the risk of its attenuation and dissipation. If people are directed to do too many things that they cannot do, some of their capacity to care is lost. Thus, a key feature of this "transmission" involves the provision of moral information and priorities to people whose actions can make a difference. In the right economy, every occupational role channels responsibility for the work's consequences. In the wrong economy, responsibility dissipates as "heat" with every transaction.

Aristotelian Business Ethics

The energy metaphor is not the usual way to talk about responsibility in business ethics, and at this stage of the book it is time to reintegrate the earlier discussions into the dominant business ethics discourses. In this chapter and the one that follows, I will trace some of these connections. The key element of the energy grid metaphor is its openness. Moral energy works across things towards diverse ends rather than being enclosed by a corporate body or a professional role. Objects provide scaffolding to establish connections with distant moral concerns. To understand why we need to seek out new scaffolding, it is worth observing the traditional institutional structures upon which closed moral systems depend.

Many business ethics scholars are inspired by Aristotle. Their devotion is ironic given the derision with which Aristotle described the businesspeople of his day: "The kind [of commerce] that has to do with exchange is justly disparaged, since it is not natural."[2] Apart from the household economy, Aristotle was decisive: profit and usury are perversions of practice. As MacIntyre notes, the tradition of Aristotelian "virtues is at variance with central features of the modern economic order."[3]

Nevertheless, while Aristotle's specific judgments may be inconsistent with the field of business ethics today, his way of judging has proven useful. Aristotle was keenly attuned to practice and experience as the processes by which virtues develop. This aspect of his thinking accounts for much of its appeal in business ethics scholarship. Not only does Aristotle show how professional activities are associated with their own virtues, but he conceives of these virtues within communities and shows how characteristics of the communities are reflected by individuals' virtuousness.

Modern philosophers have returned to Aristotle because his concept of ethics is characteristically different from the rule-oriented judgments found in recent deontological and teleological thought. In the 1950s, Anscombe challenged philosophical ethics for talking of obligations without a religious belief system that obliges.[4] To her, this language of rule following is a vestigial appendage of an earlier era when there was agreement on divine authority. In the decades since Anscombe began her work on intentionality, many philosophical pragmatists have worked from the premise that ethics is more about doing than it is deciding, and that developing positive moral habits may be more important than passing out-of-context judgments on whether certain actions are responsible. Pragmatists put practice before theory, and allow principles to be taken up and discarded in its service. Doing so makes it more difficult to develop an ethics of blame, but more honest in accounting for the everyday struggles that people experience in living with the choices they make.

The trouble with both pragmatism and virtue ethics is that neither defines a domain of moral achievement to which we can strive. In Aristotelian virtue, one does not strive to be virtuous; one seeks happiness and finds virtue along the way. To be sure, as Dewey argued above (see Chapter 5), one can find new objectives in practice. While that is significant for an ethic that builds on experience, it is not enough. Practice does not provide us with an external evaluative standard. Instead, pragmatism acts as if every worker, craftsperson, manager, and consumer is too caught up in what she is doing and how she is doing it to ask how the pieces fit together. I wish to argue that practical responsibility attaches to moral scaffolding, that is, to a structural notion of how society fits together and allocates responsibility. If we want to improve professional ethics, we need to improve the scaffolding.

Ethics for a Closed Society

Aristotle argues that people must play different roles within a society in order for the society to be just and efficient. Each different role has different virtues attached to it, but not all roles are created equal. The people who govern a society are involved in a practice that produces the highest virtues. As such, statesmen maintain rule by earning the favor of the citizens and they learn virtue in the process. Though Aristotle is no great advocate of democracy, he is equally opposed to tyranny, and suggests that just rule must strike a balance.

A key difference between Aristotle's conception of governance and the one I propose is that Aristotle emphasizes justice as a distinct role, whereas I propose that the demands of justice are diffused across social strata. Aristotle assigns the task of comprehending the constitution to a small class of individuals rather than distributing this function across the wider public.

If Aristotle is right that the only people who comprehend justice within a society are those who have experience in balancing the needs and competing interests of that community, then justice is the kind of virtue that only a few people will practice. It follows that the people who know justice best may not be businesspeople. This presents a significant problem for Aristotelian business ethics, but the problem can be stated even more generally. In an open society, most people do not have experience balancing competing interests, especially not the competing interests of those on the margins. As such, in Aristotelian terms, justice has few practitioners in modern life.

In Aristotle's epoch, the pieces of a community actually seemed to fit together. From the start of the second book of his *Politics*, Aristotle's polis is a unitary thing, a place-bound community that shares a single constitution among a common citizenry. He uses the imagery of the body and its organs. He discusses the importance of its size both in territorial and population terms, advocating moderation between too large and too small. "It is difficult, perhaps impossible, for an overly populated city-state to be well-governed …. For law is a kind of organization, and … an excessively large number of things cannot share in organization."[5] While Aristotle's city is small, it must be large enough to be self-sufficient, and also for agreement to be bounded within space. In *Ethics*, Aristotle argues that agreement is only significant when it occurs among people who are together within a physically bounded space.[6]

Modern life is messier. This book was written for a British press by an American living in Russia. Its story is no more cosmopolitan than many things we consume today. Aristotle knew the world was round, but he could not have imagined a technological system that would allow ideas and actions to circulate the world instantaneously, and he could not imagine the extent to which communities would cease to be small, autonomous, and spatially separated entities. Now that our actions reach so far beyond the communities that we inhabit, the interdependence that Aristotle's model relies upon is no longer realized. The fact that our actions reach so far afield is significant for ethics because the consequences do not always come back to us. Reach is an even more serious problem for business ethics because the consequences of managers' actions are especially unlikely to come back to them.

Consider how today's senior executives experience reality. Many businesses are isolated from global responsibility by complex supply chain networks, obscure ownership structures, joint ventures, securitization, and a maze of other boundaries that obfuscate rather than clarify who owes what to whom. Many people who make all of their money from oil go to work in clean white shirts and nicely pressed suits because their work holds materials at a distance. The gap between actions and consequences is personal as well. Many managers would have to look across both organizational boundaries and the divisions of geography, culture, and class to see the most serious consequences of the businesses they run. Because so much of our communication and action is mediated, managers' actions are not taking place within a community that looks anything like Aristotle's polis. Instead, managers interface with a divided public "who never are and never can be united in an actual situation or organization."[7] Worse yet, because careers involve moves between firms, if negative consequences are realized after a delay, the manager whose decisions caused those consequences may have moved on. If Aristotle is right that we only know virtue through the context that facilitates practical wisdom, both intellectual and moral, then he may also be right to denigrate business virtues, both in his time and in ours.

Beyond Cultural Closure

There are four plausible responses to the elitism and cultural closure that Aristotelian virtue seems to depend upon. First, Aristotle might be wrong about labor and the kinds of virtues that are found in different kinds of work. Justice may be more ubiquitous than he believes. Second, we might be able to make people see their responsibilities differently by changing the narrative about them. Third, because societies are now more flexible and overlapping, necessity may have spurred us all to take more seriously the demands of justice that we author in our own small ways. And fourth, perhaps Aristotle is right and managers are the new statesmen.

I begin with the first response. Aristotle assumes that a laborer will not appreciate the demands of justice because the laborer is not practiced in it, but perhaps justice is everywhere open for observation. Perhaps there are similarities across scale so that we can learn to understand justice at a wider scale by understanding what is just in a particular way. This is an un-Aristotelian way of thinking that resonates much more with the Platonic conception of society against which Aristotle seems to have been arguing. In this book, I have argued that looking closer at things can help us to recognize needs and values of people and natural systems. That claim certainly rests on the assumption that ethics is everywhere and that everyone is capable of discovering it if they will just pay attention. We may not comprehend the whole pattern of society, but if there are similarities across scale, then we can develop sensibilities from our own experiences that apply to the whole. Think, for instance, of John Ruskin's aesthetic arguments against rote artistic labor.[8] Ruskin believed that some things were more beautiful than others because their style reflects the way they were made. He finds art more beautiful that is made by artists who craft in a self-directed manner than art that is made to consistently replicate a fixed product. The former treats its creators as autonomous persons who can explore the patterns of life, whereas the latter treats them as machines.[9] This suggests a resonance between the artist and the art critic, as if they can understand one another without needing to do the same work. Nothing could be less Aristotelian than the view that everyday craft labor can help a person to understand justice. On the contrary, Aristotle wrote, "it is impossible to engage in virtuous pursuits while living the life of a vulgar craftsman or a hired laborer."[10] Indeed, Aristotle imagines that slaves are better off than the laboring classes because slaves have more contact with their betters. But virtue ethics has moved beyond Aristotle in many interesting ways, and definitions of virtue are now open to possibilities that Aristotle did not imagine. Alzola defines virtue as involving "higher-order desires and values, beliefs, framing capacities, emotions, and enduring patterns of behavior that have any bearing on moral matters."[11] Some experiences may be occupation-specific, but many others may cut across occupations in different ways. Alzola argues that we cannot allow situations to create the categories of virtue, because doing so would rob virtues of meaning and normative force.

The second possibility for moving beyond the situation-bound experiential impasse of narrow occupations with wide moral consequences is to change the way that we talk about ethics and occupational responsibility. Aristotelians like Solomon and pragmatists like Freeman look to narratives as a way of honing business conduct and highlighting business virtues. They believe that telling the right stories

about business, about the way that businesses thrive through cooperation and the good that business does in the world, can help us to
increase our expectations and aspirations for what businesses do. This
helps us to escape Aristotelian elitism in two ways: it creates a medium
through which managers can develop the empathy and system awareness that managing responsibly calls upon, and it involves people in
a reflective activity that goes beyond their usual practice. What we
experience is very often shaded by how we talk about our experiences
and what stories we tell about them. Telling the right stories may help us
to represent nobler virtues and to aspire towards them.

A third response would focus on the ahistorical application of
Aristotelian thought. Things are different now, and perhaps people
are now also different. Because societies are now more flexible and
overlapping, the task of crafting the state may actually be distributed
more than it was in Aristotle's time. Dewey describes the dynamic
process by which problems form publics. Though it is not usually
a countable noun, Dewey uses the plural form of "public" to represent
the overlapping and emergent communities that are defined by shared
concerns.

Institutions are solutions to prior problems that stuck around.
Whereas the fixity of a just order is a mainstay of Aristotelian political
thought, Dewey emphasizes flexibility, arguing that new problems are
not always adequately covered by prior ways of organizing political
action. Once we take the problems as dynamic and changing, we can
move beyond Aristotle. We can take some elements of his thought,
prioritizing practical experience for example, but also recognize the
importance of allowing new problems to dictate new ways of structur-
ing group responses to certain experiences. This is essentially the
response favored by the present argument, as you will see below.

The fourth response is to embrace Aristotle's elitism rather than
setting it aside. Perhaps senior managers actually have experience
that provides them with a wider view, and perhaps this experience
makes them more attuned to a wider set of interests than everyman.
As I write, this theory of government is being put to the test in the
Trump administration, but the preliminary evidence hardly reinforces
the elite wisdom hypothesis. At the very least, wealthy Americans seem
to be out of touch. Betsy DeVos, for example, is the first US secretary of
education to neither attend nor send her children to public schools.
Insofar as Aristotle's theory of elite justice involves experience, lacking

context seems to demonstrate how this theory is misapplied to today's governing elites. Brooke Harrington, a scholar who studies contemporary elite wealth and its management, has attempted to reconcile Trump's cabinet with a history of American elite leadership:

The problem with these prospective leaders is not their money. It's that they – like Trump – seem more interest in what their country can do for them than in what they can do for their country.[12]

Scholars sometimes try to justify excessive executive compensation by emphasizing the bewildering complexity of the modern firm. They argue that only a truly great person could comprehend this complexity. As a consequence, CEOs earn all-star wages. Countering this narrative are the facts that internal hires are often very successful as managers, that managers are often poorly informed if they do not figure out how to channel information through their subordinates and to partition managerial tasks, and that many managers do not actually have a wide range of experiences beyond discussions about financing, strategy, shareholder relations, etc. In any case, I see little appeal in a modern elitist account of justice and responsibility. To the greatest extent possible, my approach to ethics seeks to devolve responsibility away from elites so that all employees can participate in the governance of a sustainable and dignified economy.

Let the Problem Make the Public

Dewey's dynamic conception of problems is a fruitful line in helping us to regroup, to reorganize the way that Aristotle treats communities. It is important to note that there is more to moral thought than practical wisdom. There is also critique, aesthetic aspiration, and noble visions of how we might live. I want to bridge the gap between practical occupation-bound experience (which produces what Dewey would call ends-in-view) and the lofty aspirations of moral theories that entirely lack a model of implementation.

Often, these two ways of thinking about ethics fail to communicate. Practice accepts the purposive aims of a narrow cultural frame; universalistic ethical doctrine aims higher and gives grounds for criticizing the wrong objectives, but is often difficult to express across situations. The challenge is to connect aspirational values with the applied wisdom that comes from experience.

Aristotle did not face this problem because, for him, the problem had different boundaries. For Aristotle, the city-state provided all the scaffolding that virtue required. The city-state was a bounded locus of problems, and the virtuous were those who solved them. Fast forward two thousand years, and our problems have grown. Climate change dwarfs even the largest political community, if a modern state can even be said to function as a community in an Aristotelian sense. It is still virtuous to solve problems, but at the same time as global problems have grown, the problems that we are asked to solve in our professions have shrunk. Nobody is asked to destroy the environment as an occupational task. They are asked to develop a machine that cuts threads into casings to go into wells to drill oil that will be piped to a refinery, made into gasoline, and burned in a car. The end-in-view is so much smaller, even though the aggregate consequences loom larger than ever.

So then, how do we reconnect our highest aims with the everyday tasks of doing a job well? Aristotle suggests that we do not. Because purposes come from practice and from the problems in view, it is only the statesman and the rulers whose experience will elevate their excellence to this level.

Dewey makes a different argument. In *The Public and Its Problems*, Dewey develops a framework for thinking about institutions and social groups as emergent phenomena that arise to respond to persistent problems that they face together. While Aristotle leans on the bounded interdependence of a self-sufficient community as the unifying force of moral life, Dewey describes how publics form episodically around issues of common concern. In time, a given public may manage to found institutions that reinforce its power and help to solve subsequent problems more readily, but these developments may also become decoupled from the communities that got them moving.

Objects present problems that publics gather around, but this is not their distinguishing feature. Publics can also gather around causes, political parties, identities, and shared narratives. What is different about objects is that once they become a gathering point, they also provide the kind of moral scaffolding that the global economy requires. With objects, we can trace our connections and gather together as communities that are both interdependent and united in a common standard of virtue. Aristotle was right. The virtue of a forester is different from the virtue of an office administrator, because their concerns differ and so should the conduct to which they aspire. But they are tied together by the paper that the administrator buys, and they ought to share the common objective of ensuring that this paper is adequately stewarded.

Looking at objects is a way of changing the narrative about virtue and professional responsibility. It is a way of shifting old alliances and building new moral communities by associating problems with new publics. Once objects bring the missing moral scaffolding, we can deal with virtues without the narrow autarkic frame of a city-state. We can deal with communities that overlap and change, and problems that draw them together. And we can find happiness in the excellence of practice that reaches as widely as it must to do something well within the wider pattern.

The proposed argument for a new materialism in business ethics changes the way that communities are shaped, and by doing so, it aims to change business virtues. If businesses took the material consequences of their actions seriously, their employees would have new experiences that might inspire new virtues. Furthermore, if people challenge each other to behave better and challenge their firms to direct resources in ways that govern the firm's expansive material responsibilities, then over time there may be more room for an extended form of virtue like the one that I propose. What I advance, in this case, is a better directed form of care.

With this view in mind, let us revisit the question of how obligations adhere to objects. We will find, as did Aristotle, that responsibilities are more adequately ascribed within occupations than to the public at large, but I begin with conscientious consumers, the vanguard of object singularization. The remainder of this chapter picks up questions from Chapter 3 and Chapter 4 that we are now prepared to answer.

Conscientious Consumption

Being aware that inanimate objects affect at-risk persons and ecologies, conscientious consumers share an intuition that these connections are conduits of moral responsibility. Because our moral, legal, political, and economic systems are not organized in a way that affirms their intuition, conscientious consumers fight an uphill battle. It seems both impractical and incorrect for these idealists to believe that their consumption can channel responsibility. Acknowledging that conscientious consumers are often unable to accomplish their conscientious goals with the resources and choices open to them does not ward off the internal critique that these consumers often fail to do what they say they ought to do. It is true that many conscientious consumers obsess over the origins of their produce and coffee, yet they use mobile phones, computers, and countless other technologies of unknown provenance. Because they cannot fully manage the consequences of their purchases, it is concluded that their approach to responsibility is ill-conceived.

The problem with this inference is that it assumes a fixed technological base. It assumes that the way that the economy is organized and held accountable will always be as it is right now. But this assumption is indefensible. Technologies are already changing in the way that we track products and materials. These changes will facilitate a different mode of accountability in the future. Because moral technologies are not fixed, new moral capabilities will emerge. As difficult as it may be today to determine where a product was made and what were the human consequences of that production, these determinations are becoming less onerous. Supply chain traceability is rapidly increasing, and so is the traceability of currency. With these advancements and their extensions, conscientious consumers may one day be able to act consistently upon their singularizing intuitions.

And yet, as I have already shown, there are limits to consumers' capacity to make informed judgments about supply chains. While they clearly perform a governance function and are likely to continue doing so in the future, the onus is not on them to maintain responsible products. There are too many things in the economy and too many nuances for each thing. Final consumers cannot be the arbiters of supply chain responsibility any more than they can be the designers or logistical coordinators of the things that they buy.

I am skeptical about conscientious consumption. Because I presume that we lack systemic knowledge of how all parts of complex living systems and societies should work together, adaptive management is a necessary aspect of object stewardship. Conscientious consumers have a limited capacity to act and monitor within supply chains. Taking actions and monitoring the consequences are the two key aspects of adaptive management. As such, their conscientiousness eventually draws upon forms of knowledge that they cannot possibly possess, so we must turn to those who can know and do more. Conscientious consumers, in turn, have an obligation to pay a price premium over irresponsible products when justice is costly. While it is possible for us to limit consumers' information processing obligations, we cannot ensure adequate resource provision for responsible production without consumers' participation.

Professionals Prioritizing Things

If consumers are not capable of adaptive management, who is? Producers who work with things may not be able to understand the entire supply chain, but they can manage objects, societies, and living systems adaptively by tracking the consequences of their actions.

Recall the argument that brought us to this point: value is personal, social, relational, useful, and ecological. Value and attention are inextricably linked. Persons, places, and things belong together as objects of value. The ethic that focuses upon them is based upon a series of insights about objects and their value. By tracing objects between places and persons, the theory lays the foundations for an alternative social ethic that is at once material in its orientation, environmental in its sensitivity, and humanistic in its application.

From the microscopic premise of looking closely at objects, we can construct an ethic with a global scope, aiming at a more responsible human society, a healthier natural environment, and a more stable economic order. The result is a new approach to ethics and an alternative scheme for economics. Both fields converge on questions of what we value and how we value it.

The move towards materials is tactile, present, and concrete. It brings things into view that might have been here all along, but it puts them in a new light and by doing so personalizes a set of moral concerns that might otherwise be abstract. The power of this moral lens depends on where we focus it. We can get lost in the details of small, meaningless things, or we can focus on substantive concerns with things that hurt people and things that could help more if they were used differently. Because objects pervade our work lives, and because there is so much we can do about them and the way that they are handled in organizational contexts, the workplace is the right place to start.

To conclude this argument, I reprise the goals that moralizing objects accomplishes. The approach contributes to governance, norms, and responsibilities within complex social systems. Focusing on the local ethics of objects lays a foundation for market governance that neither corrupts nor is corrupted by the political system. I can merge the questions of how a person ought to behave and how a person ought to expect others to behave because we have a systemic account of how we allocate responsibilities. Managers, employees, and regulators can extract meaningful answers to the challenging moral dilemmas of business ethics by focusing on things. For example, Volkswagen can understand that it is both a car manufacturer and an emissions company, and find no contradiction in these roles. Having reached these conclusions, professionals must expand the way that they understand themselves. The process of stewardship often draws upon expertise, information, and awareness that consumers do not possess and are not likely to gain in the future.

In fact, object singularization is already well underway. We can see the signs of singularization on a Wrigley gum wrapper that contains a pictorial guide to gum consumption, as if the gum is telling its own story of how it wants to be used: put the gum in your mouth, then into the wrapper, then into a waste bin. We can see the singularization of technology in computer marketing, where components are advertised for their nontoxic ingredients, which are only relevant if one plans to eat the laptop or to take responsibility for its disposal long after purchase. We can find singularization in fair-trade coffee, chocolate, and gold. In a lifetime, one could not describe all of the small ways in which people already show concern for objects, their origins, and their disposal. The great majority of these examples go beyond the requirements of the law. Wrigley is not responsible for its customers littering, and many states have no requirements for computer recycling. Fair-trade labeling regimes cross jurisdictions much more easily than the extraterritorial reach of the law because their moral logic is not constrained by the reach of political authority.

Showing concern means valuing objects whether they are persons, places, or things. Persons are worthy of consideration, but not uniquely worthy. Things, alone and in sets, also warrant concern. The importance of a place may come from the community of persons who live there, from the ecology that thrives there, or both. Valuing people, things, and the biological capacity of places provides a comprehensive object value framework. Looking to the flow of resources through these ecologies charts a roadmap of responsibility.

At the center of this whole moral apparatus are the working professionals who choose to dedicate a part of their lives to a given commercial activity. It is these people who we entrust with the responsible care of our world's resources, because they have an opportunity to study the resources that they use carefully enough to know how to use them responsibly.

In the discussion of Aristotle's communitarianism above, I worried that virtues could not emerge or thrive in an ill-defined community where the roles are plastic and the consequences far-reaching. Objects provide an interesting solution to this problem by defining the boundaries of overlapping and interdependent communities in a suitably malleable and comprehensive way. As I will argue in Chapter 8, this solution allows us to sustain some of the key arguments being put forth today in business ethics research. For example, in a recent article, Kennedy, Kim, and Strudler argue that managerial hierarchies and respect for authority can be justified on Confucian grounds according to the performance afforded by the hierarchy. However:

To the extent that high-ranking individuals are committed to achieving these performances in a way that undermines one or more lower-ranking individuals' ability to live the good life, the authority of high-ranking individuals is inconsistent with the lower-ranking individuals' dignity.[13]

Their argument speaks to a deep and often overlooked question in management, namely, the question of why people should consent to be managed. They describe a harmoniousness that functional hierarchies can achieve, drawing analogies with orchestras as organizations that require collective submission to an ordering force.

Harmony is also an important aesthetic and practical principle for Aristotle. In his work, obedience to authority is conditional on a leader's conduct and the extent to which the leader is able to balance competing interests. In both of these communitarian conceptions, objectives are established and sustained by an internal standard of conduct, balance, and order. The resonance between the subordinate's justifiable reason for action and the purpose of the broader organization gives the subordinate a reason to follow. But these kinds of resonances are less observable and less consequential when they sound across organizational boundaries. Kennedy and coauthors argue that their model applies across organizational boundaries nonetheless, but only insofar as an external consideration is relevant to the reasons given by the community surrounding the organization and those who are directly subject to its managers' authority.

I argue for something much more radical: a reconfiguration of the conception of the organizational community in order to ensure that the full reach of the organization's consequences are treated with concern. As I will argue in Chapter 8, the moral scaffolding that objects provide can extend dominant business ethics narratives in the directions that they must necessarily extend, not only to respect established stake-holders but to decide who ought to be a stakeholder.

Still, Kennedy, Kim, and Strudler provide a helpful example of how a justification for managerial authority can be at once compelling and conditional, how it can assert a cause for action and demand ongoing scrutiny from the moral person subjected to it. When professionals prioritize things, they discover new reasons for taking certain actions, and according to these reasons, they may have new grounds for dis-obedience. At the same time, the management of objects' consequences is a complicated enough business that none of us can do it alone. Just as object stewardship is a cause for insubordination, it is also a cause for the establishment of new managerial priorities that can help organiza-tions to more effectively manage objects.

The Spirit of Business Ethics

Chapter 3 introduced several topics in business ethics to identify pro-blems that are difficult for established approaches to solve. In this chapter, I have already discussed an Aristotelian approach to business ethics and used it as a foundation for proposing the professionalization of object stewardship. In this context, a brief survey of the field is in order. This section locates stakeholder theory within business ethics and shows how objects can clarify questions of stakeholder identifica-tion and governance.

The discipline of business ethics emerged in the late nineteenth century, at about the same time as business schools became prevalent. It has been a consistent presence ever since.[14] In this time, business ethicists have questioned and taught the norms of capitalism. The study of bourgeois ethics has a much longer history, pockets of which date back to the end of the Middle Ages.[15] Its most vibrant tradition today persists in business schools. This academic discipline took shape through the efforts of moral philosophers, management theorists, social psychologists, sociologists, legal scholars, theologians, and even a few Marxists. Starting in the late 1960s, business schools began to introduce courses on social issues, and from the 1970s, the first research and textbooks began to appear. Since that time, the subject has taken an increasingly prominent, though not fully integrated, position in the business curriculum.[16] With the expansion of global corporate power, the decline of the regulatory state, and the recurrence of corporate scandals, business ethics continues to grow in importance.

The two main streams of business ethics research trace from normative and empirical roots. On the normative side, philosophers apply ethical theory to the business environment or develop normative theories for the business context. On the empirical side, social scientists articulate and test explanatory theories for how and why businesses behave as they do. This includes efforts to explain organization-level behavior like corporate social responsibility, fraud, and corporate volunteerism. It also includes individual and group-level processes involved in organizational citizenship, whistleblowing, and organizational deviance.

Business ethics research is diverse in its approach, but unified in a sense of purpose. An essay commemorating the first 1,500 articles in the Journal of Business Ethics was titled "The Quest to Improve the Human Condition."[17] Many ethics scholars, whether social science researchers or normative theorists, are interested in more than truth and accurate description; they want to make a difference. In these goals, academic business ethics joins numerous professional associations, legal regimes, public policy institutes, educational institutions, private firms, and individual business leaders working to make business responsible. For the great majority of these actors, business ethics constitutes a range of responsibilities that goes beyond the strictures described by Weber, but how far beyond is subject to considerable debate (see Chapter 3, Dispirited Capitalism).

Chapter 3 surveyed three different accounts of the relationship between responsibilities and institutional structures. First, for Weber, the relationship between responsibility and economy is historically contingent. The needs of a capitalist economy did not create norms; instead, norms allowed the economy to develop. Contingent or not, Weber believed that the norms that perpetuate capitalism are here to stay. Second, for Heath, responsibilities arise from the need to help certain systems to function in morally adequate ways. Heath does not advocate a moral foundation for efficiency, but he suggests that within the context of a capitalist economy, efficiency ought to be promoted. Heath demands more from businesses than Weber expects the capitalist logic to require, but Heath still finds few obligations for firms beyond legal compliance. The third account of the relationship between responsibilities and institutional structures suggests that substantive moral concerns ought to apply to business actions as much as any other human action. According to normative stakeholder theory, there is no special moral sphere in which business operates that allows businesspeople to ignore moral duties to the people with whom they do business. According to theories of corporate responsibility, the duties that individual persons have to take care of others, so-called duties of rescue, also apply to organizations. These duties go beyond business interests when the firm can use its unique competencies to promote an important cause. Each of these three relationships prescribes different norms and values for a capitalist economy.

This section addresses and reformulates a set of problems in stakeholder theory and corporate responsibility. While I find great value in these approaches, I agree with their critics that they are not easily maintained through systems of social control. I propose an ideal model of optimal stakeholder salience, and then consider how objects might be brought into the business ethics discourse to work towards this ideal.

If we take as granted that both markets and states can fail, and that people are responsible when they do fail, the result is a call to action. Dysfunctional states and markets compromise fairness, basic human rights, and ecological sustainability. Too much is at stake for the global economy to operate dysfunctionally. If the spirit of capitalism is broken, it is ours to fix. We owe it to ourselves, to the worst off, and to the natural environment to demand more from the state and the market. But what should we demand? And from whom?

Chapters 3 and 4 developed the tension that the market and the state often fail to fulfill their objectives. In Chapters 5 and 6, I outlined a more positive alternative where responsibility could be focused and allocated without reliance on legal boundaries. I showed that material objects help us to decide what to demand and from whom in a way that criticizing state actions and market failures cannot. Now I return to the context of business ethics and state and market failures to see if we are better prepared to work through their limitations.

Stakeholder Theory

The unifying humanism of business ethics scholarship finds direct expression in the stakeholder approach, perhaps the most important theory in the field. Stakeholder theory posits that numerous constituencies are important to firms, and that a firm's market worth and contribution to society expand as it creates value for these constituencies. The theory tasks managers with the moral and occupational duty to care for these stakeholders (see the Introduction and Chapter 8).

On the moral side of the approach, stakeholder identification[18] decides for whom managers should care based upon ethical criteria. By acting in the interests of parties who are morally legitimate and deserving of concern, a firm can fulfill its ethical duties. This means, at a minimum, that the firm pursues the interests of all its collaborators. On the social science side, researchers observe the factors that make managers perceive people or groups as stakeholders. They also examine the extent to which caring for different stakeholders creates a competitive advantage for firms that do so.

Critics of stakeholder theory express a version of this research question as a concern when they complain that there is nothing to maximize in stakeholder management; no single group comes first. Whereas markets are thought to have clear and certain accountability mechanisms, at least in the ideal case, stakeholder theory leaves multiple competing interests and little certainty about which should be addressed first.[19] A move towards the vagaries of competing interests seems to be a move away from the juridical character of ethics achieved in other fields. Jensen, who advances this view, is concerned that managers will behave opportunistically if they are not constrained by the certainty of fixed organizational goals. However, contra Jenson, sometimes people do the right thing when they are trusted to do so. Kacperczyk finds that when shareholders lose power through antitakeover provisions, managers use their newfound autonomy to improve stakeholder relations using environmental management and other initiatives. This ends up improving the corporation's performance with respect to its shareholders, who at first seemed wronged by the antitakeover provisions.[20] An extensive research literature now links nonfinancial motives to the interests of other legitimate stakeholder groups, suggesting that managers are not merely opportunists and that shareholders are not the exclusive object for managers to serve, two conclusions that broadly contradict the principal-agent model's assumptions.[21]

Stakeholder doctrine is rarely articulated as an institutionalized formulation of care. Most of what is written about stakeholders looks from the firm out to society, rather than from society into the firm. The shareholder primacy debate has spilled over from management to corporate law, and there the topic is more often pursued as a question of public policy. Nevertheless, as I will discuss in Chapter 8, corporate law is still primarily formal in nature, and it tends to focus on either the contractual actions of founders or the formal procedures that facilitate these contractual actions.

Try to imagine what a stakeholder society looks like. If every businessperson were to take responsibility for her stakeholders, would the whole economy be responsible? Though there is evidence to suggest that businesses can make money by doing more good for stakeholders, the extension that the market will provide all the motivations necessary to develop a just economy is implausible. The inclusive goals of stakeholder theory blunt capitalism's sharpest edges by giving managers reason to limit uncompensated externalities, to care for customers, and to provide value to employees. Sometimes stakeholder analysis even suggests that managers ought to take responsibility for vulnerable upstream suppliers. Nevertheless, many stakeholders remain vulnerable whenever their interests contradict the profit motive.

As I discussed above (see Chapter 3, Interpreting Market Failures), an increasingly prominent approach to business ethics argues that the field should focus on market failures.[22] A critic of stakeholder theory, Heath claims that moral obligations emerge when markets fail, and that absent these conditions firms should be free to compete. I have already suggested that this approach leaves moral agents out of practice when they need to decide to act on moral rather than market intuitions. Thus, while Heath and I agree that market failures cut holes in the certainty that one can profit from creating value for stakeholders or even shareholders, we disagree as to whether this means that managers and responsible businesspeople need to understand market failures in order to cue the moral script.

The approach that I will propose does not ask managers to discern when markets work and when they do not. Chapter 8 returns to Heath's criticism of stakeholder theory. Heath argues that the range of stakeholder theorists are not sufficiently attuned to shareholder claims, and that they either demand too much or demand the wrong things from managers. I suggest that affixing stakeholder theory's scope criterion to material objects establishes a range of moral obligations that are substantive, extralegal, and not based upon market failures, thereby improving the prescriptive power of business ethics arguments.

Another criticism of stakeholder theory concerns the underlying moral procedure that begins with a preselected group of relevant people and ends with a moral insight. Critics view stakeholder identification as the destination of a moral inquiry rather than the point of departure. Orts and Strudler, for instance, argue that stakeholder theory is a useful heuristic, but that it lacks the substance to produce a comprehensive humanistic and ecological doctrine for business ethics.[23] The limitations that they describe might be overcome with input patched in from other ethical systems, an approach for which there is precedent.[24] But if patching is to be the basis for stakeholder theory, any structural accountability that works from it must also be patched. As such, stakeholder theory has little potential to gain what Durkheim called a juridical character or for laws to be based upon this approach.

Nevertheless, if we think of stakeholder theory as an aspiration to be satisfied by an augmented system of governance, as a destination rather than a departure, then we have a standard against which to judge the moral conclusions that we reach through a new approach to business ethics. This is one of many such standards that business ethics provides. Business ethicists equate corporations with communities to encourage cooperation and mutual respect.[25] They suggest that self-respect and certain forms of autonomy are necessary components of a moral business,[26] and that creativity is an essential feature of solving the ethical problems that arise within the business context.[27] These insights provide valuable outcomes for a theory of organizational responsibility that intends to shape institutional inputs.

What these standards cannot provide is a means of achievement, other than teaching and theorizing, to steer the economy on the course that theory proposes. As long as short-sighted firms continue to externalize costs onto other parties,[28] many ethical theories will be lost to practice. As long as those who serve a firm or incur a firm's costs are not its employees or managers and lack interpersonal connections to those who are, ethical theories will fail to remedy the harms that they suffer. If corporations are communities, they are gated communities. Locating their gates cannot determine who is wrongfully excluded, or how they might best be included.

Optimal Stakeholder Salience

In an influential article on the structure of stakeholder theory, Mitchell, Agle, and Wood distinguish between stakeholder identification as a moral activity and stakeholder salience as a behavioral process.[29] They put forward three features that are likely to affect a stakeholder's salience and influence: power, legitimacy, and urgency. I focus here on power and legitimacy because urgency is one of many stakeholder assets, like proximity, media access, and connectedness, which determine the extent to which legitimate stakeholders have the power to get their voices heard.

A second modification to the Mitchell, Agle, and Wood model allows for the scope of legitimacy and power to change, as well as the extent to which they overlap. This understanding derives from Jones' and Wicks' convergence argument. They suggest that stakeholder research can be "unabashedly normative" yet also descriptively powerful.[30] Jones made an important earlier contribution to stakeholder research by advancing the claim that an instrumental stakeholder approach makes decisions through both moral and economic inputs.[31] Combining these ingredients with a theory of object responsibility and accountability gives us a sketch of things to come.

A value system that prioritizes object origins as a point of legitimation for different stakeholder groups and structurally empowers these groups in a targeted way solves the three basic variables in the stakeholder model. A brief summary and diagram will help to clarify this solution.

Figure 7.1: Empowering Legitimate Stakeholders represents the size of the population that has power over a firm, the size of the population that deserves power over the firm, and the extent to which these two

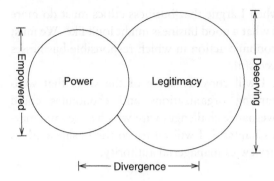

Figure 7.1 Empowering Legitimate Stakeholders

populations overlap. Taken as a static model, some stakeholders have power, some have legitimacy, and some have both.

The model is much more powerful when its dynamics are in play. However, not all of the pieces can move; some are fixed. I suggest that the scope of legitimate stakeholder groups is fixed, exogenously determined by the moral deservingness of some parties. Whoever deserves to profit and whoever deserves not to be harmed by a firm is a legitimate stakeholder in these terms. Until a firm creates new obligations or satisfies old ones, the legitimate expectations of extant stakeholders will not change. Power, on the other hand, is determined by features in the environment, like laws, economic resources, market positions, and organizational processes. Ideally, power would be allocated exclusively to legitimate stakeholders so that the circles perfectly overlap. When the circles do not overlap, it indicates that some stakeholders have more power than they deserve because some of their fellow stakeholders are disempowered. The empowerment of legitimate stakeholders depends upon narrowing the gap between the stakeholders who have power and those who deserve power.

Singularization speaks to this problem by providing inputs for the three main variables in the system. It sets the scope of the deserving according to the direct and indirect impact of physical objects bought and sold by a given business. Supply chain consciousness, if it can be made into a salient normative feature of the wider economy, might thereby narrow the gap between those who deserve power and those who have it. Notice that this alignment is not only an act of the firm as a matter of moral identification, but also a by-product of the wider economic structure that makes the right stakeholders salient. This is what I have in mind when I argue that business ethics must do more than shape ideas about what a good business might look like. We must advance a theory of economic action in which responsible businesses are identifiable and successful.

In the next section, I will consider some of the ways that well-managed, object-stewarding organizations and economies could improve upon basic governance challenges with which states and markets struggle. Then, in Chapter 8, I will return to the business ethics literature and to the purview of managerial authority.

Material Responsibility Versus Alternatives

I have argued that objects ought to be morally sticky, and that professionals should learn to recognize the obligations that adhere to them. This amounts to arguing that obligations do adhere to objects. However, in my thinking, this argument is not justifiable by any property of either objects or morality. I make no basic ontological claim about objects that shows why users should be caretakers of the things that they use. I simply state that it is practically efficient and convenient for us to organize ourselves in this way, which comprehensively allocates responsibility for all things with which people deal.

The next move in the argument is crucial because it shows the kinds of problems that objects can resolve. Objects connect social and ecological criticism with people, even distant people. As these people trace their connections to social and ecological harm through objects, they recognize a sense of personal responsibility for these harms. This recognition makes no reference to the ascribed responsibilities from the market and the state. This is telling. It shows how objects elide people and responsibilities when states and markets fail to do so.

Questions remain. For instance, while I told a story of how objects are cared for, I have not wrapped this story into an institutional package. I have not explored the specific role that firms and states might play in encouraging object care. Aspects of object care may also apply to market behaviors and to legal theories on duties of care within property theory, but I stop short of developing these possibilities. I am comfortable with the more fundamental contention that professional responsibilities and workplace obligations ought to be expanded according to the consequences of the physical stuff with which we work.

Now that we have arrived at this object-focused professionalism and more clearly specified how it operates as a standard of conduct, we are left with a final task in the assessment of its relative merit. This conclusion locates object responsibility within the range of answers to the question, "Who owes what to whom?" It establishes evaluative standards for different answers to that question. Once we compare traditionalism, authoritarianism, and the welfare state, we find that object-guided responsibility is comprehensive, voluntary, and efficient. However, it is not capable of fairly distributing burdens to help, and it depends upon voluntary participation because it does not adequately motivate action.

Who Owes What to Whom?

To frame this concluding analysis, it should be understood that object stewardship solves a certain problem. While an object focus highlights moral concerns in terms of consequences, rights, etc., it is more of a medium than a message. Looking closely may facilitate understanding, value, and empathy, but there is no substitute for the kinds of normative principles and values that help us to differentiate between the good, the bad, the right, and the wrong.

At the same time, these principles are often poorly directed. Ethical principles usually clarify what would be better without specifying who ought to make it better. Bernard Williams once described the way that language facilitates these kinds of normative claims. He gives the example, "The room ought to be swept."[32] I might describe this scenario as an aimless ought, a normative claim that is asserted without it being directed towards anyone in particular. The room should be swept, but who should do the sweeping? Many moral rights are asserted in this way. People are said to have the right to free speech, but only the government is tasked with protecting these rights, and at least constitutional speech protections are only asserted as a limit on legislative authority rather than a substantive positive right. Newspapers, for example, have no obligation to give their ink away for free to a speaker who has something that she wishes to say.

On my account, objects provide a missing piece of scaffolding, ascribing a presumptive role in governing the global economy to many specific people for many specific things. They direct aimless oughts by localizing the community of concern that should play a role in improving a state of affairs. In turn, objects help everyone else to pass judgment on a dysfunctional material chain. We can raise our expectations, demanding that certain firms and employees involve themselves in governing their supply chains. In a very general way, objects answer the question of who owes what to whom. If there is an object that could cause harm, all of its makers and users owe it to potential victims to minimize the risk of that harm. To determine whether this is a good answer to our question, we should first consider some of the criteria by which answers should be judged.

Standards of Evaluation

Who owes what to whom? While this is a question for ethics, it is usually answered by the political economy. Many social obligations are doled out by ownership rights, prior commitments, assets, and debts. As Adam Smith famously observed, exchange rather than benevolence accounts for the preponderance of interpersonal motivations, especially between strangers.[33]

I am interested in how a specific obligation is put upon a specific person. It may be helpful to differentiate between the obligation to help and the obligation not to cause harm; these are handled differently in different contexts, and the proposed theory does much less for positive obligations than it does for negative ones. Let us set aside the kinds of transactional resources that people have at their disposal, which allow them to help themselves. Instead, we will be interested in who is expected to mitigate a given harm that has been caused and who will be expected to help when someone lacks resources to help themselves.

We will explore how different systems have answered these questions in the next section. But from the start, I want to be clear about some of the characteristics of a good answer.

- First, in answering who owes what to whom, we ought to specify people who are obliged to help and to mitigate harm. To minimize aimless oughts, obligations must attach to individuals.
- Second, our answer should leave some room for people to voluntarily adopt the obligations that are put upon them. If people are forced into roles that they would not choose for themselves and are

not especially qualified to fulfill according to some collective preference, then our system will produce one injustice in order to
reduce another.

- Third, obligations should be distributed fairly. Those who owe
should be capable of meeting their obligations for both helping
others and for avoiding causing them harm.
- Fourth, our answer to the question of who owes what to whom
should facilitate efficient specialization. Those who can most capably satisfy positive obligations should be compensated for doing
so, and there ought to be incentives in place for the people who are
best able to satisfy obligations to be involved in the activities that
most efficiently make use of their talents.
- Fifth, there must be accountability for harm. If private misconduct
creates an obligation, it is best for the perpetrator to be the one who
makes amends, pays restitution, and mitigates in the future.
- Sixth, the obligations must be comprehensive such that areas of
moral concern are adequately doled out and none are left unmet.

The answer to the question of who owes what to whom should be
specific, voluntary, fair, specialized, accountable, and comprehensive.

Welfare Capitalism

Welfare capitalism is today's dominant institutional form determining
who owes what to whom. I will focus on three aspects: the welfare
state, professional responsibility, and corporate social responsibility.
These elements often overlap within the aegis of the state, the law,
professional bodies, property rights, and branded corporate social
responsibility initiatives that civil society activism helps to inspire.
Together, this combined activity amounts to what Ostrom calls "polycentric governance,"[34] and it is the best that we have. Some combination of voluntary philanthropy, state financing, legal sanctions, and
public pressure mitigates harm and provides beneficence.

First, the welfare state. I already discussed the welfare state extensively in the context of the high expectations that people have for it
and the disappointments that they often experience when it fails to
reach its potential. Welfare states allocate resources and curtail harm
through regulation. When these regulations and resources are adequate, the welfare state meets most of the evaluative standards listed

above. It allocates specific responsibilities to individuals to pay taxes and obey the law. Participation in the welfare state is not voluntary, but at least these responsibilities can be fairly allocated such that taxes are administered fairly and the rule of law is upheld. Welfare states can facilitate specialization in the way that they regulate and in the way that they spend public resources. Regulations can ensure accountability for the harm that people cause with their work. However, all of these possibilities are merely that: glimmers of hope that tantalize while the practical activities of welfare states most often miss the mark. So, while it is possible for a welfare state to create specific obligations, to avoid forcing too many invo-luntary duties, to fairly allocate responsibilities, to encourage labor specialization and maintain accountability, the fact is that no welfare state currently administers a comprehensive allocation of responsi-bility such that someone is responsible for every harm within the economy and someone is responsible for all the beneficent acts that we could agree are worth undertaking. Moreover, the least capable states are so limited in their resources or so vexed by their elites that they may not satisfy any single evaluative criterion listed above.

Let us consider professional responsibility next. Where professional bodies exist, they create certain positive duties for their members and they define what kind of conduct is viewed as harmful. It is not only the professional body, but the whole professional system, including the training process, system of credentials, professional journals, etc. Sociologists study these professions as a special type of occupational organization, and it is clear that most kinds of work will never enjoy the internal controls or the barriers to entry that the legal and medical professions maintain. But in exchange for wage premiums, these professions do self-police and maintain an internal normative system.

Do professions determine who owes what to whom in a way that is specific, voluntary, fair, specialized, accountable, and comprehensive? Specific, yes. If there is a profession, it does often elaborate specific expectations for individual practitioners. Voluntary, yes. Positive obli-gations, like humanitarian work undertaken by Doctors without Borders or pro bono legal aid, are usually undertaken voluntarily at the firm level or the individual level. Fair, no. Professionalism does not have a distributive mechanism that ensures that those who are most able to help will contribute according to their abilities, though informal

Table 7.1 *An Evaluative Comparison of Elements of the Welfare State*

	Welfare state	Professionalization	CSR	Combined
Targeted responsibility	–	–	–	–
Voluntary obligations	–	+	+	+
Distributive fairness	+/–	–	–	+/–
Efficient specialization	+/–	+	+/–	+/–
Accountability for harm	+/–	+/–	–	+/–
Comprehensiveness	–	–	–	–

norms do demand more legal aid from the most successful firms. Specialized, yes. Professionals are specialized by definition, and as expertise increases, subdisciplines also emerge. Accountability depends on the profession and the way that it is organized, but it is certainly possible for professions to create a locus of accountability for specific professionalized activities. Comprehensive, no. The professions that include positive obligations to help and accountability for causing harm are exceptional, and most occupations are not organized in this way. Most workplace behavior is not governed by norms of professionalism.

Likewise, corporate social responsibility (CSR) is the exception rather than the rule. Like professional responsibility, CSR is primarily voluntary and relies heavily on reputational motivations.[35] CSR can allow for efficient specialization where firms make use of their special capabilities to help.[36] But the demands of CSR are weak and superficial. It does not hold firms accountable for the harm they cause, does not distribute burdens fairly, and is not comprehensive.

How do these overlapping institutions fare according to the evaluative standards proposed above? In isolation, they do not fare especially well, but when taken together, they perform better.

When combined, the welfare state, professional responsibility, and CSR can perform admirably. However, even at their best, none of these systems is institutionally tuned for the question that object-based responsibility is most capable of answering. None of these systems ensures that all unmet obligations are designated as someone's responsibility. For that, we need object stewardship.

The opposition in this comparison is not necessary. Indeed, we might eventually singularize objects in order to better focus CSR activities and in order to better regulate business activity within the welfare state, but the obligations themselves and their satisfaction is not the state's responsibility. If the argument sustained here is taken seriously, we are all responsible for our things when the state fails to make someone responsible for them.

Governing Every Thing

While the proposed materialism obliges responsibilities that exhaustively account for the human impact on the natural environment and on human societies, it lacks a juridical character. People are responsible for everything, but they are legally responsible for only the forms of stewardship that the law demands of them.

Between legal and moral responsibility, some gaps are cavernous. Even as numerous school shootings and firearm-based terrorist incidents have shown guns and bullets to carry a weighty moral cost, gun sales are booming and prices remain low. If the argument in this book is taken seriously, everyone who makes, sells, or buys a weapon shares responsibility for the harm that it causes. According to this argument, weapons and ammunition are too cheap, too widely available, and too casually handled to minimize the injuries that they cause. Taking care of these dangerous things should at least involve a much more concerted effort to ensure the state of mind of the people who have access to them.

Guns are an exception, and it would be very unfortunate if we allowed the behavior of the worst offenders to taint the way that we understand all commercial activity. Many industries have been quite innovative in thinking about how their products can be made safer and less environmentally harmful. For example, Honda is experimenting with designs to make cars safer for the pedestrians that they sometimes hit, acknowledging an unfortunate fact and trying to minimize the harm that results.[37] These kinds of innovations demonstrate a real concern for the consequences of a product, and I suspect that there are more firms showing such concern than there are firms that entirely lack it.

We are unprepared to govern everything. We need companies and the professionals who work for them to take on the task of thinking creatively about their products and materials. We need them to look upstream and down, to find the harms and risks, and to mitigate them. No law will overcome what Adorno called "the preponderance of the object" better than human ingenuity and empathy. We must act as stewards, even when the law does not force us to do so.

A Plan of Action

While governing everything is beyond our reach, every employee is capable of caring for objects within the scope of her work. This section outlines a practical approach to object care to demonstrate the feasibility of object stewardship.

There is much work to be done in making sense of objects and their consequences. Up to this point, I have discussed these tasks as scientific and humanitarian, involving powers of observation and empathy. The professionalization of object care depends on both aspects. Provided that professionals are sufficiently aware and willing to care, there are many opportunities for them to do so through the objects with which they work.

To specify what employees can do as object stewards, consider a few basic steps. The key elements of object stewardship involve focusing on objects, exploring their consequences, reaching out to the people and communities who share an interest in the same objects, taking action, and recursively refocusing on new objects. This book made a case for object stewardship, but professionals will need to adapt the way that they approach object care within their organizations and industries.

In the *focus* phase, professionals must decide what objects present the most significant risks and opportunities for improving the consequences of the work that they do. The main factors in making such an assessment relate to the seriousness of the consequences associated with a particular object and the volume of a firm's dealings with that object. The product of these factors determines the extent of the consequences in an object category. According to these consequences, a firm and its employees may decide to focus on one object rather than another. Some objects may be discovered indirectly through organizational activities and expenditures. For example, firms that spend significant resources on travel may need to address the ecological consequences of its travel policies, even though the firm does not directly purchase jet fuel.

In the *exploration* phase, professionals assess the damage and try to discover unrealized possibilities for the benevolent use of things. McDonough and Braungart, for instance, suggest that designers should look for closed loops in which materials can be reused without the need to break them down to their primary components.[38] It may not be immediately apparent how best to develop products for remanufacturability or which objects should be the targets of these innovations, but this exploratory phase will inform employees' priorities in adopting or avoiding particular uses of things.

As this chapter has emphasized, one of the causes for object singularization is the unrealized potential of commerce as an extensive community of concern. In the *outreach* phase, professionals assess the extent of these communities and develop them in ways that enrich their capabilities. It is clear that we need to work together to collect information about the way that things are being produced, used, and discarded. Community organizing is a key occupational demand of object stewardship. The labor involved in developing these connections, especially where they cross cultural boundaries, explains why we must not expect every employee to take an interest in every object. On the contrary, it is necessary that professionals focus their time, energy, and relationships.

In the *action* phase, professionals implement the insights that they have assembled. Action can be constructive or destructive; it can promote relationships or discontinue them. Contrary to stakeholder theory, which maintains a relatively fixed conception of an organization's community, object stewardship can perturb organizational communities, product designs, and business strategies in response to an assessment of the extended consequences of a given activity or material use.

In time, firms that work at object care will resolve the pressing problems of the first objects that they attempt to steward. Once stewardship efforts yield results, and harms that once brought a given object to the firm's attention are now being abated, it is time for the firm to look elsewhere. In the *refocus* phase, professionals return to the first phase to ask, "What is next?" Here, their stakeholder networks and object awareness are likely to provide helpful insights about new stewardship projects. The platform is recursive because the scope of a firm's network and the consequences of its material impact cannot be addressed comprehensively all at once.

There is a tension between this practical limit of organizational action and the gross ascription of blame to organizational entities.

I have argued that firms and individual employees are, at least to some extent, responsible for the harms caused by their objects. Yet here I am arguing for prioritization and incrementalism. It may be frustrating to acknowledge, but ethics sometimes works this way. Some outcomes are morally regrettable: we are responsible for some things that are beyond our capacity to resolve.

Many philosophers deny the possibility of moral regret, believing instead that "can implies ought." To do so, they must adopt the kind of rule-oriented morality that was critiqued above (see the discussion of Anscombe in Chapter 7, Aristotelian Business Ethics). However, our ethic of object stewardship leaves room for regret. It is not a matter of following rules, but of discovering opportunities for taking care of others so that they (and we) might thrive in the process. Williams presents a formulation of agent-focused moral regret that fits well with the kinds of responsibilities described above. As he explains:

The sentiment of agent-regret is by no means restricted to voluntary agency. It can extend far beyond what one intentionally did to almost anything for which one was causally responsible in virtue of something one intentionally did.[39]

I have described a causal world where material actions stretch far beyond the scope of individuals' intentions. Object stewardship is not meant to create unrealistic demands or responsibilities so daunting that they dissuade action. Instead, stewardship seeks possibilities and honest appraisals of what we now regret to motivate action that we might not experience these regrets in the future.

Conventional moral theories often focus on blame and regret, on the negative case for morality. But the focus here must turn to positive potential, to the chance to accomplish a more just and good society. In this society, professionals' work should challenge and inspire them with new problems that engage their full moral and cognitive powers.

Chapter 8 discusses core ideas in business ethics to show that looking more closely at objects can lead to interesting new possibilities for that discipline. It presents an account of how organizational expectations are established, and argues that objects provide supportive scaffolding for determining the scope of an organization's responsibilities.

8 | *Materiality for Business Ethics*

In mainstream management theory, the notion that firms are organized around physical stuff has considerable precedent. The resource-based view (RBV) characterizes firms according to their idiosyncratic assets. RBV scholars largely study firms' capabilities to conceive and implement strategies, but they also emphasize firms' resources as physical capital in their locations, plants, and access to materials.[1] Hart extends the RBV by emphasizing that important firm resources rely upon the natural environment.[2] Access to materials, for example, is directly dependent upon the ecological conditions that produce them.

In Hart's natural-resource-based view, pollution prevention is the most basic level at which firms can become cognizant of their natural resource dependences. Some firms will go further to focus on product stewardship or even sustainable development. Hart's argument paved the way for management scholars to recognize the crucial role that environmental resources play. In this analysis, both sustainable development and pollution prevention are eventual results of a firm's material cognizance.

While resources matter to some RBV scholarship, there is also a sense among management scholars that materials are immaterial. Research on virtual organizations contends that many of the "brick and mortar" fixtures of organizational activities are becoming less significant. As Gilder declares:

The central event of the twentieth century is the overthrow of matter. In technology, economics, and the politics of nations, wealth in the form of physical resources is steadily declining in value and significance. The powers of mind are everywhere ascendant over the brute force of things.[3]

Gilder goes on to describe the way that microchips have overthrown the materiality of objects because they are made from resources that are so abundant in nature. The irony of this example is that, while it is true that one of the most expensive parts of a chip is its design and that

274

the materials themselves are abundant, a massive material infrastructure is necessary to transform these mundane resources into their final form. Even very mundane resources, like breathable air, become extremely complex and resource intensive when it must be purified and cleaned of all the particles that would ordinarily be airborne. Gilder fails to appreciate the networks of materials that go into the design, production, use, and disposal of microchips. The fact that the physical plants in which chips are manufactured are extraordinarily expensive is a basic demonstration that microprocessors do not make themselves. Intel's conversion of an Israeli semiconductor chip fabrication plant to the 10 nm node was expected to cost $6 billion.[4] New fab plants in this class were expected to cost as much as $12 billion.[5] These expenses demonstrate that the sand and aluminum that go into the chips are only the surface of a deep material undertaking that brings together labor, equipment, and energy to make semiconductors.

Still, those who deny the precedence of materials are right about one thing: wealth is no longer being amassed through exclusively material means. Ideas do matter, now more than ever. In this book, I have argued that materials can help us to understand the scope of our actions' consequences so that our ideas do not become disconnected from their consequences. This argument is primarily concerned with moving beyond a bounded conception of responsibility. I wish to deny the sufficiency of an interpersonal ethic of care, the insufficiency of which is already demonstrable on both social and ecological grounds. The alternative that I propose is that we expand the circles of moral regard through the physical things with which we deal.

This chapter traces the implications of the singularization argument through some key debates within the business ethics literature, where objects have received even less attention than in mainstream management. I already introduced some key business ethics ideas within a discussion of its limitations (see Chapter 3). I argued that business ethics is very often hindered by its own pragmatism, and by the practical constraints placed on its normative aspirations. But in the chapters since, I have reconstructed a pragmatic approach that finds new values and aspirations by looking closer at material things. I translated the notion of stewardship into an ethic of care that applies to individual objects and to assemblages of objects gathered together by ecosystems and societies. Finally, I showed how these developments could address three key examples of market, regulatory, and ethical failures: inequality, climate change, and finance.

Now I return to business ethics to demonstrate that objects warrant consideration in many different normative theories, perhaps not in the way that we decide that basic concepts like moral autonomy and meaningful work are significant, but certainly in the way that we distribute the responsibility for promoting these ends. The specific question here is whether objects should play a role in defining managerial goals. I will show that objects have a role to play in managerial responsibility, and perhaps in the way that we understand organizational governance as well.

Directed Care

One of the challenges in business ethics is to direct the moral regard that we demand from businesses. Consider the Christian dictate "Love thy neighbor." As discussed above, it is sometimes morally compelling to treat corporations as communities, but the shape of these communities and their boundaries are a major hindrance to the application of the community metaphor. It seems obvious that we should treat people with care, but as long as our global system of production ensures that the people who make our things are not our neighbors, this ethic of care collapses. The modern economy ensconces many managers into elite corporate "neighborhoods," and if an ethic of care cannot stretch beyond their gates, its results will only privilege the privileged. An unjustifiably proximate ethic of care allows managers to ignore massive distributional gaps in broader supply chains and to focus instead on similar others. However, many business ethics scholars have argued that firms remain associated with these distant consequences and that the suffering they cause should not be disassociated from their actions.

In contrast, an object focus cuts across firms. It denies moral relevance to firms' boundaries. When we trace threads of responsibility across the economy and see where they lead, we expand the horizons of our moral landscapes and weave ourselves into a different moral order. We form new communities and establish new aspirations for what it means to behave responsibly.

The object focus involves a radical reconfiguration in the locus of responsibility for individual employees and business enterprises, but its implications for business ethics are not nearly so sweeping. In fact, almost any of the well-established ideas about corporate and personal responsibility for helping others, respecting rights, and avoiding harm can be focused through this new object lens. This chapter summarizes a set of useful ideas developed in the past few decades to promote corporate responsibility and discusses an illustrative case that will demonstrate the relevance of object stewardship to the business ethics literature.

I focus on the specification of organizational and managerial objectives through stakeholder engagement and fiduciary duties. This topic is itself a massive and contentious subdiscipline within management research. My treatment will be brief and evocative rather than complete. My intention is to show how a more vibrant treatment of objects clarifies key ideas in the domain of business ethics. I will leave unanswered the question of whether traditional legal structures need to be altered around the firm and its legal governance. Likewise, I will say little about the kinds of managerial interventions that could help establish object stewardship as a key organizational priority. My focus is on the way that we think about firms and what we expect from them.

What Are Firms For?

Businesses have many faces. To their customers, they present a brand, for example, one that emphasizes product quality. To investors, they may present a different brand that emphasizes profitability with low costs and high revenues. In this way, businesses manage different audiences, convincing regulators that their primary goal is to follow the law and convincing employees that the firm is really a community that takes care of its own. The best firms manage to be all of these things, exceeding the demands of multiple heterogeneous audiences. But what is the defining purpose of an entity that serves so many masters, an entity that has an interest in making each of them feel as if they are the most important of all? This is a more difficult question to answer.

One way to answer this question is to look at how corporations came into being and how they are created today. Enterprises' historical origin and legal structure help to demarcate their competing objectives. In this vein, Orts proposes a legal theory of the firm, suggesting that the law has a special capacity to balance and maintain multiple competing priorities that cannot be maximized in an economic sense.[6] His argument speaks directly to some of the topics that concern us here, like the location of a firm's boundaries, but we work from opposite sides of the law. Whereas Orts takes the law as a source of insight, I take it as a feature of the regulatory and social environment that ought to be justified. Orts emphasizes the corporate form's profound dependence on the law. I agree that the firm is an artifact of law, but I question whether our analysis of this legal fiction can resolve the attendant problems of accountability that arise within firms. In my account, if the kinds of corporations that the law facilitates fail to broker a sustainable future, then these firms, and perhaps the laws that maintain them, have a demonstrable defect. This does not imply that the law should necessarily be changed or that a better arrangement will be forthcoming, but it suggests an evaluative lens that we might utilize to judge employees, firms, industries, and the whole legal institutional complex.

While these broad claims are possible implications of the object-focused approach to organizational responsibility, much more work needs to be done to direct this approach into an alternative institutional apparatus. To avoid stretching the argument too thin, I wish to bracket these questions. Some elements of business law, like legal personhood, strike commentators as offensive to the basic aspirations of democracy. And yet, as Orts demonstrates, there is a more complicated dance between entitlements and responsibilities playing out in the creation of legal fictions. Whether the law should protect objects from misuse is an important question, but it will take us far afield from the matter at hand. We should first decide whether it is helpful to use objects to gather organizational responsibilities as a way of extending and recasting the dominant analytic frameworks.

In thinking about what firms are for, a second point of departure, beyond the law, begins with the recognition that firms want things. As Painter-Morland has argued, following Deleuze and Guattari, capitalism is a desiring machine.[7] This account flattens some distinctions between different social and technological entities by realizing that many different things have wants. Accordingly, firms are goal-seeking entities that meet or disappoint internal and external benchmarks. Painter-Morland's account belies a strict teleology, as does her source material. Rather than being bound up in a narrow and prescribed purpose, firms are characterized by dynamic flows. No single entity governs this process, nor should any single entity define its purpose.

Deleuze and Guattari write that "a society is defined by its amalgamations, not by its tools."

Painter-Morland focuses on amalgamations of people, doubting the application of blame from group to individual:

An individual employee's sense of morality is related to and influenced by the tacit understanding of propriety that informs organizational protocols. When an individual participates in an organizational system, he/she is part of a complex circuit of reciprocal influence, which runs in and out of the individual's moral sensibilities along multiple channels. [T]hese lines of influence cannot be disconnected. [The employee] remains largely unaware.[8]

While objects cannot wholly alleviate the tendency that people have to think and moralize in groups, they can help individuals within organizations to form different groups, gathering around objects to ensure proper conduct. As we think about amalgamations instead of tools, we begin to see that assemblages of things are already working to define the way that we understand corporate responsibility. In business ethics, many researchers have tried to make sense of the firm as a moral quantity. Doing so forces us to face a number of difficult questions. Is the firm blameworthy? If it is blameworthy, can blame be spread onto employees who are themselves innocent? By what criteria can we determine whether a firm intends to do something or whether it is just an employee who transgresses?

Again, as Orts demonstrates, the law has established precedents for answering these questions, for deciding when entities are liable and when individuals are liable for entities. Here, the law accomplishes something that objects cannot. An object focus cannot account for the decisions that people make and the way that they act together as a community, but it can help us to see how people are sorted into and out of groups. It can call into question some groupings as disingenuous and overly narrow, and it can draw people out of their organizations and into supply chain structures that span the scope of their shared responsibilities.

To see how important this is for contemporary business ethics, consider the area of corporate governance, broadly construed. Donaldson recently argued that theories of corporate governance are neglectful of key moral concepts. He shows that even the most positivistic accounts of how firms are organized, like Oliver Williamson's, rely upon normatively laden language with concepts like "good" and "workable," but:

Even if Williamson assigned the terms good and workable full normative status, he would nonetheless need to answer some key questions. Good for whom? Are some actors more important than others?[9]

Likewise, in agency theory, Donaldson finds that general obligations are neglected. Firms are treated as cost control structures. The question of participants' obligations to others is rarely asked or answered. In both these cases, Donaldson uses corporate boundary problems to show that ostensibly factual matters – how large is the firm and how is it structured – can only be answered with the help of key moral conclusions.

In Donaldson's main constructive proposal for governance theorists, he suggests that firms may be characterized by different "identities" according to which they are organized to address certain issues:

For efficiently satisfying property rights and securing the fulfillment of con-tractual obligations, theories of organizational economics that emphasize the minimization of transaction costs involving, for example, the deterrence of opportunism may serve as useful governance tools. On the other hand, for properly answering questions about corporate citizenship or employee rights, some form of market-responsive stakeholder theory might be preferable.[10]

My approach to objects provides a new identity for firms and their participants or a standard against which other identities can be eval-uated for completeness. If we take objects seriously, then managers and shareholders cannot simply define away their responsibilities for upstream and downstream obligations. Objects provide a new stan-dard for determining the scope of the firm's moral regard.

Now, a person might question whether we should not just look to the law to fix these boundaries. Can't the law decide? In some cases, it can. Orts' institutionalism is certainly not an apology for the status quo; he has constructed a standard against which laws, on his view, ought to be judged. But others are less critical of the status quo, and the boundary problems that Donaldson outlines cannot be isolated from the main ideologies of business practice. Banerjee makes an argument akin to Donaldson's when he criticizes the mainstream conception of stake-holder identification. Where empiricists rely upon a descriptive notion of "legitimacy" to define who deserves to be a stakeholder, they some-times accept an evaluative standard that is not morally defensible. As Banerjee notes, powerful people and powerful firms often control the system of legitimation through the state. Taking up the example of apartheid South Africa, Banerjee laments the fact that empirical approaches to stakeholder theory only criticize the misuse of violence by civil society groups without recognizing that the state and corporations can also misuse violence. In this discussion of "stakeholder colonialism," extractive industries feature prominently. Their actions are juxtaposed with indigenous communities who have a justifiable claim to the places where they live, yet "the history of interactions between indigenous communities and the corporate sector ... is marked with blood, violence, death and dispossession."[11]

Both Banerjee and Donaldson deal with the question of how inclusive a firm ought to be. Banerjee presents a difficult case in the violation of indigenous peoples' rights. These rights are often violated with the help of local authorities, perhaps even within the guise of legislative and democratic legitimacy. No empirical governance theory is capable of dealing with the heterogeneous mass of dependents that firms actually affect. If the law defines their interests as irrelevant and violently asserts an organization's right to dispossess, mainstream governance theory would reach a similar conclusion. Objects offer a new empirical input, regrouping the obligations for which firms are responsible regardless of traditional or authoritarian legal boundaries.

At the same time, there is a question of overreach, of whether we ascribe responsibilities to people who are incapable of acting upon them. Corporate law and the regulatory systems that interact with corporate legal structures tend to be extremely conservative in their ascriptions of blame. As Laufer has argued, a legally unnecessary emphasis has been placed on finding individuals who intended some wrongful act.[12] Painter-Morland explains their concerns, suggesting that often individuals are incapable of intending an organization's actions because they do not fully comprehend them and because they are a part of an organization's flows. In my view, none of this matters from an object stewardship perspective. There is a question of whether a given object's use is associated with a given set of harms, and if the answer is affirmative, then all of those who stand to benefit from that harm share in some obligations regardless of their intentions. The case is not strong enough to send someone to prison for someone else's failure to act as a steward of the natural environment, but it is strong enough to call into question the profits that they earn from that business enterprise.

So, this will be my approach in the following sections. I will use objects to append interested parties that firms can harm to the list of relevant constituencies, and then I will fall back upon Donaldson's bundled set of corporate identities. A firm can be a contractual entity that minimizes transaction costs, a community, and a personal project of some leader. It can be all of those things, so long as that firm is also an entity that takes care of the objects that are entrusted to it.

Organizational Teleologies

Deciding what firms are for involves describing an end or purpose for corporate entities. Yet the work that we have done to better understand objects will now complicate any attempt to understand managers and firms in a simple, teleological way. To understand why, let us explore an argument about teleology and its limits.

It is hard not to treat objects teleologically because it seems so natural to do so. The fact that we name and categorize things according to their uses demonstrates the expansive applicability of teleological concepts. For example, an ironing board is described by its characteristic application, ironing, rather than by an intricate description of its form: "locking scissor-legged table with elongated top." Even when a use is not implied by a name, many nouns are associated with specific verbs. Scissors cut, crops feed, and ovens bake. These same pairings apply also to professionals for whom a bounded set of verbs describes both their activities and the purposes of those activities. Doctors interview, advise, suture, and inject, but these are not ends; the fact that doctors heal is what matters about their work.

These teleological pairings are a part of our most basic understanding of objects and a prominent aspect of what we need to know in order to decide how to deal with things and people. Indeed, understanding the tasks for which a tool is best suited can help us to decide how to use it and how not to use it. For example, what makes scissors useful in cutting fabrics and other materials with soft fibers is the fact that they are very sharp. Less floppy materials, like paper, do not require the same degree of sharpness, and because these materials include hard ingredients, they can dull scissors, making them less useful for fabric. In the use of scissors for cutting paper and fabric, teleological categories collide. Cloth scissors cannot cut paper without losing their capacity to cut cloth. As a consequence, there are different kinds of scissors for cloth and paper. And, just as tools like scissors become more specialized, so does labor. A fragmentation of professional skills coincides with an ever-expanding range of supporting products.

Given the configuration of these tools and the people who wield them, we might expect that tools would play a key role in how we understand occupational responsibilities. In many professions, this is the case. Lawyers learn about protecting confidentiality by not taking sensitive information from the office, doctors learn about safeguarding addictive painkillers from drug-seeking patients, and firefighters learn to take care of a breathing apparatus. The intricacies of these categories reflect the narrow specifics of different organizations with different purposes. And as purposes have grown more specific, the residual category of workplace responsibility has grown increasingly important. Indeed, management scholars had to invent a new category of occupational responsibility, organizational citizenship behavior, to describe all the work that people do across their occupational boundaries and outside their craft specializations.[13]

As useful as it may be to think about uses, there are a few key problems with this teleological thinking, particularly when it is applied to moral categories and to persons. First, no object has a singular purpose. The entrepreneurship literature on bricolage describes many adaptations that resource-limited firms utilize in order to accomplish their goals. Bricoleurs make use of the materials around them according to their personal goals, not the limited descriptions of what objects are meant to do. In this case, objects are as much shaped by the bricoleur's purposes as the purposes are shaped by the available objects. Such creativity is not limited to entrepreneurs. For example, at a shipping office in Novosibirsk, I once saw a manila folder that had been stapled into the form of a waste basket. Weber named the file as a key bureaucratic technology for its system of order, but clearly folders have purposes beyond paper storage. The possibilities of entrepreneurial and bureaucratic bricolage exceed the narrow, teleological boundaries of a unified and singular purpose.

The second problem with teleological thinking is that it cannot appreciate the meaning of things that choose their own ends. People are not like scissors that belong to one task or another: they are capable of choosing between tasks. To think of people as moral agents, we must ascribe some value to their purposes, and we must make room for them to decide. If we have to say what a person "is for," then it might be best, in terms of moral autonomy, to say that the purpose of a person is that which they choose. Thus, in a sense, managers are for whatever they choose to be for, and this is as it should be. We can always ask a moral question about what choices would be praiseworthy and responsible, and we can value responsibility as the realization of one's moral freedom, but this is not the same as stating that a person's ends are defined by moral law.[14] Nor can we say that a person's purposes are defined by her organization. Organizations do generate purposes for their members, but this genesis must not overwhelm members' capacity to have their own reasons and to pursue them preferentially when an organization fails to apprehend what it ought to do.

The third limitation of teleological thinking is its presumptuousness. Our systems are too complex to reliably predict how one element will interact with others. Interactions between the biotic and abiotic elements of living systems are only predictable within a given range of previously observed conditions; new extremes yield unpredictable results. The uses and consequences of spaces and structures within social life change dynamically such that a street can be a site of an affectionate kiss, a traffic accident, and a transaction within minutes. Even written laws and public institutions with explicit and codified purposes can change over time, meshing or abrading as different actors within them make use of their organizational authority in new and creative ways. We can disaggregate the elements of these systems to bring them together in a controlled context, isolating fungi from roots or employees from teams, but we will still only be seeing part of the picture. There are $n(n+1)$ dyads of organisms in a diverse ecosystem; this makes an immense set of possibilities. Triadic interactions are exponentially greater. It is pure hubris to imagine that we can consistently delimit objects' purposes. We must not be too confident in our teleological imaginations.

All of this is a preamble to the main question. What kinds of purposes can we ascribe to firms and the people who direct them? To date, the main descriptions of managerial and organizational purpose fall into three categories: personal-contractual, efficient, and communitarian. Rather than overturning these categories, I wish to show how all three descriptions of managerial obligations can be improved by understanding the lively role that objects play within them.

Personal-Contractual

The first way to understand firms' objectives is to understand the objectives of the people who create firms and the people to whom they make commitments. A founding team begins with a goal or vision, and managerial theorists are increasingly aware that these purposive orientations can leave an impression on a firm's culture. Thus, one way to parse a firm's purpose is to recognize the personal and idiosyncratic nature of the things that people within firms want. These desires evolve as firms develop, spreading out through the contractual and property relations that give the corporation its legal form. Founders may change their minds, or they may allocate resources to people who are permitted to autonomously develop parts of an organization and to make commitments on its behalf. Founders and the managers who they hire make commitments to funders, employees, and customers, and these commitments are bundled together within the business entity. I label this account of a firm's purposes as the "personal-contractual" aspect because the firm's purposes are described by the contracts between people and the firm, as well as the sum of their personal and shared aspirations.

There is considerable debate in the business ethics literature on the extent to which stakeholder relationships can be understood as a direct entailment of the personal-contractual (property-based) conception of the firm. Donaldson and Preston argue that property relations involve bundles of rights over the things that someone owns, and that if we understand these rights correctly, they imply that the owners of a corporation share rights and obligations with many other parties to the firm.[15] However, it is more common to perceive the focus on shareholders and owners' rights as antithetical to a broader moral conception of the firm. Even in Donaldson and Preston's work, there is an outer boundary to the responsibilities that are accessible by unbundling property rights. Beyond this threshold, a party is no longer connected, via ownership and its attendant rights and responsibilities, to a firm as its stakeholder. This is the point of stakeholder exclusion, a point at which the law would generally find no reason to hold that a firm had a binding motivation to take a party's interests into consideration when making decisions. Most of the protracted supply chain relationships that concern conscientious consumers fall outside of this boundary. Regardless of whether an excluded party is harmed by the firm's market behavior, she stands outside the strategic and legalistic bounds of the firm. There is a great deal of overlap between the contractual extent of a firm, the inclusive scope of its community, and the reach of its consequences. Nevertheless, I will differentiate between a firm's contractual, communitarian, and consequentialist boundaries. I argue that objects can help to broaden both the contractual and communitarian boundaries to a range that is defensible in consequentialist terms.

The teleology behind the personal-contractual understanding of a firm derives its force from a liberal conception of individual economic actors as autonomous agents. Believing in individuals' free choice leads many scholars to promote an economy in which employment and organization is voluntary on all sides. Hence, a firm's telos is tied up in the free choices of its members. Beginning with Adam Smith's description of the "propensity to truck, barter, and exchange," many economists sought to naturalize economic life as an appropriate sphere of human activity.[16] It is easy to see how these arguments have taken root. We want to understand firms as associations among individuals who share a common purpose by choice because this idea of economic life affirms a number of positive values. It makes room for innovation, achievement, and group solidarity. The alternatives do not provide the same self-determination when employees work as forced labor in the only job that they are permitted to hold or when they work within hereditary roles handed down by fixed social systems. More controversially, when employers are not able to dismiss employees, relocate, and otherwise determine the scope of their relationships, it is also sometimes suggested that they are not as free as they should be.

To illustrate just how personal the behavior of large firms can become, consider the religious motivations that are ascribed to firms through their owners. I already discussed the case of Chick-fil-A (see Chapter 3), a fast food restaurant that made headlines by taking a public stance against gay rights on religious grounds. Chick-fil-A is a characteristic example of the personal-contractual specification of corporate purposes that can only be understood in light of the specific history of the founding family within the firm. Likewise, the retailer Hobby Lobby took a prominent position in a political debate over the Affordable Care Act by arguing that the health insurance that the firm was being forced to provide to its employees violated the firm's religious convictions. As I will discuss in the next section, the idea that firms serve their owners has been depersonalized into a fiduciary responsibility for shareholder wealth maximization, but doing so changes the game, stripping shareholders of many of the qualities that belong to them as moral persons.

There are grounds for some disagreement as to whether the libertarian conception of the firm is liberal at all. When we emphasize the freedom of employees, shareholders, managers, suppliers, and customers to contract as they choose, we lean towards a "do what you want" libertarianism that accepts all formulations of power by the mere fact of the seemingly consensual agreements that gave rise to them. Samuel Freeman makes this argument with a focus on political libertarianism:

What is striking about libertarians' conception of political power is its resemblance to feudalism .... Feudalism is a system of personal political dependence that is based on a network of private contractual agreements. Under feudalism, the elements of political authority are powers that are held personally by individuals, not by enduring political institutions. These powers are held as a matter of private contractual right .... Liberalism evolved in great part by rejecting the idea of privately exercised political power.[17]

Freeman urges caution in allowing the seeming openness of free markets and exchange to inspire an unwarranted confidence in the protection of individuals' rights under these conditions. While his argument is most immediately applicable as a defense of the state's regulatory capacity, it applies here as well in the context of the personal-contractual aspect of an organization's purposes.

This "liberal" conception of the firm as a nexus of contracts is as much an aspiration as it is a statement of fact. Often, organizational members are not as free to choose to engage with a firm as the contract-by-consent discourse suggests. While it is true that workers are formally free to choose where to work, they become increasingly entangled in a firm and its way of doing things as they make firm-specific investments in skills and knowledge. That they do so is essential for the firm and the skillful economy that firms create. Nevertheless, it comes at a significant personal cost. The more that an employee's skills are specific to a given firm and the less easily she can choose to work elsewhere, the more beholden she becomes to whatever arbitrariness there may be in that firm's personal-contractual purposes and to the hierarchy that maintains them. The idea that people are free agents who can move fluidly between employment opportunities is partially true, but if this notion is reified and essentialized, it leaves us with the misimpression that workplaces are and should be disassociated social settings where strangers make temporary use of one another.

A significant line of inquiry in management research now works against this harshly individualistic perspective. Stewardship-oriented management theorists argue that firms thrive when employees care about each other, feel safe taking risks, and believe that they are a part of something worthwhile.[18] To be clear, there is no either/or in the way that the personal-contractual purposes of a firm are specified. Firms can be organized around shared interests and common purposes with a desire to maintain employees' well-being and they can also be built around founders' arbitrary and selfish interests. The personal-contractual category does not imply that firms will be good or bad; it explains the etiology of their purposes in personal terms.

In corporate law, debate continues as to whether the law should favor a certain conception of how firms work and in whose interests they operate. Hansmann takes a perspective that is most consistent with the personal-contractual argument developed here, suggesting that firms can be formed in different ways depending on how their founders and early participants wish to share risk.[19] Others are more partisan. In the next section, I will discuss the normative aspiration shared by many corporate law theorists that business should be efficient. One of the leading conceptions of business from an efficiency perspective views the corporation as a way of solving a coordination problem between shareholders and managers. According to this principal-agent model, managers will tend to behave opportunistically if not monitored and controlled. The corporate structure provides this monitoring and control through the incentives that it doles out to managers. Arguing against this model, Blair and Stout propose a team production theory.[20] They suggest that everyone who invests in firm-specific resources, whether through firm-specific human capital or through the provision of other resources, is jointly trusting the entity to fairly distribute resources and trusting its leadership to act in the interests of the team. While these perspectives are partisan in the sense that they argue for power to be concentrated or shared, each also accounts for a specific etiology of the firm. Hansmann belongs to the personal-contractual camp. Principal-agent theories belong to the efficiency camp discussed in the next section, and team production theorists belong to the communitarian camp in the section after that. While laws do shape firms in important ways, it would make more sense to decide what firms are for and then let the law facilitate that purpose than to begin with the law's demands. As such, let us consider the personal-contractual etiology from an object-oriented perspective.

How can the object-centered approach deepen our understanding of firms' personal-contractual purposiveness? I suggest three main possibilities. First, objects belong to an important range of firm purposes that bring people together, and it makes sense to recognize the relationship that these objects have to people as we account for the things that people are trying to do within firms. Objects are also purposes. Companies want to build a better bike, car, or spatula, and their activities cannot be explained without a focus on the character and qualities of these objects.

Second, objects are part of what makes human capital specific to a firm. Consider the situated peculiarities of the place where a firm operates, the history of its facility, the software it has implemented, and the machines it has purchased and then modified for its production. These features determine key aspects of employees' lives and conduct in ways that are only partially transferable to other firms. The objects and their history are as much a part of the firm as an organizational delineation of tasks or the personnel who work together. Indeed, the physical objects may be the least transient part of the organization; we should recognize them as durable entities that shape firm-specific entanglements.

Third, the nexus of contracts view of the firm seems to imply that firms are disembodied and abstract "legal fictions," but the object-centered view emphasizes the physical and embodied nature of organizing. This includes the ergonomics of the way that people work in different spaces and the physicality of the people who work there. Since Foucault began observing the critical symbolic use of bodies in maintaining a state's power,[21] many researchers have taken note of the embodied meaning of the way that physical persons are placed at work. Contrary to the abstract idealization of firms as agreements, we find dense systems of expectations where demands are placed on a person's body and the things with which it is adorned. In one workplace, a person needs to wear shoes with antislip soles. In another, a woman must wear high heels that are 2–4 inches tall.[22] It is tempting for firms to translate all of this into contractual power, but the real issues are physical. In a minor scandal that emerged about a receptionist who was sent home from a London accounting office for wearing flat shoes, the problem was physical discomfort, not symbolic decorum. Tangible objects have tangible consequences; they are not legally fictitious, and we would do well to avoid imagining them away as we seek to render the firm into its most abstract theoretical form. Indeed, a promising line of inquiry into the nature of the firm has sought to describe it in terms of its natural resource footprint.[23] Accordingly, the firm is a nexus of physical stuff as much as it is a nexus of contracts.

Efficient

Most scholars do not understand firms as the specific product of capricious owners who can do as they choose. It is arguably the case that corporate governance scholarship is not interested in owners' preferences at all. Instead, scholars understand owners as abstract actors by compressing their diverse interests into a single ruling desire to maximize the market value of their assets. The upside of this abstract treatment is that it lends itself to the competitive marketization of organizational activities, and insofar as this approach inspires firms to innovate and become more efficient, to cut costs, and to produce new products, numerous social benefits may be the direct result. However, as to the specific question of whether a firm should always maximize shareholder wealth, endorsing such a view involves a big leap of faith and a little dose of chicanery.

The leap of faith is the main subject of this section. Advocates of a shareholder wealth maximization (SWM) norm believe that firms serve their shareholders best by doing anything that they can to increase the firm's net present value. They believe that when firms behave in this way, markets perform efficiently in the service of a public good. These two beliefs go hand in hand. Private motives would be quite difficult to justify without social utility, and without firms' service of private motives, they would be perennially undercapitalized. And yet, the social performance of the shareholder wealth maximization criterion is rarely questioned systematically. I will discuss this problem in detail below.

I will not focus on a second discontinuity in shareholder wealth maximization that results from firms disregarding shareholders' distinctive identities, but let us consider it in passing. If firms' interests are determined solely by the business consequences of their strategies, many things may seem permissible that would be entirely inconsistent with the interests of some shareholders.

In American publicly traded companies, shareholders belong to every possible identity group: they are women, gay, transgender, black, immigrants, and foreign nationals. Some drive hybrids and measure their carbon footprints, and some drive diesel trucks and are proud of their Southern heritage. Some eat meat and some are vegetarians. A firm may not appease all of these groups, some of whom hold deeply inconsistent political and moral judgments, but the personal-contractual view holds that each firm is beholden to the combined preferences and public scrutiny of its shareholders.

The most devastating critique of shareholder wealth maximization focuses on the fact that this criterion does not consistently produce social value. Nevertheless, even if we were to accept that shareholders were the key actors and that they have rights regardless of the social consequences, we would still be at a loss to explain why shareholders are not accorded the respect that would acknowledge their specific interests. It is both disingenuous and inaccurate to act as if shareholders are not people.

In this text, I have tried to put people back into their contexts, their bodies, and the flows of material things that surround them. The same particularities that I try to reassert for objects are even more compellingly owed to individual persons, whose preferences and interests are not mere abstractions. Firms can take a more honest approach by developing principled responses to the social and political issues they face, allowing principles to be tried out in the court of public opinion that the capital markets provide. But when firms act as if their shareholders are not people, they cancel the only moral reason we have for taking corporations seriously: the people who they serve.

Let us return to the leap of faith involved in imagining that profit-maximizing corporations maximize public welfare by seeking to increase shareholder wealth. This claim depends on a number of assumptions that have been widely criticized by business scholars as well as civil society groups. I already considered these limitations as a rationale for why consumers might seek an alternative specification of responsibility and why they may come to believe that markets do not work, or do not work well enough on their own (see Chapter 3, Mistrusting Markets). Recall that externalities, negative and positive, are a fundamental problem for the social welfare consequences of profit-seeking organizational conduct. Public welfare suffers whenever firms benefit from producing negative externalities that are not priced into their market actions and whenever firms fail to produce outputs that would generate public goods because they are unable to profit from doing so.

An object focus responds to the purported efficiency of shareholder wealth maximization by connecting object-based harms with specific firms to properly ascribe responsibilities to entities and by providing an appropriate moral lens for reflecting upon objects' consequences where efficiency alone will not suit. I discuss each of these issues in the following paragraphs.

An object focus does its most powerful normative work by associating externalities with specific firms and employees. Whereas a cynical positivist might imagine that a lax regulatory environment and a permissive corporate culture entitles both firms and employees to produce negative externalities, I have argued to the contrary. I showed ways that many people find themselves responsible for the material consequences of the work that they do. Absent this specification, it is common for externalities to occur that are not allocated to any individual actors. The goal is to comprehensively allocate responsibilities for not causing harm, so that some individual or group accepts responsibility for each moral duty. In this sense, object stewardship acts like a moral matchmaker, consistently pairing off the responsibilities that would otherwise be widowed by the market and the regulatory state.

I will not overstate this result. I have not proposed a scheme to sanction positive and negative externalities. But even if these sanctions are never forthcoming, even without incentives to take responsibility for a full complement of material things, objects can still provide a helpful tool for those managers and employees who wish to voluntarily behave responsibly and those other stakeholders who wish to demand that they do so. Absent an object focus, one cannot easily decide where profits should end and the work of managing resources responsibly should begin. Economists long for an efficient equilibrium at which optimum regulation produces optimum externalities. Too much regulation would be too costly to enforce without returning sufficient value in the resultant reduction in externalities. Too little regulation leaves value on the table by failing to deter the organizational actions that cost more harm to society than it costs to deter them. The standard economic approach follows a similar line for the firms, which optimize the level of their compliance in the face of regulatory and reputational costs.

The argument for a shareholder wealth maximization norm among managers depends on effective regulation and on accurate information. Absent the specific conditions under which effective regulation and reputation effects lead managers to internalize all externalities, the SWM norm gives no cause for direct nonlegal responsibilities among managers. If the state and reputations do not force firms to behave responsibly, shareholder wealth maximization will certainly not cover the responsibility deficit. One of the arguments sustaining the SWM norm is that managers cannot be trusted to make the evaluative judgments about right and wrong that organizational responsibility implies. This argument is strained by the fact that almost all aspects of management require managers to make evaluative judgments of this kind, not only in normative matters but also in marketing, HR, strategy, etc. Still, if the argument has any credence, it is defeated by the prospect of an object-delineated conception of organizational responsibility. Let us assume that objects specify the extents of organizational responsibility. If so, organizations are not duty-bound to do good in the world. It is enough for organizations to take care of the objects entrusted to them. If they did this, it should reduce the tendency of managers to corruptly draw resources from the firm in pursuit of their own pet projects.

The second aspect of the object focus that cuts across the shareholder wealth maximization conception of organizational responsibility is the moralization of diverse persons and objects in noninstrumental terms. The efficiency narrative fails to appreciate the moral motivations shared by many individuals on both sides of the regulatory nexus. Regulations are often born in passionate and pathos-laden language rather than cold calculations. For example, in the early 1980s, Candy Lightner founded Mothers Against Drunk Drivers after her daughter was killed by a serial offender. The organization went on to play a leading role in the moralization of alcohol sales and consumption. Similarly, the deaths of children in accidental and mass shootings feature prominently in today's gun control debate. The evaluative disconnect between an efficiency-based approach to regulation and the stewardship approach that I endorse is most obvious in these extreme cases. For example, young children have limited economic value. Society has yet to invest resources in them or their futures and nobody depends upon them. Since children are expensive, a household may actually be enriched by a death of a child, but thinking in these terms demonstrates the poverty of insight that a pure efficiency argument brings to important social issues. The calculative perspective misses the point that ethics places demands upon us regardless of whether these demands are costly to implement. The protection of children exemplifies the kind of responsibility that is shared by the whole society. Their suffering is the most serious indictment of the social system that creates it, not because of children's' economic value but because of the value that we place in them as people who are related to other people in a dense network of value.

To be clear, economists also love their children, and some approaches to economics can understand the preferences that people have for others' welfare functions. Moreover, firms' most serious social-value-destroying actions are likely to result in market and perhaps legal sanctions, so there are often prudential reasons why managers are unwilling to overstep moral limits in pursuit of profit. The more modest claim that I wish to advance is that managerial theory and pedagogy often displace these kinds of priorities. Even though the law gives leeway for managers to act in the interests of employees,[24] business schools still theorize and teach finance as if firms are exclusively beholden to shareholders.

The shareholder primacy camp continues to hold a dominant position in both financial theory and corporate governance. When it comes to the dominant narrative in corporate governance, shareholders are stripped of their moral and political identities. What is left is a person who wants nothing more than to have more money either today or, at some premium, in the future. This thin conception of a person's interests is transmitted into the firm's purposes by the same basic rationale that motivated the personal-contractual approach to a firm's purposes, but this impersonal-contractual formulation lacks the very possibility of a conscience. Once shareholders are morally hamstrung, the promotion of their interests excuses callousness, undermining the moral purposes that might otherwise inspire the firm and its shareholders.

These desires provide firms with what is now taken to be the best-established criterion for corporate performance: long-term value. Because financial theory gives a good deal of credit to the information processing capacity of markets, the presumption is that an increase of share price will reflect future value of shareholders and an increase in long-term value. This second conception of firms' purposes is a major product of economic and financial research. It finds for firms no higher purpose than the maximization of shareholder value, and ascribes that purpose to firms regardless of the specific preferences of the individuals involved.

For many financial theorists, corporations have an objective function. Their task is to maximize shareholder value, a task that is conveniently describable by a mathematical function. Of course, economists have a long history of ascribing purposes to agents that represent an incomplete approximation of what the agents themselves would choose. The mathematical architecture that now dominates the field of economics requires numerous assumptions about what individuals want, as if we all had ordered preferences that are independent, monotonic, and concave.

When it comes to abstract theory, there is no treatment of the firm that is less grounded and more tendentious than the theory of the efficient firm. The problem is not efficiency per se, but the failure to ask the lingering question: "Efficient for whom?" The answer, it must be said, is that publicly traded firms that serve the interests of their shareholders are, by definition, efficient in their service of capital and only conditionally efficient in the service of social utility. Some of these firms fail to serve the interests of their shareholders because they are poorly governed and because their managers seek their own benefit. In these cases, firms may pursue an awkward combination of elite managers' and shareholders' abstract interests. It is the interplay between these interests that has captured the greater part of academic attention in the study of corporate finance and corporate governance, all the while assuming that society at large would benefit from firms that maximize shareholder value.

An object focus can introduce a proviso to the shareholder value criterion to clarify the order in which benefit ought to be distributed. In the next section, I discuss stakeholder approaches to management. We will see that firms can focus on wider communities and that this focus may improve firms' performance. Stakeholder management does little to de-escalate the conflict between shareholders and managers, but it should clarify expectations for everything else. Specifically, as Freeman has argued most forcefully, firms should benefit everyone with whom they interact. Objects will help us to specify the scope of these interactions to guarantee that the right stakeholders are included in the moral calculus that justifies corporate dividends and executive compensation.

A final note on efficiency from an object perspective. While scholars often emphasize firms' efficiency, calculated as revenue in excess of cost or as comparative cost advantage for the same output, resource efficiency and the efficient use of objects provide an alternative. We can ask whether firms waste the material things that they manage, whether they leave their landscapes less capable of supporting life, whether they make forests into lasting sources of value or junk mail. Too much corporate activity is relegated to a vacuous standard of conduct based on the internal dynamics of a given firm. All of the people who invest and work for a given firm are essentially on the same team. Their internal conflicts are about as meaningful to the rest of us as the results of a scrimmage between players on the same football team. The real question is not who wins within a firm, but who wins outside of it, and that outcome is much more acutely realized in the material legacies of a firm's products, equipment, and property than it is in the distribution of wealth among its elites.

Communitarian

Firms take on an internal orientation when shareholders take primacy, either as specific persons with concrete interests or as abstract actors whose interests are assumed to be pecuniary. The firm looks to its funders to determine how they wish it to behave. The legal compliance and reputation orientations described in the previous section expand the domain slightly, but still relegate managerial intentions to a largely instrumental position. In the past three decades, managerial theorists and business ethics scholarship has taken a communitarian turn. Increasingly, the internalist account of organizational purposes is being supplanted by an argument that firms ought to serve a diverse set of external audiences, which we call stakeholders.

Most approaches to business ethics focus on people, that is, on the obligations that businesses have to employees, customers, suppliers, and investors. We use the concept of a stakeholder as a shorthand for the practical and moral content of a diverse and dynamic class of relationships between businesses and their communities. None of this is simple. There is a question as to whether corporations are the kind of entity that can possess moral obligations.[25] Even if corporations are not that kind of entity, there is a question as to whether sanctions can be used to change the way that corporations behave.[26] There are questions about how stakeholders ought to be identified and prioritized.[27] And there are questions about how corporations that fail their stakeholders are to be brought to account.[28] If you successfully answer these questions, you might get back to the basic intuition that businesses ought to take care of the people that need them and of the people that the businesses need.

The usual approach to stakeholder theory contributes to this intuition by focusing on the nature of stakeholder relationships and showing how useful and praiseworthy it is to develop such relationships. It is useful to develop positive stakeholder relationships because corporations depend upon people who labor on their behalf, buy their products, and invest in them. Keep these people happy and the firm will thrive. This utility-focused approach is called instrumental stakeholder theory because the stakeholder concept is being deployed as an instrument of the profit-maximizing firm.[29] But not all approaches to stakeholder theory are instrumental, and many are guided by principles beyond profit. From a normative perspective, developing positive stakeholder relationships is praiseworthy because it creates bonds of reciprocity and mutualism upon which a thriving economy depends.[30] It is praiseworthy because firms have obligations to the people who support them, and these obligations ought to be fulfilled.

Whether normative or instrumental, most approaches to stakeholder theory accept as a foregone conclusion that we actually know who the stakeholders are or who they ought to be. This is a strange assumption, particularly in light of the shifting boundaries around firms. Many corporations rely upon other entities to store their data, clean their floors, respond to their phone calls, print their materials, manufacture their products, service their installations, and to conduct the great majority of the apparent activities that belong to the firm itself. In one sense, this is a triumph of task specialization within the corporate ecology: firms are able to develop and maintain expertise relevant to more specific and specialized classes of activities so that each business will focus on a core set of activities. The logistical scope of the supply chains of many modern firms is such that a design firm may be completely circumvented in the delivery of finished goods, hotels may not wash or own the sheets on their beds or the carpet on their floors, and many people are not employed by the companies where they physically work.

From a moral perspective, these shifting borders seem arbitrary. The mutualistic insight in stakeholder theory is that so long as these people are involved in an activity that works towards a common purpose, so long as they depend upon one another, they ought to be concerned with each other's well-being. It should not matter whether a firm is connected to a person as an employee, subcontractor, onshore laborer, or offshore laborer. But despite a nice line of arguments to express the moral sensibility of interdependence that obliges organizational actors to behave fairly towards others, this sensibility is hardly winning the day. The boundaries between firms are difficult to pierce in legal terms.

Should it be otherwise? Many advocates of business ethics distrust legalistic approaches to corporate responsibility. They appreciate the flexibility and autonomous organization that voluntary approaches to ethicality rely upon. In defending a libertarian conception of stakeholder theory, Freeman and Phillips nevertheless conclude that liberal precepts preclude firms from causing harm to third parties without their consent.[31] This takes us a significant step beyond the efficiency focus described above, but to take this step, additional information is required. Most significantly, there is a question of scope. In a causal universe where actions cascade to have far-reaching consequences, how far must one look to see the scope of her actions?

The stakes of determining the scope of firms' consequences increase once we recognize the adversarial nature of organizational responsibility. Firms compete. The firms that can reduce the scope of their responsibilities will thereby reduce their apparent costs. When Waste Management changed the way that it depreciated its trash cans, it gave itself the appearance of profit without actually changing anything about its business conduct. Analogously, gaming stakeholder scope criteria is like moral earnings management. Firms underrepresent the intensity of corporate obligations to outsiders and they seem more responsible by doing so. This leads to one of the key complaints about stakeholder theory, that it suffers from "the taint of moral laxity."[32]

Joseph Heath argues that business ethics has failed to appreciate the importance of the competitive context in which business professionals operate by instead acting as if everyone is obligated to maximize social obligations in the same way. In doing so, we have misrepresented the lessons learned from developing stakeholder relations within the law. While it is true that states have developed legal protections for employees, customers, and others for more than a century to ward off firm conduct, Heath argues that these protections are not signs of law favoring a stakeholder model, but instead serve as indicators of a law that seeks to fix market failures. Following Goodpaster,[33] Heath provides a thoughtful account of business responsibility that gives recognition to a basic problem in the allocation of moral responsibility:

Being a loyal fiduciary involves showing *partiality* toward the interests of one group, not an impartial concern for the interests of all .... Part of the unwillingness to accept this line of reasoning stems from a rejection of the idea that there might be an institutional "division of moral labor," such that not everyone is morally responsible for everything at all times. Many of the most subtle and difficult questions in professional ethics involves [sic] dealing with the way that obligations are divided up and parceled out to different individuals occupying different institutional roles.[34]

In pitting partiality against impartiality, Heath demands precisely the innovation that an object focus provides. Asking managers to avoid causing harm within their extended networks of material relations is not akin to asking them to remedy the world's woes. The kind of stewardship that I propose does not make such boundless moral claims. Instead, when we demand partiality to things, we create a bounded set of interpersonal obligations. We ask that businesses be partial, but we discourage a form of partiality that puts business profit before stewardship.

Whether this undermines the stakeholder concept depends on what we take from it. For Heath, stakeholder theory tends to be either too strong, in that it denies partiality, or too weak, in that it denies a firm's obligations to vulnerable and poorly organized outsiders. The language of market failures, he contends, is better suited to chart the middle course. However, I find value in the stakeholder narrative as a way to gather information about the characters of the corporate drama and to use that information as an input in an evolving moral calculus. Whether calculated according to residual shareholder value or not, what is most important from an ethical perspective is that the calculus is inclusive. It needs to push firms to avoid harms and to seek to provide positive value. There is no better way for firms to become inclusive in the stakeholders they identify than by caring for objects. As long as profits do not come at the expense of stewardship and harm mitigation, I am not opposed to the profit motive. A substantive professional responsibility to mitigate harm is a demanding moral burden, and its adoption would challenge both managers and financial theorists.

  This book is about the business ethics of material things. Everyone manages things. We deliver, fix, sort, file, shelve, prepare, cook, clean, launder, manufacture, mine, mix, wash, plant, remove, sort, create, and destroy things. With so many things in our lives, it is amazing that they receive so little attention. This book argues that material things can guide the scope of our moral communities, helping us to understand where our actions have consequences, and target the individuals and organizations who ought to be accountable. To realize our humanist and environmentalist aspirations for businesses, we need to understand the way that people and organizations fit into a material world, and the most basic appraisal of this recognition comes through the avoidance of harm.

  Business ethics is a field of sharp contradictions, compelling aspirations, and disappointing delivery. If we can believe the business press and the most optimistic scholarship, there is a revolution underway; businesses are becoming responsible. With the rise of corporate social responsibility, sustainable business, and impact investment, every possible combination of the words "community," "social," "green," and "sustainable" has now been appended to the standard business lexicon. It is the golden age of conscientious capitalism.

  Heartening as these claims may seem, ill tidings of corporate irresponsibility contradict them. Indeed, new corporate scandals seem to pop up on an almost daily basis. Fines and earnings misstatements that used to be counted in the millions or tens of millions now frequently run into the billions of dollars. These scandals are offset by authentic and impressive efforts to use business for social and environmental good. We seem to be caught in a cycle. Firms break laws, spill oil, release private information, sell unsafe products, launder money, evade taxes, manipulate governments, and mistreat employees. Yet they also provide jobs, make useful products, clean up the environment, support government services, improve product safety, protect privacy, pay taxes, and respect employees. The cataclysmic crash of high hopes and regrettable results makes corporate responsibility a beguiling subject. Firms tease us with the possibility of an ethical economy, but there is little consistency in their actions.

The concept of corporate responsibility implies that responsibility comes from firms, that firms are the proper unit of analysis for thinking about economic responsibility. We have many reasons to expect a lot from firms. They wield unimaginable resources and accomplish astounding technological feats. We invest so much time and attention into these firms that we cannot help but hope that our efforts will be put to good use. Alas, our hopes are often misplaced, and as we realize this, we begin to search for an entity that can make firms behave better.

Amidst rising cynicism, government is the next place to turn. Regulatory authority is often useful in guiding firms towards a more responsible future. We can thank regulation for the end of child labor, the forty-hour-work week, and a drastic reduction in lead poisoning across America. And yet, government is at least as likely as firms to disappoint its constituents. Governments are porous structures. Representatives are susceptible to campaign financing incentives and outright corruption. Likewise, regulatory agencies are dependent upon the firms that they are meant to regulate. The current status of corporate responsibility is as much an indictment of the regulatory state as it is of the structure of corporate governance.

This is where material objects come in. Objects can help us to decide who ought to be responsible for what. One of the biggest problems in establishing an ethical economy is the allocation of responsibility. As long as we cannot agree on who ought to do what, on whether the state or the firm is responsible for cleaning up after a messy economy, it will be difficult for us to efficiently allocate resources to the most pressing social and environmental problems.

Every approach shares this challenge. Whether you begin with professional norms, positive organizational culture, regulatory incentives, or personal obligations, each strategy requires us to somehow parse the collective responsibilities that we have to help and not to harm. We need to decide who is responsible to whom for what. We need to distribute these responsibilities to the right organizations and people, and the distributions need to be reasonable, plausible, appropriate, and specific.

For a variety of reasons, it is difficult to decide who is responsible for what. The interplay between state responsibility and corporate responsibility yields one problem in the allocation of responsibility that has haunted business ethics. Donaldson, who wrote one of the first books examining the normative obligations that corporations have within different kinds of states, argues that firms need to be careful of the context in which they do business, and that depending on the adequacy of the state, a firm may be obligated to do more.[35] It is easy enough to specify certain responsibilities for certain entities, but it is much more difficult to conceive of an overarching scheme that is comprehensive so that all responsibilities add up without creating a significant moral remainder of collective duties for which no one is responsible.

In a novel way, this book deals with the question of how business ethics allocates responsibility. Where business ethics has been a largely humanistic discipline, I am proposing a change that reflects a different kind of humanism. To focus on the dynamic system of material relations in which businesses are embedded is to locate people as well, as agents and patients who can help and harm. I suggest that objects already provide businesses with a handrail that guides them to the specific sites where they are responsible. This object-focused responsibility can become a lens for deploying both utilitarian and deontological approaches to business ethics. In this sense, the objects themselves need not have any moral content, as long as they can guide us to subjects who do.

An object focus is an important step in a much longer progression of moral foci. Over time, as economies and social systems have grown more complex, the best-established nexus of responsibility, the kin group or family, has endured. The question that we face in modern society is where else we become responsible, where else we should invest ourselves in trying to create a just world. Gradually, responsibility gathers in new institutional forms: a captain is responsible for her ship, a tradesperson for her craft, a professional for her client, a shepherd for her flock, and a manager for her firm. Unfortunately, most locations of responsibility generalize poorly. For example, if we prioritize being responsible to members of our own religious communities, there will be many gaps. Likewise, while liberal philosophy has invested a significant amount of moral and political imagination in the responsibilities of citizens within states, these moral communities exert influence in ways that exceed the scope of the citizen-communities within them. A global world needs a global allocative scheme, and flows of material things provide one. Allocating global responsibility may seem grandiose, but an object focus is also extremely specific. It manages to substantiate a particularistic form of ethics that can deal with the details of specific corporate blunders.

Managing Things

Material things can be useful in orienting managers to behave responsibly in the interest of shareholders and other organizational stakeholders by establishing moral limits and making the expanse of an organization's consequences more concrete. Things can also produce a less anthropocentric description of what firms ought to do and how managers ought to work. Drucker famously argued that firms thrive by serving their customers, not shareholders, and that efficient and effective customer service will eventually produce corporate profits.[36] Though the shareholder wealth maximization language may dominate in classrooms and financial circles, Drucker's description of managerial responsibility is probably better at characterizing the role that firms play in a consumer society. Firms make things, and if they make their customers happy by making their products, they get to make more of their products for more customers.

I have been critical of this consumer society and its endless array of poorly organized material waste. This critique applies directly to the organizational quest to satisfy customer interests. Insofar as customers take a narrow view of their things, enjoying products temporarily until they carelessly throw them away, customer satisfaction and ecological catastrophe go hand in hand. Object stewardship can soften the blow of these costs by shifting focus towards consequences that are otherwise unrecognized. It is possible to go one step further, to imagine that managers conceive of their work as primarily a duty of object stewardship. Once this duty is satisfied, firms can deliver residual profits to shareholders and deliver excellent products to customers.

As I conceive of it, stewardship-centered management does not deny the importance of employees, shareholders, customers, suppliers, and community members, but it finds a place for them according to the flows of material things. It allows the needs of the material ecology to play a central role in how products are designed, how manufacturing is organized, how delivery and recycling are set up, and how new products are introduced. In ecological terms, some things should not be sold, even though customers are willing to buy them. A focus on material things and their ecologies of value denies the possibility that any stakeholder priority, whether shareholder, customer, or employee, can be used as a justification for ignoring the harm we cause.

The main features of object-centered management have already been presented. I ask that managers guide employees and organizations to sustain the value of material things, not just the ones that they sell, but the ones that they use as well. In the sustainable design literature, the notion of cradle-to-cradle design[37] highlights the ways that things can be made with an eye to their unmaking and their remaking. Contrary to recycling, which tends to be a resource-intensive way to reclaim materials that are often degraded in the process, cradle-to-cradle design tries to make use of materials that can be directly converted into another important use rather than constantly downcycling the value of key inputs.

But this is a chapter about business ethics, and here I wish to outline a few other matters that seem to follow from a material managerialism. First, there are themes around corporate moral agency and collective responsibility. Painter-Morland has argued that causal structures within firms are too complex to ascribe responsibility to individuals, and that it is more appropriate to recognize that whole organizations have desires.[38] This, of course, creates a problem of agency that Painter-Morland tries to address through key managerial innovations, moving beyond codes of conduct to establish organizational forms where numerous people can spontaneously take responsibility. As she correctly observes, there is a difference between individual-focused, blame-based responsibility and the dynamic possibilities of people working together to solve problems. Blame requires closure, hierarchy, and legalistic norms, whereas working together requires people to spontaneously and openly accept responsibility in order to accomplish shared goals. The closure of blame is often inconsistent with the openness of action. Painter-Morland seeks to make room for the spontaneous form of responsibility, but I argue that organizations still need guidance to delineate roles and to ensure that important consequences are properly managed.

Using objects to map obligations across the economy to organizations and to people within organizations makes room for dynamic and spontaneous forms of moral agency, while at the same time creating a road map to see where the agency ought to have occurred in cases of corporate moral failures. Object stewardship bridges an important gap in business ethics theorizing between managerialism as a professionalized form of leadership and other kinds of occupational activities. Managerial responsibility, like the stake-holder model critiqued above, tends towards either exhaustive or severely circumscribed responsibility. Either the "buck stops" at the top of the hierarchy, in which case an authority figure is somehow responsible for many things that are seemingly beyond her or his control, or responsibility bounces around an organization across uncharted paths such that everyone can always point the finger at someone else.

The uncertain and ambiguous responsibilities of professionals like managers, doctors, and lawyers are tacitly contrasted with craft specialists whose work is assumed to be static and its consequences comprehensible. The roles played by builders, chefs, cashiers, and manufacturers do not receive the scrutiny from moral theorists that managers receive because we act as if the moral lessons of these positions are obvious and bounded. But in fact, these positions present the same questions of moral boundaries that challenges the scope of managerial responsibility. Should the home builder worry about the contributions made by her trade to the waste stream? Should the chef care where the ingredients are grown and by whom they are picked? Should the manufacturer consider components' health and safety consequences? The boundaries between professional roles, transactions, firms, and jurisdictions open up moral gaps that only objects can fill. Yet we somehow miss the role that objects can play. It appears that managers are not so different from craftspeople, that we are all entangled in a common fabric of commerce. There is room for expertise in many different aspects, but the global sense of responsibility for things cannot be isolated. It flows along the same paths that objects follow.

Volkswagen's Emissions

Philosophers are predisposed to favor reason as the standard by which morality and thought are judged. Perhaps they are right. Reason is accountable to itself. In its reflective nature, it provides an internal mechanism for its own improvement. Reason is also social; it allows us to provide justifications that other people can evaluate and that we, as a society, can reflect upon. It is hard to provide a similar accounting for emotion.

Nevertheless, psychologists increasingly emphasize that human cognitive machinery is deeply emotional. One's sense of purity is perhaps the most intriguing and least rationally justifiable of these emotions. In one social psychological experiment, Zhong and Liljenquist asked participants to describe an unethical deed from their past.[39] Participants in the treatment condition washed their hands with an antiseptic wipe, while others did not. At the end of the experiment, everyone was asked to help a person in need, but those who had washed their hands were 33 percent less likely to agree to help. Obviously, it is not reasonable for an antiseptic wipe to decide whether one should or should not render aid, and yet this is the physical, tactile power of a clean conscience.

In environmental marketing, narratives of purity and cleanliness give brands access to some of these very basic moral emotions. Volkswagen's marketing of its diesel engines will go down in history as one of the most spectacular misuses of the cleanliness/purity narrative. The one thing that Volkswagen wanted the American public to think about its Jetta TDI diesel engine is that it was clean. A series of commercials in 2009 showed an elderly woman placing her white scarf in front of the tail pipe of a running car to demonstrate the cleanliness of the car's exhaust. The engine was branded as the "TDI clean diesel." Another commercial bragged about the model's fuel economy, claiming the contradictory features that the car "really hauls" but its diesel engine runs clean. In all of these commercials, the new Volkswagen models are white, an inconvenient color for a car, but one that people are psychologically predisposed to link with moral purity.[40]

Volkswagen will not have the last laugh. In late 2015, the company admitted to installing software controlling these "clean diesel" engines to detect emissions test conditions so that its cars could pass the tests but pollute on the road. Cars with this software spew plumes of nitrogen oxides and particulates at ten to forty times the regulatory limits. The scandal swirling around these cars is deeply incongruous with the Volkswagen brand in America, which focuses on the company's supposedly environmentally friendly technology.

Volkswagen's misconduct was brazen, obstinate, and initially unapologetic. When independent researchers established the discrepancies between real world and test pad emissions, Volkswagen pushed an ineffective software update as its remedy and failed to disclose the root cause of poor performance. It was not until regulators threatened to withhold certification from Volkswagen's new fleet of diesels, effectively banning them from the US market, that Volkswagen finally came clean. Though Volkswagen attempted to blame a small group of employees as if they were an unauthorized cabal, later reports indicated a systematic scheme with emails using code words, referring to the cheat as "acoustic software" to put regulators off the trail.[41]

Dieselgate is only the latest episode in a decades-long game of cat and mouse between car manufacturers and regulators. Since the Clean Air Act of 1970 first specified pollution control systems, the auto industry has introduced several controversial technologies that undermine regulatory intent in pursuit of performance. The Clean Air Act contains a clever prohibition against devices that are mainly utilized to avoid adhering to regulation. It prohibits car companies from installing parts and components "where a principal effect of the part or component is to bypass, defeat, or render inoperative any ... element of design ... in compliance with regulation."[42] Fortunately, this gives regulators a solid basis in law to pursue Volkswagen.

All of this is interesting, but to focus on Volkswagen's misconduct and the regulators' triumph is to miss the deeper lesson of the diesel debacle for the way that we think about business ethics. Again and again, we choose to represent firms as abstract legal entities, human communities, and managerial hierarchies. Again and again, we try to frame the problems of corporate irresponsibility as if they are always problems with people. However, as is very often the case, this is a story about the mismanagement of material things. Rather than denying the moral emotions that motivate people, I try to focus these emotions on real, material conditions. Consumers' desire to drive clean cars could have positive consequences, but first we need to provide them with enough understanding about the material circumstances in which cars are produced and used for them to deploy their emotions consistently. Likewise, producers can use their own moral emotions and their own purity sensibilities if they will just understand that managing materials is a major part of business responsibility. To that end, let us follow this case a bit further as a demonstration of the power of the object-centered approach to business ethics.

Diesel fuel is a remarkably dense source of energy. By mass, it is almost 90 percent carbon.[43] While gasoline engines rely upon carburetors or fuel injectors to mix air and fuel which is then ignited by electronic spark, diesel engines burn without a spark: when fuel and air are forced together with enough pressure and heat, the mixture ignites. The emissions profile of an engine is a consequence of the fuel being burned, the specific characteristics of the way that it is burned, and the emissions control system, which can include additional devices where impurities, pollution, and unburnt fuel react before escaping the tail pipe. But from the start, the entire system must work with the properties of the fuel, which depends in turn on the length of the carbon chains and how easy it is to vaporize in the combustion chamber of an engine.

While diesel engines provide a thermodynamic efficiency that makes them an effective strategy for converting fuel into work, their emissions tend to produce significant NO_x and particulate emissions. This is caused by two related problems: the overall mixture of air and fuel is too lean to utilize the standard catalytic converter technology that minimizes pollution from exhaust in spark engines, and the localized site of combustion is too rich for fuel to burn cleanly in diesels. In combustion, a fuel mixture is either rich or lean depending on whether it has lots of fuel or lots of oxygen. Spark engines usually run on a rich fuel mixture, which means that most of the oxygen is used up by the combustion in the cylinder. After the engine, spark exhaust is forced through a reaction site where it becomes hot enough that many impurities are destroyed. Unfortunately, this catalytic converter technology only works well for exhaust that has very little oxygen in it. Diesel engines usually run with much more oxygen than the fuel requires, which leaves too much oxygen for the spark engine's catalytic converter to function. At the same time, because diesel fuel is difficult to aerosolize, large droplets and high temperatures in diesel combustion are associated with the emissions problems that Volkswagen engineers have been trying to solve.[44]

Why do we care about mono-nitrogen oxides and particulate pollution? This book advances a materialist conception of responsibility. It suggests that we can rethink business ethics by considering the way that the things we make, buy, and sell react with the natural environment and its people. In short, objects guide us to understand the scope of a firm's social and environmental responsibilities. The Volkswagen debacle provides a characteristic illustration of how actions and materials come together to create responsibilities. In the case of diesel emissions, we care about them because the particles they release have a significant impact on human health and environmental welfare. Diesel emissions include sooty particulates that are so small that they pierce deep into lung tissue of those who breathe them in. NO_x also reacts with air in intense sunlight to form dangerous surface ozone, an element of smog that is harmful to both human and plant health. It may be hard to determine exactly whose lives are affected by a mobile pollution source like a car, but in the aggregate, Volkswagen cannot deny the role of its product in the creation of undesirable emissions and social harm.[45]

I have argued that companies like Volkswagen need to reinvent themselves. They need to understand and take moral ownership for the diesel fuel their cars will burn and for the particles and gases that they will exhaust. One of Volkswagen's clean diesel commercials juxtaposed the diesel's engine sound with a hybrid's quiet exhaust. That commercial failed to explain that every time an engine makes a loud sound from rapid acceleration, the car's pollution controls are being overwhelmed. The Jetta commercial characterizes the doublespeak of every major car company operating today. They want to have it both ways: to promote their product with a masculine projection of power, noise, and speed, but to also suggest that their cars are clean and safe. To add to Volkswagen's woes, the Federal Trade Commission has joined the suit, claiming that Volkswagen's representations about the sustainability of its cars were false claims.[46]

Imagine the alternative. Imagine that Volkswagen embraced the scope of its social and environmental impact through the extensive network of its cars and their material relations. Employees who write software would realize that they are not in the business of passing emissions tests. Instead, they are in the business of minimizing the harm that their cars will cause and making cars that are better for their owners, for the natural environment, and for the people who breathe particles from Volkswagen's exhaust pipes. Everything that Volkswagen has done since the scandal has failed to appreciate the partnership that the firm needs to develop with its drivers in order to mitigate automotive pollution. They have sold their customers and themselves on a fleet of environmentally sustainable race cars, and now the firm and its drivers must choose between environmental performance and automotive performance. The way to make that choice is by appreciating the meaning of things, by weighing the consequences of different kinds of emissions in different circumstances.

When diesel-powered ships are at sea, they shut down their pollution controls, producing more of certain emissions and less of others.

Whether this is responsible or not depends on the local and global impact of the action, on the way that the emissions affect living systems and onshore communities. Shouldn't it be the same with Volkswagen's engines? NO_x emissions are a more serious threat when exposed to sun in hot and densely populated areas; why should we expect a universal fix to a local problem? Unfortunately for Volkswagen, the firm missed an opportunity to be a real leader in pollution controls. It failed to recognize the complex and local interactions and to mitigate them in adaptive and creative ways. Now, the firm seems to be jumping on board with electric cars. If this is their direction, we can only hope that they take environmental factors like power generation technologies and battery disposal more seriously in the next generation of cars, that their employees and managers alike take responsibility for monitoring their firm's conduct and the consequences of its objects.

A materialist approach to business ethics is hardly utopian. It is founded on a way that people already think about moral problems and the scope of their responsibilities, and it gives cause for us to infuse a new kind of scientific and ecological literacy into many kinds of work. That alone would significantly reconstitute the professional and technological competencies that we expect from people in the workplace. It would force Volkswagen, its marketing team, and its dealerships to immerse themselves in a more technical and critical account of their products' ecological performance. This is the real lesson that Volkswagen should learn from its scandal. Obviously, the dishonesty and fraud were indefensible, but the wrong that the firm did was material.

Wrapping Up

This book describes a wide range of organizational objects in diverse settings. We explored trees in forests, car exhaust under the sun, climate change among the poor, and shoes among the rich. We considered mobile devices in education, porches in neighborhoods, global e-waste in distant junkyards, and elephant tusks in Sri Lanka.

The range is wide enough to confirm that a mere description of objects and forms of object care cannot determine how we ought to behave towards different classes of things. Fortunately, along the way we have developed some tools: singularization to recognize the unique attributes of things and to take responsibility for specific objects, stewardship as a form of evaluative caretaking, critique as a way to keep from allowing the state and the market to set the standard of conduct, ecosystems and societies as networks in which things come to have and sustain value, object-focused consequentialism as a wide-angle lens for gathering the moral considerations that belong together within a given set of material consequences, and pragmatism as a way to iteratively enhance the values to which we aim and the tools with which we act.

All this brings us to the end, where we realize that we can care for material things. We can ask Volkswagen to take responsibility for its cars' emissions. We can ask individual employees to take a keen interest in the material footprint of their work.

Still, there are limits to this argument. While the intentions of designers and creators can have significant impact, it is only through collaboration across the supply chain that the most significant results will be achieved. The same holds for technological solutions to social problems more broadly:

Seeking salvation through tools alone is no more viable as a political strategy than addressing the ills of capitalism by cultivating a public appreciation of arts and crafts. Society is always in flux, and the designer can't predict how various political, social, and economic systems will come to blunt, augment, or redirect the power of the tool that is being designed.[47]

We must not invest our hopes in the gimmickry that objects alone solve problems. That is not the point. It is human beings who decide how to use objects. Object stewards can regulate the consequences of their work far better than people who do not exercise such control.

A further limitation is the absence of an institutional framework that provides either positive or negative incentives for object stewardship. While I have conceived of an approach to organizing objects that distributes the burdens of care, many forms of innovation in object governance require additional investment. Firms tend to seize the opportunity to reduce costs by improving ecological efficiency, but once they have undertaken the available cost-effective projects, the remaining opportunities to improve ecological performance tend to produce returns at higher costs after significant delays, which reduces the likelihood of implementation.[48] I have not solved this problem or proposed an institutional infrastructure that could do so. Distributing the responsibility for object stewardship is a way to inspire organizational action. But when stewardship demands are stymied by managers and shareholders who fail to acknowledge their responsibilities, object stewardship is likely to fail. Norm enforcement and incentives are beyond the scope of the present account, which more readily justifies than governs.

That being said, responsibilities often precede institutional infrastructure to facilitate them. The reason that business ethics is such an interesting field of study is precisely this: the market does create tensions between responsibility and the bottom line. The challenge is not to imagine these tensions away or to settle for the status quo, but to locate people who are conscientious enough to strive for the responsible objective, even when the incentives fail. In the end, we may have to reorganize our economies and laws to distribute responsibilities for the stewardship of objects. But until we do, we must continue to admonish each other to do the right thing.

Take care.

Endnotes

Introduction

1. Robert C. Solomon, *Ethics and Excellence: Cooperation and Integrity in Business* (New York: Oxford University Press, 1993), 187.
2. Sherwin B. Nuland, *The Doctors' Plague: Germs, Childbed Fever, and the Strange Story of Ignác Semmelweis* (New York: W.W. Norton, 2003), 191.
3. Jane Bennett, *Vibrant Matter: A Political Ecology of Things* (Durham, NC: Duke University Press, 2010), preface, paragraph 7.
4. Bruno Latour, *Politics of Nature: How to Bring the Sciences into Democracy* (Cambridge, MA: Harvard University Press, 2004), Chapter 2, Third Division between Humans and Nonhumans: Reality and Recalcitrance, paragraph 6 (emphasis in original).
5. Ian Hodder, *Entangled: An Archaeology of the Relationships between Humans and Things* (Malden, MA: Wiley-Blackwell, 2012).
6. Corey Watts, "A Brewing Storm: The Climate Change Risks to Coffee," *The Climate Institute*, August 2016, www.climateinstitute.org.au/verve/_resources/TCI_A_Brewing_Storm_FINAL_WEB270916.pdf.
7. Too little credit is given to the ways that minorities define mainstream culture. Often, rights that would be protected for mainstream artists are weakly protected on the cultural margins. For instance, the musical group Enigma's most popular song, "Return to Innocence," sampled, without acknowledgement, a recording made by seventy-year-old aboriginal Taiwanese farmers who were barely compensated for making the recording.
8. See Fred Myers, "Some Properties of Art and Culture: Ontologies of the Image and Economies of Exchange," in *Materiality*, ed. Daniel Miller (Durham, NC: Duke University Press, 2005), 88–117.
9. "The Hidden Water We Use," *National Geographic*, http://environment.nationalgeographic.com/environment/freshwater/embedded-water, accessed May 3, 2015.
10. Michael Pollan, *The Botany of Desire: A Plant's Eye View of the World* (New York: Random House, 2001), Introduction, paragraph 3.

11. John Ryder, "The Use and Abuse of Modernity: Postmodernism and the American Philosophic Tradition," *Journal of Speculative Philosophy*, 7 no. 2 (1993): 93.

12. Theodor W. Adorno, *Negative Dialectics* (New York: Continuum, 1973), 183.

13. Daniel Miller, *Material Culture and Mass Consumption* (Oxford; New York: Blackwell, 1987), 240.

14. Karl Marx, *Grundrisse: Foundations of the Critique of Political Economy* (London: Penguin Classics, 1993).

15. Bennett, *Vibrant Matter*.

16. Steven Shapin, Simon Schaffer, and Thomas Hobbes, *Leviathan and the Air-Pump: Hobbes, Boyle, and the Experimental Life* (Princeton, NJ: Princeton University Press, 1985), 440.

17. Michel Foucault, *Discipline and Punish: The Birth of the Prison*, trans. Alan Sheridan (New York: Vintage, 1977).

18. Hodder, *Entangled*.

19. Shiping Tang, "Foundational Paradigms of Social Sciences," *Philosophy of the Social Sciences*, 41 no. 2 (2011): 218.

20. Aihwa Ong and Stephen J. Collier, eds., *Global Assemblages: Technology, Politics, and Ethics as Anthropological Problems* (Malden, MA: Blackwell, 2005).

21. Ian Bogost, *Alien Phenomenology, Or, What It's Like to be a Thing* (Minneapolis: University of Minnesota Press, 2012), Chapter 3, Metaphor and Obligation, paragraph 18.

22. R. Edward Freeman, Jeffery S. Harrison, Andrew C. Wicks, Bidhan L. Parmar, and Simone de Colle, *Stakeholder Theory: The State of the Art* (Cambridge: Cambridge University Press, 2010).

23. Robert A. Phillips and Joel Reichart, "The Environment as a Stakeholder? A Fairness-Based Approach," *Journal of Business Ethics*, 23 no. 2 (2000): 185–197.

24. Robert A. Phillips, "Ethics and Network Organizations," *Business Ethics Quarterly*, 20 no. 3 (2010): 533–543.

25. Richard B. Sobol, *Bending the Law: The Story of the Dalkon Shield Bankruptcy* (Chicago: University of Chicago Press, 1991), 408.

26. John Ruskin, *Unto This Last and Other Writings*, ed. Clive Wilmer (London: Penguin, 1997).

27. Laurel Neme, "One Country Will Destroy Its Ivory—and Pray for Elephants," *National Geographic*, January 25, 2016, http://news .nationalgeographic.com/2016/01/160125-sri-lanka-elephants-buddhism-ivory-stockpile-cites.

28. Philosophers and lawyers use the term "persons" for entities worthy of moral and political respect to reference a theory of moral personhood.

"Persons" may sound strange, but "peoplehood" would be worse, so philosophers write about "persons" and "personhood." In this text, "persons" refers to individual entities capable of planning, evaluating and carrying out intentional acts. Personhood, in this way, is constitutive of morality and responsibility. However, personhood is not the only rationale justifying moral respect. There are good reasons to take care of entities that are not human or even sentient without confusing these entities with persons.

1 The Singularization of Everything

1. For full technological disclosure, I drafted this book on an iPad using the Pages app, and then revised and expanded using Scrivener on a laptop.
2. *Foxconn: An Exclusive Inside Look*, ABC News, 2012.
3. Marilyn Strathern, *Property, Substance & Effect: Anthropological Essays on Persons and Things* (London: Athlone Press, 1999).
4. Marcel Mauss, *The Gift* (London: Routledge, 1990), 16.
5. See Hodder, *Entangled*. Hodder contrasts things and objects, using the etymology of objects to treat them as a category for things that block or inhibit action. Though the concept is conceptually important, ordinary language makes few distinctions between things and objects, except perhaps in classes of things that are too abstract to be treated as an object. Even these are objects of the mind. In any case, I do not maintain the distinction here.
6. Charles Duhigg and David Barboza, "In China, Human Costs are Built into an iPad," *New York Times*, January 25, 2012.
7. Greg Campbell, "Blunt Trauma: Marijuana, the New Blood Diamonds," *New Republic*, July 13, 2013. Journalists have shown an interest in how drug supply chains connect with harm. Rajeev Syal, "Drug Money Saved Banks in Global Crisis, Claims UN Advisor," *Observer*, December 13, 2009. Likewise, journalists have explored the connections with global commerce.
8. Seth Stevenson, "The Greatest Paper Map of the United States You'll Ever See," *Slate*, January 2, 2012.
9. Heather Timmons and J. Adam Huggins, "New York Manhole Covers, Forged Barefoot in India," *New York Times*, November 26, 2007.
10. Kim Severson, "More Choice, and More Confusion, in Quest for Healthy Eating," *New York Times*, September 8, 2012. Food is perhaps the most frequent form of object-centered journalism, and the attention has greatly increased under the scrutiny of local food movements. Editorial, "From Farm to Landfill," *New York Times*, September 29,

2012. Interest also focuses on how food is wasted. "One Insecticide, from Field to Table," *New York Times*, May 7, 1990. A much longer tradition considers the health risks from foods origins, especially through technological changes in farming.

11. Stephanie Strom, "A Sweetheart Becomes Suspect; Looking Behind Those Kathie Lee Labels," *New York Times*, June 27, 1996. Sweatshops are the quintessential target of journalistic muckraking in the developing world, and clothing production has been particularly notorious/attractive because it connects with prominent brands and known labels.

12. John H. Cushman, "Nike Pledges to End Child Labor and Apply U.S. Rules Abroad," *New York Times*, May 13, 1998; Steven Greenhouse, "Nike Shoe Plant in Vietnam is Called Unsafe for Workers," *New York Times*, November 8, 1997.

13. Editorial, "Harvest of Weapons Thrown into the Sea," *New York Times*, July 19, 1931. Guns are another persistently moralized object. Interest in their disposal can be traced back to the early 1930s, and the tradition persists. Al Baker, "Where Illegal Guns Can Do No More Harm," *New York Times*, June 3, 2008; Pam Belluck, "Seeing Crime Guns Destroyed Gives Solace to Victims' Families," *New York Times*, January 4, 2006.

14. Sari Horwitz, "Cigarette Smuggling Linked to Terrorism," *Washington Post*, June 8, 2004.

15. Gardiner Harris, "The Safety Gap," *New York Times*, October 31, 2008. Pharmaceuticals are highlighted for the places that make them and for the life cycle concerns raised by their disposal. See Maine Department of Environmental Protection [press release], "Pharmaceutical Drugs found in Landfill Water," www.maine.gov/tools/whatsnew/index.php?topic=DEP±News&id=88993&v=Article.

16. Steve Mullis, "'Profoundly Sorry' HSBC Reaches $1.9B Settlement in Money-Laundering Case," *NPR*, December 10, 2012; Shahien Nasiripour and Kara Scannell, "UK Banks Hit by Record 2.6 Bn US Fines," *Financial Times*, December 11, 2012. Money laundering is a persistent theme of moralization and object concern, but recent cases at HSBC, Standard Chartered, and JPMorgan Chase represent settlements at an unforeseen scale and illustrate the major institutional complicity in the money laundering process.

17. "Under this law, a chattel was deemed to be a deodand whenever a coroner's jury decided that it had caused the death of a human being. Deodands were automatically forfeit to the crown. The term 'deodand' derives from the Latin phrase *deo dandum*, which means 'to be given to God'." Anna Pervukhin, "Deodands: A Study in the Creation of

Common Law Rules," *The American Journal of Legal History*, 47 no. 3 (July 2005): 237.

18. D. I. C. Ashton-Cross, "Liability in Roman Law for Damage Caused by Animals," *Cambridge Law Journal*, 11 no. 3 (1953): 395.

19. Oliver Wendell Holmes, Jr., *The Common Law* (Boston: Little, Brown and Company, 1881). Within the Roman legal tradition of noxal surrender, instruments that result in a human death were taken as deodand, or as cursed objects forfeit to the crown. Holmes documents numerous examples of how objects are taken to be blameworthy in early common law cases. In his view, this is done to "gratify the passion of revenge. Learned men have been ready to find a reason in the personification of inanimate nature common to savages and children, and there is much to confirm this view. Without such a personification, anger towards lifeless things would have been transitory, at most" (285).

20. See Igor Kopytoff, "The Cultural Biography of Things: Commoditization as Process," in *The Social Life of Things: Commodities in Cultural Perspective*, ed. Arjun Appadurai (Cambridge: Cambridge University Press, 1986), 64–94; Lucien Karpik, *Valuing the Unique: The Economics of Singularities* (Princeton, NJ: Princeton University Press, 2010), 10. The term "singularity" is used by some anthropologists and economic sociologists. While my use of it has a similar meaning, I theorize that it can be applied to a much wider range of objects than some other scholars might.

21. John Ruskin, *Unto This Last and Other Writings*, ed. Clive Wilmer (London: Penguin, 1997), 84.

22. *Commodity, n.*, OED Online (Oxford University Press), accessed October 27, 2012. The word commodity itself has divergent meanings. Sometimes there is little or no distinction between a "commodity" and a "good" or "product." It stands simply for something that is sold. For example, in the Oxford English Dictionary, a commodity is defined as "a thing of use or advantage to mankind; esp. in pl. useful products, material advantages, elements of wealth... A kind of thing produced for use or sale, an article of commerce, an object of trade; in pl. goods, merchandise, wares, produce. Now esp. food or raw materials, as objects of trade." In contrast, Marx described the quality standardization implied in the meaning of "commodity" as something more specific (see below).

23. See Sidney W. Mintz, *Sweetness and Power: The Place of Sugar in Modern History* (New York: Penguin Books, 1985); Kenneth Pomeranz, *The World that Trade Created: Society, Culture, and the World Economy* (Armonk, NY: M.E. Sharpe, 1999). Though the list of commodities traded on large and regional exchanges has expanded to

include oil and a much longer list of goods if wholesale markets are included, commodities markets are still most focused upon raw materials, precious metals, food, and energy.

24. "One cannot tell by the taste of wheat whether it has been raised by a Russian serf, a French peasant, or an English capitalist." Karl Marx, *A Contribution to the Critique of Political Economy*, trans. N. I. Stone, 2nd ed. (Chicago: Charles H. Kerr & Company, 1904), 20.

25. Paul Bloom, *How Pleasure Works: The New Science of Why We Like What We Like* (New York: Norton, 2010), preface paragraph 5.

26. Georg Simmel, *The Philosophy of Money*, trans. Tom Bottomore, David Frisby, and Kaethe Mengelberg (New York: Rutledge, 1978), 163. Simmel's treatment of money often emphasizes the way that money is commodified and fungible, which is inconsistent with the notion of singularities, but his work also shows real sensitivity to the material properties of social life.

27. Bloom's aforementioned volume is a good start in this literature. See also Chapter 8 in Dan Ariely, *Predictably Irrational, Revised and Expanded Edition: The Hidden Forces that Shape our Decisions* (New York: HarperCollins, 2009), for a discussion of endowment effects and the meaning that some owners quickly ascribe to their property.

28. I use the term "conscientious consumer" in lieu of the somewhat more common category of "conscious consumer" because I prefer to emphasize the application of one's moral conscience to consumer decisions. Later in this text, I will describe how attention (consciousness) plays an important role in conscientiousness. In common use, these terms are practically indistinguishable.

29. David Vogel, *The Market for Virtue: The Potential and Limits of Corporate Social Responsibility* (Washington, DC: Brookings Institution Press, 2005).

30. See Gary Gereffi, John Humphrey, and Timothy Sturgeon, "The Governance of Global Value Chains," *Review of International Political Economy*, 12 no. 1 (2005): 78–104. Numerous structural components maintain supply chain characteristics. See David L. Levy, "Political Contestation in Global Production Networks," *Academy of Management Review*, 33 no. 4 (2008): 943–963. Yet these characteristics occur within a globally contested and often failing regime.

31. Graeme Auld, *Constructing Private Governance: The Rise and Evolution of Forest, Coffee, and Fisheries Certification* (New Haven: Yale University Press, 2014). Auld's account takes seriously the market conditions under which governance forms emerge and are sustained. While I will discuss some of these conditions, I am more interested in understanding the role that objects play as a gathering point for moral

considerations than in the interplay between certification and market competition. I take the question of whether a general system of object governance would be desirable to run in parallel with the question of how such systems can and do (mal)function.

32. Paul W. Hirt, *A Conspiracy of Optimism: Management of the National Forests since World War Two* (Lincoln, NE: University of Nebraska Press, 1994), 416.
33. David A. Perry, "The Scientific Basis of Forestry," *Annual Review of Ecology and Systematics*, 29 (1998): 435–466.
34. Ibid.
35. Samuel P. Hays, *Wars in the Woods: The Rise of Ecological Forestry in America* (Pittsburgh, PA: University of Pittsburgh Press, 2007), 3.
36. Tim Ingold, "Bringing Things Back to Life: Creative Entanglements in a World of Materials," *NCRM Working Paper. Realities* / Morgan Centre, University of Manchester. (2010, unpublished), 4.
37. William L. Balée, *Footprints of the Forest: Ka'Apor Ethnobotany – The Historical Ecology of Plant Utilization by an Amazonian People* (New York: Columbia University Press, 1999).
38. M. Kat Anderson, *Tending the Wild: Native American Knowledge and the Management of California's Natural Resources* (Berkeley: University of California Press, 2005), 167.
39. Robert S. Seymour and Malcolm L. Hunter, Jr., "Principles of Ecological Forestry," in *Maintaining Biodiversity in Forest Ecosystems*, ed. Malcolm L. Hunter, Jr. (Cambridge: Cambridge University Press, 1999).
40. W. J. Bond, F. I. Woodward, and G. F. Midgley, "The Global Distribution of Ecosystems in a World without Fire," *New Phytologist*, 165 no. 2 (2005): 525–538.
41. Perry, *The Scientific Basis of Forestry*, 441.
42. Paul Hawken, Amory B. Lovins, and L. Hunter Lovins, *Natural Capitalism: Creating the Next Industrial Revolution* (Boston: Little, Brown and Co., 1999).
43. John Mazzone and John Pickett, *The Household Diary Study: Mail Use and Attitudes in FY 2009* (Washington, DC: United States Postal Service, 2010), http://about.usps.com/studying-americans-mail-use/household-diary/2009/fullreport-pdf/usps-hds-fy09.pdf.
44. John Muir, "The American Forests," *The Atlantic*, 1897, www.theatlantic.com/magazine/archive/1897/08/the-american-forests/305017.
45. "God has cared for these trees, saved them from drought, disease, avalanches, and a thousand straining, leveling tempests and floods; but he cannot save them from fools, – only Uncle Sam can do that." Ibid.

46. Michael R. Clark and Joelyn Sarrah Kozar, "Comparing Sustainable Forest Management Certifications Standards: A Meta-Analysis," *Ecology and Society*, 16 no. 1 (2011): 3–27, www.ecologyandsociety .org/vol16/iss1/art3.

47. Lars H. Gulbrandsen, "Overlapping Public and Private Governance: Can Forest Certification Fill the Gaps in the Global Forest Regime?" *Global Environmental Politics*, 4 no. 2 (2004): 75–99.

48. Mireya Navarro, "Environmental Groups Spar Over Certifications of Wood and Paper Products," *New York Times*, September 11, 2009, www.nytimes.com/2009/09/12/science/earth/12timber.html.

49. Saskia Ozinga, *Behind the Logo: An Environmental and Social Assessment of Forest Certification Schemes* (Gloucestershire, UK: Forests and the European Resource Network, 2001), www.fern .org/sites/fern.org/files/Behind%20the%20logo.pdf.

50. ForestEthics, *Certified Greenwash: Inside the Sustainable Forestry Initiative's Deceptive Eco-Label*, 2010, http://forestethics.org/downloads/ SFI-Certified-Greenwash_Report_ForestEthics.pdf.

51. Ibid.

52. Benjamin Cashore, Graeme Auld, and Deanna Newsom, "The United States' Race to Certify Sustainable Forestry: Non-State Environmental Governance and the Competition for Policy-Making Authority," *Business and Politics*, 5 no. 3 (2004): 1–259.

53. Ray C. Anderson, *Mid-Course Correction: Toward a Sustainable Enterprise: The Interface Model* (Atlanta, GA: Peregrinzilla Press, 1998), 72.

54. Charles W. Schmidt, "Face to Face with Toy Safety: Understanding an Unexpected Threat," *Environmental Health Perspectives*, 116 no. 2 (2008): A70.

55. Michael Pirson and Deepak Malhotra, "Unconventional Insights for Managing Stakeholder Trust," *MIT Sloan Management Review*, 49 no. 4 (2008): 50.

56. Paul W. Beamish and Hari Bapuji, "Toy Recalls and China: Emotion vs. Evidence," *Management and Organization Review*, 4 no. 2 (2008): 197–209.

57. Pirson and Malhotra, "Unconventional Insights for Managing Stakeholder Trust," 50.

58. David Barboza, "Scandal and Suicide in China: A Dark Side of Toys," *New York Times* (August 23, 2007), C1.

59. Centers for Disease Control and Prevention, "Multistate Outbreak of Salmonella Infections Associated with Peanut Butter and Peanut Butter-Containing Products: United States, 2008–2009," *Morbidity and*

Mortality Weekly Report, 58 (January 29, 2009): 85–90, http://ftp.cdc .gov/pub/publications/mmwr/wk/mm58e0129.pdf.

60. Gardiner Harris, "Salmonella was Found at Peanut Plant Before," *New York Times*, A15, January 28, 2009.
61. Missy Ryan, "One in Four Americans 'Very Worried' about China Imports," *Reuters*, September 19, 2007, http://uk.reuters.com/article/ 2007/09/19/uk-usa-foodsafety-poll-idUKN1818311820070919.
62. Barboza, "Scandal and Suicide in China."
63. Ivan Muñoz, Cristina Gazulla, Alba Bala, Rita Puig, and Pere Fullana, "LCA and Ecodesign in the Toy Industry: Case Study of a Teddy Bear Incorporating Electric and Electronic Components," *The International Journal of Life Cycle Assessment*, 14 no. 1 (2009): 64–72.
64. Ibid., 68.
65. US Environmental Protection Agency, 2013, "Climate Change and Waste," www.epa.gov/climatechange/climate-change-waste.
66. Alan Barrett and John Lawlor, "Questioning the Waste Hierarchy: The Case of a Region with a Low Population Density," *Journal of Environmental Planning and Management*, 40 no. 1 (1997): 19–36.
67. Clemen Rasmussen and Dorte Vigsø, eds., *Rethinking the Waste Hierarchy* (Copenhagen: Environmental Assessment Institute, 2005).
68. US Environmental Protection Agency, 2013, "Municipal Solid Waste," www.epa.gov/epawaste/nonhaz/municipal/index.htm.
69. Katie Campbell and Ken Christensen, "Where Does America's E-Waste End Up? GPS Tracker Tells All," *PBS Newshour*, May 20, 2016, www.pbs.org/newshour/updates/america-e-waste-gps-tracker-tells-all-earthfix/
70. Margarita Svetlova, Sara R. Nichols, and Celia A. Brownell, "Toddlers' Prosocial Behavior: From Instrumental to Empathic to Altruistic Helping," *Child Development*, 81 no. 6 (2010): 1814–1827.
71. Gavin Hilson, "Fair Trade Gold: Antecedents, Prospects and Challenges," *Geoforum*, 39 no. 1 (2008): 386–400.
72. Viviana A. Zelizer, *The Social Meaning of Money* (New York: Basic Books, 1994), 5.
73. Humeyra Pamuk, Steve Stecklow, Babak Dehghanpisheh, and Can Sezer, "Special Report – Golden Loophole: How an Alleged Turkish Crime Ring Helped Iran," *Reuters*, April 29, 2014, www.reuters.com/article/us-iran-turkey-special-report-idUSBREA3S07120140429
74. Hawken, Lovins, and Lovins, *Natural Capitalism: Creating the Next Industrial Revolution*.
75. Julian Lincoln Simon, *Hoodwinking the Nation* (New Brunswick, NJ: Transaction, 1999), 140.

76. G. Robinson Gregory, *Resource Economics for Foresters* (New York: Wiley, 1987), 477.
77. Jon M. Conrad, *Resource Economics*, 2nd ed. (New York: Cambridge University Press, 2010), 285.
78. For example, Donald A. MacKenzie, *An Engine, Not a Camera: How Financial Models Shape Markets* (Cambridge, MA: MIT Press, 2006), 377.
79. Robert K. Merton, "The Unanticipated Consequences of Purposive Social Action," *American Sociological Review*, 1 no. 6 (1936): 894–904.
80. Hawken, Lovins, and Lovins, *Natural Capitalism: Creating the Next Industrial Revolution*, 396.
81. Michael C. Jensen, "Value Maximization, Stakeholder Theory, and the Corporate Objective Function," *Business Ethics Quarterly*, 12 no. 2 (2002): 235–256.

2 Singularization Schema

1. See Marlieke T. R. van Kesteren, Dirk J. Ruiter, Guillén Fernández, and Richard N. Henson, "How Schema and Novelty Augment Memory Formation," *Trends in Neurosciences*, 35 no. 4 (2012): 211–219. Recent work in neuroscience argues that schemas are important to the storage of both novel and congruent information.
2. See, for example, Sandra L. Bem, "Gender Schema Theory: A Cognitive Account of Sex Typing," *Psychological Review*, 88 no. 4 (1981): 354–364.
3. Mark W. Baldwin, "Relational Schemas and the Processing of Social Information," *Psychological Bulletin*, 112 no. 3 (1992): 461–484.
4. Miller, *Material Culture and Mass Consumption*, 178.
5. Andrew Sayer, "(De)commodification, Consumer Culture, and Moral Economy," *Environment and Planning D: Society and Space*, 21 (2003): 343.
6. Ferruccio Rossi-Landi, "Commodities as Messages," in *Recherches sur les systèmes signifiants*, ed. J. Rya-Debove, Warsaw Symposium (The Hague: Mouton, 1968). Cited in Lee V. Cassanelli, "Qat: Changes in the Production and Consumption of a Quasilegal Commodity in Northeast Africa," in *The Social Life of Things: Commodities in Cultural Perspective*, ed. Arjun Appadurai (Cambridge: Cambridge University Press, 1986), 224.
7. Kopytoff, "The Cultural Biography of Things," 85.
8. George A. Akerlof, "The Market for 'Lemons': Quality Uncertainty and the Market Mechanism," *The Quarterly Journal of Economics*, 84 no. 3 (1970): 488–500.

9. Daniel Miller, *A Theory of Shopping* (Cambridge, MA: Polity Press, 1998); Daniel Miller, "The Poverty of Morality," *Journal of Consumer Culture*, 1 no. 2 (2001): 225–243.

10. Barry Schwartz, *The Paradox of Choice: Why More is Less* (New York: Ecco, 2004), 265.

11. Gary Wolf, "Steve Jobs: The Next Insanely Great Thing," *Wired Digital Magazine* (1996), www.wired.com/1996/02/jobs-2.

12. Ibid.

13. Erving Goffman, *Asylums: Essays on the Social Situation of Mental Patients and Other Inmates* (Garden City, NY: Anchor Books, 1961), 386.

14. Nicholas Epley, Adam Waytz, and John T. Cacioppo, "On Seeing Human: A Three-Factor Theory of Anthropomorphism," *Psychological Review*, 114 no. 4 (2007): 864.

15. Ibid., 880.

16. Jean Piaget and Jacques Vonèche, *The Child's Conception of the World* (Lanham, MD: Rowman & Littlefield Pub Incorporated, 2007).

17. Immanuel Kant, *Groundwork for the Metaphysics of Morals* (New Haven, CT: Yale University Press, 2002).

18. Morela Hernandez, "Toward an Understanding of the Psychology of Stewardship," *Academy of Management Review*, 37 (2012): 174.

19. Gabriel Abend, *The Moral Background: An Inquiry into the History of Business Ethics* (Princeton, NJ: Princeton University Press, 2014), 341.

20. Jennifer Welchman, "A Defence of Environmental Stewardship," *Environmental Values*, 21 (2012).

21. See Stephen Jay Gould, "The Golden Rule: A Proper Scale for Our Environmental Crisis," *Natural History*, 99 no. 9 (1990): 24. See also James Lovelock, "The Fallible Concept of Stewardship of the Earth," in *Environmental Stewardship*, ed. R. J. Berry (London: T&T Clark, 2006).

22. Bernard Williams, *Morality: An Introduction to Ethics*, ed. Canto (Cambridge: Cambridge University Press, 1993), xvii.

23. *Up*, directed by Pete Docter and Bob Peterson (Buena Vista, FL: Pixar Animation Studios and Walt Disney Pictures, 2009).

24. "Any heart that isn't moved by this lyrical passage must be made of stone." Joe Morgenstern, "Reaching for the Sky, 'Up' Fails to Soar," *Wall Street Journal*, May 14, 2009.

25. "I think they are emotionally manipulative in a fundamentally dishonest way. I do not think the people making the films are necessarily dishonest, but they do not seem attuned to what their stories are saying …. One example, in the opening montage of 'Up,' you're essentially being strong-armed into shedding tears about Carl and Ellie. To me, it was

grotesquely sentimental and a lot of people were looking for an excuse to break into tears, and obviously this was for them ... There's a sentimentality in most Pixar pictures that are [sic] very manipulative and completely unconvincing to me. They are congratulating their audience for feeling these synthetic emotions and, to me, that's offensive." Michael Barrier, cited in Jordan Zakarin, "Animated Man: Cartoon Expert Michael Barrier Decries Pixar, Computers," *The Huffington Post*, February 25, 2011, www.huffingtonpost.com/2011/02/25/anima ted-man-cartoon-expe_n_828319.html. Emotional manipulation was a theme in reviews as well. "'Up' deals with adult ideas in ways that children can accept: it's all about dreams deferred, the loss of loved ones and the way disappointments sometimes reveal hidden opportunities for happiness. But as great as all of that sounds, 'Up' has the quality of a vacation package masquerading as a journey. Everything in it seems meticulously calibrated to get an effect out of us." Stephanie Zacharek, "'Up': Pixar's Latest is Bursting with Charming Visual Touches and Life-Affirming Messages, So Why Does it Feel so Cold?" *Salon*, May 29, 2009, www.salon.com/2009/05/29/up_review.

26. *Toy Story*, directed by John Lasseter (Buena Vista, FL: Pixar Animation Studios and Walt Disney Pictures, 1995); *Toy Story 2*, directed by John Lasseter, Ash Brannon and Lee Unkrich (Buena Vista, FL: Pixar Animation Studios and Walt Disney Pictures, 1999); *Toy Story 3*, directed by Lee Unkrich (Buena Vista, FL: Pixar Animation Studios and Walt Disney Pictures, 2010).

27. For the most important children's narrative demonstrating this problem, see Shel Silverstein, *The Giving Tree* (New York: Harper & Row, 1964).

28. *WALL-E*, directed by Andrew Stanton (Buena Vista, FL: Pixar Animation Studios and Walt Disney Pictures, 2008).

29. Slavoj Žižek, "Nobody Has to be Vile," *The London Review of Books*, April 6, 2006, www.lrb.co.uk/v28/n07/slavoj-zizek/nobody-has-to-be-vile.

3 The Power of Negative Thinking

1. Norman Vincent Peale, *The Power of Positive Thinking* (New York: Prentice-Hall, 1952), 276.

2. Herbert Marcuse, "A Note on Dialectic (1960)," in Andrew Feenberg and William Leiss, eds., *The Essential Marcuse: Selected Writings of Philosopher and Social Critic Herbert Marcuse* (Boston: Beacon Press, 2007), 63.

3. Ibid., 64.

4. See N. Craig Smith, *Morality and the Market* (London: Routledge, 1990). Smith's argument focuses on the rationale that places consumers in a position of power. As he explains, "Consumer sovereignty is the key to this study[,] the basis for the argument[, and] the rationale for capitalism." And yet, as Smith acknowledges, this sovereign power is not always easy for consumers to wield. The present argument also supports ethical purchase behavior, but I will emphasize professional expertise and intermediary responsibility to a much greater extent than I do the obligations of final purchasers.

5. See, for example, Patrick De Pelsmacker, Liesbeth Driesen, and Glenn Rayp, "Do Consumers Care about Ethics? Willingness to Pay for Fair-Trade Coffee," *Journal of Consumer Affairs*, 39 no. 2 (2005): 363–385. There is a great deal of research on consumer willingness to pay for responsible products. This research covers various aspects of the consumer motivations for responding to ecological and social brand appeals. For a comprehensive review of the fair-trade research undertaken thus far, see Veronika A. Andorfer and Ulf Liebe, "Research on Fair Trade Consumption: A Review," *Journal of Business Ethics*, 106 no. 4 (2012): 415–435. Here, I am interested in the broader strategy of conscientious consumption rather than the specific psychological or behavioral impetus.

6. See Monroe Friedman, "A Positive Approach to Organized Consumer Action: The 'Buycott' as an Alternative to the Boycott," *Journal of Consumer Policy*, 19 no. 4 (1996): 439–451. Conscientious consumption is an economic and political act, yet neither of these spheres can explain the behavior. Friedman describes activists' conscientious consumer movements as a "buycott", a pro-organizational expression of favor that, like a boycott, goes beyond the mere quality of the product. Deirdre Shaw, Terry Newholm and Roger Dickinson, "Consumption as Voting: An Exploration of Consumer Empowerment," *European Journal of Marketing*, 40 no. 9 (2006): 1049–1067. More generally, the metaphor of a purchase as a vote has become very common. Together, these processes seem to expand the sphere of consumer sovereignty into a realm traditionally reserved for actual sovereignty.

7. See in general Pippa Norris, ed., *Critical Citizens: Global Support for Democratic Government* (Oxford: Oxford University Press, 1999). Institutional trust is a concept that political scientists use to explain important aspects of the way that citizens relate to states. There has been a marked and persistent decline in institutional trust in government and in political leaders within industrialized societies. See Arthur Miller and Ola Listhaug, "Political Performance and Institutional Trust," in *Critical Citizens: Global Support for*

Democratic Government, ed. Pippa Norris (Oxford: Oxford University Press, 1999), 2014–2016. This decline relates in particular to frustrations with the perceived efficacy of institutions.

8. Miller, *The Dialectics of Shopping*.
9. Sayer, "(De)commodification, Consumer Culture, and Moral Economy."
10. Andrew Sayer, *Why Things Matter to People: Social Science, Values and Ethical Life* (Cambridge: Cambridge University Press, 2011).
11. Joseph A. Schumpeter, *The Theory of Economic Development* (New Brunswick, NJ: Transaction, 1934).
12. Friedrich A. Hayek, *The Fatal Conceit: The Errors of Socialism* (Chicago: University of Chicago Press, 1988).
13. See, for example, Ronald H. Coase, "The Problem of Social Cost," *Journal of Law and Economics*, 3 (October 1960): 1–44. Coase argues that markets can handle social costs provided that property rights are in place. Our analysis will suggest that the incidence of externalities needs to be carefully allocated in order to justify economic entitlements.
14. C. Edwin Baker, *Media, Markets, and Democracy* (Cambridge: Cambridge University Press, 2002). Newspapers are another example of a positive externality. As Baker argues, newspaper consumption helps democracy to work, improves market performance, and makes your neighbors more interesting to talk to; all three of these benefits are enjoyed by people who do not have to buy the paper themselves.
15. Carl Shapiro, "Consumer Information, Product Quality, and Seller Reputation," *The Bell Journal of Economics*, 13 no. 1 (1982): 20–35. For example, if there is a lag in the information that consumers receive about products through seller reputation, then consumers will make inefficient decisions while they are misinformed.
16. Akerlof, "The Market for Lemons," 488–500.
17. See George J. Stigler, *The Organization of Industry* (Chicago: University of Chicago Press, 1968), 67. In an early definition of barriers to entry, Stigler focuses on the higher cost function borne by entrants. Harold Demsetz, "Barriers to Entry," *The American Economic Review*, 72 no. 1 (1982): 47–57. Demsetz notes that barriers to entry are essential to markets and that property itself can be conceived as such a barrier. There is no practical way to distinguish between the sorts of barriers that are necessary and those that undermine consumer sovereignty, at least none that relies upon a gap between marginal revenue and marginal cost. Legal attempts to determine intentionality are similarly problematic. See Michael E. Porter, "How Competitive Forces Shape Strategy," *Harvard Business Review* (March-April 1979): 137. As difficult as it can be to make policy regarding barriers

to entry, the conceptual meaning can be at least somewhat clearer: when structural features or market strategies limit entry, competition decreases and sellers benefit. Whether this is monopolistic greed or good business strategy depends on the situation.

18. Marshall W. Meyer and Lynn G. Zucker, *Permanently Failing Organizations* (Beverly Hills, CA: Sage Publications, Inc., 1989).

19. "Not every transaction fits comfortably into the classical-contracting scheme. In particular, long-term contracts executed under conditions of uncertainty are ones for which complete presentation is apt to be prohibitively costly if not impossible. Problems of several kinds arise. First, not all future contingencies for which adaptations are required can be anticipated at the outset. Second, the appropriate adaptations will not be evident for many contingencies until the circumstances materialize." Oliver E. Williamson, "Transaction-Cost Economics: The Governance of Contractual Relations," *Journal of Law and Economics*, 22 no. 2 (1979): 237. See also Oliver E. Williamson, *The Economic Institutions of Capitalism: Firms, Markets, Relational Contracting* (New York: Free Press, 1985), and Ronald H. Coase, "The Nature of the Firm," *Economica*, 4 no. 16 (1937): 386–405.

20. Allen E. Buchanan, *Ethics, Efficiency, and the Market* (Totowa, NJ: Rowman & Allanheld, 1985), 135.

21. As Stiglitz noted in his Nobel lecture, "Information imperfections are pervasive in the economy: indeed, it is hard to imagine what a world with perfect information would be like." Peter Englund, ed., *Prize Lectures in Economic Sciences 2001–2005* (Singapore: World Scientific Publishing Co., 2008), 488.

22. For another example based on imperfect information, see Michael Rothschild and Joseph Stiglitz, "Equilibrium in Competitive Insurance Markets: An Essay on the Economics of Imperfect Information," *The Quarterly Journal of Economics*, 90 no. 4 (1976): 629–649.

23. "Groups have a stronger incentive to adopt or develop norms that externalize costs than those that merely maximize joint welfare without producing negative externalities." Eric A. Posner, "Law, Economics, and Inefficient Norms," *University of Pennsylvania Law Review*, 144 (1995–1996): 1723.

24. Michael E. Porter, *Competitive Strategy: Techniques for Analyzing Industries and Competitors* (New York: Free Press, 1980), 396.

25. Jeffrey F. Jaffe, "Special Information and Insider Trading," *The Journal of Business*, 47 no. 3 (1974): 410–428. For instance, market actors may trade on special information to which they have access as insiders.

26. See Robert H. Nelson, *Economics as Religion: From Samuelson to Chicago and Beyond* (University Park, PA: Pennsylvania State University Press, 2002). Economics as science should be contrasted against economics as religion. There is an ideological approach to economic orthodoxy that still derives its major conclusions from the aforementioned assumptions.

27. Herbert Alexander Simon, *Administrative Behavior: A Study of Decision-Making Processes in Administrative Organization*, 3rd ed. (New York: Free Press, 1976), 364.

28. Coase, "The Nature of the Firm," 386–405; Oliver E. Williamson, "The Theory of the Firm as Governance Structure: From Choice to Contract," *Journal of Economic Perspectives*, 16 no. 3 (2002): 171–195.

29. Amos Tversky and Daniel Kahneman, "Judgement Under Uncertainty: Heuristics and Biases," in *Judgement Under Uncertainty: Heuristics and Biases*, eds. Daniel Kahneman, Paul Slovic, and Amos Tversky (Cambridge: Cambridge University Press, 1974); George A. Akerlof and Rachel E. Kranton, "Economics and Identity," *The Quarterly Journal of Economics*, 115 no. 3 (2000): 715–753.

30. Senate Permanent Subcommittee on Investigations, "Gas Prices: How Are They Really Set?," *Senate Hearing* 107–509 (April 30 and May 2, 2002); Senate Permanent Subcommittee on Investigations, "U.S. Strategic Petroleum Reserve: Recent Policy has Increased Costs to Consumers But Not Overall U.S. Energy Security," *Senate Committee Print* 108–118 (March 5, 2003); Senate Permanent Subcommittee on Investigations, "The Role of Market Speculation in Rising Oil and Gas Prices: A Need to Put the Cop Back on the Beat," *Senate Committee Print* 109–165 (June 27, 2006).

31. Senate Permanent Subcommittee on Investigations, "Excessive Speculation in the Natural Gas Market," *Senate Hearing* 110–235 (June 25 and July 9, 2007).

32. Senate Permanent Subcommittee on Investigations, "Excessive Speculation in the Wheat Market," *Senate Hearing* 110–235 (June 25 and July 9, 2007).

33. Senate Permanent Subcommittee on Investigations, "Wall Street Bank Involvement with Physical Commodities," *Senate Hearing and Report* (November 20 and 21, 2014).

34. Senate Permanent Subcommittee on Investigations, "Wall Street Bank Involvement with Physical Commodities," *Senate Hearing and Report* 250 (November 20 and 21, 2014).

35. Ibid., 10.

36. David Kocieniewski, "A Shuffle of Aluminum, but to Banks, Pure Gold," *New York Times*, July 20, 2013.

37. Joseph Heath, *Morality, Competition, and the Firm: The Market Failures Approach to Business Ethics* (New York: Oxford University Press, 2014), 10.

38. Ted Robert Gurr, Keith Jaggers, and Will H. Moore, "The Transformation of the Western State: The Growth of Democracy, Autocracy, and State Power Since 1800," *Studies in Comparative International Development*, 25 no. 1 (1990): 73–108. Democratic and economic development play a complex and intertwined role in the development of the modern state. Democracies like the United States and France are leading examples of the drastic expansion of state power that occurred in the late colonial period as a by-product of both economic and political change. In the process, democracy took control that monarchies could not have hoped to maintain and markets gained traction in goods and services that were previously provided by household production. It is difficult to say whether the market expanded the state or vice versa.

39. John Stuart Mill, *Considerations on Representative Government* (New York: Cosimo, 2008), 51.

40. Amartya Sen, *Development as Freedom* (New York: Knopf, 1999), 152.

41. Alexis de Tocqueville, *Democracy in America*, trans. Harvey C. Mansfield and Delba Winthrop (Chicago: University of Chicago Press, 2000).

42. Bernard Manin, *The Principles of Representative Government* (Cambridge: Cambridge University Press, 1997), 243. The framers of the US Constitution demonstrated a deep ambivalence regarding democracy. Their solution was a representative form of government that is particularly open to elite participants.

43. David Lublin, *The Paradox of Representation: Racial Gerrymandering and Minority Interests in Congress* (Princeton, NJ: Princeton University Press, 1997), 159; Samuel Issacharoff, "Gerrymandering and Political Cartels," *Harvard Law Review*, 116 no. 2 (2002): 593–648. Political redistricting has been a major source of debate, both in its use to facilitate the election of minority candidates and in its use to reinforce the strength of political power.

44. See, for instance, Diane Stone, "Recycling Bins, Garbage Cans or Think Tanks? Three Myths Regarding Policy Analysis Institutes," *Public Administration*, 85 no. 2 (2007): 259–278. There is considerable opacity in the interactions that eventually write and edit law. And, while formal boundaries purportedly divide scientific analysis of policy from

the political process that produces it, the boundaries are not as clear as theory would suggest.

45. Mark A. Smith, *American Business and Political Power: Public Opinion, Elections, and Democracy* (Chicago: University of Chicago Press, 2000), 245. The question of how business power influences legislative outcomes is not by any means resolved. The simple claim that business interests are organized and through their aggregate power are able to control the political process can be summarily dismissed. As Smith has argued, the business community's interests are fractured, and when they are not the legislature tends to win and lose elections based upon these very issues. In other words, elected officials act on behalf of elite business interests and against the will of the people at great political peril. However, this does not resolve the question of how business shapes political sentiments and perceptions among the electorate, an outcome greatly exacerbated by unlimited political action committee funding.

46. See, for example, Ernesto Dal Bó, "Regulatory Capture: A Review," *Oxford Review of Economic Policy*, 22 no. 2 (2006): 217–218.

47. David Vogel, "The Private Regulation of Global Corporate Conduct: Achievements and Limitations," *Business & Society*, 49 no. 1 (2010): 73.

48. Neil Postman, *Amusing Ourselves to Death: Public Discourse in the Age of Show Business* (New York: Penguin Books, 1985), 184; Norman E. Bowie, "A Kantian Theory of Meaningful Work," *Journal of Business Ethics*, 17 no. 9 (1998): 1083–1092.

49. Manin, *The Principles of Representative Government*, 243.

50. Russell J. Dalton and Martin P. Wattenberg, *Parties Without Partisans: Political Change in Advanced Industrial Democracies* (Oxford: Oxford University Press, 2000), 314.

51. Russ Choma, "One Member of Congress = 18 American Households: Lawmakers' Personal Finances Far From Average," *Center for Responsive Politics*, January 12, 2015, www.opensecrets.org/news/2015/01/one-member-of-congress-18-american-households-lawmakers-personal-finances-far-from-average. According to the Center for Responsive Politics, the median net worth of Congressional representatives' households is more than eighteen times the median net worth of American households.

52. Lawrence Lessig, *Republic, Lost: How Money Corrupts Congress–and a Plan to Stop It* (New York: Twelve, 2011), 383.

53. Richard L. Hasen, "*Citizens United* and the Illusion of Coherence," *Michigan Law Review*, 109 (2010): 581.

54. Adam Bonica, Nolan McCarty, Keith T. Poole, and Howard Rosenthal, "Why Hasn't Democracy Slowed Rising Inequality?" *Journal of Economic Perspectives*, 27 no. 3 (2013): 103–123.
55. Nolan McCarty, Keith T. Poole, and Howard Rosenthal, *Polarized America: The Dance of Ideology and Unequal Riches*, 2nd ed. (Cambridge: MA, MIT Press 2016).
56. Edmund L. Andrews, "Greenspan Concedes Error on Regulation," *New York Times* 24 (2008), B1. The 2008 financial crisis was a particularly sharp rebuke of the deregulation agenda in banking. Alan Greenspan, whose leadership of the Federal Reserve gave preference to markets over regulation, described his disappointment in the wake of the crisis. In a statement to a Congressional committee on oversight he admitted, "Those of us who have looked to the self-interest of lending institutions to protect shareholders' equity, myself included, are in a state of shocked disbelief . . .. This modern risk-management paradigm held sway for decades . . .. The whole intellectual edifice, however, collapsed in the summer of last year."
57. See, for example, Wendell Potter, *Deadly Spin: An Insurance Company Insider Speaks Out on How Corporate PR is Killing Health Care and Deceiving Americans* (New York: Bloomsbury Press, 2010), 277. Potter worked in public relations for a major healthcare firm. He argues in the book, as he did before Congress, that firms mislead regulators and consumers about their practices while undermining regulatory alternatives.
58. See Robert M. Lawless, Angela K. Littwin, Katherine M. Porter, John A. E. Pottow, Deborah Thorne, and Elizabeth Warren, "Did Bankruptcy Reform Fail? An Empirical Study of Consumer Debtors," *American Bankruptcy Law Journal* 82 (2008): 349–406. The 2005 Bankruptcy Abuse Prevention and Consumer Protection Act is one example of the aggressive policy-shaping efforts of the consumer credit industry. The law was sold by its advocates as a measure that would protect consumers from the irresponsible use of bankruptcy by high income individuals who use bankruptcy strategically. However, after the law went into effect, there was no change in the income profile of consumers declaring bankruptcy. While there was a reduction in bankruptcy filings overall, those who filed for bankruptcy after 2005 were relatively more indebted than those who filed before the law was passed. This clear victory for credit card companies, whose balance sheets are directly impacted by bankruptcy proceedings, was one more step in a long history of increases in American household debt that does not seem to serve the public interest.

59. William G. Tierney, "Too Big to Fail: The Role of For-Profit Colleges and Universities in American Higher Education," *Change: The Magazine of Higher Learning*, 43 no. 6 (2011): 32. Regulation has not kept pace with the rapid expansion of for-profit postsecondary education. As one scholar explains: "Over the last few years, the for-profit industry has fought virtually every regulation that the Department of Education has proposed. While it has begun to reform itself to some degree and is more open to external research than when I first began studying it a decade ago, its philosophy is largely libertarian and market-driven. The assumption is that the market has self-correcting mechanisms that will take care of any problems and that disreputable institutions will go out of business. The role of the government, in this view, is little more than to provide subsidies to students/consumers to facilitate the growth of the companies. [W]hile the for-profit institutions should — indeed, must — have a place at the postsecondary table, they also need to accept the responsibility and oversight that participation in postsecondary education demands."

60. Charles Tilly, "Globalization Threatens Labor's Rights," *International Labor and Working-Class History*, no. 47 (1995): 4. Throughout history, globalization has hindered labor rights. As Tilly stated succinctly, "globalization threatens established rights of labor through its undermining of state capacity to guarantee those rights."

61. James A. Piazza, "Globalizing Quiescence: Globalization, Union Density and Strikes in 15 Industrialized Countries," *Economic and Industrial Democracy*, 26 no. 2 (2005): 289–314. Data on labor contestation amidst globalization show that globalization decreases strikes, but that the effect is mediated by unionization.

62. See Charles Heckscher and Françoise Carré, "Strength in Networks: Employment Rights Organizations and the Problem of Co-Ordination," *British Journal of Industrial Relations*, 44 no. 4 (2006): 605–628. One example is the Coalition of Immokalee Workers, which has managed to organize among fast food chains that buy large quantities of the tomatoes that their workers grow. Increasingly, these network approaches serve as supplements to declining union power.

63. Quoted from a meeting on April 8, 2003 between DeLay and students from the University of Pennsylvania.

64. "Chronology: Former House Majority Leader Tom DeLay," *New York Times*, www.nytimes.com/ref/washington/delay-timeline.html, accessed October 1, 2016.

65. R. Jeffrey Smith, "The DeLay-Abramoff Money Trail," *Washington Post*, December 31, 2005.

66. Max Weber, *The Protestant Ethic and the Spirit of Capitalism*, ed. Talcott Parsons (New York: Charles Scribner's Sons, 1958).

67. Solomon, *Ethics and Excellence*.

68. See Robert H. Frank, "If Homo Economicus Could Choose His Own Utility Function, Would He Want One with a Conscience?" *The American Economic Review*, 77 no. 4 (1987): 593–604. It is enough for a conscience to have a positive economic value.

69. Joshua D. Margolis and James P. Walsh, "Misery Loves Companies: Rethinking Social Initiatives by Business," *Administrative Science Quarterly*, 48 no. 2 (2003): 268–305.

70. Tim Rowley and Shawn Berman, "A Brand New Brand of Corporate Social Performance," *Business & Society*, 39 no. 4 (2000): 397–418.

71. Franz Mehring, *The Lessing Legend*, trans. A. S. Grogan (New York: Critics Group Press, 1938).

72. "Engels to Franz Mehring," *Marx and Engels Correspondence 1893*, trans. Donna Torr (London: International Publishers, 1968).

73. Karl Polanyi, *Dahomey and the Slave Trade: An Analysis of an Archaic Economy*, Vol. 42 (Seattle: University of Washington Press, 1966), xvii.

74. Thomas Donaldson and Thomas W. Dunfee, *Ties that Bind: A Social Contracts Approach to Business Ethics* (Cambridge, MA: Harvard Business School Press, 1999).

75. George G. Brenkert, "Freedom, Participation and Corporations: The Issue of Corporate (Economic) Democracy," *Business Ethics Quarterly*, 2 no. 3 (1992): 251–269; Andrew Crane, David Knights, and Ken Starkey, "The Conditions of our Freedom: Foucault, Organization, and Ethics," *Business Ethics Quarterly*, 18 no. 3 (2008): 299–320.

76. Nien-hê Hsieh, "Rawlsian Justice and Workplace Republicanism," *Social Theory and Practice*, 31 no. 1 (2005): 115–142.

77. Jeffrey Moriarty, "How Much Compensation Can CEOs Permissibly Accept?" *Business Ethics Quarterly*, 19 no. 2 (2009): 235–250.

78. James C. Scott, *Seeing Like a State: How Certain Schemes to Improve the Human Condition Have Failed* (New Haven: Yale University Press, 1999).

79. R. Edward Freeman, *Strategic Management: A Stakeholder Approach* (Cambridge: Cambridge University Press 2010) Chapter 3, The "Rational" Level: Stakeholder Maps, paragraph 2.

80. Ibid., Chapter 3, The "Rational" Level: Stakeholder Maps, paragraph 7.

81. Adolf Augustus Berle and Gardiner Means, *The Modern Corporation and Private Property* (New York: The Macmillan Company, 1933).

82. Henry Hansmann and Reinier Kraakman, "Toward Unlimited Shareholder Liability for Corporate Torts," *The Yale Law Journal*, 100 no. 7 (1991): 1879–1934.

83. Jeffrey N. Gordon, "Executive Compensation and Corporate Governance in Financial Firms: The Case for Convertible Equity-Based Pay," *Columbia Law and Economics Working Paper* no. 373 (July 9, 2010), http://ssrn.com/abstract=1633906.

84. Francisco H. Ferreira and Norbert Schady, "Aggregate Economic Shocks, Child Schooling and Child Health," *World Bank Research Observer*, 24 no. 2 (2008): 147–181.

85. Kenneth E. Goodpaster, "Business Ethics and Stakeholder Analysis," *Business Ethics Quarterly*, 1 no. 1 (1991): 63.

86. John Rawls, *A Theory of Justice* (New York: Oxford University Press, 1999). Rawls' approach to justice, for instance, is presented as ideal theory without regard for how a better world is accomplished. As such, the agents in a Rawlsian system of justice have much more limited natural duties of justice than they would have if he meant to describe a state that would quickly realize just institutions.

87. Archon Fung, "Deliberation Before the Revolution: Toward an Ethics of Deliberative Democracy in an Unjust World," *Political Theory*, 33 no. 3 (2005): 397–419.

88. David Hume, *A Treatise of Human Nature*, ed. P. H. Nidditch (Oxford: Clarendon Press, 1978).

89. G. E. Moore, *Principia Ethica* (Cambridge: Cambridge University Press, 1903), 232.

90. Robert B. Cialdini, Raymond R. Reno, and Carl A. Kallgren, "A Focus Theory of Normative Conduct: Recycling the Concept of Norms to Reduce Littering in Public Places," *Journal of Personality and Social Psychology*, 58 no. 6 (1990): 1015–1026.

91. Yuen Yuen Ang, "Authoritarian Restraints on Online Activism Revisited: Why 'I-Paid-A-Bribe' Worked in India but Failed in China," *Comparative Politics*, 47 no. 1 (2014): 21–40.

92. Emile Durkheim, *The Division of Labor in Society* (New York: Free Press, 1997), xxxii.

93. Robert Jackall, *Moral Mazes: The World of Corporate Managers*, 20th anniversary ed. (New York: Oxford University Press, 2010), 294.

94. Donaldson and Dunfee, *Ties that Bind*.

95. Ibid.

96. Diana B. Henriques, *The Wizard of Lies: Bernie Madoff and the Death of Trust* (New York: Times Books/Henry Holt and Co., 2011), 217.

97. US Securities and Exchange Commission, *Investigation of Failure of the SEC to Uncover Bernard Madoff's Ponzi Scheme*, Report No. OIG-509, US Securities and Exchange Commission Office of Investigations, August 31, 2009. www.sec.gov/news/studies/2009/oig-509.pdf.

98. cf. Heath, *Morality, Competition, and the Firm*.

99. Stephen Hilgartner and Charles L. Bosk, "The Rise and Fall of Social Problems: A Public Arenas Model," *American Journal of Sociology*, 94 no. 1 (1988): 53–78.

100. In his 2009 Society for Business Ethics presidential address, Phillips noted how campus activists extended corporate responsibility: "What I was seeing was the president of a university being held responsible for how one of its licensees' sub-contractors' sub-contractors treated its employees." Robert A. Phillips, "Ethics and Network Organizations," *Business Ethics Quarterly* (2010): 533–34.

101. Richard E. Wokutch, "Nike and Its Critics," *Organization and Environment*, 14 no. 2 (2001): 207.

102. Jennifer L. Burns and Debora L. Spar, "Hitting the Wall: Nike and International Labor Practices," *Harvard Business Review Case Study* 700–047, January 19, 2000.

103. Richard M. Locke, "The Promise and Perils of Globalization: The Case of Nike," in *Management: Inventing and Delivering its Future*, eds. Richard Schmalensee and Thomas A. Kochan (Cambridge, MA: MIT Press, 2003), 39–70.

104. Greg Campbell, *Blood Diamonds: Tracing the Deadly Path of the World's Most Precious Stones* (Boulder, CO: Westview Press, 2002).

105. J. Andrew Grant and Ian Taylor, "Global Governance and Conflict Diamonds: The Kimberley Process and the Quest for Clean Gems," *The Round Table: The Commonwealth Journal of International Affairs*, 93 no. 375 (2004): 385–401.

106. Norbert Elias, *Power and Civility*, 1st American ed., Vol. 2 (New York: Pantheon Books, 1982), 376.

107. James E. Post, Lee E. Preston, and Sybille Sauter-Sachs, *Redefining the Corporation: Stakeholder Management and Organizational Wealth* (Stanford, CA: Stanford Business Books, 2002), 320; Robert A. Phillips and Craig B. Caldwell, "Value Chain Responsibility: A Farewell to Arm's Length," *Business and Society Review*, 110 no. 4 (2005): 345–370.

108. James H. Davis, F. David Schoorman, and Lex Donaldson, "Toward a Stewardship Theory of Management," *Academy of Management Review*, 22 no. 1 (1997): 20–47.

109. See Myrna Wulfson, "The Ethics of Corporate Social Responsibility and Philanthropic Ventures," *Journal of Business Ethics*, 29 no. 1–2

(2001): 135–145. This form of stewardship is raised in considering what justifications managers can use for philanthropic activity since they serve as "trustees" or "stewards" of organizational resources.

110. Tor Guimaraes and Kevin Liska, "Exploring the Business Benefits of Environmental Stewardship," *Business Strategy and the Environment*, 4 no. 1 (1995): 9–22.

111. Robert Phillips, *Stakeholder Theory and Organizational Ethics* (San Francisco, CA: Berrett-Koehler, 2003), 200. R. Edward Freeman, Jeffrey S. Harrison, Andrew C. Wicks, Bidhan L. Parmar, and Simone de Colle, *Stakeholder Theory: The State of the Art* (Cambridge: Cambridge University Press, 2010). Stakeholder theory suggests that firms owe duties to numerous constituencies, and that an important part of management is building value within these stakeholder networks. Stewardship agrees and grounds the importance in a system of object flows, accountability, and property relations.

112. Donaldson and Dunfee, *Ties that Bind*. Where Donaldson and Dunfee look for norms within communities, we will look to object stewardship as an evaluative standard against which norms can be evaluated and adopted.

113. Kim Severson, "Chick-fil-A Thrust Back into Spotlight on Gay Rights," *New York Times*, sec. A13, July 26, 2012.

114. See Carlos J. Torelli, Alokparna Basu Monga and Andrew M. Kaikati, "Doing Poorly by Doing Good: Corporate Social Responsibility and Brand Concepts," *Journal of Consumer Research*, 38 no. 5 (2012): 948–963.

115. Kant, *Groundwork for the Metaphysics of Morals*.

116. Robert Axelrod, "An Evolutionary Approach to Norms," *The American Political Science Review*, 80 no. 4 (1986): 1095–1111.

117. Joel Feinberg, *The Moral Limits of the Criminal Law* (New York: Oxford University Press, 1984).

118. Brian C. Briggeman and Jayson L. Lusk, "Preferences for Fairness and Equity in the Food System," *European Review of Agricultural Economics*, 38 no. 1 (2011): 1–29.

119. Phillips, *Ethics and Network Organizations*.

4 Three Failures in Regulated Markets

1. See, for example, A. T. Flegg, "Inequality of Income, Illiteracy and Medical Care as Determinants of Infant Mortality in Underdeveloped Countries," *Population Studies*, 36 no. 3 (1982): 441–458.

2. You Jong-sung and Sanjeev Khagram, "A Comparative Study of Inequality and Corruption," *American Sociological Review*, 70 no. 1 (2005): 136–157.
3. Thomas Piketty. *Capital in the Twenty-First Century*, trans. Arthur Goldhammer (Cambridge, MA: Harvard University Press, 2013).
4. C. K. Prahalad, *The Fortune at the Bottom of the Pyramid* (Upper Saddle River, NJ: Wharton School Publishing, 2005), 401.
5. "Power in organizations has always been closely associated with inequality whether in terms of class, as for example in the ownership-control debate, or in terms of discrimination regarding age, race, sex, sexuality, religion, or other disadvantages." David Knights, "Power at Work in Organizations" in *The Oxford Handbook of Critical Management Studies*, eds. Mats Klvesson, Todd Bridgman, and Hugh Willmott (Oxford: Oxford University Press, 2009), 158.
6. Douglas S. Massey, *Categorically Unequal: The American Stratification System* (New York: Russell Sage Foundation, 2007), 36.
7. Dionne Searcey, "What's the Asbestos Risk Today?," *Wall Street Journal*, March 11, 2013.
8. Timmons and Huggins, *New York Manhole Covers, Forged Barefoot in India*.
9. Xia Huo et al., "Elevated Blood Lead Levels of Children in Guiyu, an Electronic Waste Recycling Town in China," *Environmental Health Perspectives*, 115 no. 7 (2007): 1113.
10. Thomas C. Buchmueller and Alan C. Monheit, "Employer-Sponsored Health Insurance and the Promise of Health Insurance Reform," *National Bureau of Economic Research*, no. 14839 (2009): 1–35, www.nber.org/papers/w14839.
11. Anmol Chaddha, "Are Bad Jobs Good for Poor People? The Wal-Mart Question," *Race, Poverty & the Environment*, 14 no. 1 (2007): 15–17; Elaine Ditsler, Peter Fisher and Colin Gordon, "On the Fringe: The Substandard Benefits of Workers in Part-Time, Temporary, and Contract Jobs," *The Commonwealth Fund*, no. 879 (2005): 1–23.
12. Barbara Ehrenreich, *Nickel and Dimed: On (Not) Getting by in America* (New York: Picador, 2011).
13. Paul Osterman and Beth Shulman, *Good Jobs America: Making Work Better for Everyone* (New York: Russell Sage Foundation, 2011).
14. Paul Hemp, "Presenteeism: At Work—But Out of It," *Harvard Business Review*, 82 no. 10 (2004): 49–58; Gunnar Aronsson, Klas Gustafsson, and Margareta Dallner, "Sick but Yet at Work: An Empirical Study of Sickness Presenteeism," *Journal of Epidemiology and Community Health*, 54 no. 7 (2000): 502–509.

15. David U. Himmelstein, Deborah Thorne, Elizabeth Warren, and Steffie Woolhandler, "Medical Bankruptcy in the United States, 2007: Results of a National Study," *The American Journal of Medicine*, 122 no. 8 (2009): 741–746.

16. State Health Access Data Assistance Center, *State-Level Trends in Employer-Sponsored Health Insurance* (Minneapolis, MN: University of Minnesota, 2013), www.rwjf.org/en/library/research/2013/04/state-level-trends-in-employer-sponsored-health-insurance.html.

17. Michael D. Kogan, Milton Kotelchuck, Greg R. Alexander, and Wayne E. Johnson, "Racial Disparities in Reported Prenatal Care Advice from Health Care Providers," *American Journal of Public Health*, 84 no. 1 (1994): 82–88.

18. Kevin Fiscella, Peter Franks, Marthe R. Gold, and Carolyn M. Clancy, "Inequality in Quality: Addressing Socioeconomic, Racial, and Ethnic Disparities in Health Care," *Journal of the American Medical Association*, 283 no. 19 (2000): 2579–2584.

19. Jonathan Kozol, *Savage Inequalities: Children in America's Schools* (New York: Crown Publishers, 1991), 262.

20. William S. Comanor and Robert H. Smiley, "Monopoly and the Distribution of Wealth," *The Quarterly Journal of Economics*, 89 no. 2 (1975): 177–194. It is difficult to estimate how the benefits and burdens of monopoly are distributed. One attempt to do so is found in the work of Comanor and Smiley, who argued in the mid-1970s that half of the wealth of the top 2.4 percent of households could be attributed to monopoly gains. Their critics contended that their estimates were high, but the authors argued that they had chosen the most conservative possible model. William S. Comanor and Robert H. Smiley, "Monopoly and the Distribution of Wealth: Revisited," *The Quarterly Journal of Economics*, 94 no. 1 (1980): 195–198; Lacy Glenn Thomas, "Monopoly and the Distribution of Wealth: A Reappraisal," *The Quarterly Journal of Economics*, 94 no. 1 (1980): 185–194. Concern with monopoly raises frequent attacks from the right and the left. For a slightly more polemical account of monopoly's consequences, see Barry C. Lynn, *Cornered: The New Monopoly Capitalism and the Economics of Destruction* (Hoboken, NJ: John Wiley & Sons, 2010), 312.

21. William Darity, "Forty Acres and a Mule in the 21st Century," *Social Science Quarterly*, 89 no. 3 (2008): 656–664.

22. Survey by Hearst Corporation and Research & Forecasts, October 20–November 2, 1986. iPOLL databank. The Roper Center for Public Opinion Research, University of Connecticut, www.ropercenter .uconn.edu/ipoll.html. One idiosyncratic demonstration of America's

belief in the right to education is the fact that, according to a 1986 poll, 75 percent of Americans wrongly believe that the US Constitution guarantees a free high school education. Only with a tragic sense of irony can the aspiration for public education find purchase within a failure in civic education.

23. Kozol makes one of the more forceful arguments against resource inequality in education funding and tax structure: "East St. Louis, like many poor cities in America, taxes itself at a very high rate. It's one of the most heavily taxed school districts in Illinois. In New Jersey, its counterpart is Camden. Camden has almost the highest property tax rate in New Jersey. But in both cases, because the property is virtually worthless, even with a high property tax, they cannot provide adequate revenues for their schools. What we ought to do ultimately is get rid of the property tax completely as the primary means of funding public education, because it is inherently unjust." Marge Scherer, "On Savage Inequalities: A Conversation with Jonathan Kozol," *Educational Leadership*, 50 no. 4 (1993): 4–9.

24. Mismanagement takes various forms, from callously disinterested school administrators, who are probably relatively rare, to the incessant reorganization of school structures under new management techniques. The latter is the more pressing concern at present: "Our schools will not improve if we continually reorganize their structure and management without regard for their essential purpose." Diane Ravitch, *The Death and Life of the Great American School System: How Testing and Choice are Undermining Education* (New York: Basic Books, 2010), 225. To this point, Kozol places the mismanagement outside of the schools themselves: "I find great teachers and often very courageous administrators struggling against formidable odds, and then finding themselves condemned by venomous politicians in Washington for failing to promote excellence." Scherer, *On Savage Inequalities: A Conversation with Jonathan Kozol*, 5.

25. "Rhee-Forming D.C. Schools: A Democrat Shakes Up Washington's Failed Public Schools," *Wall Street Journal*, November 22, 2008. Community violence, food access, and parental participation in education can all directly influence educational attainment. Nevertheless, many education reformers fail to recognize or address the relationship between poverty and educational attainment.

26. James S. Coleman, "Social Capital in the Creation of Human Capital," *American Journal of Sociology*, 94 (1988): S95–S120.

27. Elaine Simon and Eva Gold, "Education as a Field for Community Organizing: A Comparative Perspective," in *The People Shall Rule: ACORN, Community Organizing, and the Struggle for Economic*

Justice, ed. Robert Fisher (Nashville, TN: Vanderbilt University Press, 2009), 63–94.

28. McCarty, Poole, and Rosenthal, *Polarized America*, Chapter 1, paragraph 10.

29. Marx pursues a number of topics related to capital reproduction in the second volume of *Das Kapital*. In his analysis, the crucial, inequality-inducing feature of capital's expansion is the way that money must inevitably commodify labor within a process of commodity fetishism. The capitalist relation, in other words, places the investor in a position to coordinate the laborer, and reduces the worker's labor to that of a commodity. Practically speaking, there are a number of features of work, compensation, and labor power that this theory is forced to dismiss, not least of which is the worker who enjoys enough occupational mobility and skilled expertise that the capitalist must compete to employ her. My object here is not to rehash tired debates about the nature of capitalist profit, but to point to specific inequality-producing features of the capitalist relationship that neither the regulatory state nor the capitalist firm are likely to vanquish.

30. Robert Nozick, *Anarchy, State, and Utopia* (New York: Basic Books, 1974).

31. Comanor and Smiley, *Monopoly and the Distribution of Wealth*, 177–194.

32. Lucian A. Bebchuk and Jesse M. Fried, *Pay without Performance: The Unfulfilled Promise of Executive Compensation* (Cambridge, MA: Harvard University Press, 2004).

33. Rakesh Khurana, *Searching for a Corporate Savior: The Irrational Quest for Charismatic CEOs* (Princeton, NJ: Princeton University Press, 2002), 295.

34. Francesco Caselli, "Technological Revolutions," *The American Economic Review*, 89 no. 1 (1999): 78–102; Giulia Faggio, Kjell G. Salvanes, and John Van Reenen, "The Evolution of Inequality in Productivity and Wages: Panel Data Evidence," *Industrial and Corporate Change* 19, no. 6 (2010): 1919–1951.

35. For a review, see Sara Wakefield and Christopher Uggen, "Incarceration and Stratification," *Annual Review of Sociology*, 36 (2010): 387–406. It is worth noting that the relationship between disadvantage and incarceration is so tight that it is often difficult to disentangle. As Wakefield and Uggen summarize: "Does imprisonment reflect societal disadvantage or cause it? Sociological research on inequality and mass incarceration clearly shows both processes at work." With endogeneity of this scope and without the help of experimental evidence, it will never be possible to show with certainty that

punishment is generating inequality rather than the reverse, but the rapid expansion of the mass incarceration experiment in the United States provides strong evidence already of deepening intergenerational effects of disadvantage that a prison sentence can cause.

36. Massey, *Categorically Unequal: The American Stratification System*, 99.
37. Bruce Western, *Punishment and Inequality in America* (New York: Russell Sage Foundation, 2006), 247.
38. Bruce Western and Katherine Beckett, "How Unregulated is the US Labor Market? The Penal System as a Labor Market Institution," *American Journal of Sociology*, 104 no. 4 (1999): 1030–1060.
39. Marianne Bertrand and Sendhil Mullainathan, "Are Emily and Greg More Employable than Lakisha and Jamal? A Field Experiment on Labor Market Discrimination," *The American Economic Review*, 94 no. 4 (September 2004): 991–1013. While it is not possible to randomly assign people to prison, it is possible to randomly assign names to resumes. Research on discrimination illustrates a profound racial effect, with white-sounding names receiving 50 percent more callbacks than black-sounding names.
40. Ian Urbina, "Despite Red Flags about Judges, a Kickback Scheme Flourished," *New York Times*, sec. A, March 27, 2009. The article describes the judges' $1.5 million yacht named "Reel Justice," a tragic symbol of the ill-gotten gains that they derived from trading "cash for kids," as the scandal has come to be known. On the other end of the scheme, serious damage was done to the lives and life prospects of the children who lost not only due process but also time and developmental stability.
41. See "Perpetual Peace: A Philosophical Sketch," in *Kant: Political Writings*, ed. Immanuel Kant (Cambridge: Cambridge University Press, 1991), 93.
42. Fredrik Hedenus and Christian Azar, "Estimates of Trends in Global Income and Resource Inequalities," *Ecological Economics*, 55 no. 3 (2005): 351–364. The Gini coefficient is one way to measure inequality. Values range from 0 to 100. At zero, a society is perfectly equal. At 100, a society would distribute all of its resources to a single person. Both Sweden and Denmark are relatively equal, with coefficients under 25. The United States is considerably less equal, with a coefficient of 45 as of 2007. In comparison, South Africa has a coefficient of 62.5 as of 2013, according to the CIA World Factbook. However, there are major problems with these measures. Most importantly, they diminish the very consequential feature of inequality: scale invariance. Whereas the Gini would treat a situation in which a poor person has $2,000 and

a wealthy person has $20,000 as equivalent to a situation in which a poor person has $1,000 and a wealthy person has $10,000, most people perceive their incomes in relative terms such that the first situation, which provides the wealthier person with much more than the poorer person, may be subjectively worse than the second situation. There are also major empirical issues with the calculations of relative income inequality. Hedenus and Azar find that global inequality has been relatively constant in purchasing power terms since the 1960s but increasing in market exchange rate terms.

43. Michel Foucault, *Discipline and Punish: The Birth of the Prison*, trans. Alan Sheridan (New York: Vintage, 1977), 11.

44. Karen McGrane, "The Rise of the Mobile-Only User," *Harvard Business Review*, May 28, 2013.

45. Michael Barris, "Marketing to Young Mobile Users: A Complex, Sensitive Topic," *Mobile Marketer*, September 30, 2014, www.mobilemarketer.com/cms/news/advertising/18808.html.

46. Steven Pinker, *The Better Angels of Our Nature: Why Violence Has Declined* (New York: Viking, 2011).

47. Brian Kahn, "Earth's CO_2 Passes the 400 PPM Threshold—Maybe Permanently," *Scientific American*, September 27, 2016, www.scientificamerican.com/article/earth-s-co2-passes-the-400-ppm-threshold-maybe-permanently. In September 2016, the monthly average was 401.03 ppm, according to the Scripps Institute for Oceanography. Scientists do not expect the monthly atmospheric average to drop below 400 ppm during our lifetimes.

48. See Susan Solomon et al., Intergovernmental Panel on Climate Change, *Climate Change 2007: The Physical Science Basis: Contribution of Working Group I to the Fourth Assessment Report of the Intergovernmental Panel on Climate Change* (Cambridge; New York: Cambridge University Press, 2007), 3. Historical CO_2 levels are measured through ice cores.

49. "Global mean temperature for the decade 2000–2009 has not yet exceeded the warmest temperatures of the early Holocene (5000 to 10,000 yr B.P.). These temperatures are, however, warmer than 82 percent of the Holocene distribution .... In contrast, the decadal mean global temperature of the early twentieth century (1900–1909) was cooler than >95 percent of the Holocene distribution. Global temperature, therefore, has risen from near the coldest to the warmest levels of the Holocene within the past century, reversing the long-term cooling trend that began ~5000 yr B.P." Shaun A. Marcott, Jeremy D. Shakun, Peter U. Clark, and Alan C. Mix, "A Reconstruction of Regional and

Global Temperature for the Past 11,300 Years," *Science*, 339 no. 6124 (2013): 1201.

50. According to the 2007 Intergovernmental Panel on Climate Change, "based on a range of models, it is likely that future tropical cyclones (typhoons and hurricanes) will become more intense, with larger peak wind speeds and more heavy precipitation associated with ongoing increases of tropical sea surface temperatures. There is less confidence in projections of a global decrease in numbers of tropical cyclones. The apparent increase in the proportion of very intense storms since 1970 in some regions is much larger than simulated by current models for that period." Solomon et al., Intergovernmental Panel on Climate Change, *Climate Change 2007: The Physical Science Basis: Contribution of Working Group I to the Fourth Assessment Report of the Intergovernmental Panel on Climate Change*, 15.

51. "Although precipitation has increased in many areas of the globe, the area under drought has also increased. Drought duration and intensity has also increased. While regional droughts have occurred in the past, the widespread spatial extent of current droughts is broadly consistent with expected changes in the hydrologic cycle under warming." Ibid., 54.

52. United Nations Development Programme (UNDP) and Khalid Malik, *Human Development Report 2013. The Rise of the South: Human Progress in a Diverse World* (New York: United Nations Development Programme, 2013).

53. Ralf Eriksson and Jan Otto Andersson, *Elements of Ecological Economics* (New York: Routledge, 2010), 36.

54. Paul W. Taylor, *Respect for Nature: A Theory of Environmental Ethics*, 25th anniversary ed. (Princeton, NJ: Princeton University Press, 2011), 61–63. It is possible to distinguish between having a good and having interests. Taylor, for instance, argues biological entities have a good that machines lack: "It is not the machine's own good that is being furthered by being kept well-oiled, but the good of certain humans for whom the machine is a means to their ends." Living things, on the other hand, do have a good such that we can act "in their interest" even though we would not say that they have interests. "They do not have interests because they are not interested in, do not care about, what happens to them. [T]hose living things that lack consciousness or, if conscious, lack the ability to make choices among alternatives confronting them … include all forms of plant life and the simpler forms of animal life." Human beings are capable of making choices, and also of realizing what will promote the good of living things that cannot make choices for themselves. In Chapter 5, I will develop a conception of ecological or

network value that does not distinguish between the good of machines and the good of plants as a basis for an instrumentalist approach to economic responsibility.

55. I refer here in general terms to countries with high per-capita GDP as industrial economies and to countries with low per-capital GDP as developing economies.

56. Hedenus and Azar, *Estimates of Trends in Global Income and Resource Inequalities*, 351–364.

57. Julian L. Simon, *The Ultimate Resource* (Princeton, NJ: Princeton University Press, 1981), 415.

58. Hawken, Lovins, and Lovins, *Natural Capitalism: Creating the Next Industrial Revolution*, 396.

59. Paul Hawken, *The Ecology of Commerce: A Declaration of Sustainability*, revised ed. (New York: Harper Business, 1993), 3.

60. See, for example, Simon, *Hoodwinking the Nation*, 140.

61. US Department of Energy, "US Household Expenditures for Gasoline Account for Nearly 4 Percent of Pretax Income," *US Energy Information Administration*, Last modified February 15, 2013, www .eia.gov/todayinenergy/detail.cfm?id=9831.

62. Hawken makes predictions that have already proven untrue, and so have many great social theorists. Those who aim to mobilize people must walk a fine line. Too much doomsday reporting runs the risk of demobilizing potential allies. Yet optimism can fly in the face of the daunting road ahead.

63. Riley E. Dunlap and Aaron M. McCright, "Organized Climate Change Denial," *The Oxford Handbook of Climate Change* (London: Oxford University Press, 2011), 144–160.

64. Seth Shulman, *Smoke, Mirrors & Hot Air: How ExxonMobil Uses Big Tobacco's Tactics to Manufacture Uncertainty on Climate Science* (Cambridge, MA: Union of Concerned Scientists, 2007).

65. Carbon Disclosure Project and Accenture, *Reducing Risk and Driving Business Value: CDP Supply Chain Report 2012–2013* (New York: Carbon Disclosure Project, 2013).

66. Keith Johnson, "How Carbon Dioxide Became a 'Pollutant'," *Wall Street Journal*, April 18, 2009.

67. Helm writes, "Business-as-usual is ... what is most likely for some time to come. Emissions are not being stabilized, but rather are on a path of rapid increase. Fossil-fuel consumption is going up, there is plenty left to exploit, and the dirtiest fossil fuel—coal — is expanding its share." Dieter Helm, "Climate-Change Policy: Why Has So Little Been Achieved?" *Oxford Review of Economic Policy*, 24 no. 2 (2008): 212.

68. Ibid., 220.

69. Nicholas Herbert Stern, *Stern Review: The Economics of Climate Change*, vol. 30. (London: HM Treasury, 2006).

70. Timothy Searchinger et al., "Use of US Croplands for Biofuels Increases Greenhouse Gases through Emissions from Land-Use Change," *Science*, 319 no. 5867 (2008): 1238–1240.

71. For a review on urban structure and energy use, see William P. Anderson, Pavlos S. Kanaroglou, and Eric J. Miller, "Urban Form, Energy and the Environment: A Review of Issues, Evidence and Policy," *Urban Studies*, 33 no. 1 (1996): 7–35.

72. Meg Marquardt, "Neutralizing the Rain: After Much Success in the Battle Against Acid Rain, Challenges Remain," *Earth* (July 2012), www.earthmagazine.org/article/neutralizing-rain-after-much-success-battle-against-acid-rain-challenges-remain.

73. For a helpful introduction to the early books describing the crisis, see Andrew W. Lo, "Reading about the Financial Crisis: A Twenty-One-Book Review," *Journal of Economic Literature*, 50 no. 1 (2012): 151–178.

74. See, for example, Jensen, "Value Maximization, Stakeholder Theory, and the Corporate Objective Function," 235–256.

75. US Financial Crisis Inquiry Commission, *The Financial Crisis Inquiry Report: Final Report of the National Commission on the Causes of the Financial and Economic Crisis in the United States*, US Independent Agencies and Commissions (2011), www.gpo.gov/fdsys/pkg/GPO-FCIC/content-detail.html.

76. Six Democratic appointees accepted the main findings, three Republican appointees wrote one dissenting view, and the last Republican appointee wrote another.

77. For one of the more critical studies of investor confidence in the wake of the dot-com boom, see Robert J. Shiller, *Irrational Exuberance* (Princeton, NJ: Princeton University Press, 2000), 296. Shiller argues that investor confidence is essential to the maintenance of price levels, and that these confidences are largely informed by historical evidence rather than any essential fact: "initial price increases ... lead to more price increases as the effect of the initial price increases feed back into yet higher prices through increased investor demand" (60).

78. Joseph A. Schumpeter, *Capitalism, Socialism and Democracy* (New York: Harper Perennial, 1942). Long before Shiller, Joseph Schumpeter argued that business growth occurs cyclically. A more specific historical account of what Shiller calls (quoting Greenspan) "irrational exuberance" can be found in Charles Mackay,

Extraordinary Popular Delusions and the Madness of Crowds (New York: Three Rivers Press, 1980).

79. See Carmen M. Reinhart and Kenneth S. Rogoff, *This Time is Different: Eight Centuries of Financial Folly* (Princeton, NJ: Princeton University Press, 2009), Chapter 13, paragraph 1. Among global crises, Reinhart and Rogoff list the crisis of 1825–1826, the panic of 1907, and the Great Depression.

80. Ibid., Chapter 16, paragraph 36.

81. Stephen W. Hawking, *A Brief History of Time: From the Big Bang to Black Holes* (Toronto; New York: Bantam Books, 1988), 198. Stephen Hawking introduces his book on the history of the universe by asking whether we know any better than the turtle theory. As the story goes, a person inquires about how the world is supported. In answer, he learns that the world sits on a platform on the back of an elephant and that the elephant stands on the back of a turtle. What supports the turtle? Another turtle. It is turtles all the way down. Geertz uses the parable to describe the infinite uncertainty of description. The more precise you try to be, the less certain you are. "Cultural analysis is intrinsically incomplete. And worse, than that, the more deeply it goes the less complete it is. It is a strange science whose most telling assertions are its most tremulously based, in which to get somewhere with the matter at hand is to intensify the suspicion, both your own and that of others, that you are not quite getting it right. But that, along with plaguing subtle people with obtuse questions, is what being an ethnographer is like." Clifford Geertz, "Thick Description: Toward an Interpretive Theory of Culture," in *The Interpretation of Cultures: Selected Essays* (New York: Basic Books, 1973), 29.

82. Benoit B. Mandelbrot, *The Fractal Geometry of Nature* (San Francisco: W.H. Freeman, 1982), 460.

83. Orly R. Shenker, "Fractal Geometry is Not the Geometry of Nature," *Studies in History and Philosophy of Science*, 25 no. 6 (1994): 967–981.

84. Christopher B. Barrett and Brent M. Swallow, "Fractal Poverty Traps," *World Development*, 34 no. 1 (2006): 1–15.

85. Ben Bernanke, "The Global Saving Glut and the US Current Account Deficit," Sandridge Lecture, Virginia Association of Economics, Richmond, Virginia, March 10 (2005).

86. China is mentioned three times in the 410 pages of the main report and three times in the thirty pages of the Republican dissent. In the main report, China is listed alongside France, Germany, and Italy, but not in the dissent.

87. Raghuram Rajan, *Fault Lines: How Hidden Fractures Still Threaten the World Economy* (Princeton, NJ: Princeton University Press, 2010), Kindle edition, 260.
88. Ibid., 86.
89. Ibid., 3.
90. Dan Fletcher, "The 50 Worst Inventions," May 27, 2010, *TIME*, www.time.com/time/specials/packages/completelist/0,29569,19919 15,00.html.
91. Upton Sinclair, *The Jungle* (New York: Doubleday, Page & Company, 1906), 4.
92. Rajan explains the macroeconomic forces that helped put large financial entities in a precariously illiquid position: "First, an enormous quantity of money flowed into low-income housing in the United States, both from abroad and from government-sponsored mortgage agencies such as Fannie Mae and Freddie Mac [the two most important GSEs]. This led to both unsustainable house price increases and a steady deterioration in the quality of mortgage loans made. Second, both commercial and investment banks took on an enormous quantity of risk, including buying large quantities of the low-quality securities issued to finance subprime housing mortgages, even while borrowing extremely short term to finance these purchases." Rajan, *Fault Lines: How Hidden Fractures Still Threaten the World Economy*, 16.
93. US Financial Crisis Inquiry Commission, *The Financial Crisis Inquiry Report: Final Report of the National Commission on the Causes of the Financial and Economic Crisis in the United States*, xii.
94. See generally George A. Akerlof and Robert J. Shiller, *Animal Spirits: How Human Psychology Drives the Economy, and Why it Matters for Global Capitalism* (Princeton, NJ: Princeton University Press, 2009), 230.
95. Gary Gorton, *Slapped by the Invisible Hand: The Panic of 2007* (Oxford; New York: Oxford University Press, 2010), 223.
96. Lo, "Reading about the Financial Crisis: A Twenty-One-Book Review," 15.
97. Akerlof and Shiller, *Animal Spirits: How Human Psychology Drives the Economy, and Why it Matters for Global Capitalism*, 37.
98. William White, "Anatomy of Crisis –The Living History of the Last 30 Years: Economic Theory, Politics and Policy," (presentation, Institute for New Economic Thinking, Cambridge University, Cambridge, April 8–11, 2010).
99. "An informational cascade occurs when it is optimal for an individual, having observed the actions of those ahead of him, to follow the behavior of the preceding individual without regard to his own information." Sushil Bikhchandani, David Hirshleifer, and Ivo Welch,

"A Theory of Fads, Fashion, Custom, and Cultural Change as Informational Cascades," *Journal of Political Economy*, 100 no. 5 (1992): 994. The concept is useful in explaining important aspects of how information asymmetries encourage herd behavior. Though it does not account for the rising prices and escalating commitment of a financial bubble, it does offer a coherent description of how a firm might struggle to find a lender as it enters bankruptcy (see 1013).

100. The growth of the term "investment vehicle" is illustrative of the vagueness of these financial concepts. Historically, the destination of an investment was relatively clear. Investment opportunities included real assets, commodities, and securities. No metaphorical vehicle was needed to deliver these to the purchaser.

101. Sections 20 and 32 of The Banking Act of 1933, also known as the Glass-Steagall Act, were repealed under the Gramm-Leach-Bliley Financial Modernization Act of 1999. These sections limited banks from issuing or selling securities beyond their core business activities or from employing people that do so.

102. Joseph Stiglitz, "Capitalist Fools," *Vanity Fair*, 51 no. 1 (2009), www.vanityfair.com/news/2009/01/stiglitz200901.

103. Alan D. Morrison and William J. Wilhelm, "The Demise of Investment Banking Partnerships: Theory and Evidence," *The Journal of Finance*, 63 no. 1 (2008): 311–350.

104. William H. Whyte, *The Organization Man* (New York: Simon and Schuster, 1956).

105. Ryan S. Burg, *Rebuilding the Iron Cage: Post-Failure Organizing in Newspapers and Investment Banks* (Philadelphia: Publicly Accessible University of Pennsylvania Dissertations, 2011), 152. I observed these ephemeral attachments in my dissertation research. As one banker who I interviewed explained, his colleagues were motivated by money in how they worked, where they worked, and how closely they affiliated with a given organization: "They were in it for the money, and that's it …. Working on the trading floor is like working for a sports team. I mean, you just go to whoever pays the highest price. And do not think about loyalty, because you're gonna get screwed."

106. Some derivatives are more difficult to price than others. In this chapter, I discuss different kinds of derivatives, including relatively pedestrian interest rate swaps. One should not blur categories between so-called "vanilla options" and exotic derivatives in describing the causes of the 2008 financial crisis. At the same time, even the most basic options contracts can create repayment constraints if too many outstanding obligations are simultaneously triggered.

107. Bethany McLean and Peter Elkind, *The Smartest Guys in the Room: The Amazing Rise and Scandalous Fall of Enron* (New York: Portfolio, 2003), 435.

108. Just as auditors are hired by the firms that they audit, ratings agencies are compensated by the bond issuers that they rate, which creates a potentially serious conflict of interest. See Jerome S. Fons, "Rating Competition and Structured Finance," *The Journal of Structured Finance*, 14 no. 3 (2008): 7–15.

109. One ongoing controversy concerns the international regulatory standards developed by the Basel Accords, a process with which the Bank for International Settlements is a core institution. Basel III addressed key aspects of bank liquidity in ways that might have fundamentally altered the standards of bank reserves. However, these measures were significantly softened after very aggressive advocacy from the finance industry. Some view this as the latest in a long line of evidence suggesting the regulatory capture of the world's central banks by the finance industry. Others suggest that the revision is reasonable and necessary for economic performance. See, for example, Andrew Ross Sorkin, "Easing of Rules for Banks Acknowledges Reality," *New York Times*, sec. B1, January 8, 2013.

110. Bank for International Settlements, *Semiannual OTC Derivatives Statistics at End-June 2012* (2012).

111. Federal Reserve Bank of New York, *Quarterly Report on Household Debt and Credit* (2017).

112. International Monetary Fund, www.imf.org/external/pubs/ft/weo/20 17/01/weodata/weorept.aspx, accessed April 28, 2017. Debt data compiled from BEA and IMF's Government Finance Statistics Yearbook and GDP data from National Statistical Office.

113. Michael Kushma, Richard Class, and Philippe Kurzweil, "The Evolution of the Global Bond Market," *Morgan Stanley Investment Focus* (2012), 11.

114. A market explanation for this trend should also account for debt performance relative to other investment opportunities and the rate of inflation.

115. Kushma, Class, and Kurzweil, "The Evolution of the Global Bond Market," 2.

116. Halah Touryalai, "Backlash: Student Loan Burden Prevents Borrowers from Buying Homes, Cars," *Forbes*, June 26, 2013.

117. Josh Mitchell, "Many Cannot Pay Student Loans," *Wall Street Journal*, sec. A2, August 6, 2013.

118. See the US Department of Education, *First Official Three-Year Student Loan Default Rates Published: Department Continues Efforts to Help Students Better Manage their Debt* (2012). The actual rate is

probably much higher since most public statistics include recent graduates whose loans are in deferral. See Meta Brown, Andrew Haughwout, Donghoon Lee, Maricar Mabutas, and Wilbert van der Klaauw, "Grading Student Loans," *Liberty Street Economics* (blog), New York Fed, March 5, 2012, http://libertystreeteconomics.newyorkfed.org/2012/03/grading-student-loans.html.

119. Chris Kirkham, "For-Profit Colleges Manage Student Loan Default Rates, Senators Call for Investigation," *Huffington Post*, December 27, 2012, www.huffingtonpost.com/2012/12/27/for-profit-colleges-student-loan-default_n_2371688.html.

120. Nasiripour and Scannell, *UK Banks Hit by Record 2.6 Bn US Fines.*

121. Patrick Jenkins, "Bank Shares Buoyed on a Sea of Scandal," *Financial Times*, January 7, 2013.

122. David Graeber, *Debt: The First 5,000 Years* (Brooklyn, NY: Melville House, 2011), Kindle edition, locations 188–194.

123. See, for example, Joseph E. Stiglitz, *Freefall: America, Free Markets, and the Sinking of the World Economy* (New York: W. W. Norton & Co., 2010); Simon Johnson and James Kwak, *13 Bankers: The Wall Street Takeover and the Next Financial Meltdown* (New York: Vintage Books, 2011); and Sofie M. M. Loyens, Remy M. J. P. Rikers, and Henk G. Schmidt, "The Impact of Students' Conceptions of Constructivist Assumptions on Academic Achievement and Drop-Out," *Studies in Higher Education*, 32 no. 5 (2007): 581–602.

5 Person, Place, and Product

1. The original argument appears in Peter Singer, "Famine, Affluence, and Morality," *Philosophy & Public Affairs*, 1 no. 3 (1972): 229–243. An extended version with a practical exploration of duties of privilege can be found in Peter Singer, *The Life You Can Save: Acting Now to End World Poverty* (New York: Random House, 2009).

2. Peter Singer, *Animal Liberation: A New Ethics for our Treatment of Animals* (New York: New York Review, 1975).

3. David T. Schwartz, *Consuming Choices: Ethics in a Global Consumer Age* (Lanham, MD: Rowman & Littlefield Publishers, 2010).

4. Ibid., chapter 5, V, paragraph 1.

5. Ibid., chapter 5, VI, paragraph 2.

6. For an interesting survey of the complex challenges involved in poverty alleviation, see Abhijit V. Banerjee and Esther Duflo, *Poor Economics: A Radical Rethinking of the Way to Fight Global Poverty* (New York: PublicAffairs, 2011).

7. Janet Poppendieck, *Sweet Charity? Emergency Food and the End of Entitlement* (New York: Viking, 1998).
8. Hodder, *Entanglement*.
9. Singer's focus on human suffering has considerable precedent. For example, as Curtin describes, "To speculate about mere theories when there is suffering in the world, [the Buddha] said, is like speculating about the origin of a poison arrow while it is still lodged in one's flesh. First remove the arrow! Questions about origins can come later." Deane Curtin, "A State of Mind Like Water: Ecosophy T and the Buddhist Traditions" in *Beneath the Surface: Critical Essays in the Philosophy of Deep Ecology*, eds. Eric Katz, Andrew Light, and David Rothenberg (Cambridge, MA: MIT Press, 2000), 253. However, Singer, at least, has moved beyond the notion that the efficiency with which we dispatch our moral obligations is insignificant. His recent work on effective altruism emphasizes these considerations to a much greater extent.
10. Maurice Merleau-Ponty, *Phenomenology of Perception*, trans. Colin Smith (London: Routledge & Kegan Paul, 1958).
11. William McDonough and Michael Braungart, *Cradle to Cradle: Remaking the Way We Make Things* (New York: North Point Press, 2002).
12. Bernard Williams, *Ethics and the Limits of Philosophy* (Cambridge, MA: Harvard University Press, 1985). Philosophers distinguish between thin and thick descriptive concepts. A thin descriptive concept is something like length, mass, or color. It is directly measurable and lacks evaluative content. Whether a six-foot man, a ten-pound weight, and a red car are good or bad is not at all determined by the adjective descriptions. In contrast, a thick descriptive concept has a mixture of measurable and evaluative attributes. Whether someone is courageous may be measured by one's actions, but courage cannot be separated from its connotation as a moral virtue. Persons and things are already thick moral concepts because they carry an evaluative weight. Persons are important, things are not. The concept of place, however, has no evaluative content. To describe somewhere as a place does not require its protection or otherwise limit its use. By the end of this book, I will suggest that moral theory needs to extend its sense of place, to thicken the concept, but first things first.
13. Kurt Gray, Joshua Knobe, Mark Sheshkin, Paul Bloom, and Lisa Feldman Barrett, "More Than a Body: Mind Perception and the Nature of Objectification," *Journal of Personality and Social Psychology*, 101 no. 6 (2011): 1207–1220.

14. Kurt Gray, Liane Young, and Adam Waytz, "Mind Perception is the Essence of Morality," *Psychological Inquiry*, 23 no. 2 (2012): 101–124.

15. Brock Bastian, Steve Loughnan, Nick Haslam, and Helena R. M. Radke, "Don't Mind Meat? The Denial of Mind to Animals Used for Human Consumption," *Personality and Social Psychology Bulletin*, 38 no. 2 (2012): 247–256.

16. Gilles Deleuze and Félix Guattari, *A Thousand Plateaus: Capitalism and Schizophrenia*, trans. Brian Massumi (London: Continuum, 1987), 322.

17. Ibid., 321.

18. Buber capitalizes It to emphasize the status of objects. See Martin Buber and Walter Arnold Kaufmann, *I and Thou* (New York: Scribner, 1970), 57–58.

19. Ibid., 64.

20. Timothy Morton, *Ecology without Nature: Rethinking Environmental Aesthetics* (Cambridge, MA: Harvard University Press, 2007), 19.

21. Buber and Kaufmann, *I and Thou*, 81. Buber argues that ordering is essentially a distancing act. "This is part of the basic truth of the human world: only It can be put in order. Only as things cease to be our You and become our It do they become subject to coordination." In his terms, "You" is a relational and comprehensive understanding of another, whereas "It" is partial, incomplete, and distanced. Ordering implies domination and control. But what if the more complete relational interaction is made into a part of the order? Would the act of ordering still necessitate subordination?

22. Richard Rorty, *Philosophy and the Mirror of Nature* (Princeton, NJ: Princeton University Press, 1979).

23. John Dewey, "Theory of Valuation" in *International Encyclopedia of Unified Science* vol. II, no. 4, ed. Otto Neurath (Chicago: University of Chicago Press, 1939), 1–66.

24. Ibid., 14.

25. Ibid., 50.

26. Ibid., 38.

27. R. Edward Freeman, "The Politics of Stakeholder Theory: Some Future Directions," *Business Ethics Quarterly*, 4 no. 4 (1994): 411.

28. Phillips, *Ethics and Network Organizations*, 534.

29. John Arthur Passmore, *Man's Responsibility for Nature: Ecological Problems and Western Traditions* (London: Duckworth, 1974), 213.

30. Jeremy Bentham, *An Introduction to the Principles of Morals and Legislation* (Oxford: Clarendon Press, 1907); Singer, *Animal Liberation: A New Ethics for our Treatment of Animals*.

31. Adam D. Galinsky, William W. Maddux, Debra Gilin, and Judith B. White, "Why it Pays to Get Inside the Head of Your Opponent:

The Differential Effects of Perspective Taking and Empathy in Negotiations," *Psychological Science*, 19 no. 4 (2008): 378–384.

32. Daniel Hart, Robert Atkins, and Debra Ford, "Urban America as a Context for the Development of Moral Identity in Adolescence," *Journal of Social Issues*, 54 no. 3 (1998): 513–530; James Youniss and Miranda Yates, "Youth Service and Moral-Civic Identity: A Case for Everyday Morality," *Educational Psychology Review*, 11 no. 4 (1999): 361–376.

33. Americus Reed II and Karl F. Aquino, "Moral Identity and the Expanding Circle of Moral Regard Toward Out-Groups," *Journal of Personality and Social Psychology*, 84 no. 6 (2003): 1270–1286.

34. Thomas Nagel, *The View from Nowhere* (Oxford: Oxford University Press, 1986), 19. Moreover, the subjectivity of perception is an enduring philosophical problem in recognizing others' minds and experiences. As Nagel explains, "Each of us is the subject of various experiences, and to understand that there are other people in the world as well, one must be able to conceive of experiences of which one is not the subject: experiences that are not present to oneself. To do this it is necessary to have a general conception of subjects of experience and to place oneself under it as an instance."

35. John Dewey, "Theory of Valuation," 8.

36. Andrew Traviss, Twitter post, October 17, 2013, 5:08 PM, https://twitter.com/andrewtraviss/status/390992747319943168

37. Recorded on October 3, 2011 using Google autocomplete suggestions.

38. I will discuss the question of whether objects have interests below.

39. Kant explains, "A good will seems to be the indispensable condition of even the worthiness to be happy." Cited in John Rawls and Barbara Herman, *Lectures on the History of Moral Philosophy* (Cambridge, MA: Harvard University Press, 2000), Kindle edition, location 2000.

40. Lee Rainie and Aaron Smith, "Social Networking Sites and Politics," *Pew Internet & American Life Project*, March 12, 2012, www.pewinternet.org/2012/03/12/social-networking-sites-and-politics. There is considerable evidence that people assume that others think as they do and share their beliefs. This explains an interesting problem with political discussions on social network websites. A Pew study found that 38 percent of respondents had been surprised by a friend's political beliefs posted online and that 18 percent had chosen to block or delete a friend because of political expression.

41. Donaldson and Dunfee, *Ties that Bind*.

42. J. J. C. Smart and Bernard Williams, *Utilitarianism: For and Against* (Cambridge: Cambridge University Press, 1973), 116. Williams

argues famously that utilitarianism cannot require an agent to discard the value of his own projects. An agent "is identified with his actions as flowing from projects or attitudes which ... he takes seriously at the deepest level, as what his life is about ... It is absurd to demand of such a man ... should just step aside from his own project and decision and acknowledge the decision which utilitarian calculation requires. It is to alienate him in a real sense from his actions and the source of his action in his own convictions."

43. For example, Bernard Williams, "Ethical Consistency," in *Problems of the Self* (Cambridge: Cambridge University Press, 1973).

44. Martha Craven Nussbaum and Amartya Sen, eds. *The Quality of Life* (Oxford: Clarendon Press, 1993), 453.

45. Arne Næss, "The Shallow and the Deep, Long-Range Ecology Movement: A Summary," in *The Selected Works of Arne Næss*, ed. Alan Drengson (Houten, the Netherlands: Springer Netherlands, 2005), 2263–2269.

46. Elaine Scarry, *On Beauty and Being Just* (Princeton, NJ: Princeton University Press, 1999), 134; Ruskin, *Unto This Last and Other Writings*.

47. Some situations and polities are fairer and respectful of rights than others. Insofar as these situations result from concerted actions, they are what I refer to as an "end state." However, this usage differs from the standard deontological/teleological distinction in ethics. Whether we refer to a responsible economy as an end state or as a standard of conduct, this normative preference has some common characteristics that differ from the modes of understanding the self and understanding others described above.

48. See Anat Zohar and Shlomit Ginossar, "Lifting the Taboo Regarding Teleology and Anthropomorphism in Biology Education—Heretical Suggestions," *Science Education*, 82 no. 6 (1998): 679–697. At least, we avoid descriptions of agency and intent in scientific practice. It can be pedagogically and grammatically useful to explain evolution as if there is some purposeful utility to phenotypical variation, even though this variation is finally attributable to random variation subject to selection pressures.

49. Bentham, *An Introduction to the Principles of Morals and Legislation*; Singer, *Animal Liberation: A New Ethics for our Treatment of Animals*.

50. Fikret Berkes, *Sacred Ecology*, 3rd ed. (New York: Routledge, 2012).

51. Christopher D. Stone, *Should Trees Have Standing? Law, Morality, and the Environment*, 3rd ed. (New York: Oxford University Press, 2010), 17.

52. Deane Curtin, "A State of Mind Like Water," 259. For example, even deep ecologists are reticent to treat nonliving things as autonomously

valuable. Though they view other living things as collaborative elements that are realizing together ("corealizing") mutual possibilities, they are not necessarily willing to include nonsentients in this process. In a discussion of Arne Naess, one of the founders of the deep ecology philosophy, Curtin describes Naess's position on material things. "To extend corealization beyond living beings is to risk nonsense; not to do so introduces dualism, the distinction between beings we can identify with and have compassion for, and those that are beyond the 'limit'." George Sessions, "David Rothenberg, Pragmatism, and the Crowley/Deep Ecology Controversy," *ISEE Newsletter*, 19 no. 2 (Spring/Summer 2008): 46. Sessions dissents from this characterization of Naess, arguing that Naess "extends the concept of living beings to the inanimate as well."

53. Graham Harman, *Towards Speculative Realism: Essays and Lectures* (Hants, UK: John Hunt Publishing, 2010), 156.

54. *Care, v.*, OED Online, Oxford University Press, accessed September 5, 2012.

55. Berenice Fisher and Joan Tronto, "Toward a Feminist Theory of Caring," in *Circles of Care: Work and Identity in Women's Lives*, eds. Emily K. Abel and Margaret K. Nelson (Albany, NY: State University of New York Press, 1990), 40.

56. See Joan C. Tronto, *Moral Boundaries: A Political Argument for an Ethic of Care* (New York: Routledge, 1993), 226.

57. Joan C. Tronto, "An Ethic of Care," Ethics in Community-Based Elder Care (2001), 61.

58. See Aristotle, *De Anima* (London: Penguin Books, 1986), book 3, chapter 3. See also Aristotle, *Aristotle's Nicomachean Ethics*, trans. Robert C. Bartlett and Susan D. Collins (Chicago: University of Chicago Press), book VII. Aristotle discusses imagination in *De Anima* and the capacity to reason in *Nicomachean Ethics*.

59. In *Summa Theologica*, Aquinas writes that "Dumb animals and plants are devoid of the life of reason whereby to set themselves in motion; they are moved, as it were by another, by a kind of natural impulse, a sign of which is that they are naturally enslaved and accommodated to the uses of others." Thomas Aquinas, *Summa Theologica*, trans. Fathers of the English Dominican Province (Ashland, OH: BookMasters, 2012), Question 64, Article 1.

60. "God, having designed man for a sociable creature, made him not only with an inclination, and under a necessity to have fellowship with those of his own kind, but furnished him also with language, which was to be the great instrument and common tie of society. Man, therefore, had by nature his organs so fashioned, as to be fit to frame articulate sounds,

which we call words. But this was not enough to produce language; for parrots, and several other birds, will be taught to make articulate sounds distinct enough, which yet by no means are capable of language." John Locke, *An Essay Concerning Human Understanding*, 2nd ed. (London: Basset, 1690), Kindle edition, book 3, locations 12–15.

61. Immanuel Kant, Peter Lauchlan Heath, and J. B. Schneewind, *Lectures on Ethics* (New York: Cambridge University Press, 1997), 212.

62. "[I]f there were such machines having the organs and the shape of a monkey or of some other animal that lacked reason, we would have no way of recognizing that they were not entirely of the same nature as these animals; whereas, if there were any such machines that bore a resemblance to our bodies and imitated our actions as far as this is practically feasible, we would always have two very certain means of recognizing that they were not at all, for that reason, true men." René Descartes, *Discourse on Method and Meditations on First Philosophy*, 4th edition trans. Donald A. Cress (Indianapolis, IA: Hackett, 1998), Kindle edition, locations 883–886.

63. Martin Heidegger, *Being and Time*, trans. John Macquarrie and Edward Robinson (London: SCM Press, 1962), 97. Heidegger's translators explain that he uses the term equipment (*Das Zeug*) "as a collective noun which is analogous to our relatively specific 'gear' (as in 'gear for fishing') or the more elaborate 'paraphernalia', or the still more general 'equipment'." My usage is not consistent with Heidegger's in any way. For Heidegger, "object" is pejorative; person is *dasein*, distinguished by a reflective character; and place is approached as an infinite universe of particularities occurring within a moment in time.

64. Ibid, 102.

65. Ibid, 98. In my account of object-based responsibility, it is important that things are used and are capable of being used in distinct ways because objects' roles in specific tasks come with moral responsibilities. Likewise, taking objects away from tasks has moral repercussions. For example, taking trees from the task of habitat creation within forests is a morally laden act precisely because trees are uniquely suited to that task. Thus, the question of whether objects' purposes are circumscribed is significant. Heidegger addresses this teleological issue with an activity-based conception of object suitability for use. Objects are uniquely suited for certain tasks and they are also bound up in the tasks to which they are put. But when we try to understand them through their uses, we take a perspective that is different from the purity of use. According to Heidegger, these two aspects can never be united. Because equipment can be both singular and plural, equipment can be

appropriated in a specific way that could not be more suitable and there can be manifold assignments for different equipment.

66. Jael drove a peg through Sisera's head with a hammer in Chapters 4 and 5 of Judges. The Beatles song "Maxwell's Silver Hammer" is an upbeat study in murder by hammer.

67. Heidegger, *Being and Time*, locations 3059–3069.

68. "If we read Heidegger's tool-analysis in the right way, the lingering priority of *Dasein* in his philosophy is vaporized, and we encounter a strange new world filled with shocking possibilities for twenty-first-century philosophy." *Dasein* is Heidegger's term for persons who are distinguished by their awareness of their own existence. Graham Harman, *Tool-Being: Heidegger and the Metaphysics of Objects* (Chicago: Open Court, 2002), 2.

69. Ibid., 2–4.

70. For an account of how philosophy can make sense of objects within networks, Latour's Actor Network Theory is certainly the most influential available resource.

71. Bogost, *Alien Phenomenology*, chapter 1, Tiny Ontology.

72. Lucas D. Introna, "Ethics and the Speaking of Things," *Theory, Culture & Society*, 26 no. 4 (2009): 25–46.

73. Michael Zimmerman, "Towards a Heideggerian Ethos for Rational Environmentalism," *Environmental Ethics*, 5 (1983): 99–131.

74. Introna, "Ethics and the Speaking of Things," 41.

75. Charles Horton Cooley, *Human Nature and the Social Order* (New York: Charles Scribner's Sons, 1902), Kindle edition, locations 2078–2079. Cooley is most famous for his concept of the looking-glass self. According to this notion of socialized self-perception, one understands oneself through the perceptions of others. "There is no sense of 'I' as in pride or shame, without its correlative sense of you, or he, or they." The shame of these murders has been recorded in these videos, as if etched permanently as a reflective judgment of the criminals.

76. "3 Guys, 1 Hammer," *Urban Dictionary*, www.urbandictionary.com/define.php?term=3%20guys%201%20hammer, accessed June 4, 2013.

77. Scarry, *On Beauty and Being Just*, 134.

6 Ecological Value

1. Warren Busscher, "Spending Our Water and Soils for Food Security," *Journal of Soil and Water Conservation*, 67 no. 3 (2012): 228.

2. Wendell Berry, *The Unsettling of America* (San Francisco: Sierra Club Books, 1977), 86.

3. Aldo Leopold, *A Sand County Almanac and Sketches Here and There* (New York: Oxford University Press, 1949), 216.

4. Charles Kellogg, *The Soils That Support Us: An Introduction to the Study of Soils and Their Use by Men* (New York: Macmillan, 1941).

5. Franklin D. Roosevelt, "Letter to all State Governors on a Uniform Soil Conservation Law," *The American Presidency Project*, February 26, 1937, www.presidency.ucsb.edu/ws/?pid=15373.

6. Quoted in Busscher, "Spending Our Water and Soils for Food Security."

7. Todd McLellan, *Things Come Apart: A Teardown Manual for Modern Living* (New York: Thames & Hudson, 2013).

8. Rick Chillot, "Bike Repair Tips from Pro Mechanics," *Bicycling*, April 30, 2010, www.bicycling.com/maintenance/bike-repair-tips.

9. Robert M. Pirsig, *Zen and the Art of Motorcycle Maintenance: An Inquiry into Values* (New York: William Morrow & Inc., 1974), Chapter 4.

10. Pirsig. *Zen and the Art of Motorcycle Maintenance*, Chapter 25.

11. Eric J. Stewart, "Growing Unculturable Bacteria," *Journal of Bacteriology*, 194 no. 16, (2012): 4151–4160.

12. Hawken, Lovins, and Lovins, *Natural Capitalism: Creating the Next Industrial Revolution*, 151.

13. Charles Darwin, *The Descent of Man* (New York: D. Appleton and Co., 1875), 126.

14. Cited in Lynn Margulis and Dorion Sagan, *What is Life?* (Berkeley: University of California Press, 1995).

15. Ibid., 78.

16. J. Craig Venter, Karin Remington, John F. Heidelberg, Aaron L. Halpern et al., "Environmental Genome Shotgun Sequencing of the Sargasso Sea," *Science*, 304, vol. 5667 (2004): 66.

17. Karen Kaplan, "Seeing Earth's Future in a Petri Dish," *Los Angeles Times*, November 24, 2007, http://articles.latimes.com/2007/nov/24/science/sci-venter24.

18. Bond, Woodward and Midgley, *The Global Distribution of Ecosystems in a World without Fire*, 525–538.

19. Robert W. Mutch, "Wildland Fires and Ecosystems–A Hypothesis," *Ecology*, 51 no. 6 (1970): 1046–1051.

20. James Lovelock, *Gaia: A New Look at Life on Earth* (Oxford: Oxford Paperbacks, 2000).

21. See, for example, Kat Anderson, *Tending the Wild: Native American Knowledge and the Management of California's Natural Resources* (Berkeley: University of California Press, 2005).

22. Irwin N. Forseth and Anne F. Innis, "Kudzu (Pueraria Montana): History, Physiology, and Ecology Combine to Make a Major

Ecosystem Threat," *Critical Reviews in Plant Sciences*, 23 no. 5 (2004): 401–413.

23. Hugh J. MacIsaac, "Potential Abiotic and Biotic Impacts of Zebra Mussels on the Inland Waters of North America," *American Zoologist*, 36 no. 3 (1996): 287–299.

24. David L. Strayer and Heather M. Malcom, "Effects of Zebra Mussels (Dreissena Polymorpha) on Native Bivalves: The Beginning of the End Or the End of the Beginning?" *Journal of the North American Benthological Society*, 26 no. 1 (2007): 111–122.

25. Harry V. Thompson and C. M. King, *The European Rabbit: The History and Biology of a Successful Colonizer* (Oxford; New York: Oxford University Press, 1994).

26. E. A. Johnson, K. Miyanishi and S. R. J. Bridge, "Wildfire Regime in the Boreal Forest and the Idea of Suppression and Fuel Buildup," *Conservation Biology*, 15 no. 6 (2001): 1554–1557.

27. Suthawan Sathirathai and Edward B. Barbier, "Valuing Mangrove Conservation in Southern Thailand," *Contemporary Economic Policy*, 19 no. 2 (2001): 109–122.

28. David W. Roscoe and Scott G. Hinch, "Effectiveness Monitoring of Fish Passage Facilities: Historical Trends, Geographic Patterns and Future Directions," *Fish and Fisheries*, 11 no. 1 (2010): 12–33. It is possible for fish to swim upstream despite dams. Extensive facilities are maintained for them to do so, but research on the effectiveness of these facilities is still incomplete.

29. For example, Passmore, *Man's Responsibility for Nature; Ecological Problems and Western Traditions*, 213.

30. Robert J. Sampson, *Great American City: Chicago and The Enduring Neighborhood Effect* (Chicago: University of Chicago Press, 2012).

31. Ioannis Armakolas, "The 'Paradox' of Tuzla City: Explaining Non-Nationalist Local Politics During the Bosnian War," *Europe-Asia Studies*, 63 no. 2 (2011): 229–261.

32. F. Mancini, F. Stecchi and G. Gabbianelli, "GIS-Based Assessment of Risk due to Salt Mining Activities at Tuzla (Bosnia and Herzegovina)," *Engineering Geology*, 109 no. 3 (2009): 170–182.

33. Fikret Berkes, "Cross-Scale Institutional Linkages: Perspectives from the Bottom Up," in *The Drama of the Commons*, eds. Elinor Ostrom and National Research Council Committee on the Human Dimensions of Global Change (Washington, DC: National Academy Press, 2002), 312.

34. Christopher McGrory Klyza and David J. Sousa, *American Environmental Policy: Beyond Gridlocks. Updated Edition* (Cambridge, MA: MIT Press, 2013), 165. This is an important condition. Many administrative applications of the adaptive management

concept have been used to push for controversial compromises amidst legislative deadlocks. In the 1990s, the Clinton administration's Forest Plan attempted such a compromise.

35. Todd Zwillich, "Quietly, Congress Extends a Ban on CDC Research on Gun Violence," *The Takeaway*, July 2, 2015, www.pri.org/stories/2015-07-02/quietly-congress-extends-ban-cdc-research-gun-violence.
36. Lysander Spooner, "Vices Are Not Crimes: A Vindication of Moral Liberty," *The Lysander Spooner Reader* (Baltimore, MD: Laissez Faire Books, 2012).
37. This is the common English phrasing of Luke 6:31.
38. Donaldson and Dunfee, *Ties that Bind*.
39. Matt McGrath, "California Methane Leak 'Largest in US History,'" BBC, February 26, 2016, www.bbc.com/news/science-environment-35659947.
40. Yevgen Yesyrkenov, "Rosneft Wins Award for Gas Flaring Reduction Efforts in Russia," *World Bank*, October 25, 2012, http://blogs.world bank.org/energy/gas-flaring-reduction-makes-life-better-for-the-peo ple-of-gubkinskiy.
41. H. A. Trexler, "The Buffalo Range of the Northwest," *The Mississippi Valley Historical Review*, 7 no. 4 (1921): 360.
42. de Tocqueville, *Democracy in America*.
43. Robert F. Sayre, *Recovering the Prairie* (Madison, WI: University of Wisconsin Press, 1999).
44. Janine Mileaf, "Between You and Me: Man Ray's Object to be Destroyed," *Art Journal*, 63 no. 1 (2004): 5–23.
45. Guy Debord and Asger Jorn, *Mémoires: Structures Portantes d'Asger Jorn* (Paris: Jean-Jacques Pauvert aux Belles Lettres, 1993).
46. Guy Debord, *The Society of the Spectacle* (New York: Zone Books, 1994).
47. Andrew Woodfield, *Teleology* (Cambridge: Cambridge University Press, 1976), 206.
48. Hodder, *Entangled*, 152.
49. Ruskin, *Unto This Last and Other Writings*.
50. Rafaela Hillerbrand and Michael Ghil, "Anthropogenic Climate Change: Scientific Uncertainties and Moral Dilemmas," *Physica D: Nonlinear Phenomena*, 237 no. 14 (2008): 2132–2138. For example, Hillerbrand and Ghil argue that uncertainty should be managed by reducing downside risk.
51. Stephen M. Gardiner, "Ethics and Global Climate Change, *Ethics*," 114 no. 3 (2004): 555–600.
52. Isaac Held, "Simplicity Amid Complexity," *Science*, 343 no. 6176 (2014): 1206–1207.

53. Hodder, *Entanglement*.
54. Heidegger, *Being and Time*.
55. Richard R. Nelson and Sidney G. Winter, *An Evolutionary Theory of Economic Change* (Cambridge, MA: Belknap Press of Harvard University Press, 1982).
56. Ross Galbreath and Derek Brown, "The Tale of the Lighthouse-Keeper's Cat: Discovery and Extinction of the Stephens Island Wren," *Notornis*, 51 (2004): 193–200. To be fair, Tibbles may not be entirely to blame. A few additional specimens of the bird were collected in the two years after the cat-collected specimens. Moreover, other cats are believed to have been brought to the island at about the same time.

7 Putting Responsibility to Work

1. See Mona Siddiqui, *Hospitality and Islam: Welcoming in God's Name* (New Haven, CT: Yale University Press, 2015). The Bible includes several sections that focus on welcoming the stranger. In Leviticus 19:34, "The stranger that dwelleth with you shall be unto you as one born among you, and thou shalt love him as thyself." In Luke 14:12–14, "When thou makest a dinner or a supper, call not thy friends, nor thy brethren, neither thy kinsmen, nor *thy* rich neighbours; lest they also bid thee again, and a recompence be made thee. But when thou makest a feast, call the poor, the maimed, the lame, the blind: And thou shalt be blessed." King James Version.
2. Aristotle, *Politics*, trans. C.D.C. Reeve (Indianapolis, Hackett, 1998), 1258b.
3. Alasdair MacIntyre, *After View: A Study in Moral Theory* (South Bend, IN: University of Notre Dame, 1984), 254.
4. G.E.M. Anscombe, "Modern Moral Philosophy," *Philosophy*, 124 no. 33 (1958): 1–19.
5. Aristotle, *Politics*. 1326a25.
6. Aristotle, *Aristotle's Nicomachean Ethics*, trans. Robert C. Bartlett and Susan D. Collins (Chicago: University of Chicago Press, 2011), 1167b.
7. Soren Kierkegaard, *The Present Age*, trans. Alexander Dru (New York: Harper & Row, 1962), 60.
8. John Ruskin, *Unto This Last and Other Writings*.
9. John Ruskin, *Praeterita* (Oxford: Oxford University Press, 2012), 7. In fact, Ruskin is a strange figure to draw upon in making this argument. Ruskin introduces himself in his autobiography this way: "I am, and my father was before me, a violent Tory of the old school." Ruskin believed in hereditary authority, and looked to elites to recognize the suffering in

society and to act in ways that would alleviate it. His faith in hierarchy and the established order makes him an unlikely hero of craft production.

10. Aristotle, *Politics*, 1278a19-20.
11. Miguel Alzola, "The Possibility of Virtue," *Business Ethics Quarterly*, 22 no. 2 (2012): 394.
12. Brooke Harrington, "Yes, Trump's Cabinet is Super Rich. That's Not Why We Should Be Worried," *Washington Post*, January 19, 2017.
13. Jessica A. Kennedy, Tae Wan Kim, and Alan Strudler, "Hierarchies and Dignity: A Confucian Communitarian Approach," *Business Ethics Quarterly*, online first, 2016, DOI: 10.1017/beq.2016.17.
14. Gabriel Abend, *The Moral Background*, 99.
15. Weber, *The Protestant Ethic and the Spirit of Capitalism*; Benjamin Franklin, *Benjamin Franklin: Autobiography & Selected Writings* (New York: Modern Library, 1981); Werner Sombart and Mortimer Epstein, *The Quintessence of Capitalism: A Study of the History and Psychology of the Modern Business Man* (London: T. F. Unwin, 1915), 400; Leon Battista Alberti, *The Family in Renaissance Florence*, trans. Renée Neu Watkins (Columbia, SC; University of South Carolina Press, 1969); Daniel Bell, *The Cultural Contradictions of Capitalism*, 20th anniversary ed. (New York: Basic Books, 1996), xviii [note 5]. Weber traces the spirit of capitalism through Benjamin Franklin to Calvinists in the wake of the Protestant Reformation. Werner Sombart argues that the bourgeois ethos emerged a few hundred years earlier in Florence, a history that he traces through Leon Battista Alberti. Daniel Bell attributes the rise of Weber's argument over Sombart's to the latter's seeming support of the Nazis in 1934 and to Sombart's unapproachable form of exposition.
16. For a history, see Richard T. De George, "The History of Business Ethics," in *The Accountable Corporation*, Marc Epstein and Kirk Hanson, eds. (Westport, CT: Praeger, 2006), vol. 2, 47–58.
17. Denis Collins, "The Quest to Improve the Human Condition: The First 1500 Articles Published in Journal of Business Ethics," *Journal of Business Ethics*, 26 no. 1 (2000): 1–73.
18. Mitchell, Agle, and Wood, *Toward a Theory of Stakeholder Identification and Salience: Defining the Principle of Who and What Really Counts*, 853–886.
19. Jensen, "Value Maximization, Stakeholder Theory, and the Corporate Objective Function," 235–256.
20. Aleksandra Kacperczyk, "With Greater Power Comes Greater Responsibility? Takeover Protection and Corporate Attention to

Stakeholders," *Strategic Management Journal*, 30 no. 3 (2009): 261–285.

21. Joseph Heath, "The Uses and Abuses of Agency Theory," *Business Ethics Quarterly*, 19 no. 4 (2009): 497–528.

22. Heath, *Morality, Competition, and the Firm*.

23. Eric W. Orts and Alan Strudler, "The Ethical and Environmental Limits of Stakeholder Theory," *Business Ethics Quarterly*, 12 no. 2 (2009): 215–233.

24. See Donaldson and Dunfee, *Ties that Bind*. Integrative Social Contracts Theory is perhaps the best example of a hybridized moral view that absorbs norms from communities, religion, and moral philosophy. Intuitionist and virtue-based theories of ethics also rely heavily on moral views that lack a unifying theme.

25. Edwin M. Hartman, *Organizational Ethics and the Good Life* (Oxford: Oxford University Press, 1996).

26. Norman E. Bowie, *Business Ethics: A Kantian Perspective* (Hoboken, NJ: Wiley-Blackwell, 1999).

27. Patricia H. Werhane, *Moral Imagination and Management Decision-Making* (New York: Oxford University Press, 1999), 146.

28. Robert A. G. Monks and Nell Minow, *Power and Accountability* (New York: HarperBusiness, 1991), 292.

29. Mitchell, Agle, and Wood, *Toward a Theory of Stakeholder Identification and Salience: Defining the Principle of Who and What Really Counts*, 853–886.

30. Thomas M. Jones and Andrew C. Wicks, "Convergent Stakeholder Theory," *Academy of Management Review*, 24 no. 2 (1999): 206.

31. Thomas M. Jones, "Instrumental Stakeholder Theory: A Synthesis of Ethics and Economics," *Academy of Management Review*, 20 no. 2 (1995): 404–437.

32. Bernard Williams, *Moral Luck: Philosophical Papers 1973–1980* (Cambridge: Cambridge University Press, 1981), 115.

33. Adam Smith, *The Wealth of Nations* (New York: Modern Library, 2000).

34. Elinor Ostrom, "Beyond Markets and States: Polycentric Governance of Complex Economic Systems," *American Economic Review*, 100 no. 3 (2010): 641–672.

35. Carol-Ann Tetrault Sirsly and Elena Lvina, "From Doing Good to Looking Even Better: The Dynamics of CSR and Reputation," *Business & Society*, online first, 2016, DOI: 10.1177/0007650315627996.

36. Thomas W. Dunfee, "Do Firms with Unique Competencies for Rescuing Victims of Human Catastrophes Have Special Obligations? Corporate

Responsibility and the AIDS Catastrophe in Sub-Saharan Africa," *Business Ethics Quarterly*, 16 no. 2 (2006): 185–210.

37. Kami Buchholz, "Honda Works to Prevent Vehicle-to-Pedestrian Accidents," *Automotive Engineering*, September 30, 2016, http://articles.sae.org/12408.

38. William McDonough and Michael Braungart, *Cradle to Cradle: Remaking the Way We Make Things*.

39. Bernard A. O. Williams and T. Nagel, "Moral Luck," *Proceedings of the Aristotelian Society, Supplementary Volumes*, 50 (1976): 124.

8 Materiality for Business Ethics

1. Jay Barney, "Firm Resources and Sustained Competitive Advantage," *Journal of Management*, 17 no. 1 (1991): 101.

2. Stuart L. Hart, "A Natural-Resource-Based View of the Firm," *Academy of Management Review*, 20 no. 4 (1995): 986–1014.

3. George Gilder, *Microcosm: A Prescient Look Inside the Expanding Universe of Economic, Social, and Technological Possibilities Within the World of the Silicon Chip* (New York: Simon & Schuster, 1989), 17.

4. Anton Shirlov, "Intel to Spend $6 Billion on 10nm Fab in Israel," *Kit Guru*, September 23, 2014, www.kitguru.net/components/cpu/anton-shilov/intel-to-spend-6-billion-on-10nm-fab-in-israel.

5. Mark Lapedus, "10 nm Fab Watch," *Semiconductor Engineering*, May 21, 2015, http://semiengineering.com/10nm-fab-watch.

6. Eric W. Orts, *Business Persons: A Legal Theory of the Firm* (Oxford: Oxford University Press, 2013).

7. Mollie Painter-Morland, "Agency in Corporations," in *Business Ethics and Continental Philosophy*, eds. Mollie Painter-Morland and René ten Bos (Cambridge: Cambridge University Press, 2011), 25.

8. Mollie Painter-Morland, *Business Ethics as Practice: Ethics as the Everyday Business of Business* (New York: Cambridge University Press, 2008), 122.

9. Thomas Donaldson, "The Epistemic Fault Line in Corporate Governance," *Academy of Management Review*, 37 no. 2 (2012): 262.

10. Ibid, 267.

11. Subhabrata Bobby Banerjee, *Corporate Social Responsibility: The Good, The Bad, and the Ugly* (Cheltenham, UK: Edward Elgar, 2007), 34.

12. William S. Laufer, *Corporate Bodies and Guilty Minds: The Failure of Corporate Criminal Liability* (Chicago: University of Chicago Press, 2006).

13. Dennis W. Organ, "Organizational Citizenship Behavior: It's Construct Clean-Up Time," *Human Performance*, 10 no. 2 (1997): 85–97.
14. For a discussion of the relationship between freedom and responsibility, see Hugh Willmott, "Organizational Culture," in *Business Ethics and Continental Philosophy*, eds. Mollie Painter-Morland and René ten Bos (Cambridge: Cambridge University Press, 2011), 86.
15. Thomas Donaldson and Lee E. Preston, "The Stakeholder Theory of the Corporation: Concepts, Evidence, and Implications," *Academy of Management Review*, 20 no. 1 (1995): 65–91.
16. Smith, *The Wealth of Nations* (New York: Modern Library, 2000).
17. Samuel Freeman, "Illiberal Libertarians: Why Libertarianism is not a Liberal View," *Philosophy and Public Affairs*, 30 no. 2 (2002): 148–149.
18. Hernandez, "Toward an Understanding of the Psychology of Stewardship," *Academy of Management Review*, 172–193.
19. Henry Hansmann, *The Ownership of Enterprise* (Cambridge, MA: Harvard University Press, 1996).
20. Margaret Blair and Lynn A. Stout, "A Team Production Theory of Corporate Law," *Virginia Law Review*, 85 no. 2 (1999).
21. Michel Foucault, *Discipline and Punish: The Birth of the Prison*, trans. Alan Sheridan (New York: Vintage, 1995).
22. *BBC News*, "High Heels Row: Firm Accused of Sexism Changes Policy," May 12, 2016, www.bbc.com/news/uk-england-london-36272893.
23. Hart, "A Natural-Resource-Based View of the Firm."
24. Eric W. Orts, "Beyond Shareholders: Interpreting Corporate Constituency Statutes," *George Washington Law Review*, 61 no. 1 (1992): 14–135.
25. David Rönnegard, "How Autonomy Alone Debunks Corporate Moral Agency," *Business and Professional Ethics Journal*, 32 no. 1–2 (2013): 77–106.
26. Amy J. Sepinwall, "Denying Corporate Rights and Punishing Corporate Wrongs," *Business Ethics Quarterly*, 25 no. 4 (2015): 517–534.
27. Ronald K. Mitchell, Bradley R. Agle, and Donna J. Wood, "Toward a Theory of Stakeholder Identification and Salience: Defining the Principle of Who and What Really Counts," *Academy of Management Review*, 22 no. 4 (1997): 853–886.
28. Laufer, *Corporate Bodies and Guilty Minds*.
29. Thomas M. Jones, "Instrumental Stakeholder Theory: A Synthesis of Ethics and Economics," *Academy of Management Review*, 20 no. 2 (1995): 404–437.
30. Robert Phillips, *Stakeholder Theory and Organizational Ethics* (San Francisco: Berrett Koehler, 2003).

31. R. Edward Freeman and Robert A. Phillips, "Stakeholder Theory: A Libertarian Defense," *Business Ethics Quarterly*, 12 no. 3 (2002): 331–349.
32. Joseph Heath, "Business Ethics Without Stakeholders," *Business Ethics Quarterly*, 16 no. 3 (2006): 542.
33. Kenneth E. Goodpaster, "Business Ethics and Stakeholder Analysis," *Business Ethics Quarterly*, 1 no. 1 (1991): 53–73.
34. Heath, "Business Ethics Without Stakeholders," 546. Emphasis in original.
35. Thomas Donaldson, *The Ethics of International Business* (Oxford: Oxford University Press, 1989).
36. Drucker writes, "The purpose of business is to create and keep a customer." Cited in Stefan Stern, "The Importance of Creating and Keeping a Customer," *Financial Times*, October 10, 2011.
37. McDonough and Braungart, *Cradle to Cradle*.
38. Painter-Morland, *Business Ethics as Practice*.
39. Chen-Bo Zhong and Katie Liljenquist, "Washing Away Your Sins: Threatened Morality and Physical Cleansing," *Science*, 313 no. 5792 (2006): 1451–1452.
40. Gary D. Sherman and Gerald L. Clore, "The Color of Sin: White and Black Are Perceptual Symbols of Moral Purity and Pollution," *Psychological Science*, 20 no. 8 (2009): 1019–1025.
41. Geoffrey Smith, "VW Emissions Scandal May Go Back As Far As 1999," *Fortune*, April 19, 2016, http://fortune.com/2016/04/19/vw-emissions-scandal-origins-1999.
42. Title 42, U.S. Code, Motor Vehicle Emissions and Fuel Standards. 7522 (a)(3)(b), as amended in Clean Air Act Amendments (1990).
43. See www.icbe.com/carbondatabase/fuels/Diesel_Info.html, accessed September 7, 2016. The source of this factoid is itself an interesting case in the labors of singularization. The International Carbon Bank & Exchange runs a database that records greenhouse gas emissions in a "bank-like environment." It is again interesting that as the pressures of sustainability mount, we are forced to think differently about our materials.
44. Dale R. Tree and Kenth I. Svensson, "Soot Processes in Compression Ignition Engines," *Progress in Energy and Combustion Science*, 33 no. 3 (2007): 272–309.
45. Geoffrey Mohan and Ben Welsh, "How Much Pollution Did VW's Emissions Cheating Create?" *Los Angeles Times*, October 9, 2015, www.latimes.com/business/la-fi-vw-pollution-footprint-20151007-htmlstory.html.

46. Sara Randazzo and Mike Spector, "FTC Sues Volkswagen Over Advertising of Diesel Vehicles: Lawsuit Positions FTC to be Part of any Global Civil Settlement," *Wall Street Journal*, March 29, 2016, www.wsj.com/articles/ftc-sues-volkswagen-over-advertising-of-diesel-vehicles-1459262536.
47. Evgeny Morozov, "Making It: Pick up a Spot Welder and Join the Revolution," *The New Yorker*, January 13, 2014, www.newyorker.com/magazine/2014/01/13/making-it-2.
48. Subhabrata Bobby Banerjee, Easwar S. Iyer, and Rajiv K. Kashyap, "Corporate Environmentalism and Its Antecedents: Influence of Industry Type," *Journal of Marketing*, 67 no. 2 (2003): 106–122; Sanjay Sharma and Harrie Vredenburg, "Proactive Corporate Environmental Strategy and the Development of Competitively Valuable Organizational Capabilities," *Strategic Management Journal*, 19 no. 8 (1998): 729–753.

Index